D0899633

IX

English Literature and Irish Politics

MATTHEW ARNOLD

ENGLISH LITERATURE AND IRISH POLITICS

Edited by R. H. Super

ANN ARBOR   THE UNIVERSITY OF MICHIGAN PRESS

Copyright © by The University of Michigan 1973
All rights reserved
ISBN 0–472–11659–2
Library of Congress Catalog Card No. 60-5018
Published in the United States of America by
The University of Michigan Press and simultaneously
in Don Mills, Canada, by Longman Canada Limited
Manufactured in the United States of America

9 5 40 45

Editor's Preface

This ninth volume of Arnold's prose is made up of his *Irish Essays and Others*, 1882 (excluding the reprinted "Prefaces to Poems" of 1853–54 which appeared in the first volume of this edition) and five of the nine essays from *Essays in Criticism*, Second Series. In addition there are a long essay on "Joseph de Maistre on Russia," discovered in the files of the *Quarterly Review* a decade or so ago by the present editor and Professor Fraser Neiman working independently, a short article on "A Genevese Judge" from *The Pall Mall Gazette*, two letters on education from *The Times*, the short Preface "On Poetry" written for *The Hundred Greatest Men*, and the short preface to Arnold's selection of Burke's writings on Irish affairs. All these last except the second letter to *The Times* and the Preface to Burke were printed in Professor Neiman's *Essays, Letters, and Reviews by Matthew Arnold* (Cambridge, Massachusetts: Harvard University Press, 1960). Arnold's selections from the writings of Wordsworth, Byron, Gray, Keats, and Burke are listed in the Appendix. The period covered by this volume is from February, 1879, to February, 1882.

The Second Series of *Essays in Criticism* was projected by Arnold and his publishers early in 1888, but his death in April of that year occurred before their plans had been completed. Unlike the First Series, it was not a collection conceived for a single purpose and unified by a pair of introductory essays composed to clarify that purpose. As published posthumously, the Second Series consists of the five essays in the present volume, dating from 1879 to 1881, and four others published in periodicals during the last few months of Arnold's life; these four will appear in the final (eleventh) volume of the present edition.

As in the eight volumes that have gone before, the text has been set from the last edition over which Arnold may have exercised any supervision. Textual variants from earlier editions are indicated in the Textual Notes; these include changes in paragraphing and changes from semicolon to full stop or the reverse, but no other changes in punctuation. Clear textual blunders are corrected, and the corrections noted.

The Critical and Explanatory Notes aim at showing the circumstances under which the essays were composed and written, explaining Arnold's allusions and indicating the sources of his quotations. If the reader does not find the information he needs for the understanding of a passage, the cause may be the editor's oversight, but it is much more likely that the editor was simply unable to supply what was needed.

The editor is indebted to his friends Professor James M. Osborn for the use of Arnold's letters to Humphry Ward (after Mr. Peter Smith had called them to my attention), Professor Hoover H. Jordan for help with Moore's *Life of Byron*, and Professor Robert Liddell Lowe for infinite pains in resolving some troublesome bibliographical points. He is grateful to former students who did some of the spadework in the annotation of individual essays: Jerome J. Donnelly, Russell R. Larson, Elliott M. Simon, Arvid F. Sponberg, and Richard L. Townsend. The volume was largely prepared during a year of study provided by the generous support of the John Simon Guggenheim Memorial Foundation, supplemented by a grant from the Horace H. Rackham School of Graduate Studies of the University of Michigan.

Contents

*Irish Essays

"Ecce, Convertimur ad Gentes"[1]

I cannot help asking myself how I come to be standing here
to-night. It not unfrequently happens to me, indeed, to be
invited to make addresses and to take part in public meetings,
—above all in meetings where the matter of interest is education; probably because I was sent, in former days, to acquaint   5
myself with the schools and education of the Continent, and
have published reports and books about them. But I make
it a general rule to decline the invitation. I am a school-
inspector under the Committee of Council on Education, and
the Department which I serve would object, and very prop-   10
erly object, to have its inspectors starring it about the country,
making speeches on education. An inspector must naturally be
prone to speak of that education of which he has particular
cognisance, the education which is administered by his own
Department, and he might be supposed to let out the views   15
and policy of his Department. Whether the inspectors really
knew and gave the Department's views or not, their speeches
might equally be a cause of embarrassment to their official
superiors.

However, I have no intention of compromising my official   20
superiors by talking to you about that branch of education
which they are concerned in administering,—elementary education. And if I express a desire that they should come to
occupy themselves with other branches of education too,
branches with which they have at present no concern, you   25
may be quite sure that this is a private wish of my own, not
at all prompted by my Department. You may rely upon it,
that the very last thing desired by that Department itself, is

[1] An Address delivered to the Ipswich Working Men's College.

I

to invade the provinces of education which are now independent of it. Nobody will ever be able to accuse the Committee of Council of carrying an Afghanistan war into those provinces, when it might have remained quietly within its own borders. There is a Latin law-maxim which tells us that it is the business of a good judge to seek to extend his jurisdiction: —*Boni judicis est ampliare jurisdictionem.* That may be characteristic of a good judge, but it is not characteristic of a British Government in domestic affairs generally, certainly not in the concerns of education.

And for this reason: because the British Government is an aristocratic government. Such a government is entirely free from the faults of what is commonly called a bureaucracy. It is not meddlesome, not fussy, not prone to seek importance for itself by meddling with everybody and everything; it is by nature disposed to leave individuals and localities to settle their own affairs for themselves as much as possible. The action of individuals and of localities, left to themselves, proves insufficient in this point and in that; then the State is forced to intervene. But what I say is, that in all those domestic matters, such as the regulation of workhouses, or of factories, or of schools, where the State has, with us, been forced to intervene, it is not our aristocratic executive which has sought the right of intervention, it is public opinion which has imposed the duty of intervention upon our aristocratic executive. Our aristocratic system may have its faults, but the mania for State-interference everywhere is not one of them. Above all, in regard to education this has been conspicuously the case. Government did not move in the matter while it could avoid moving.

Of course, even when it was at last obliged to move, there were some people to be found who cried out against it for moving. In the early days of the Committee of Council, one clergyman wrote that he was not going to suffer Lord John Russell, "or any other Turkish Bashaw," to send an inspector into his schools; and Archdeacon Denison threatened, as is well known, to have the poor inspector drowned in a horsepond. But these were eccentric men, living in a fantastic world of their own. To men who inhabit the real world, it was abundantly apparent that our Government moved in the matter of public education as late as it could, that it moved as slowly as it could, as inoffensively as it could; and that throughout, instead of stimulating public opinion to give it additional powers, it has confined itself to cautiously accepting and discharging the functions which public opinion has insisted on laying upon it.

You may be sure that this will continue to be the case; that if more part in public education comes to be assigned to the Government in this country, it is not that the Government seeks it, it is that the growth of opinion will compel the Government to undertake it. So that if I speak of the desirableness of extending to a further class of Schools the action of the State, it is well understood that I am not, as in bureaucratic Prussia I might be, revealing the secret aims and ambitions of the Education Department. All the aims of that Department have been clearly manifested to be the other way.

Well, but why am I here? I am here, in the first place, because I heard that your Working Men's College, which holds its annual meeting to-night, and which I was asked to address, is the largest body of the kind in England. Bodies of this kind, with their classes, their lectures, their libraries, their aspirations, are a testimony, however poor and imperfect may be the use often made of them, they are, as it seems to me, a testimony, they are a profession of faith, which is both affecting and valuable. They are a profession of belief in the saving power of light and intelligence, a profession of belief in the use and in the practicability of trying to know *oneself* and the world, *to follow*, as Dante says, *virtue and knowledge*.

No one can accuse us English, as a nation, of being too forward with such professions of faith in the things of the mind. No one can accuse us of not showing ourselves enough aware, how little good may in many cases come from professions of this sort, how much they may disappoint us, what a contrast their performance often is to their promise, how much they often bring with them which is hollow and nonsensical. We are very shy, as every one knows, of all public homage to the power of science and letters. We have no National Institute.

In a short time there will be held in Paris a reception, as it is
called, of one of the most famous men of letters in France, or indeed in all Europe,—M. Renan,—at the French Academy. That
reception, and the discourse of the new member, will be for
5   our neighbours over in France one of the very foremost events
of the year. Hardly any parliamentary field-day will call forth
greater interest and excitement. Every one will want to be
present, every one will be eager to know what is said, every
one will discuss what is said. We English keenly feel the
10   unreality, as we call it, which attends displays of this kind. We
prefer that our own celebrations should be for incidents of a
more practical character; should be such as the dinner and
speechifying, for instance, at the opening of the annual season
for the Buckhounds.

15   But above all, we are on our guard against expecting too
much from institutions like this Working Men's College.
We are reminded what grand expectations Lord Brougham
and the other friends of knowledge cheap and popular, the
founders of the Mechanics' Institutes, held out; what tall talk
20   they indulged in; and we are told to look and see how little has
come of it all. Nature herself fights against them and their
designs, we are told. At the end of his day, tired with his labour,
the working man in general cannot well have the power, even
if he have the will, to make any very serious and fruitful efforts
25   in the pursuit of knowledge. Whatever high professions these
institutions may start with, inevitably their members will come,
it is said, to decline upon a lower range of claim and endeavour.
They will come to content themselves with seeking mere amusement and relaxation from their Institute. They will visit its
30   reading-rooms merely to read the newspapers, to read novels;
and they are not to be blamed for it.

No, perhaps they are not to be blamed for it, even if this does
happen. And yet the original, lofty aspiration, the aspiration
after the satisfactions, solace, and power which are only to be
35   got from true knowledge, may have been right after all. In spite
of the frequent disappointment, the constant difficulty, it may
have been right. For to arrive at a full and right conception of
things, to know one's self and the world,—which is knowledge;

then to act firmly and manfully on that knowledge,—which is
virtue; this is the native, the indestructible impulse of the spirit
of man. All the high-flown commonplaces about the power of
knowledge, and about the mind's instinctive desire of it, have
their great use, whenever we can so put them as to feel them ani-   5
mating and inspiring to us. For they are true in themselves; only
they are discredited by being so often used insincerely. The
profession of faith of institutes like your College, that knowledge
is power, that there is an intelligible law of things, that the
human mind seeks to arrive at it, and that our welfare depends   10
on our arriving at it and obeying it, this profession of faith, I say,
is sound in itself, it is precious, and we do well to insist upon it.
It puts in due prominence a quality which does not always get
enough regard in this country,—intelligence.

Goethe, the great poet of Germany, and the greatest critic,   15
perhaps, that has ever lived, went so far as to say boldly of our
nation (which, notwithstanding, he highly esteemed and admired): *Der Engländer ist eigentlich ohne Intelligenz*—"The
Englishman is, properly speaking, without intelligence." Goethe
by no means meant to say that the Englishman was stupid. All   20
he meant was, that the Englishman is singularly without a keen
sense of there being an intelligible law of things, and of its
being our urgent business to ascertain it and to make our doings
conform to it. He meant that the Englishman is particularly
apt to take as the rule of things what is customary, or what   25
falls in with his prepossessions and prejudices, and to act upon
this stoutly and without any misgiving, as if it were the real
natural rule of things. He meant that the Englishman does not
much like to be told that there is a real natural rule of things,
presenting itself to the intelligence; to be told that our action,   30
however energetic, is not safe unless it complies with this real
and intelligible rule. And I think Goethe was right here, and
that the Englishman, from his insularity, and from his strength,
and from some want of suppleness in his mind, does often
answer to the description which Goethe gives of him.   35

Now it is a grave thing, this indifference to the real natural
and rational rule of things, because it renders us very liable to
be found fighting against nature, and that is always calamitous.

And so I come at last to the entire reason for my being here to-night. There is a point in which our action, as a community, seems to me quite at variance with what the rational rule of things would prescribe, and where we all suffer by its being thus at variance. I have tried in vain for twenty years to make the parties most directly concerned see the mischief of the present state of things. I want to interest you in the matter. I speak to you as a Working Men's College, the largest in England, representing the profession of faith that what we need is intelligence, the power to see things as they really are, and to shape our action accordingly. I look upon you, I say, as representing that profession of faith, and representing it as entertained by the class of working men. You, too, are concerned in the failure which I want to remedy, though not directly concerned in it. But you *are* concerned in it, and that gravely; we are all gravely concerned in it.

You will, I am sure, suffer me to speak to you with perfect frankness, even though what I say should offend some of those who hear me. My address is to the class of working men; but there are present before me to-night, I know, hearers from other classes too. However, the only possible use of my coming here would be lost if I did not speak to you with perfect frankness. I am no politician. I have no designs upon your borough, or upon any borough, or upon parliamentary honours at all. Indeed, I have no very ardent interest,—if you will allow me to speak for a moment of myself and of what interests me, —in politics in their present state in this country. What interests me is English civilisation; and our politics in their present state do not seem to me to have much bearing upon that.

English civilisation,—the humanising, the bringing into one harmonious and truly humane life, of the whole body of English society,—that is what interests me. I try to be a disinterested observer of all which really helps and hinders that. Certain hindrances seem to me to be present with us, and certain helps to be wanting to us. An isolated observer may easily be mistaken, and his observations greatly require the test which other minds can exert upon them. If I fail to carry you with me in what seems to me to be perfectly clear, that is against the

soundness of my observations and conclusions. But that I may
have the chance of carrying you with me, it is necessary that
I should speak to you with entire frankness. Then it will appear
whether your aid, or the aid of any among you, is to be had for
removing what seems to me one great hindrance, and for pro-   5
viding what seems to me one great help, to our civilisation.

For twenty years, then,—ever since I had to go about the
Continent to learn what the schools were like there, and observed at the same time the people for whom the schools
existed and the conditions of their life, and compared it with   10
what was to be found at home,—ever since that time, I have
felt convinced that for the progress of our civilisation, here
in England, three things were above all necessary:—a reduction
of those immense inequalities of condition and property
amongst us, of which our land-system is the base; a genuine   15
municipal system; and public schools for the middle classes. I
do not add popular education. Even so long as twenty years
ago, popular education was already launched. I was myself
continually a witness of the progress it was making; I could see
that the cause of popular education was safe. The three points,   20
then, were reduction of our immense inequalities of condition
and property, a municipal system extended all through the
country, and public schools for the middle classes. These
points are hardly dreamed of in our present politics, any one
of them.   25

Take the first of the three. Mr. Gladstone, who ought to
know, ridicules the very notion of a cry for equality in this
country; he says that the idea of equality has never had the
slightest influence upon English politics; nay, that, on the
contrary, we have the religion of inequality. There is, indeed,   30
a little bill brought forward in Parliament year after year,—
the Real Estates Intestacy Bill,—which proposes that there
should be equality in the division of a man's land amongst his
children after his death, in case he happens to die without a
will. It is answered, that if a man wants his land to go thus   35
equally amongst his children, he has only just to take the
trouble of making a will to that effect; and that, in the absence of a will, his land had better follow the rule of the pres-

ent general system of landed inheritance in this country, a
system which works well. And nothing more is said, except,
perhaps, that one hears a few timid words of complaint about
the hardship inflicted upon younger children by this system.

5   But, for my part, I am not so much concerned about the
younger children. My objection to the present system is not
on their account; but because I think that, putting their supposed natural rights quite out of the question, the present
system does not work well now at all, but works altogether

10   badly. I think that now, however it may have worked formerly, the system tends to materialise our upper class, vulgarise
our middle class, brutalise our lower class. If it does not do
that, I have no other objection to make to it. I do not believe
in *any* natural rights; I do not believe in a natural right, in

15   each of a man's children, to his or her equal share of the
father's property. I have no objection to the eldest son taking
all the land, or the youngest son, or the middle daughter, on
one condition: that this state of things shall really work well,
that it shall be for the public advantage.

20   Once our present system of landed inheritance had its real
reason and justification,—it worked well. When the modern
nations of Europe were slowly building themselves up out of
the chaos left by the dissolution of the Roman empire, a number of local centres were needed for the process, with a strong

25   hereditary head-man over each; and this natural need the
feudal land-system met. It seems to me, it has long seemed to
me, that, the circumstances being now quite changed, our
system of immense inequalities of condition and property
works not well but badly, has the natural reason of things not

30   for it but against it. It seems to me that the natural function
is gone for which an aristocratic class with great landed
estates was required; and that when the function is gone, and
the great estates with an infinitely multiplied power of minis-
tering to mere pleasure and indulgence remain, the class own-

35   ing them inevitably comes to be materialised, and the more so
the more the development of industry and ingenuity augments
the means of luxury.

The action of such a class materialises all the class of newly

enriched people as they rise. The middle class, having above
them this materialised upper class, with a wealth and luxury
utterly out of their reach, with a standard of social life and
manners, the offspring of that wealth and luxury, seeming
utterly out of their reach also, are inevitably thrown back   5
too much upon themselves, and upon a defective type of
civilisation. The lower class, with the upper class and its standard of life still farther out of their reach, and finding nothing
to attract them or to elevate them in the standard of life of the
middle classes, are inevitably, in their turn, thrown back upon   10
themselves, and upon a defective type of civilisation. I speak
of classes. In all classes, there are individuals with a happy
nature and an instinct for the humanities of life, who stand
out from their class, and who form exceptions.

Now, the word *vulgarised* as applied to the middle class,   15
and *brutalised* as applied to the lower class, may seem to you
very hard words. And yet some of you, at any rate, will feel
that there is a foundation for them. And whether you feel it
or not, the most competent, the most dispassionate observers
feel it, and use words about it much more contemptuous and   20
harsher than mine. The question is not, whether you or I may
feel the truth of a thing of this kind; the question is, whether
the thing is really so. I believe that it is so; that with splendid
qualities in this nation at large, that with admirable exceptions
to be found in all classes, we at present do tend to have our   25
higher class in general materialised, our middle class vulgarised,
and our lower class brutalised; and that this tendency we owe
to what Mr. Gladstone calls our religion of inequality.

True, no one here in England combines the fact of the
defects in our civilisation with the fact of our enormous in-   30
equality. People may admit the facts separately; the inequality,
indeed, they cannot well deny; but they are not accustomed
to combine them. But I saw, when I began to think about these
matters, that elsewhere the best judges combined this fact of
great social imperfection with the fact of great inequality. I   35
saw that Turgot, the best and wisest statesman whom France
has ever had, himself one of the governing and fortunate class,
made inequality answerable for much of the misery of the

modern nations of Europe. "Everywhere," says Turgot, "the laws have favoured that inequality of fortunes which corrupts a certain number, to doom the rest to degradation and misery." Vehement as this language sounds, I saw that the spectacle France is described as presenting, under the old system, was enough to account for it. I saw that the French peasants, under that system, were described by a sober and grave authority as presenting the appearance of a number of puny, dingy, miserable creatures, half clad and half articulate, creeping about on the surface of the ground and feebly scratching it. I saw that Tocqueville, coming after the French Revolution, and a severe judge of its faults and of the faults of democracy, spoke of inequality much as Turgot spoke of it. "The common people is more uncivilised in aristocratic countries," says Tocqueville, "than in others, because there, where persons so powerful and so rich are met with, the weak and the poor feel themselves overwhelmed, as it were, with the weight of their own inferiority; not finding any point by which they may recover equality, they despair of themselves altogether, and suffer themselves to fall into degradation."

And then I saw the French peasant of the present day, who has been made by equality. There is a chorus of voices from all sides in praise of his condition. First, let us take, as in duty bound, your principal, Mr. Barham Zincke, who has been staying in a French peasant's home this last summer, and has published in the *Fortnightly Review*, in two delightful articles which ought to be reprinted in a cheap form, an account of what he beheld.[1] Your principal says that "the dense peasant population of the Limagne,"—the region where he was staying, in the heart of France,—"are, speaking of them as a body, honest, contented, hard-working, hardy, self-respecting, thrifty, and self-supporting." He gives a charming account of their manners and courtesy, as well as of their prosperity; and he pronounces such a population to be a State's greatest wealth. Prince Bismarck appears to agree with your principal, for he declares that the social condition of France seems to have greater elements of soundness,—this well-being of the French

[1] See *Fortnightly Review* for November and December 1878.

peasant counting foremost among them all,—than the social condition of any other nation of Europe. A learned Belgian economist, M. de Laveleye, chimes in with Prince Bismarck and with your principal, and declares that France, being the country of Europe where the soil is more divided than anywhere else except in Switzerland and Norway, is, at the same time, the country where material well-being is most widely spread, where wealth has of late years increased most, and where population is least outrunning those limits which, for the comfort and progress of the working classes themselves, seem necessary. Finally, I come back again to another countryman of our own, Mr. Hamerton, who lives in France. He speaks of the French peasant just as your principal speaks of him, and he ends by saying: "The interval between him and a Kentish labourer is enormous." What, that black little half-human creature of the times before the Revolution, feebly scratching the earth's surface, and sunk far below the point which any English peasantry ever sank to, has now risen to this, that the interval between him and a Kentish labourer,— no such bad specimen of our labourers either,—is enormous! And this has been brought about by equality.

Therefore, both the natural reason of the thing and also the proof from practical experience seem to me to show the same thing: that for modern civilisation some approach to equality is necessary, and that an enormous inequality like ours is a hindrance to our civilisation. This to me appears so certain, that twenty years since, in a preface to a book about schools, I said that I thought so. I said the same thing more at length quite lately, in a lecture[1] at the Royal Institution, an institution which has been stigmatised by a working man as being "the most aristocratic place in England." I repeat it here because it is a thing to be thought over and examined in all its bearings, not pushed away out of sight. If our inequality is really unfavourable to our civilisation, sooner or later this will be perceived generally, and our inequality will be abated. It will be abated by some measure far beyond the scope of our present

---

[1] Published in the *Fortnightly Review* for March 1878, and reprinted in *Mixed Essays* with the title *Equality*.

politics, whether by the adoption of the French law of bequest,
which now prevails so widely upon the Continent, or, as Mr.
Mill thought preferable, by fixing the maximum of property
which any one individual may take by bequest or inheritance,
5   or in some other manner. But this is not likely to come in our
time, nor is it to be desired that such a change should come
while we are yet ill prepared for it. It is a matter to which I
greatly wish to direct your thoughts, and to direct the thoughts
of all who think seriously. I enlarge upon it to-night, because it
10   renders so very necessary a reform in another line, to which
I shall come finally. But it is not itself a matter where I want
to enlist your help for a positive present measure of reform.

   Neither is the matter which I am next going to mention a
matter of this kind. My second point, you remember, was the
15   extension of municipal organisation throughout the whole
country. No one in England seems to imagine that municipal
government is applicable except in towns. All the country
districts are supposed to require nothing more than the parish
vestry, answering to that sort of mass-meeting of the parish-
20   ioners in the churchyard, under the presidency of the parson,
after service on Sundays, which Turgot describes in the
country districts of France before the Revolution. Nothing,
as I have frequently said, struck me more, both in France and
elsewhere on the Continent, than the working of the munici-
25   pality and municipal council as established everywhere, and
to observe how it was the basis of all local affairs, and the
right basis. For elementary schools, for instance, the municipal basis is undoubtedly the natural and right one; and we
are embarrassed, and must be embarrassed, so long as we have
30   not the municipal basis to use for them in the rural districts of
this country. For the peasant, moreover, for the agricultural
labourer, municipal life is a first and invaluable stage in political education; more helpful by far, because so much more
constant, than the exercise of the parliamentary franchise. So
35   this is my second point to which I should like members of
institutions like yours to turn their thoughts, as a thing very
conducive to that general civilisation which it is the object
of all cultivating of our intelligence to bring about. But this,

too,—the establishment of a genuine municipal system for the whole country,—will hardly, perhaps, come in our time; men's minds have not yet been sufficiently turned to it for that. I am content to leave this also as a matter for thought with you.

Not so with my third point, where I hope we may actually get something done in our time. I am sure, at all events, we *need* to get something actually done towards it in our time. I want to enlist your interest and help towards this object,— towards the actual establishment of public schools for the middle classes.

The topics which suggest themselves to me in recommendation of this object are so numerous that I hardly know which of them to begin with; and yet I have occupied your attention a good while already, and I must before long come to an end of my discourse. As I am speaking to a Working Men's College, I will begin with what is supposed to have most weight with people; I will begin with the direct interests in this matter of yourselves and your class. By the establishment of public schools for the middle classes, I mean an establishment of the same kind as we now have for popular education. I mean the provision by law, throughout the country, of a supply of properly guaranteed schools, in due proportion to the estimated number of the population requiring them; schools giving secondary instruction, as it is called,—that fuller and higher instruction which comes after elementary instruction, —and giving it at a cost not exceeding a certain rate.

Now for your direct interest in the matter. You have a direct interest in having facilities to rise given to what M. Gambetta, that famous popular leader in France, calls the new social strata. This rise is chiefly to be effected by education. Promising subjects come to the front in their own class, and they pass then, by a second and higher stage of education, into the class above them, to the great advantage of society. It is hardly too much to say that you and your class have in England no schools by which you can accomplish this rise if you are worthy of it.

In France they exist everywhere. Your principal tells us, that he found in the village where he was staying in the

Limagne, six village lads, peasants' children, who were attending the secondary schools in Clermont. After all their losses,
after all the milliards they have had to pay to Germany, the
French have been laying out more and more in the last few
years on their public secondary schools; and they do not
seem so much worse off in their pecuniary condition at this
moment than practical nations which make no such expenditure. At this very time a commission is sitting in France, to
consider whether secondary instruction may not be brought
into closer connection with elementary instruction than it is
at present, by establishing schools more perfectly fitted than
the present secondary schools to meet the wants of the best
subjects who rise from the schools below.

Now, you often see the School Boards, here in this country,
doing what is in my opinion an unwise thing, making the
programme of their elementary schools too ambitious. The
programme of the elementary school should be strictly limited.
Those who are capable and desirous of going higher should do
it either by means of evening classes such as you have here, or
by means of secondary schools. But why do the School Boards
make this mistake?—for a mistake I think it is, and it gives occasion to the enemies of popular education to represent it as
an unpractical and pretentious thing. But why do they make
the mistake? They make it because, in the total absence in
this country of public secondary schools, and in the inconvenience arising from this state of things, they are driven to
make some attempt to supply the deficiency. Discourage,
then, the School Boards in their attempt to make the elementary
school what it cannot well be; but make them join with you
in calling for public secondary schools, which will accomplish
properly what they are aiming at.

But all this is socialism, we are told. An excellent man, Professor Fawcett, tells us that the most marked characteristic of
modern socialism is belief in the State. He tells us that socialism and recourse to the action of the State go always together.
The argument is an unfortunate one just at this moment, when
the most judicious of French newspapers, the *Journal des
Débats,* informs us that in France, which we all consider a

hotbed of State-action and of centralisation, socialism has quite
disappeared. However, this may perhaps turn out not to be
true. At any rate, Professor Fawcett says that the working
men of this country cannot be too much cautioned against
resort to the State, centralisation, bureaucracy, and the loss   5
of individual liberty; that the working class cannot be too
much exhorted to self-reliance and self-help.

Well, I should have thought that there had been no lack of
cautions and exhortations in this sense to us English, whether
we are working men or whatever we may be. Why, we have   10
heard nothing else ever since I can remember! And ever since
I was capable of reflection I have thought that such cautions
and exhortations might be wanted elsewhere, but that giving
them perpetually in England was indeed carrying coals to
Newcastle. The inutility, the profound inutility, of too many   15
of our Liberal politicians, comes from their habit of for ever
repeating, like parrots, phrases of this kind. In some countries
the action of the State is insufficient, in others it is excessive.
In France it is excessive. But hear a real Liberal leader, M.
Gambetta, in reply to the invectives of *doctrinaires* against   20
the State and its action. "I am not for the abuses of centralisation," said M. Gambetta at Romans, "but these attacks on *the
State*, which is France, often make me impatient. I am a defender of *the State*. I will not use the word centralisation;
but I am a defender of the national *centrality*, which has made   25
the French nation what it now is, and which is essential to our
progress." Englishmen are not likely, you may be sure, to let
the State encroach too much; they are not likely to be not
lovers enough of individual liberty and of individual self-
assertion. Our dangers are all the other way. Our dangers   30
are in exaggerating the blessings of self-will and self-assertion,
in not being ready enough to sink our imperfectly informed
self-will in view of a large general result.

Do not suffer yourselves, then, to be misled by declamations
against the State, against bureaucracy, centralisation, socialism,   35
and all the rest of it. The State is just what Burke very well
called it, long before M. Gambetta: *the nation in its collective
and corporate character*. To use the State is simply to use co-

operation of a superior kind. All you have to ask yourselves is whether the object for which it is proposed to use this co-operation is a rational and useful one, and one likely to be best reached in this manner. Professor Fawcett says that socialism's first lesson is, that the working man can acquire capital without saving, through having capital supplied to him by the State, which is to serve as a fountain of wealth perennially flowing without human effort. Well, to desire to use the State for that object is irrational, vain, and mischievous. Why? Because the object itself is irrational and impossible. But to use the State in order to get, through that high form of co-operation, better schools and better guaranteed schools than you could get without it, is rational, because the object is rational. The schools may be self-supporting if you like. The point is, whether by their being public schools, State schools, they are or are not likely to be better schools, and better guaranteed, than you could get in any other way. Indisputably they are likely to be better, and to give better guarantees. Well, then, this use of the State is a use of co-operation of a very powerful kind for a good and practicable purpose; and co-operation in itself is peculiarly of advantage, as I need not tell you, to the middling and ill off. Rely upon it that we English can use the State without danger; and that for you to be deceived by the cry against State-interference is to play the game of your adversaries, and to prolong for yourselves a condition of certain inferiority.

But I will ask you to do more than to consider your own direct interest in the establishment of public schools for the middle classes. I will ask you to consider the general interest of the community. The friends and flatterers of the middle classes,—and they have many friends and flatterers,—have been in the habit of assuring us, that the predominance of the middle classes was all that we required for our well-doing. Mr. Bright, a man of genius, and who has been a great power in this country, has always seemed to think that to insure the rule of the middle classes in this country would be to bring about the millennium. Perhaps the working class has not been without its flatterers too, who have assured it that it ought to rule

because it was so admirable. But you will observe, that my
great objection to our enormous inequality, and to our aristocratic system, is not that it keeps out from power worthier
claimants of it, but that it so grievously mars and stunts both
our middle class and our lower class, so keeps them in imper-   5
fection. It is not the faults and imperfections of our present
ruling class itself which strike me so much. Its members have
plenty of faults and imperfections, but as a whole they are the
best, the most energetic, the most capable, the honestest upper
class which the world has ever seen. What strikes me is the bad   10
effect of their rule upon others.

The middle classes cannot assume rule as they are at present,
—it is impossible. And yet in the rule of this immense class, this
class with so many correspondences, communications, and openings into the lower class, lies our future. There I agree with   15
Mr. Bright. But our middle class, as it is at present, *cannot* take
the lead which belongs to it. It has not the qualifications.
Seriousness it has, the better part of it; it may even be said to
have sacrificed everything to seriousness. And of the seriousness
and of the sense for conduct in this nation, which are an invalu-   20
able treasure to it, and a treasure most dangerously wanting
elsewhere, the middle classes are the stronghold. But they have
lived in a narrow world of their own, without openness and
flexibility of mind, without any notion of the variety of powers
and possibilities in human life. They know neither man nor the   25
world; and on all the arduous questions presenting themselves
to our age,—political questions, social questions, the labour question, the religious question,—they have at present no light, and
can give none. I say, then, they *cannot* fill their right place as
they are now; but you, and I, and every man in this country,   30
are interested in their being able to fill it.

How are they to be made able? Well, schools are something.
Schools are not everything; and even public schools, when you
get them, may be far from perfect. Our public elementary
schools are far from perfect. But they throw into circulation   35
year by year among the working classes,—and here is the great
merit of Mr. Forster's Act,—a number of young minds trained
and intelligent, such as you never got previously; and this must

tell in the long run. Our public secondary schools, when we get them, may be far from perfect. But they will throw into circulation year by year, among the middle classes, a number of young people with minds instructed and enlarged as they
5   never are now, when their schools are, both socially and intel- lectually, the most inadequate that fall to the lot of any middle class among the civilised nations of Europe. And the improve- ment so wrought must tell in the end, and will gradually fit the middle classes to understand better themselves and the world,
10 and to take their proper place, and to grasp and treat real politics,—politics far other than their politics of Dissent, which seem to me quite played out. This will be a work of time. Do not suppose that a great change of this kind is to be effected off hand. But we may make a beginning for it at once, and a good
15 beginning, by public schools for the middle classes.

For twenty years I have been vainly urging this upon the middle classes themselves. Now I urge it upon you. Comprehend, that middle-class education is a great democratic reform, of the truest, surest, safest kind. Christianity itself was such a reform.
20 The kingdom of God, the grand object of Jesus Christ, the grand object of Christianity, is mankind raised, as a whole, into har- mony with the true and abiding law of man's being, living as we were meant to live. Those of old who had to forward this work found the Jewish community,—to whom they went first,—nar-
25 row, rigid, sectarian, unintelligent, of impracticable temper, their heads full of some impossible politics of their own. Then they looked around, and they saw an immense world outside the Jew- ish community, a world with a thousand faults, no doubt, but with openness and flexibility of mind, new and elastic, full of
30 possibilities;—and they said: *We turn to the Gentiles!* Do not be affronted at being compared to the Gentiles; the Gentiles were the human race, the Gentiles were the future. Mankind are called in one body to the peace of God; that is the Christian phrase for civilisation. We have by no means reached that consummation
35 yet; but that, for eighteen centuries, we have been making way towards it, we owe to the Gentiles and to those who turned to them. The work, I say, is not nearly done yet; and our Judaic and unelastic middle class in this country is of no present

service, it seems, for carrying it forward. Do you, then, carry
it forward yourselves, and insist on taking the middle class with
you. You will be amply repaid for the effort, in your own
fuller powers of life and joy, in any event. We may get in our
time none of the great reforms which we have been talking   5
about; we may not even get public schools for the middle
classes. But we are always the better, all of us, for having aimed
high, for having striven to see and know things as they really
are, for having set ourselves to walk in the light of that knowledge, to help forward great designs, and to do good. "Consider   10
whereunto ye are born! ye were not made to live like brutes,
but to follow virtue and knowledge."

A Speech at Eton[1]

The philosopher Epictetus, who had a school at Nicopolis in
Epirus at the end of the first century of our era, thus apostro-
phises a young gentleman whom he supposes to be applying to
him for education:—

5   "Young sir, at home you have been at fisticuffs with the man-
servant, you have turned the house upside down, you have been
a nuisance to the neighbours; and do you come here with the
composed face of a sage, and mean to sit in judgment upon the
lesson, and to criticise my want of point? You have come in
10 here with envy and chagrin in your heart, humiliated at not
getting your allowance paid you from home; and you sit with
your mind full, in the intervals of the lecture, of how your
father behaves to you, and how your brother. What are the
people down at home saying about me?—They are thinking:
15 Now he is getting on! they are saying: He will come home a
walking dictionary!—Yes, and I should like to go home a walking dictionary; but then there is a deal of work required, and
nobody sends me anything, and the bathing here at Nicopolis
is dirty and nasty; things are all bad at home, and all bad here."
20   Nobody can say that the bathing at Eton is dirty and nasty.
But at Eton, as at Nicopolis, the moral disposition in which the
pupil arrives at school, the thoughts and habits which he brings
with him from home and from the social order in which he
moves, must necessarily affect his power of profiting by what
25 his schoolmasters have to teach him. This necessity is common
to all schooling. You cannot escape from it here any more
than they could at Nicopolis. Epictetus, however, was fully

1 Address delivered to the Eton Literary Society.

persuaded that what he had to teach was valuable, if the mental
and moral frame of his pupils were but healthy enough to permit
them to profit by it. I hope the Eton masters have the same
conviction as to the native value of what they teach. But you
know how many doubters and deniers of the value of a classical   5
education we nowadays meet with. Let us put aside all that is
said of the idleness, extravagance, and self-indulgence of the
schoolboy. This may pair off with the complaint of Epictetus
about the unsatisfactory moral state of his pupil. But with us
there are many people who go on and say: "And when the   10
schoolboy, in our public schools, does learn, he learns nothing
that is worth knowing."

It is not of the Eton schoolboy only that this is said, but of
the public schoolboy generally. We are all in the same boat,—all
of us in whose schooling the Greek and Latin classics fill the   15
principal place. And it avails nothing, that you try and appease
the gainsayer by now acquainting yourselves with the diameter
of the sun and moon, and with all sorts of matters which to us
of an earlier and ruder generation were unknown. So long as
the Greek and Latin classics continue to fill, as they do fill, the   20
chief place in your school-work, the gainsayer is implacable
and sticks to his sentence: "When the boy does learn, he learns
nothing that is worth knowing."

Amidst all this disparagement, one may well ask oneself
anxiously what is really to be said on behalf of studies over   25
which so much of our time is spent, and for which we have,
many of us, contracted a fondness. And after much consideration I have arrived at certain conclusions, which for my own
use I find sufficient, but which are of such extreme simplicity
that one ought to hesitate, perhaps, before one produces them to   30
other people. However, such as they are, I have been led to
bring them out more than once, and I will very briefly rehearse
them now. It seems to me, firstly, that what a man seeks
through his education is to get to know himself and the world;
next, that for this knowledge it is before all things necessary   35
that he acquaint himself with the best which has been thought
and said in the world; finally, that of this *best* the classics of
Greece and Rome form a very chief portion, and the portion

most entirely satisfactory. With these conclusions lodged safe in one's mind, one is staunch on the side of the humanities.

And in the same spirit of simplicity in which these conclusions have been reached, I proceed further. People complain that the significance of the classics which we read at school is not enough brought out, that the whole order and sense of that world from which they issue is not seized and held up to view. Well, but the best, in literature, has the quality of being in itself formative,—silently formative; of bringing out its own significance as we read it. It is better to read a masterpiece much, even if one does that only, than to read it a little, and to be told a great deal about its significance, and about the development and sense of the world from which it issues. Sometimes what one is told about the significance of a work, and about the development of a world, is extremely questionable. At any rate, a schoolboy, who, as they did in the times of ignorance at Eton, read his Homer and Horace through, and then read them through again, and so went on until he knew them by heart, is not, in my opinion, so very much to be pitied.

Still that sounding phrase, "the order and sense of a world," sends a kind of thrill through us when we hear it, especially when the world spoken of is a thing so great and so interesting as the Græco-Roman world of antiquity. If we are not deluded by it into thinking that to read fine talk about our classical documents is as good as to read the documents themselves, the phrase is one which we may with advantage lay to heart. I remember being struck, long ago, with a remark on the Greek poet Theognis by Goethe, who did not know Greek well and had to pick out its meaning by the help of a Latin translation, but who brought to everything which he read his powerful habits of thought and criticism. "When I first read Theognis," says Goethe, in substance, "I thought him querulous and morbid, and disliked him. But when I came to know how entirely his poetry proceeded from the real circumstances of his life, from the situation of parties in Megara, his native city, and from the effects of that situation upon himself and his friends, then I read him with quite another feeling." How very little do any of us treat the poetry of Theognis and other ancients in that fashion! was my thought after reading Goethe's criticism. And earlier still I remember being struck at hearing a schoolfellow, who had left the sixth form at Rugby for Cambridge, and who had fallen in somewhere with one of Bunsen's sons, who is now a member of the German Parliament,—at hearing this school-fellow contrast the training of George Bunsen, as we then called him, with our own. Perhaps you think that at Rugby, which is often spoken of, though quite erroneously, as a sort of opposition establishment to Eton, we treated the classics in a high philosophical way, and traced the sequence of things in ancient literature, when you at Eton professed nothing of the kind. But hear the criticism of my old schoolfellow. "It is wonderful," said he; "not only can George Bunsen construe his Herodotus, but he has a view of the place of Herodotus in literary history, a thing none of us ever thought about." My friend spoke the truth; but even then, as I listened to him, I felt an emotion at hearing of the place of Herodotus in literary history. Yes, not only to be able to read the admirable works of classical literature, but to conceive also that Graeco-Roman world, which is so mighty a factor in our own world, our own life, to conceive it as a whole of which we can trace the sequence, and the sense, and the connection with ourselves, this does undoubtedly also belong to a classical education, rightly understood.

But even here, too, a plain person can proceed, if he likes, with great simplicity. As Goethe says of life: Strike into it anywhere, lay hold of it anywhere, it is always powerful and interesting,—so one may almost say of classical literature. Strike into it where you like, lay hold of it where you like, you can nearly always find a thread which will lead you, if you follow it, to large and instructive results. Let us to-night follow a single Greek word in this fashion, and try to compensate our-selves, however imperfectly, for having to divert our thoughts, just for one evening's lecture, from the diameter of the sun and moon.

The word I will take is the word *eutrapelos, eutrapelia.* Let us consider it first as it occurs in the famous Funeral Oration put by Thucydides into the mouth of Pericles. The word stands there for one of the chief of those qualities which have made

Athens, says Pericles, "the school of Greece;" for a quality by
which Athens is eminently representative of what is called
Hellenism: the quality of flexibility. "A happy and gracious
flexibility," Pericles calls this quality of the Athenians; and it
5 is no doubt a charming gift. Lucidity of thought, clearness and
propriety of language, freedom from prejudice and freedom
from stiffness, openness of mind, amiability of manners,—all
these seem to go along with a certain happy flexibility of nature,
and to depend upon it. Nor does this suppleness and flexibility
10 of nature at all necessarily imply, as we English are apt to
suppose, a relaxed moral fibre and weakness. In the Athenian
of the best time it did not. "In the Athenians," says Professor
Curtius, "the sense of energy abhorred every kind of waste of
time, their sense of measure abhorred bombast and redundancy,
15 and their clear intelligence everything partaking of obscurity or
vagueness; it was their habit in all things to advance directly
and resolutely to the goal. Their dialect is characterised by a
superior seriousness, manliness, and vigour of language."
    There is no sign of relaxation of moral fibre here; and yet,
20 at the same time, the Athenians were eminent for a happy and
gracious flexibility. That quality, as we all know, is not a
characteristic quality of the Germanic nations, to which we ourselves belong. Men are educable, and when we read of the
abhorrence of the Attic mind for redundancy and obscurity of
25 expression, its love for direct and telling speech, and then think
of modern German, we may say with satisfaction that the circumstances of our life have at any rate educated us into the use
of straightforward and vigorous forms of language. But they
have not educated us into flexibility. All around us we may
30 observe proofs of it. The state of Ireland is a proof of it. We
are rivals with Russia in Central Asia, and at this moment it is
particularly interesting to note how the want of just this one
Athenian quality of flexibility seems to tell against us in our
Asiatic rivalry with Russia. "Russia," observes one who is
35 perhaps the first of living geographers,—an Austrian, Herr von
Hellwald,—"possesses far more shrewdness, *flexibility*, and con-
geniality than England; qualities adapted to make the Asiatic
races tractable." And again: "There can be no dispute which

of the two, England or Russia, is the more civilised nation. But it is just as certain that the highly civilised English understand but indifferently how to raise their Asiatic subjects to their own standard of civilisation; whilst the Russians attain, with their much lower standard of civilisation, far greater results amongst the Asiatic tribes, whom they know how to assimilate in the most remarkable manner. Of course they can only bring them to the same level which they have reached themselves; but the little which they can and do communicate to them counts actually for much more than the great boons which the English do not know how to impart. Under the auspices of Russia the advance in civilisation amongst the Asiatics is indeed slow and inconsiderable, but steady, and suitable to their natural capacities and the disposition of their race. On the other hand, they remain indifferent to British civilisation, which is absolutely incomprehensible to them."

Our word "flexibility" has here carried us a long way, carried us to Turkestan and the valleys of the Jaxartes and Oxus. Let us get back to Greece, at any rate. The generation of Pericles is succeeded by the generation of Plato and Aristotle. Still the charming and Athenian quality of *eutrapelia* continues to be held in high esteem. Only the word comes to stand more particularly for flexibility and felicity in the give-and-take of gay and light social intercourse. With Aristotle it is one of the virtues: the virtue of him who in this pleasant sort of intercourse, so relished by the Greeks, manages exactly to hit the happy and right mean; the virtue opposed to buffoonery on the one side, and to morose rusticity, or clownishness, on the other. It is in especial the virtue of the young, and is akin to the grace and charm of youth. When old men try to adapt themselves to the young, says Plato, they betake themselves, in imitation of the young, to *eutrapelia* and pleasantry.

Four hundred years pass, and we come to the date of the Epistle to the Ephesians. The word *eutrapelia* rises in the mind of the writer of that Epistle. It rises to St. Paul's mind, and he utters it; but in how different a sense from the praising and admiring sense in which we have seen the word used by Thucydides and Aristotle! *Eutrapelia*, which once stood for

that eminently Athenian and Hellenic virtue of happy and
gracious flexibility, now conveys this favourable sense no
longer, but is ranked, with filthiness and foolish talking, among
things which are not convenient. Like these, it is not to be even
5   so much as once named among the followers of God: "neither
filthiness, nor foolish talking, nor jesting (*eutrapelia*), which
are not convenient."

This is an extraordinary change, you will say. But now, as
we have descended four hundred years from Aristotle to St.
10   Paul, let us ascend, not four hundred, not quite even one hundred years, from Thucydides to Pindar. The religious Theban
poet, we shall see (and the thing is surely very remarkable),
speaks of the quality of *eutrapelia* in the same disapproving and
austere way as the writer of the Epistle to the Ephesians. The
15   young and noble Jason appears at Iolcos, and being questioned
about himself by Pelias, he answers that he has been trained
in the nurture and admonition of the old and just Centaur,
Chiron. "From his cave I come, from Chariclo and Philyra, his
stainless daughters, who there nursed me. Lo, these twenty
20   years am I with them, and there hath been found in me neither
deed nor word that is not convenient; and now, behold, I am
come home, that I may recover my father's kingdom." The
adjective *eutrapelos*, as it is here used in connection with its two
nouns, means exactly a word or deed, in Biblical phrase, *of*
25   *vain lightness*, a word or deed *such as is not convenient.*

There you have the history of the varying use of the words
eutrapelos, eutrapelia. And now see how this varying use gives
us a clue to the order and sense, as we say, of all that Greek
world so nearly and wonderfully connected with us, so pro-
30   foundly interesting for us, so full of precious lessons.

We must begin with generalities, but we will try not to lose
ourselves in them, and not to remain amongst them long.
Human life and human society arise, we know, out of the
presence in man of certain needs, certain instincts, and out of
35   the constant endeavour of these instincts to satisfy and develop
themselves. We may briefly sum them up, these needs or instincts, as being, first and foremost, a general instinct of expansion; then, as being instincts following diverse great lines,

which may be conveniently designated as the lines of conduct, of intellect and knowledge, of beauty, of social life and manners. Some lines are more in view and more in honour at one time, some at another. Some men and some nations are more eminent on one line, some on another. But the final aim, of making our own and of harmoniously combining the powers to be reached on each and all of these great lines, is the ideal of human life. And our race is for ever recalled to this aim, and held fast to it, by the instinct of self-preservation in humanity.

The ideal of human life being such as it is, all these great and diverse powers, to the attainment of which our instincts, as we have seen, impel us, hang together,—cannot be truly possessed and employed in isolation. Yet it is convenient, owing to the way in which we find them actually exhibiting themselves in human life and in history, to treat them separately, and to make distinctions of rank amongst them. In this view, we may say that the power of conduct is the greatest of all the powers now named; that it is even three-fourths of life. And wherever much is founded amongst men, there the power of conduct has surely been present and at work, although of course there may be and are, along with it, other powers too.

Now, then, let us look at the beginnings of that Greece to which we owe so much, and which we may almost, so far as our intellectual life is concerned, call the mother of us all. "So well has she done her part," as the Athenian Isocrates truly says of her, "that the name of Greeks seems no longer to stand for a race but to stand for intelligence itself; and they who share in Hellenic culture are called Greeks even before those who are merely of Hellenic blood."

The beginnings of this wonderful Greece, what are they?

Greek history begins for us with the sanctuaries of Tempe and Delphi, and with the Apolline worship and priesthood which in those sanctuaries under Olympus and Parnassus established themselves. The northern sanctuary of Tempe soon yielded to Delphi as the centre of national Hellenic life and of Apolline religion. We are accustomed to think of Apollo as the awakener and nourisher of what is called genius, and so from the very first the Greeks, too, considered him. But in those

earliest days of Hellas, and at Delphi, where the hardy and serious tribes of the Dorian Highlands made their influence felt, Apollo was not only the nourisher of genius, he was also the au-thor of every higher moral effort. He was the prophet of his
5   father Zeus, in the highest view of Zeus, as the source of the ideas of moral order and of right. For to this higher significance had the names of Zeus and Phœbus,—names originally derived from sun and air,—gradually risen. They had come to designate a Father, the source of the ideas of moral order and of right; and
10 a Son, his prophet, purifying and inspiring the soul with these ideas, and also with the idea of intellectual beauty.

Now, the ideas of moral order and of right which are in human nature, and which are, indeed, a main part of human life, were especially, we are told, a treasure possessed by the
15 less gay and more solitary tribes in the mountains of Northern Greece. These Dorian tribes were Delphi's first pupils. And the graver view of life, the thoughts which give depth and solem-nity to man's consciousness, the moral ideas, in short, of con-duct and righteousness, were the governing elements in the
20 manner of spirit propagated from Delphi. The words written up on the temple at Delphi called all comers to *soberness and righteousness.* The Doric and Æolic Pindar felt profoundly this severe influence of Delphi. It is not to be considered as an influence at war with the idea of intellectual beauty;—to men-
25 tion the name of Pindar is in itself sufficient to show how little this was, or could be, the case. But it was, above all, an influence charged with the ideas of moral order and of right.

And there were confronting these Dorian founders of Hellas, and well known to them, and connected with them in manifold
30 ways, other Greeks of a very different spiritual type; the Asiatic Greeks of Ionia, full of brilliancy and mobility, but over whom the ideas of moral order and of right had too little power, and who could never succeed in founding among themselves a serious and powerful state. It was evident that the great source
35 of the incapacity which accompanied, in these Ionians of Asia, so much brilliancy, that the great enemy in them to the *Halt*, as Goethe calls it, the steadiness, which moral natures so highly prize, was their extreme mobility of spirit, their gay lightness,

their *eutrapelia*. For Pindar, therefore, the word *eutrapelos*, expressing easy flexibility and mobility, becomes a word of stern opprobrium, and conveys the reproach of vain folly.

The Athenians were Ionians. But they were Ionians transplanted to Hellas, and who had breathed, as a Hellenic nation, the air of Delphi, that bracing atmosphere of the ideas of moral order and of right. In this atmosphere the Athenians, Ionian as they were, imbibed influences of character and steadiness, which for a long while balanced their native vivacity and mobility, distinguished them profoundly from the Ionians of Asia, and gave them men like Aristides.

Still, the Athenians were Ionians. They had the Ionian quickness and flexibility, the Ionian turn for gaiety, wit, and fearless thinking, the Ionian impatience of restraint. This nature of theirs asserted itself, first of all, as an impatience of *false* restraint. It asserted itself in opposition to the real faults of the Dorian spirit,—faults which became more and more manifest as time went on; to the unprogressiveness of this spirit, to its stiffness, hardness, narrowness, prejudice, want of insight, want of amiability. And in real truth, by the time of Pericles, Delphi, the great creation of the Dorian spirit, had broken down, and was a witness to that spirit's lack of a real power of life and growth. Bribes had discredited the sanctity of Delphi; seriousness and vital power had left it. It had come to be little more than a name, and what continued to exist there was merely a number of forms.

Now then was the turn of the Athenians. With the idea of conduct, so little grasped by the Ionians of Asia, still deeply impressed on their soul, they freely and joyfully called forth also that pleasure in life, that love of clear thinking and of fearless discussion, that gay social temper, that ease and lightness, that gracious flexibility, which were in their nature. These were their gifts, and they did well to bring them forth. The gifts are in themselves gifts of great price, like those other gifts contributed by the primitive and serious Dorian tribes, their rivals. Man has to advance, we have seen, along several lines, and he does well to advance along them. "In the morning sow thy seed, and in the evening withhold not thine hand; for thou knowest not whether shall prosper, either this or that, or whether they both shall be alike good."

And at this moment Thucydides, a man in whom the old virtue and the new reason were in just balance, has put into the mouth of Pericles, another man of the same kind, an encomium on the modern spirit, as we may call it, of which Athens was the representative. By the mouth of Pericles, Thucydides condemned old-fashioned narrowness and illiberality. He applauded enjoyment of life. He applauded freedom from restraint. He applauded clear and fearless thinking,—the resolute bringing of our actions to the rule of reason. His expressions on this point greatly remind me of the fine saying of one of your own worthies, "the ever-memorable Mr. John Hales, of Eton College." "I comprise it all," says Hales, "in two words: *what* and *wherefore*. That part of your burden which contains *what*, you willingly take up. But that other, which comprehends *why*, that is either too hot or too heavy; you dare not meddle with it. But I must add that also to your burden, or else I must leave you for idle persons; for without the knowledge of *why*, of the grounds or reasons of things, there is no possibility of not being deceived." It seems to me not improbable that Hales had here in his mind the very words of the Funeral Oration: "We do not esteem discussion a hurt to action; what we consider mischievous is rather the setting oneself to work without first getting the guidance of reason." Finally, Thucydides applauded the quality of nature which above all others made the Athenians the men for the new era, and he used the word *eutrapelos* in its proper and natural sense, to denote the quality of happy and gracious flexibility.

Somewhat narrowed, so as to mean especially flexibility and adroitness in light social intercourse, but still employed in its natural and favourable sense, the word descends, as we saw, to Plato and Aristotle. Isocrates speaks of the quality as one which the old school regarded with alarm and disapproval; but, nevertheless, for him too the word has evidently, in itself, just the same natural and favourable sense which it has for Aristotle and Plato.

I quoted, just now, some words from the Book of Ecclesiastes, one of the wisest and one of the worst understood books in the Bible. Let us hear how the writer goes on after the words which I quoted. He proceeds thus: "Truly the light is sweet, and a pleasant thing it is for the eyes to behold the sun; yea, if a man live many years, let him rejoice in them all; and let him remember the days of darkness, for they shall be many. All that is future is vanity. Rejoice, O young man, in thy youth, and let thy heart cheer thee in the days of thy youth, and walk in the ways of thine heart and in the sight of thine eyes;—but know thou that for all these things God will bring thee into judgment." Let us apply these admirable words to the life and work of the Athenian people.

The old rigid order, in Greece, breaks down; a new power appears on the scene. It is the Athenian genius, with its freedom from restraint, its flexibility, its bold reason, its keen enjoyment of life. Well, let it try what it can do. Up to a certain point it is clearly in the right; possibly it may be in the right altogether. Let it have free play, and show what it can do. "In the morning sow thy seed, and in the evening withhold not thine hand; for thou knowest not whether shall prosper, either this or that, or whether they both shall be alike good." Whether the old line is good, or the new line, or whether they are both of them good, and must both of them be used, cannot be known without trying. Let the Athenians try, therefore, and let their genius have full swing. "Rejoice; walk in the ways of thine heart and in the sight of thine eyes;—*but know thou that for all these things God will bring thee into judgment.*" In other words: Your enjoyment of life, your freedom from restraint, your clear and bold reason, your flexibility, are natural and excellent; but on condition that you know how to live with them, that you make a real success of them.

And a man like Pericles or Phidias seemed to afford promise that Athens would know how to make a real success of her qualities, and that an alliance between the old morality and the new freedom might be, through the admirable Athenian genius, happily established. And with such promise before his eyes, a

serious man like Thucydides might well give to the new freedom the high and warm praise which we see given to it in the
Funeral Oration.

But it soon became evident that the balance between the old
morality and the new freedom was not to be maintained, and
that the Athenians had the defects, as the saying is, of their
qualities. Their minds were full of other things than those
ideas of moral order and of right on which primitive Hellas had
formed itself, and of which they themselves had, as worshippers
in the shadow of the Parnassian sanctuary, once deeply felt the
power. These ideas lost their predominance. The predominance
for Athens,—and, indeed, for Hellas at large,—of a national
religion of righteousness, of grave ideas of conduct and moral
order, predominating over all other ideas, disappeared with the
decline of Delphi, never to return. Not only did these ideas
lose exclusive predominance, they lost all due weight. Still, indeed, they inspired poetry; and then, after inspiring the great
Attic poets, Æschylus and Sophocles, they inspired the great
Attic philosophers, Socrates and Plato. But the Attic nation,
which henceforth stood, in fact, for the Hellenic people, could
not manage to keep its mind bent sufficiently upon them. The
Attic nation had its mind bent on other things. It threw itself
ardently upon other lines, which man, indeed, has to follow,
which at one time, in Greece, had not been enough followed,
of which Athens strongly felt the attraction, and on which it
had rare gifts for excelling. The Attic nation gave its heart to
those powers which we have designated, for the sake of brevity
and convenience, as those of expansion, intellect, beauty, social
life and manners. Athens and Greece allowed themselves to be
diverted and distracted from attention to conduct, and to the
ideas which inspire conduct.

It was not that the old religious beliefs of Greece, to which
the ideas that inspire conduct had attached themselves, did not
require to be transformed by the new spirit. They did. The
greatest and best Hellenic souls, Anaxagoras, Pericles, Phidias,
Sophocles, Socrates, Plato, felt, and rightly felt, that they did.
The judicious historian of Greece, whom I have already quoted,
Professor Curtius, says expressly: "The popular faith was

everywhere shaken, and a life resting simply on the traditionary notions was no longer possible. A dangerous rupture was at hand, unless the ancient faith were purged and elevated in such a manner as to meet the wants of the age. Mediators in this sense appeared in the persons of the great poets of Athens." Yes, they appeared; but the current was setting too strongly another way. Poetry itself, after the death of Sophocles, "was seized," says Professor Curtius, "by the same current which dissolved the foundations of the people's life, and which swept away the soil wherein the emotions of the classical period had been rooted. The old perished; but the modern age, with all its readiness in thought and speech, was incapable of creating a new art as a support to its children."

Socrates was so penetrated with the new intellectual spirit that he was called a sophist. But the great effort of Socrates was to recover that firm foundation for human life, which a misuse of the new intellectual spirit was rendering impossible. He effected much more for after times, and for the world, than for his own people. His amount of success with Alcibiades may probably be taken as giving us, well enough, the measure of his success with the Athenian people at large. "As to the susceptibility of Alcibiades," we are told, "Socrates had not come too late, for he still found in him a youthful soul, susceptible of high inspirations. But to effect in him a permanent reaction, and a lasting and fixed change of mind, was beyond the power even of a Socrates." Alcibiades oscillated and fell away; and the Athenian people, too, and Hellas as a whole, oscillated and fell away.

So it came to pass, that after Æschylus had sadly raised his voice to deprecate "unblessed freedom from restraint," and after complaints had been heard, again and again, of the loss of "the ancient morality and piety," of "the old elements of Hellas, reflection and moderation, discipline and social morality," it came to pass that finally, at the end of the Peloponnesian war, "one result," the historian tells us, "one result alone admitted of no doubt; and that was, the horribly rapid progress of the demoralisation of the Hellenic nation."

Years and centuries rolled on, and, first, the Hellenic genius

issued forth invading and vanquishing with Alexander; and
then, when Rome had afterwards conquered Greece, conquered
the conquerors, and overspread the civilised world. And still,
joined to all the gifts and graces which that admirable genius
brought with it, there went, as a kind of fatal accompaniment,
moral inadequacy. And if one asked why this was so, it seemed
as if it could only be because the power of seriousness, of
tenacious grasp upon grave and moral ideas, was wanting. And
this again seemed as if it could only have for its cause, that these
Hellenic natures were, in respect of their impressionability,
mobility, flexibility, under the spell of a graceful but dangerous
fairy, who would not let it be otherwise. "Lest thou shouldst
ponder the path of life," says the Wise Man, "*her ways are
moveable, that thou canst not know them.*" Then the new and
reforming spirit, the Christian spirit, which was rising in the
world, turned sternly upon this gracious flexibility, changed
the sense of its name, branded it with infamy, and classed it,
along with "filthiness and foolish talking," among "things which
are not convenient."

Now, there you see the historical course of our words *eutrapelos, eutrapelia*, and a specimen of the range, backwards and
forwards, which a single phrase in one of our Greek or Latin
classics may have.

And I might go yet further, and might show you, in the
mediæval world, *eutrapelia*, or flexibility, quite banished, clear
straightforward Attic thinking quite lost; restraint, stoppage,
and prejudice, regnant. And coming down to our own times, I
might show you fearless thinking and flexibility once more,
after many vicissitudes, coming into honour; and again, perhaps,
not without their accompaniment of danger. And the moral
from all this,—apart from the particular moral that in our
classical studies we may everywhere find clues which will lead
us a long way,—the moral is, not that flexibility is a bad thing,
but that the Greek flexibility was really not flexible enough,
because it could not enough bend itself to the moral ideas which
are so large a part of life. Here, I say, is the true moral: that
man has to make progress along diverse lines, in obedience to
a diversity of aspirations and powers, the sum of which is truly

his nature; and that he fails and falls short until he learns to advance upon them all, and to advance upon them harmoniously.

Yes, this is the moral, and we all need it, and no nation more than ours. We so easily think that life is all on one line! Our nation, for instance, is above all things a political nation, and is apt to make far too much of politics. Many of us,—though not so very many, I suppose, of you here,—are Liberals, and think that to be a Liberal is quite enough for a man. Probably most of you here will have no difficulty in believing that to be a Liberal is not alone enough for a man, is not saving. One might even take,—and with your notions it would probably be a great treat for you,—one might take the last century of Athens, the century preceding the "dishonest victory" of the Macedonian power, and show you a society dying of the triumph of the Liberal party. And then, again, as the young are generous, you might like to give the discomfited Liberals a respite, to let the other side have its turn; and you might consent to be shown, as you could be shown in the age of Trajan and of the Antonines, a society dying of the triumph of the Conservative party. They were excellent people, the Conservative Roman aristocracy of that epoch;—excellent, most respectable people, like the Conservatives of our own acquaintance. Only Conservatism, like Liberalism, taken alone, is not sufficient, is not of itself saving.

But you have had enough for one evening. And besides, the tendencies of the present day in education being what they are, before you proceed to hear more of this sort of thing, you ought certainly to be favoured, for several months to come, with a great many scientific lectures, and to busy yourselves considerably with the diameter of the sun and moon.

Wordsworth[1]

I remember hearing Lord Macaulay say, after Wordsworth's death, when subscriptions were being collected to found a memorial of him, that ten years earlier more money could have been raised in Cambridge alone, to do honour to Wordsworth, than was now raised all through the country. Lord Macaulay had, as we know, his own heightened and telling way of putting things, and we must always make allowance for it. But probably it is true that Wordsworth has never, either before or since, been so accepted and popular, so established in possession of the minds of all who profess to care for poetry, as he was between the years 1830 and 1840, and at Cambridge. From the very first, no doubt, he had his believers and witnesses. But I have myself heard him declare that, for he knew not how many years, his poetry had never brought him in enough to buy his shoe-strings. The poetry-reading public was very slow to recognise him, and was very easily drawn away from him. Scott effaced him with this public, Byron effaced him.

The death of Byron seemed, however, to make an opening for Wordsworth. Scott, who had for some time ceased to produce poetry himself, and stood before the public as a great novelist; Scott, too genuine himself not to feel the profound genuineness of Wordsworth, and with an instinctive recognition of his firm hold on nature and of his local truth, always admired him sincerely, and praised him generously. The influence of Coleridge upon young men of ability was then powerful, and was still gathering strength; this influence told entirely in favour of Wordsworth's poetry. Cambridge was a place

[1] The preface to *The Poems of Wordsworth*, chosen and edited by Matthew Arnold, 1879.

where Coleridge's influence had great action, and where Wordsworth's poetry, therefore, flourished especially. But even amongst the general public its sale grew large, the eminence of its author was widely recognised, and Rydal Mount became an object of pilgrimage. I remember Wordsworth relating how one of the pilgrims, a clergyman, asked him if he had ever written anything besides the *Guide to the Lakes*. Yes, he answered modestly, he had written verses. Not every pilgrim was a reader, but the vogue was established, and the stream of pilgrims came.

Mr. Tennyson's decisive appearance dates from 1842. One cannot say that he effaced Wordsworth as Scott and Byron had effaced him. The poetry of Wordsworth had been so long before the public, the suffrage of good judges was so steady and so strong in its favour, that by 1842 the verdict of posterity, one may almost say, had been already pronounced, and Wordsworth's English fame was secure. But the vogue, the ear and applause of the great body of poetry-readers, never quite thoroughly perhaps his, he gradually lost more and more, and Mr. Tennyson gained them. Mr. Tennyson drew to himself, and away from Wordsworth, the poetry-reading public, and the new generations. Even in 1850, when Wordsworth died, this diminution of popularity was visible, and occasioned the remark of Lord Macaulay which I quoted at starting.

The diminution has continued. The influence of Coleridge has waned, and Wordsworth's poetry can no longer draw succour from this ally. The poetry has not, however, wanted eulogists; and it may be said to have brought its eulogists luck, for almost every one who has praised Wordsworth's poetry has praised it well. But the public has remained cold, or, at least, undetermined. Even the abundance of Mr. Palgrave's fine and skilfully chosen specimens of Wordsworth, in the *Golden Treasury*, surprised many readers, and gave offence to not a few. To tenth-rate critics and compilers, for whom any violent shock to the public taste would be a temerity not to be risked, it is still quite permissible to speak of Wordsworth's poetry, not only with ignorance, but with impertinence. On the Continent he is almost unknown.

I cannot think, then, that Wordsworth has, up to this time, at all obtained his deserts. 'Glory,' said M. Renan the other day, 'glory after all is the thing which has the best chance of not being altogether vanity.' Wordsworth was a homely man, and 5 himself would certainly never have thought of talking of glory as that which, after all, has the best chance of not being altogether vanity. Yet we may well allow that few things are less vain than *real* glory. Let us conceive of the whole group of civilised nations as being, for intellectual and spiritual purposes, 10 one great confederation, bound to a joint action and working towards a common result; a confederation whose members have a due knowledge both of the past, out of which they all proceed, and of one another. This was the ideal of Goethe, and it is an ideal which will impose itself upon the thoughts of our modern 15 societies more and more. Then to be recognised by the verdict of such a confederation as a master, or even as a seriously and eminently worthy workman, in one's own line of intellectual or spiritual activity, is indeed glory; a glory which it would be difficult to rate too highly. For what could be more beneficent, 20 more salutary? The world is forwarded by having its attention fixed on the best things; and here is a tribunal, free from all suspicion of national and provincial partiality, putting a stamp on the best things, and recommending them for general honour and acceptance. A nation, again, is furthered by recognition of 25 its real gifts and successes; it is encouraged to develop them further. And here is an honest verdict, telling us which of our supposed successes are really, in the judgment of the great impartial world, and not in our own private judgment only, successes, and which are not.

30 It is so easy to feel pride and satisfaction in one's own things, so hard to make sure that one is right in feeling it! We have a great empire. But so had Nebuchadnezzar. We extol the 'unrivalled happiness' of our national civilisation. But then comes a candid friend, and remarks that our upper class is materialised, 35 our middle class vulgarised, and our lower class brutalised. We are proud of our painting, our music. But we find that in the judgment of other people our painting is questionable, and our music non-existent. We are proud of our men of science. And

here it turns out that the world is with us; we find that in the judgment of other people, too, Newton among the dead, and Mr. Darwin among the living, hold as high a place as they hold in our national opinion.

Finally, we are proud of our poets and poetry. Now poetry is nothing less than the most perfect speech of man, that in which he comes nearest to being able to utter the truth. It is no small thing, therefore, to succeed eminently in poetry. And so much is required for duly estimating success here, that about poetry it is perhaps hardest to arrive at a sure general verdict, and takes longest. Meanwhile, our own conviction of the superiority of our national poets is not decisive, is almost certain to be mingled, as we see constantly in English eulogy of Shakespeare, with much of provincial infatuation. And we know what was the opinion current amongst our neighbours the French—people of taste, acuteness, and quick literary tact—not a hundred years ago, about our great poets. The old *Biographie Universelle* notices the pretension of the English to a place for their poets among the chief poets of the world, and says that this is a pretension which to no one but an Englishman can ever seem admissible. And the scornful, disparaging things said by foreigners about Shakespeare and Milton, and about our national over-estimate of them, have been often quoted, and will be in every one's remembrance.

A great change has taken place, and Shakespeare is now generally recognised, even in France, as one of the greatest of poets. Yes, some anti-Gallican cynic will say, the French rank him with Corneille and with Victor Hugo! But let me have the pleasure of quoting a sentence about Shakespeare, which I met with by accident not long ago in the *Correspondant*, a French review which not a dozen English people, I suppose, look at. The writer is praising Shakespeare's prose. With Shakespeare, he says, 'prose comes in whenever the subject, being more familiar, is unsuited to the majestic English iambic.' And he goes on: 'Shakespeare is the king of poetic rhythm and style, as well as the king of the realm of thought; along with his dazzling prose, Shakespeare has succeeded in giving us the most varied, the most harmonious verse which has ever sounded upon the

human ear since the verse of the Greeks.' M. Henry Cochin, the
writer of this sentence, deserves our gratitude for it; it would
not be easy to praise Shakespeare, in a single sentence, more
justly. And when a foreigner and a Frenchman writes thus of
5   Shakespeare, and when Goethe says of Milton, in whom there
was so much to repel Goethe rather than to attract him, that
'nothing has been ever done so entirely in the sense of the
Greeks as *Samson Agonistes*,' and that 'Milton is in very truth
a poet whom we must treat with all reverence,' then we under-
10 stand what constitutes a European recognition of poets and
poetry as contradistinguished from a merely national recognition, and that in favour both of Milton and of Shakespeare the
judgment of the high court of appeal has finally gone.

I come back to M. Renan's praise of glory, from which I
15 started. Yes, real glory is a most serious thing, glory authenti-
cated by the Amphictyonic Court of final appeal, definitive
glory. And even for poets and poetry, long and difficult as may
be the process of arriving at the right award, the right award
comes at last, the definitive glory rests where it is deserved.
20 Every establishment of such a real glory is good and wholesome
for mankind at large, good and wholesome for the nation which
produced the poet crowned with it. To the poet himself it can
seldom do harm; for he, poor man, is in his grave, probably,
long before his glory crowns him.

25 Wordsworth has been in his grave for some thirty years, and
certainly his lovers and admirers cannot flatter themselves that
this great and steady light of glory as yet shines over him. He is
not fully recognised at home; he is not recognised at all abroad.
Yet I firmly believe that the poetical performance of Words-
30 worth is, after that of Shakespeare and Milton, of which all the
world now recognises the worth, undoubtedly the most considerable in our language from the Elizabethan age to the
present time. Chaucer is anterior; and on other grounds, too,
he cannot well be brought into the comparison. But taking the
35 roll of our chief poetical names, besides Shakespeare and Milton,
from the age of Elizabeth downwards, and going through it,—
Spenser, Dryden, Pope, Gray, Goldsmith, Cowper, Burns,
Coleridge, Scott, Campbell, Moore, Byron, Shelley, Keats (I

mention those only who are dead),—I think it certain that Wordsworth's name deserves to stand, and will finally stand, above them all. Several of the poets named have gifts and excellences which Wordsworth has not. But taking the performance of each as a whole, I say that Wordsworth seems to me to have left a body of poetical work superior in power, in interest, in the qualities which give enduring freshness, to that which any one of the others has left.

But this is not enough to say. I think it certain, further, that if we take the chief poetical names of the Continent since the death of Molière, and, omitting Goethe, confront the remaining names with that of Wordsworth, the result is the same. Let us take Klopstock, Lessing, Schiller, Uhland, Rückert, and Heine for Germany; Filicaia, Alfieri, Manzoni, and Leopardi for Italy; Racine, Boileau, Voltaire, André Chenier, Béranger, Lamartine, Musset, M. Victor Hugo (he has been so long celebrated that although he still lives I may be permitted to name him) for France. Several of these, again, have evidently gifts and excellences to which Wordsworth can make no pretension. But in real poetical achievement it seems to me indubitable that to Wordsworth, here again, belongs the palm. It seems to me that Wordsworth has left behind him a body of poetical work which wears, and will wear, better on the whole than the performance of any one of these personages, so far more brilliant and celebrated, most of them, than the homely poet of Rydal. Wordsworth's performance in poetry is on the whole, in power, in interest, in the qualities which give enduring freshness, superior to theirs.

This is a high claim to make for Wordsworth. But if it is a just claim, if Wordsworth's place among the poets who have appeared in the last two or three centuries is after Shakespeare, Molière, Milton, Goethe, indeed, but before all the rest, then in time Wordsworth will have his due. We shall recognise him in his place, as we recognise Shakespeare and Milton; and not only we ourselves shall recognise him, but he will be recognised by Europe also. Meanwhile, those who recognise him already may do well, perhaps, to ask themselves whether there are not in the case of Wordsworth certain special obstacles which hinder or delay his due recognition by others, and whether these obstacles are not in some measure removable.

The *Excursion* and the *Prelude*, his poems of greatest bulk, are by no means Wordsworth's best work. His best work is in his shorter pieces, and many indeed are there of these which are of first-rate excellence. But in his seven volumes the pieces of high merit are mingled with a mass of pieces very inferior to them; so inferior to them that it seems wonderful how the same poet should have produced both. Shakespeare frequently has lines and passages in a strain quite false, and which are entirely unworthy of him. But one can imagine his smiling if one could meet him in the Elysian Fields and tell him so; smiling and replying that he knew it perfectly well himself, and what did it matter? But with Wordsworth the case is different. Work altogether inferior, work quite uninspired, flat and dull, is produced by him with evident unconsciousness of its defects, and he presents it to us with the same faith and seriousness as his best work. Now a drama or an epic fill the mind, and one does not look beyond them; but in a collection of short pieces the impression made by one piece requires to be continued and sustained by the piece following. In reading Wordsworth the impression made by one of his fine pieces is too often dulled and spoiled by a very inferior piece coming after it.

Wordsworth composed verses during a space of some sixty years; and it is no exaggeration to say that within one single decade of those years, between 1798 and 1808, almost all his really first-rate work was produced. A mass of inferior work remains, work done before and after this golden prime, imbedding the first-rate work and clogging it, obstructing our approach to it, chilling, not unfrequently, the high-wrought mood with which we leave it. To be recognised far and wide as a great poet, to be possible and receivable as a classic, Wordsworth needs to be relieved of a great deal of the poetical baggage which now encumbers him. To administer this relief is indispensable, unless he is to continue to be a poet for the few only,—a poet valued far below his real worth by the world.

There is another thing. Wordsworth classified his poems not according to any commonly received plan of arrangement, but

according to a scheme of mental physiology. He has poems of
the fancy, poems of the imagination, poems of sentiment and
reflection, and so on. His categories are ingenious but far-
fetched, and the result of his employment of them is unsatisfactory. Poems are separated one from another which possess 5
a kinship of subject or of treatment far more vital and deep
than the supposed unity of mental origin which was Wordsworth's reason for joining them with others.

The tact of the Greeks in matters of this kind was infallible.
We may rely upon it that we shall not improve upon the 10
classification adopted by the Greeks for kinds of poetry; that
their categories of epic, dramatic, lyric, and so forth, have a
natural propriety, and should be adhered to. It may sometimes
seem doubtful to which of two categories a poem belongs;
whether this or that poem is to be called, for instance, narrative 15
or lyric, lyric or elegiac. But there is to be found in every good
poem a strain, a predominant note, which determines the poem
as belonging to one of these kinds rather than the other; and
here is the best proof of the value of the classification, and of
the advantage of adhering to it. Wordsworth's poems will 20
never produce their due effect until they are freed from their
present artificial arrangement, and grouped more naturally.

Disengaged from the quantity of inferior work which now
obscures them, the best poems of Wordsworth, I hear many
people say, would indeed stand out in great beauty, but they 25
would prove to be very few in number, scarcely more than
half a dozen. I maintain, on the other hand, that what strikes
me with admiration, what establishes in my opinion Wordsworth's superiority, is the great and ample body of powerful
work which remains to him, even after all his inferior work has 30
been cleared away. He gives us so much to rest upon, so much
which communicates his spirit and engages ours!

This is of very great importance. If it were a comparison of
single pieces, or of three or four pieces, by each poet, I do not
say that Wordsworth would stand decisively above Gray, or 35
Burns, or Coleridge, or Keats, or Manzoni, or Heine. It is in
his ampler body of powerful work that I find his superiority.
His good work itself, his work which counts, is not all of it, of

course, of equal value. Some kinds of poetry are in themselves
lower kinds than others. The ballad kind is a lower kind; the
didactic kind, still more, is a lower kind. Poetry of this latter
sort counts, too, sometimes, by its biographical interest partly,
5   not by its poetical interest pure and simple; but then this can
only be when the poet producing it has the power and importance of Wordsworth, a power and importance which he assuredly did not establish by such didactic poetry alone.
Altogether, it is, I say, by the great body of powerful and
10   significant work which remains to him, after every reduction
and deduction has been made, that Wordsworth's superiority
is proved.

    To exhibit this body of Wordsworth's best work, to clear
away obstructions from around it, and to let it speak for itself,
15   is what every lover of Wordsworth should desire. Until this has
been done, Wordsworth, whom we, to whom he is dear, all of us
know and feel to be so great a poet, has not had a fair chance
before the world. When once it has been done, he will make his
way best, not by our advocacy of him, but by his own worth and
20   power. We may safely leave him to make his way thus, we who
believe that a superior worth and power in poetry finds in mankind a sense responsive to it and disposed at last to recognise it.
Yet at the outset, before he has been duly known and recognised,
we may do Wordsworth a service, perhaps, by indicating in what
25   his superior power and worth will be found to consist, and in
what it will not.

    Long ago, in speaking of Homer, I said that the noble and
profound application of ideas to life is the most essential part of
poetic greatness. I said that a great poet receives his distinctive
30   character of superiority from his application, under the conditions immutably fixed by the laws of poetic beauty and poetic
truth, from his application, I say, to his subject, whatever it may
be, of the ideas

          'On man, on nature, and on human life,'

35   which he has acquired for himself. The line quoted is Wordsworth's own; and his superiority arises from his powerful use,

in his best pieces, his powerful application to his subject, of ideas
'on man, on nature, and on human life.'

Voltaire, with his signal acuteness, most truly remarked that
'no nation has treated in poetry moral ideas with more energy
and depth than the English nation.' And he adds: 'There, it 5
seems to me, is the great merit of the English poets.' Voltaire
does not mean, by 'treating in poetry moral ideas,' the composing moral and didactic poems;—that brings us but a very
little way in poetry. He means just the same thing as was meant
when I spoke above of 'the noble and profound application of 10
ideas to life'; and he means the application of these ideas under
the conditions fixed for us by the laws of poetic beauty and
poetic truth. If it is said that to call these ideas *moral* ideas is to
introduce a strong and injurious limitation, I answer that it is
to do nothing of the kind, because moral ideas are really so main 15
a part of human life. The question, *how to live*, is itself a moral
idea; and it is the question which most interests every man, and
with which, in some way or other, he is perpetually occupied.
A large sense is of course to be given to the term *moral*. Whatever bears upon the question, 'how to live,' comes under it. 20

> 'Nor love thy life, nor hate; but, what thou liv'st,
> Live well; how long or short, permit to heaven.'

In those fine lines Milton utters, as every one at once perceives,
a moral idea. Yes, but so too, when Keats consoles the forward-
bending lover on the Grecian Urn, the lover arrested and pre- 25
sented in immortal relief by the sculptor's hand before he can
kiss, with the line,

> 'For ever wilt thou love, and she be fair'—

he utters a moral idea. When Shakespeare says, that

> 'We are such stuff 30
> As dreams are made of, and our little life
> Is rounded with a sleep,'

he utters a moral idea.

Voltaire was right in thinking that the energetic and profound treatment of moral ideas, in this large sense, is what
distinguishes the English poetry. He sincerely meant praise, not
dispraise or hint of limitation; and they err who suppose that
5   poetic limitation is a necessary consequence of the fact, the fact
being granted as Voltaire states it. If what distinguishes the
greatest poets is their powerful and profound application of
ideas to life, which surely no good critic will deny, then to
prefix to the term ideas here the term moral makes hardly any
10 difference, because human life itself is in so preponderating a
degree moral.

It is important, therefore, to hold fast to this: that poetry is
at bottom a criticism of life; that the greatness of a poet lies in
his powerful and beautiful application of ideas to life,—to the
15 question: How to live. Morals are often treated in a narrow
and false fashion; they are bound up with systems of thought
and belief which have had their day; they are fallen into the
hands of pedants and professional dealers; they grow tiresome
to some of us. We find attraction, at times, even in a poetry
20 of revolt against them; in a poetry which might take for its
motto Omar Kheyam's words: 'Let us make up in the tavern
for the time which we have wasted in the mosque.' Or we find
attractions in a poetry indifferent to them; in a poetry where
the contents may be what they will, but where the form is
25 studied and exquisite. We delude ourselves in either case; and
the best cure for our delusion is to let our minds rest upon that
great and inexhaustible word *life*, until we learn to enter into
its meaning. A poetry of revolt against moral ideas is a poetry
of revolt against *life;* a poetry of indifference towards moral
30 ideas is a poetry of indifference towards *life*.

Epictetus had a happy figure for things like the play of the
senses, or literary form and finish, or argumentative ingenuity,
in comparison with 'the best and master thing' for us, as he
called it, the concern, how to live. Some people were afraid of
35 them, he said, or they disliked and undervalued them. Such
people were wrong; they were unthankful or cowardly. But
the things might also be over-prized, and treated as final when
they are not. They bear to life the relation which inns bear to

home. 'As if a man, journeying home, and finding a nice inn on the road, and liking it, were to stay for ever at the inn! Man, thou hast forgotten thine object; thy journey was not *to* this, but *through* this. "But this inn is taking." And how many other inns, too, are taking, and how many fields and meadows! but as places of passage merely. You have an object, which is this: to get home, to do your duty to your family, friends, and fellow-countrymen, to attain inward freedom, serenity, happiness, contentment. Style takes your fancy, arguing takes your fancy, and you forget your home and want to make your abode with them and to stay with them, on the plea that they are taking. Who denies that they are taking? but as places of passage, as inns. And when I say this, you suppose me to be attacking the care for style, the care for argument. I am not; I attack the resting in them, the not looking to the end which is beyond them.'

Now, when we come across a poet like Théophile Gautier, we have a poet who has taken up his abode at an inn, and never got farther. There may be inducements to this or that one of us, at this or that moment, to find delight in him, to cleave to him; but after all, we do not change the truth about him,—we only stay ourselves in his inn along with him. And when we come across a poet like Wordsworth, who sings

> 'Of truth, of grandeur, beauty, love and hope,
> And melancholy fear subdued by faith,
> Of blessed consolations in distress,
> Of moral strength and intellectual power,
> Of joy in widest commonalty spread'—

then we have a poet intent on 'the best and master thing,' and who prosecutes his journey home. We say, for brevity's sake, that he deals with *life*, because he deals with that in which life really consists. This is what Voltaire means to praise in the English poets,—this dealing with what is really life. But always it is the mark of the greatest poets that they deal with it; and to say that the English poets are remarkable for dealing with it, is only another way of saying, what is true, that in poetry the English genius has especially shown its power.

Wordsworth deals with it, and his greatness lies in his dealing
with it so powerfully. I have named a number of celebrated
poets above all of whom he, in my opinion, deserves to be
placed. He is to be placed above poets like Voltaire, Dryden,
5   Pope, Lessing, Schiller, because these famous personages, with a
thousand gifts and merits, never, or scarcely ever, attain the
distinctive accent and utterance of the high and genuine poets—

'Quique pii vates et Phœbo digna locuti,'

at all. Burns, Keats, Heine, not to speak of others in our list,
10   have this accent;—who can doubt it? And at the same time
they have treasures of humour, felicity, passion, for which in
Wordsworth we shall look in vain. Where, then, is Wordsworth's superiority? It is here: he deals with more of *life* than
they do; he deals with *life*, as a whole, more powerfully.
15   No Wordsworthian will doubt this. Nay, the fervent Wordsworthian will add, as Mr. Leslie Stephen does, that Wordsworth's poetry is precious because his philosophy is sound;
that his 'ethical system is as distinctive and capable of systematic
exposition as Bishop Butler's'; that his poetry is informed by
20   ideas which 'fall spontaneously into a scientific system of
thought.' But we must be on our guard against the Wordsworthians, if we want to secure for Wordsworth his due rank
as a poet. The Wordsworthians are apt to praise him for the
wrong things, and to lay far too much stress upon what they
25   call his philosophy. His poetry is the reality, his philosophy,—
so far, at least, as it may put on the form and habit of 'a scientific
system of thought,' and the more that it puts them on,—is the
illusion. Perhaps we shall one day learn to make this proposition
general, and to say: Poetry is the reality, philosophy the illusion.
30   But in Wordsworth's case, at any rate, we cannot do him justice
until we dismiss his formal philosophy.
The *Excursion* abounds with philosophy, and therefore the
Excursion is to the Wordsworthian what it never can be to the
disinterested lover of poetry,—a satisfactory work. 'Duty exists,'
35   says Wordsworth, in the *Excursion;* and then he proceeds
thus—

> '. . . Immutably survive,
> For our support, the measures and the forms,
> Which an abstract Intelligence supplies,
> Whose kingdom is, where time and space are not.'

And the Wordsworthian is delighted, and thinks that here is a sweet union of philosophy and poetry. But the disinterested lover of poetry will feel that the lines carry us really not a step farther than the proposition which they would interpret; that they are a tissue of elevated but abstract verbiage, alien to the very nature of poetry.

Or let us come direct to the centre of Wordsworth's philosophy, as 'an ethical system, as distinctive and capable of systematic exposition as Bishop Butler's'—

> '. . . One adequate support
> For the calamities of mortal life
> Exists, one only;—an assured belief
> That the procession of our fate, howe'er
> Sad or disturbed, is ordered by a Being
> Of infinite benevolence and power;
> Whose everlasting purposes embrace
> All accidents, converting them to good.'

That is doctrine such as we hear in church too, religious and philosophic doctrine; and the attached Wordsworthian loves passages of such doctrine, and brings them forward in proof of his poet's excellence. But however true the doctrine may be, it has, as here presented, none of the characters of *poetic* truth, the kind of truth which we require from a poet, and in which Wordsworth is really strong.

Even the 'intimations' of the famous Ode, those corner-stones of the supposed philosophic system of Wordsworth,—the idea of the high instincts and affections coming out in childhood, testifying of a divine home recently left, and fading away as our life proceeds,—this idea, of undeniable beauty as a play of fancy, has itself not the character of poetic truth of the best kind; it has no real solidity. The instinct of delight in Nature and her beauty had no doubt extraordinary strength in Wordsworth himself as a child. But to say that universally this instinct is mighty in childhood, and tends to die away afterwards, is to say what is extremely doubtful. In many people, perhaps with the majority of educated persons, the love of nature is nearly imperceptible at ten years old, but strong and operative at thirty. In general we may say of these high instincts of early childhood, the base of the alleged systematic philosophy of Wordsworth, what Thucydides says of the early achievements of the Greek race: 'It is impossible to speak with certainty of what is so remote; but from all that we can really investigate, I should say that they were no very great things.'

Finally, the 'scientific system of thought' in Wordsworth gives us at last such poetry as this, which the devout Wordsworthian accepts—

> 'O for the coming of that glorious time
> When, prizing knowledge as her noblest wealth
> And best protection, this Imperial Realm,
> While she exacts allegiance, shall admit
> An obligation, on her part, to *teach*
> Them who are born to serve her and obey;
> Binding herself by statute to secure,
> For all the children whom her soil maintains,
> The rudiments of letters, and inform
> The mind with moral and religious truth.'

Wordsworth calls Voltaire dull, and surely the production of these un-Voltairian lines must have been imposed on him as a judgment! One can hear them being quoted at a Social Science Congress; one can call up the whole scene. A great room in one of our dismal provincial towns; dusty air and jaded afternoon daylight; benches full of men with bald heads and women in spectacles; an orator lifting up his face from a manuscript written within and without to declaim these lines of Wordsworth; and in the soul of any poor child of nature who may have wandered in thither, an unutterable sense of lamentation, and mourning, and woe!

'But turn we,' as Wordsworth says, 'from these bold, bad men,' the haunters of Social Science Congresses. And let us be on our guard, too, against the exhibitors and extollers of a 'scientific system of thought' in Wordsworth's poetry. The poetry will never be seen aright while they thus exhibit it. The cause of its greatness is simple, and may be told quite simply. Wordsworth's poetry is great because of the extraordinary power with which Wordsworth feels the joy offered to us in nature, the joy offered to us in the simple primary affections and duties; and because of the extraordinary power with which, in case after case, he shows us this joy, and renders it so as to make us share it.

The source of joy from which he thus draws is the truest and most unfailing source of joy accessible to man. It is also accessible universally. Wordsworth brings us word, therefore, according to his own strong and characteristic line, he brings us word

' Of joy in widest commonalty spread.'

Here is an immense advantage for a poet. Wordsworth tells of what all seek, and tells of it at its truest and best source, and yet a source where all may go and draw for it.

Nevertheless, we are not to suppose that everything is precious which Wordsworth, standing even at this perennial and beautiful source, may give us. Wordsworthians are apt to talk as if it must be. They will speak with the same reverence of *The Sailor's Mother*, for example, as of *Lucy Gray*. They do their master harm by such lack of discrimination. *Lucy Gray* is a beautiful success; *The Sailor's Mother* is a failure. To give aright what he wishes to give, to interpret and render successfully, is not always within Wordsworth's own command. It is within no poet's command; here is the part of the Muse, the inspiration, the God, the 'not ourselves.' In Wordsworth's case, the accident, for so it may almost be called, of inspiration, is of peculiar importance. No poet, perhaps, is so evidently filled with a new and sacred energy when the inspiration is upon him; no poet, when it fails him, is so left 'weak as is a breaking wave.' I remember hearing him say that 'Goethe's poetry was not inevitable enough.' The remark is striking and true; no line in Goethe, as Goethe said himself, but its maker knew well how it came there. Wordsworth is right, Goethe's poetry is not inevitable; not inevitable enough. But Wordsworth's poetry, when he is at his best, is inevitable, as inevitable as Nature herself. It might seem that Nature not only gave him the matter for his poem, but wrote his poem for him. He has no style. He was too conversant with Milton not to catch at times his master's manner, and he has fine Miltonic lines; but he has no assured poetic style of his own, like Milton. When he seeks to have a style he falls into ponderosity and pomposity. In the *Excursion* we have his style, as an artistic product of his own creation; and although Jeffrey completely failed to recognise Wordsworth's real greatness, he was yet not wrong in saying of the *Excursion*, as a work of poetic style: 'This will never do.' And yet magical as is that power, which Wordsworth has not, of assured and possessed poetic style, he has something which is an equivalent for it.

Every one who has any sense for these things feels the subtle turn, the heightening, which is given to a poet's verse by his genius for style. We can feel it in the

' After life's fitful fever, he sleeps well '—

of Shakespeare; in the

' . . . though fall'n on evil days,
On evil days though fall'n, and evil tongues'—

of Milton. It is in the incomparable charm of Milton's power of poetic style which gives such worth to *Paradise Regained*, and makes a great poem of a work in which Milton's imagination does not soar high. Wordsworth has in constant possession, and at command, no style of this kind; but he had too poetic a nature, and had read the great poets too well, not to catch, as I have already remarked, something of it occasionally. We find it not only in his Miltonic lines; we find it in such a phrase as this, where the manner is his own, not Milton's—

' . . . the fierce confederate storm
Of sorrow barricadoed evermore
Within the walls of cities ;'

although even here, perhaps, the power of style, which is undeniable, is more properly that of eloquent prose than the subtle heightening and change wrought by genuine poetic style. It is style, again, and the elevation given by style, which chiefly makes the effectiveness of *Laodameia*. Still the right sort of verse to choose from Wordsworth, if we are to seize his true and most characteristic form of expression, is a line like this from *Michael*—

> ' And never lifted up a single stone.'

There is nothing subtle in it, no heightening, no study of poetic style, strictly so called, at all; yet it is expression of the highest and most truly expressive kind.

Wordsworth owed much to Burns, and a style of perfect plainness, relying for effect solely on the weight and force of that which with entire fidelity it utters, Burns could show him.

> 'The poor inhabitant below
> Was quick to learn and wise to know,
> And keenly felt the friendly glow
> And softer flame;
> But thoughtless follies laid him low
> And stain'd his name.'

Every one will be conscious of a likeness here to Wordsworth; and if Wordsworth did great things with this nobly plain manner, we must remember, what indeed he himself would always have been forward to acknowledge, that Burns used it before him.

Still Wordsworth's use of it has something unique and unmatchable. Nature herself seems, I say, to take the pen out of his hand, and to write for him with her own bare, sheer, penetrating power. This arises from two causes: from the profound sincereness with which Wordsworth feels his subject, and also from the profoundly sincere and natural character of his subject itself. He can and will treat such a subject with nothing but the most plain, first-hand, almost austere naturalness. His expression may often be called bald, as, for instance, in the poem of

Resolution and Independence; but it is bald as the bare mountain tops are bald, with a baldness which is full of grandeur.

   Wherever we meet with the successful balance, in Wordsworth, of profound truth of subject with profound truth of
5 execution, he is unique. His best poems are those which most
perfectly exhibit this balance. I have a warm admiration for
Laodameia and for the great *Ode;* but if I am to tell the very
truth, I find *Laodameia* not wholly free from something artificial, and the great *Ode* not wholly free from something declam-
10 atory. If I had to pick out poems of a kind most perfectly to
show Wordsworth's unique power, I should rather choose
poems such as *Michael, The Fountain, The Highland Reaper.*
And poems with the peculiar and unique beauty which distinguishes these, Wordsworth produced in considerable number;
15 besides very many other poems of which the worth, although
not so rare as the worth of these, is still exceedingly high.

   On the whole, then, as I said at the beginning, not only is
Wordsworth eminent by reason of the goodness of his best
work, but he is eminent also by reason of the great body of
20 good work which he has left to us. With the ancients I will not
compare him. In many respects the ancients are far above us,
and yet there is something that we demand which they can
never give. Leaving the ancients, let us come to the poets and
poetry of Christendom. Dante, Shakespeare, Molière, Milton,
25 Goethe, are altogether larger and more splendid luminaries in
the poetical heaven than Wordsworth. But I know not where
else, among the moderns, we are to find his superiors.

   To disengage the poems which show his power, and to present them to the English-speaking public and to the world, is
30 the object of this volume. I by no means say that it contains all
which in Wordsworth's poems is interesting. Except in the case
of *Margaret,* a story composed separately from the rest of the
Excursion, and which belongs to a different part of England,
I have not ventured on detaching portions of poems, or on
35 giving any piece otherwise than as Wordsworth himself gave it.
But under the conditions imposed by this reserve, the volume
contains, I think, everything, or nearly everything, which may
best serve him with the majority of lovers of poetry, nothing
which may disserve him.

I have spoken lightly of Wordsworthians; and if we are to get Wordsworth recognised by the public and by the world, we must recommend him not in the spirit of a clique, but in the spirit of disinterested lovers of poetry. But I am a Wordsworthian myself. I can read with pleasure and edification *Peter Bell*, and the whole series of *Ecclesiastical Sonnets*, and the address to Mr. Wilkinson's spade, and even the *Thanksgiving Ode;*—everything of Wordsworth, I think, except *Vaudracour and Julia*. It is not for nothing that one has been brought up in the veneration of a man so truly worthy of homage; that one has seen him and heard him, lived in his neighbourhood, and been familiar with his country. No Wordsworthian has a tenderer affection for this pure and sage master than I, or is less really offended by his defects. But Wordsworth is something more than the pure and sage master of a small band of devoted followers, and we ought not to rest satisfied until he is seen to be what he is. He is one of the very chief glories of English Poetry; and by nothing is England so glorious as by her poetry. Let us lay aside every weight which hinders our getting him recognised as this, and let our one study be to bring to pass, as widely as possible and as truly as possible, his own word concerning his poems: 'They will co-operate with the benign tendencies in human nature and society, and will, in their degree, be efficacious in making men wiser, better, and happier.'

The Irish University Question

To the EDITOR *of the* TIMES.

SIR,—Grattan said just before his death, now more than 50 years ago, "England is not our country; it will take a century before she becomes so."

We shall all agree that for the Irish to feel themselves of one country with us is just what is most desirable both for us and for them. But, if it is to come about within a century of Grattan's death, we have no time to lose.

Let us look honestly into whatever keeps us apart: The Irish say that in our treatment of their demand for a Catholic University they have a signal grievance. Some of us maintain that there is no grievance at all. Others think that there is a grievance, but that it is a very slight one.

It happens, Sir, that I have had to make myself acquainted with the provision for University education in a good many countries, and on that ground you will, perhaps, allow me to say something about this disputed Irish grievance. It seems to me that the Irish have a very real grievance. It is a grievance to which I find no parallel elsewhere in Europe. It is a grievance which must perpetually remind Ireland that she is a conquered country. Finally, it is a grievance which must be the more irritating from the manner in which it is denied or excused.

First, there is nothing like it, so far as I know, elsewhere in Europe. The established European type of University instruction is an instruction where a young man, Protestant or Catholic, may expect, in religion and in debatable matters such as philosophy or history, to find teachers of his own communion. Minorities have University instruction of this type as well as majorities. Take Catholic France. The Protestants in France are now less, I believe, than a thirty-sixth part of the nation. France has lost Strasburg, the great centre of Protestant instruction. But the French Protestants have still the Theological Faculty, as it is called, of Montauban. This faculty has eight chairs. Four of them are in various branches of what we commonly term divinity; but the other four are in philosophy, Hebrew, Greek and advanced Latin, natural sciences. In all the chairs of this faculty the professors are Protestants. They are every one of them appointed by the State and paid by the State.

Take Protestant Prussia. In the Rhine Province there is a large Catholic population. Accordingly, in the University of Bonn there is a Catholic faculty of theology as well as a Protestant; and for philosophy and history there is a system of double chairs; so that in these debatable matters the student, Protestant or Catholic, may find teachers of his own communion. Here, too, the professors are all of them appointed and salaried by the State. The University buildings, collections, and library the students have in common.

Let us come to England. Here we find a University instruction of the same type. Oxford and Cambridge are places where the religious instruction is that of the Church of England, and where it would be impossible to find a Roman Catholic filling one of the chairs of philosophy or history. The Scotch Universities are places where the religious instruction is Presbyterian, and where it would be impossible to find a Roman Catholic filling one of the chairs of philosophy or history. Our University instruction is provided partly by direct State payment of professors, but mainly from old endowments. Endowments, however, may most certainly be called a form of public and national support, inasmuch as the nation assigns, regulates, and in some cases withdraws them.

We cross to Ireland. There the Protestant minority has in Trinity College a place publicly endowed where the religious instruction is Protestant, and where it would be impossible to find a Roman Catholic filling one of the chairs of philosophy or history.

But in Ireland the Catholics are more than three-fourths of
the nation; and they desire a University where the religious
instruction is Catholic, and where debatable matters, such as
philosophy and history, are taught by Catholics. They are
offered something quite different, which they will not have.
Then they are told that a University of the kind they want they
must found and maintain for themselves, if they are to have it
at all. But in France the State provides, even for the Protestant
minority, a University instruction of the type that the Irish
Catholics want. In Prussia the State provides it for the Catholic
minority. In England and Scotland old endowments have been
made to follow the will of the majority, and supplemented by
State grants they provide the majority with a University instruction of the type that the Irish Catholics want. In Ireland, so
far are old University endowments from following the will of
the majority, that they follow, as every one knows, that of the
minority. At Trinity College, Dublin, the Irish Protestants have
a University instruction of the type that the Irish Catholics
want. Trinity College is endowed with confiscated Catholic
lands and occupies the site of a suppressed monastery. The
Catholic majority in Ireland is neither allowed the use of the old
endowments to give it a University instruction such as it desires,
and such as in England and Scotland we make the old endowments give us, nor is it allowed the aid of State grants.

There is really nothing like it, I repeat, in Europe. To treat
the Irish Catholics in this way is really to have one weight and
measure for ourselves and another for the Irish. It is, however
we may dress the thing up to our own minds, to treat Ireland
still as a conquered country. It is a survival from the state of
things when no Irish Catholic might own a horse worth more
than £5. The Irish cannot but feel it to be so.

The way in which, in order to cheat our consciences, we
deny or excuse the wrong inflicted can only make it more
irritating to the sufferers. A Scotch member pleads that Scotland stipulated at the Union for the maintenance in the Universities of certain State grants to religion—grants which would
not be conceded afresh now. How it must stimulate the feeling
for Home Rule to hear of the Scotch nation thus stipulating

for what it wanted and preserving it in virtue of such stipula-
tion, while in Ireland the desires of the majority in a like
matter are to be overridden now because they have been overridden always! Or we plead that we cannot now aid a Catholic
University in Ireland because we have made the English and   5
Scotch Universities and Trinity College, Dublin, undenominational. Perhaps this must be to a Catholic the most irritating plea
of all. We have waited until our Universities have become
thoroughly of the character that suits us, and then, when the
Anglican character of the English Universities, the Presbyterian 10
character of the Scotch Universities, has got thoroughly established and is secure for the next generation or two, at any rate,
we throw open our doors, declare tests and subscriptions
abolished, pronounce our Universities to be now perfectly
undenominational, and say that, having made them so, we are   15
precluded from doing anything for the Irish Catholics. It is as
if our proceedings had had for their very object to give us
an arm against the Irish Catholics. But an Irish Catholic may
say, "All we want is an undenominational University just like
yours. Give us a University where the bulk of the students are 20
Catholic, where the bulk of the teachers are Catholic, and we
will undertake to be open to all comers, to accept a conscience
clause, to impose no tests, to be 'perfectly undenominational.' "
We will not give him the chance.

It is said that the Government Bill is "something more than 25
a full satisfaction of all that is reasonable in the Irish Catholic
claims." The Government Bill is like the chameleon; it keeps
changing as one gazes at it. It seems admitted that even in the
lowest view of the Irish Catholic claims it is not an adequate
satisfaction of them to give Ireland an Examining Board all to 30
herself, instead of an Examining Board with its headquarters
in London. Nor is a system of prizes and competitions what is
wanted. Too much of these is even less salutary, probably, for
the young Irishman than for the young Englishman. But such
a system by itself is plainly insufficient. *The Times* has truly 35
said that some of the best subjects for University training are
to be found among those who are capable of taking a creditable
degree but not capable of winning University prizes. But it

seems that, besides prizes for competition, there will be grants
to assist students who can reach a certain standard, and here,
perhaps, is an indirect mode for conveying State help to a
Catholic University. The student who passes will hand over
5   his grant to the University as the price of instruction for his
next year and for another grant. It is not unlikely that in the
hope of thus working the Government Bill the Irish Catholics
may accept it. They must judge for themselves. My object,
Sir, in this letter is not to discuss the Government Bill. My
10   object is simply to bring home to the mind of the English
public that in the matter of University education the Irish
Catholics have a great and real grievance, and what it is. At
present we have one weight and measure for ourselves, another
for them. But a spirit of equitableness on this question is visibly
15   growing. Among the country gentlemen on the Ministerial
side there is still found, indeed, in larger numbers than one
might have expected, a spiritual progeny of Sir Edward
Knatchbull. But almost everywhere else, among politicians,
among the Dissenters, in the newspapers, in society, there is a
20   manifest and a most encouraging advance in the fairness of
mind with which this question is treated. We begin to acknowledge to ourselves that as to their higher education the Irish
Catholics are not equitably dealt with and to seek to help them
indirectly. More may not at this moment be possible. But some
25   day we shall surely perceive that both they and we should be
gainers—both their culture and our influence upon it—by our
consenting to help them directly.

I am, Sir, your obedient servant,
MATTHEW ARNOLD

On Poetry

(Preface to *The Hundred Greatest Men*)

The men who are the flower and glory of our race are to pass here before us, the highest manifestations, whether on this line or on that, of the force which stirs in every one of us—the chief poets, artists, religious founders, philosophers, historians, scholars, orators, warriors, statesmen, voyagers, leaders in mechanical invention and industry, who have appeared amongst mankind. And the poets are to pass first. Why? Because, of the various modes of manifestation through which the human spirit pours its force, theirs is the most adequate and happy.

The fact of this superior adequacy of poetry is very widely felt; and, whether distinctly seized or no, is the root of poetry's boundless popularity and power. The reason for the fact has again and again been made an object of inquiry. Partial explanations of it have been produced. Aristotle declared poetry to be more philosophical and of more serious worth than history, because poetry deals with generals, history with particulars. Aristotle's idea is expanded by Bacon, after his own fashion, who extols poetry as "submitting the shews of things to the desires of the mind," to the desires for "a more ample greatness, a more exact goodness, and a more absolute variety, than can be found in the nature of things." No man, however, can fully draw out the reasons why the human spirit feels itself to attain to a more adequate and satisfying expression in poetry than in any other of its modes of activity. For to draw them out fully we should have to go behind our own nature itself, and that we can none of us do. Portions of them we may seize, but not more; Aristotle and Bacon themselves have not succeeded in seizing more than portions of them. And at one time, probably, and to one set of observers, one ground of the primordial and incontestable fact before us comes clearest into light; at another, and to other observers, another.

For us to-day, what ground for the superiority of poetry is the most evident, the most notable? Surely its solidity. Already we have seen Aristotle prefer it to history on this very ground. Poetry has, says he, a higher wisdom and a more serious worth
5   than history. Compare poetry with other efforts of the human spirit besides history. Compare it with art. It is more intellectual than art, more interpretative. Along with the plastic representation it utters the idea, it thinks. Poetry is often called art, and poets are classed with painters and sculptors as artists. But
10   Goethe has with profound truth insisted on the difference between them. "Poetry is held to be art," he says, "and yet it is not, as art is, mechanism, mechanical. I deny poetry to be an art. Neither is it a science. Poetry is to be called neither art nor science, but genius." Poetry is less artistic than the arts, but in
15   closer correspondence with the intelligential nature of man, who is defined, as we know, to be "a thinking animal;" poetry thinks, and the arts do not.

But it thinks emotionally, and herein it differs from science, and is more of a stay to us. Poetry gives the idea, but it gives it
20   touched with beauty, heightened by emotion. This is what we feel to be interpretative for us, to satisfy us—thought, but thought invested with beauty, with emotion. Science thinks, but not emotionally. It adds thought to thought, accumulates the elements of a synthesis which will never be complete until
25   it is touched with beauty and emotion; and when it is touched with these, it has passed out of the sphere of science, it has felt the fashioning hand of the poet. So true is this, that the more the follower of science is a complete man, the more he will feel the refreshment of poetry as giving him a satisfaction which
30   our nature is always desiring, but to which his science can never bring him. And the more an artist, on the other hand, is a complete man, the higher he will appreciate the reach and effectualness which poetry gains by being, in Goethe's words, not art but genius; by being from its very nature forbidden to
35   limit itself to the sphere of plastic representation, by being forced to talk and to think.

Poetry, then, is more of a stay to us than art or science. It is more explicative than art, and it has the emotion which to science is wanting. But the grand sources of explication and emotion, in the popular opinion, are philosophy and religion. Philosophy—the love of wisdom—is indeed a noble and immortal aspiration in man. But the philosophies, the constructions of systematic thought which have arisen in the endeavour to satisfy this aspiration, are so perishable that to call up the memory of them is to pass in review man's failures. We have mentioned Goethe, the poet of that land of philosophies, Germany. What a series of philosophic systems has Germany seen since the birth of Goethe! and what sort of a stay is any one of them compared with the poetry of Germany's one great poet? So necessary, indeed, and so often shown by experience, is the want of solidity in constructions of this kind, that it argues, one may say, a dash of the pedant in a man to approach them, except perhaps in the ardour of extreme youth, with any confidence. And the one philosopher who has known how to give to such constructions, not indeed solidity, but charm, is Plato, the poet among philosophers, who produces his abstractions like the rest, but produces them more than half in play and with a smile.

And religion? The reign of religion as morality touched with emotion is indeed indestructible. But religion as men commonly conceive it—religion depending on the historicalness of certain supposed facts, on the authority of certain received traditions, on the validity of certain accredited dogmas—how much of this religion can be deemed unalterably secure? Not a dogma that does not threaten to dissolve, not a tradition that is not shaken, not a fact which has its historical character free from question. Compare the stability of Shakspeare with the stability of the Thirty-Nine Articles! Our religion has materialised itself in the fact—the supposed fact; it has attached its emotion to the fact. For poetry the idea is everything; the rest is its world of illusion, of divine illusion; it attaches its emotion to the idea, the idea *is* the fact. The strongest part of our religion to-day is its unconscious poetry. The future of poetry is immense, because in conscious poetry, where it is worthy of its high destinies, our race, as time goes on, will find an ever surer and surer stay.

The French Play in London

English opinion concerning France, our neighbour and rival, was formerly full of hostile prejudice, and is still, in general, quite sufficiently disposed to severity. But, from time to time, France or things French become for the solid English public the object of what our neighbours call an *engouement*,—an infatuated interest. Such an *engouement* Wordsworth witnessed in 1802, after the Peace of Amiens, and it disturbed his philosophic mind greatly. Every one was rushing to Paris; every one was in admiration of the First Consul:—

> "Lords, lawyers, statesmen, squires of low degree,
>   Men known and men unknown, sick, lame, and blind,
>   Post forward all like creatures of one kind,
> With first-fruit offerings crowd to bend the knee,
> In France, before the new-born majesty."

All measure, all dignity, all real intelligence of the situation, so Wordsworth complained, were lost under the charm of the new attraction:—

> " 'Tis ever thus. Ye men of prostrate mind,
>   A seemly reverence may be paid to power;
>   But that's a loyal virtue, never sown
>   In haste, nor springing with a transient shower.
> When truth, when sense, when liberty were flown,
>   What hardship had it been to wait an hour?
> Shame on you, feeble heads, to slavery prone!"

One or two moralists there may still be found, who comment in a like spirit of impatience upon the extraordinary attraction

64

exercised by the French company of actors which has lately left us. The rush of "lords, lawyers, statesmen, squires of low degree, men known and men unknown," of those acquainted with the French language perfectly, of those acquainted with it a little, and of those not acquainted with it at all, to the performances at the Gaiety Theatre,—the universal occupation with the performances and performers, the length and solemnity with which the newspapers chronicled and discussed them, the seriousness with which the whole repertory of the company was taken, the passion for certain pieces and for certain actors, the great ladies who by the acting of Mdlle. Sarah Bernhardt were revealed to themselves, and who could not resist the desire of telling her so,—all this has moved, I say, a surviving and aged moralist here and there amongst us to exclaim: "Shame on you, feeble heads, to slavery prone!" The English public, according to these cynics, have been exhibiting themselves as men of prostrate mind, who pay to power a reverence anything but seemly; we have been conducting ourselves with just that absence of tact, measure, and correct perception, with all that slowness to see when one is making oneself ridiculous, which belongs to the people of our English race.

The nice sense of measure is certainly not one of Nature's gifts to her English children. But then we all of us fail in it, we natives of Great Britain; we have all of us yielded to infatuation at some moment of our lives; we are all in the same boat, and one of us has no right to laugh at the other. I am sure I have not. I remember how in my youth, after a first sight of the divine Rachel at the Edinburgh Theatre, in the part of Hermione, I followed her to Paris, and for two months never missed one of her representations. I, at least, will not cast a stone at the London public for running eagerly after the charming company of actors which has just left us; or at the great ladies who are seeking for soul and have found it in Mdlle. Sarah Bernhardt. I will not quarrel with our newspapers for their unremitting attention to these French performances, their copious criticism of them; particularly when the criticism is so interesting and so good as that which the *Times* and the *Daily News* and the *Pall Mall Gazette*

have given us. Copious, indeed!—why should not our newspapers be copious on the French play, when they are copious
on the Clewer case, and the Mackonochie case, and so many
other matters besides, a great deal less important and interesting,
5   all of them, than the *Maison de Molière?*

So I am not going to join the cynics, and to find fault with
the *engouement,* the infatuation, shown by the English public
in its passion for the French plays and players. A passion of
this kind may be salutary, if we will learn the lessons for us
10 with which it is charged. Unfortunately, few people who feel
a passion think of learning anything from it. A man feels a
passion, he passes through it, and then he goes his way and
straightway forgets, as the Apostle says, what manner of man
he was. Above all, this is apt to happen with us English, who
15 have, as an eminent German professor is good enough to tell
us, "so much genius, so little method." The much genius
hurries us into infatuations; the little method prevents our
learning the right and wholesome lesson from them. Let us
join, then, devoutly and with contrition, in the prayer of the
20 German professor's great countryman, Goethe, a prayer which
is more needful, one may surely say, for us than for him: "God
help us, and enlighten us for the time to come! that we may
not stand in our own way so much, but may have clear notions
of the consequences of things!"

25 To get a clear notion of the consequences which do in reason
follow from what we have been seeing and admiring at the
Gaiety Theatre, to get a clear notion of them, and frankly to
draw them, is the object which I propose to myself here. I am
not going to criticise one by one the French actors and
30 actresses who have been giving us so much pleasure. For a
foreigner this must always be a task, as it seems to me, of
some peril. Perilous or not, it has been abundantly attempted;
and to attempt it yet again, now that the performances are
over and the performers gone back to Paris, would be neither
35 timely nor interesting. One remark I will make, a remark
suggested by the inevitable comparison of Mdlle. Sarah Bernhardt with Rachel. One talks vaguely of genius, but I had never
till now comprehended how much of Rachel's superiority was

purely in intellectual power, how eminently this power counts
in the actor's art as in all art, how just is the instinct which led
the Greeks to mark with a high and severe stamp the Muses.
Temperament and quick intelligence, passion, nervous mobility,
grace, smile, voice, charm, poetry,—Mdlle. Sarah Bernhardt
has them all. One watches her with pleasure, with admiration,
—and yet not without a secret disquietude. Something is wanting, or, at least, not present in sufficient force; something which
alone can secure and fix her administration of all the charming
gifts which she has, can alone keep them fresh, keep them
sincere, save them from perils by caprice, perils by mannerism.
That something is high intellectual power. It was here that
Rachel was so great; she began, one says to oneself as one
recalls her image and dwells upon it,—she began almost where
Mdlle. Sarah Bernhardt ends.

But I return to my object,—the lessons to be learnt by us
from the immense attraction which the French company has
exercised, the consequences to be drawn from it. Certainly we
have something to learn from it, and something to unlearn.
What have we to unlearn? Are we to unlearn our old estimate
of serious French poetry and drama? For every lover of poetry
and of the drama, this is a very interesting question. In the great
and serious kinds of poetry, we used to think that the French
genius, admirable as in so many other ways it is, showed radical
weakness. But there is a new generation growing up amongst us,
—and to this young and stirring generation who of us would
not gladly belong, even at the price of having to catch some of
its illusions and to pass through them?—a new generation which
takes French poetry and drama as seriously as Greek, and for
which M. Victor Hugo is a great poet of the race and lineage
of Shakspeare.

M. Victor Hugo is a great romance-writer. There are people
who are disposed to class all imaginative producers together,
and to call them all by the name of poet. Then a great romance-
writer will be a great poet. Above all are the French inclined
to give this wide extension to the name poet, and the inclination
is very characteristic of them. It betrays that very defect which
we have mentioned, the inadequacy of their genius in the higher

regions of poetry. If they were more at home in those regions, they would feel the essential difference between imaginative production in verse and imaginative production in prose too strongly to be ever inclined to call both by the common name of poetry. They would perceive with us, that M. Victor Hugo, for instance, or Sir Walter Scott, may be a great romance-writer, and may yet be by no means a great poet.

Poetry is simply the most delightful and perfect form of utterance that human words can reach. Its rhythm and measure, elevated to a regularity, certainty, and force very different from that of the rhythm and measure which can pervade prose, are a part of its perfection. The more of genius that a nation has for high poetry, the more will the rhythm and measure which its poetical utterance adopts be distinguished by adequacy and beauty. That is why M. Henry Cochin's remark on Shakspeare, which I have elsewhere quoted, is so good: "Shakspeare is not only," says M. Henry Cochin, "the king of the realm of thought, he is also the king of poetic rhythm and style. Shakspeare has succeeded in giving us the most varied, the most harmonious verse, which has ever sounded upon the human ear since the verse of the Greeks."

Let us have a line or two of Shakspeare's verse before us, just to supply the mind with a standard of reference in the discussion of this matter. We may take the lines from him almost at random:—

> "Five hundred poor I have in yearly pay,
> Who twice a day their wither'd hands hold up
> Toward heaven, to pardon blood; and I have built
> Two chantries, where the sad and solemn priests
> Sing still for Richard's soul."

Yes, there indeed is the verse of Shakspeare, the verse of the highest English poetry; there is what M. Henry Cochin calls "the majestic English iambic!" We will not inflict Greek upon our readers, but every one who knows Greek will remember that the iambic of the Attic tragedians is a rhythm of the same high and splendid quality.

Which of us doubts that imaginative production, uttering itself in such a form as this, is altogether another and a higher

thing from imaginative production uttering itself in any of the
forms of prose? And if we find a nation doubting whether there
is any great difference between imaginative and eloquent production in verse and imaginative and eloquent production in
prose, and inclined to call all imaginative producers by the   5
common name of poets, then we may be sure of one thing:
namely, that this nation has never yet succeeded in finding
the highest and most adequate form for poetry. Because, if it
had, it could never have doubted of the essential superiority of
this form to all prose forms of utterance. And if a nation has   10
never succeeded in creating this high and adequate form for
its poetry, then we may conclude that it is not gifted with
the genius for high poetry; since the genius for high poetry
calls forth the high and adequate form, and is inseparable from
it. So that, on the one hand, from the absence of conspicuous   15
genius in a people for poetry, we may predict the absence of an
adequate poetical form; and on the other hand, again, from
the want of an adequate poetical form, we may infer the want
of conspicuous national genius for poetry.

And we may proceed, supposing that our estimate of a na-   20
tion's success in poetry is said to be much too low, and is called
in question, in either of two ways. If we are said to underrate,
for instance, the production of Corneille and Racine in poetry,
we may compare this production in power, in penetrativeness,
in criticism of life, in ability to call forth our energy and joy,   25
with the production of Homer and Shakspeare. M. Victor
Hugo is said to be a poet of the race and lineage of Shakspeare,
and I hear astonishment expressed at my not ranking him much
above Wordsworth. Well, then, compare their production, in
cases where it lends itself to a comparison. Compare the poetry   30
of the moonlight scene in *Hernani*, really the most poetical
scene in that play, with the poetry of the moonlight scene in
the *Merchant of Venice*. Compare

> ". . . Sur nous, tout en dormant,
> La nature à demi veille amoureusement"—   35

with

> "Sit, Jessica; look how the floor of heaven
> Is thick inlaid with patines of bright gold!"

Compare the laudation of their own country, an inspiring but also a trying theme for a poet, by Shakspeare and Wordsworth on the one hand, and by M. Victor Hugo on the other. Compare Shakspeare's

"This precious stone set in the silver sea,
    This blessed plot, this earth, this realm, this England"—

or compare Wordsworth's

"We must be free or die, who speak the tongue
    That Shakspeare spake, the faith and morals hold
    Which Milton held . . ."

with M. Victor Hugo's

"Non, France, l'univers a besoin que tu vives!
    Je le redis, la France est un besoin des hommes."

Who does not recognise the difference of spirit here? And the difference is, that the English lines have the distinctive spirit of high poetry, and the French lines have not.

Here we have been seeking to attend chiefly to the contents and spirit of the verses chosen. Let us now attend, so far as we can, to form only, and the result will be the same. We will confine ourselves, since our subject is the French play in London, to dramatic verse. We require an adequate form of verse for high poetic drama. The accepted form with the French is the rhymed Alexandrine. Let us keep the iambic of the Greeks or of Shakspeare, let us keep such verse as,

"This precious stone set in the silver sea,"

present to our minds. Then let us take such verse as this from *Ruy Blas:*—

"Le comte d'Onate, qui l'aime aussi, la garde
    Et comme un majordome et comme un amoureux.
    Quelque reître, une nuit, *gardien peu langoureux,*
    Pourrait bien," etc. etc.

or as this, from the same:—

> "Quant à lutter ensemble
> Sur le terrain d'amour, *beau champ qui toujours tremble,*
> De fadaises, mon cher, je sais mal faire assaut."

The words in italics will suffice to give us, I think, the sense
of what constitutes the fatal fault of the rhyming Alexandrine
of French tragedy,—its incurable artificiality, its want of the
fluidity, the naturalness, the rapid forward movement of true
dramatic verse. M. Victor Hugo is said to be a cunning and
mighty artist in Alexandrines, and so unquestionably he is; but
he is an artist in a form radically inadequate and inferior, and
in which a drama like that of Sophocles or Shakspeare is
impossible.

It happens that in our own language we have an example of
the employment of an inadequate form in tragedy and in elevated poetry, and can see the result of it. The rhymed ten-
syllable couplet, the heroic couplet as it is often called, is such
a form. In the earlier work of Shakspeare, work adopted or
adapted by him even if not altogether his own work, we find
this form often employed:—

> "Alas! what joy shall noble Talbot have
> To bid his young son welcome to his grave?
> Away! vexation almost stops my breath
> That sundered friends greet in the hour of death.
> Lucy, farewell; no more my future can
> But curse the cause I cannot aid the man.
> Maine, Blois, Poitiers and Tours are won away
> 'Long all of Somerset and his delay."

Traces of this form remain in Shakspeare's work to the last,
in the rhyming of final couplets. But because he had so great a
genius for true tragic poetry, Shakspeare dropped this necessarily inadequate form and took a better. We find the rhymed
couplet again in Dryden's tragedies. But this vigorous rhetorical
poet had no real genius for true tragic poetry, and his form is
itself a proof of it. True tragic poetry is impossible with this

inadequate form. Again, all through the eighteenth century this form was dominant as the main form for high efforts in English poetry; and our serious poetry of that century, accordingly, has something inevitably defective and unsatisfactory. When it rises out of this, it at the same time adopts instinctively a truer form, as Gray does in the *Elegy*. The just and perfect use of the ten-syllable couplet is to be seen in Chaucer. As a form for tragedy, and for poetry of the most serious and elevated kind, it is defective. It makes real adequacy in poetry of this kind impossible; and its prevalence, for poetry of this kind, proves that those amongst whom it prevails have for poetry of this kind no signal gift.

The case of the great Molière himself will illustrate the truth of what I say. Molière is by far the chief name in French poetry; he is one of the very greatest names in all literature. He has admirable and delightful power, penetrativeness, insight; a masterly criticism of life. But he is a comic poet. Why? Had he no seriousness and depth of nature? He had profound seriousness. And would not a dramatic poet with this depth of nature be a tragedian if he could? Of course he would. For only by breasting in full the storm and cloud of life, breasting it and passing through it and above it, can the dramatist who feels the weight of mortal things liberate himself from the pressure, and rise, as we all seek to rise, to content and joy. Tragedy breasts the pressure of life. Comedy eludes it, half liberates itself from it by irony. But the tragedian, if he has the sterner labour, has also the higher prize. Shakspeare has more joy than Molière, more assurance and peace. *Othello*, with all its passion and terror, is on the whole a work animating and fortifying; more so a thousand times than *George Dandin*, which is mournfully depressing. Molière, if he could, would have given us Othellos instead of George Dandins; let us not doubt it. If he did not give Othellos to us, it was because the highest sort of poetic power was wanting to him. And if the highest sort of poetic power had been not wanting to him but present, he would have found no adequate form of dramatic verse for conveying it, he would have had to create one. For such tasks Molière had not power; and this is only another way of saying that for the highest tasks in poetry the genius of his nation appears to have not power. But serious spirit and great poet that he was, Molière had far too sound an instinct to attempt so earnest a matter as tragic drama with inadequate means. It would have been a heart-breaking business for him. He did not attempt it, therefore, but confined himself to comedy.

The *Misanthrope* and the *Tartuffe* are comedy, but they are comedy in verse, poetic comedy. They employ the established verse of French dramatic poetry, the Alexandrine. Immense power has gone to the making of them; a world of vigorous sense, piercing observation, pathetic meditation, profound criticism of life. Molière had also one great advantage as a dramatist over Shakspeare; he wrote for a more developed theatre, a more developed society. Moreover he was at the same time, probably, by nature a better *theatre-poet* than Shakspeare; he had a keener sense for theatrical situation. Shakspeare is not rightly to be called, as Goethe calls him, an epitomator rather than a dramatist; but he may rightly be called rather a dramatist than a theatre-poet. Molière,—and here his French nature stood him in good stead,—was a theatre-poet of the very first order. Comedy, too, escapes, as has been already said, the test of entire seriousness; it remains, by the law of its being, in a region of comparative lightness and of irony. What is artificial can pass in comedy more easily. In spite of all these advantages, the *Misanthrope* and the *Tartuffe* have, and have by reason of their poetic form, an artificiality which makes itself too much felt, and which provokes weariness. The freshness and power of Molière are best felt when he uses prose, in pieces such as the *Avare*, or the *Fourberies de Scapin*, or *George Dandin*. How entirely the contrary is the case with Shakspeare; how undoubtedly is it his verse which shows his power most! But so inadequate a vehicle for dramatic poetry is the French Alexandrine, that its sway hindered Molière, one may think, from being a tragic poet at all, in spite of his having gifts for this highest form of dramatic poetry which are immeasurably superior to those of any other French poet. And in comedy, where Molière thought he could use the Alexandrine, and where he did use it with splendid power, it yet in a considerable degree hampered and lamed him, so that this true and great poet is actually most satisfactory in his prose.

If Molière cannot make us insensible to the inherent defects of French dramatic poetry, still less can Corneille and Racine. Corneille has energy and nobility, Racine an often Virgilian sweetness and pathos. But while Molière in depth, penetrativeness, and powerful criticism of life, belongs to the same family as Sophocles and Shakspeare, Corneille and Racine are quite of another order. We must not be misled by the excessive estimate of them among their own countrymen. I remember an answer of M. Sainte-Beuve, who always treated me with great kindness, and to whom I once ventured to say that I could not think Lamartine a poet of very high importance. "He was important to *us*," answered M. Sainte-Beuve. In a far higher degree can a Frenchman say of Corneille and Racine: "They were important to *us*." Voltaire pronounces of them: "These men taught our nation to think, to feel, and to express itself." *Ces hommes enseignèrent à la nation à penser, à sentir et à s'exprimer.* They were thus the instructors and formers of a society in many respects the most civilised and consummate that the world has ever seen, and which certainly has not been inclined to underrate its own advantages. How natural, then, that it should feel grateful to its formers, and should extol them! "Tell your brother Rodolphe," writes Joseph de Maistre from Russia to his daughter at home, "to get on with his French poets; let him have them by heart,—the inimitable Racine above all; never mind whether he understands him or not. I did not understand him, when my mother used to come and sit on my bed, and repeat from him, and put me to sleep with her beautiful voice to the sound of this incomparable music. I knew hundreds of lines of him before I could read; and that is why my ears, having drunk in this ambrosia betimes, have never been able to endure common stuff since." What a spell must such early use have had for riveting the affections; and how civilising are such affections, how honourable to the society which can be imbued with them, to the literature which can inspire them! Pope was in a similar way, though not at all in the same degree, a forming and civi-

lising influence to our grandfathers, and limited their literary
taste while he stimulated and formed it. So, too, the Greek
boy was fed by his mother and nurse with Homer; but then in
this case it was Homer!

We English had Shakspeare waiting to open our eyes, when-
soever a favourable moment came, to the insufficiencies of
Pope. But the French had no Shakspeare to open their eyes to
the insufficiencies of Corneille and Racine. Great artists like
Talma and Rachel, whose power, as actors, was far superior
to the power, as poets, of the dramatists whose work they were
rendering, filled out with their own life and warmth the parts
into which they threw themselves, gave body to what was
meagre, fire to what was cold, and themselves supported the
poetry of the French classic drama rather than were supported
by it. It was easier to think the poetry of Racine inimitable
when Talma or Rachel was seen producing in it such inimitable
effects. Indeed French acting is so good, that there are few
pieces, excepting always those of Molière, in the repertory of
a company such as that which we have just seen, where the
actors do not show themselves to be superior to the pieces they
render, and to be worthy of pieces which are better. *Phèdre*
is a work of much beauty, yet certainly one felt this in seeing
Rachel in the part of Phèdre. I am not sure that one feels it in
seeing Mdlle. Sarah Bernhardt as Phèdre, but I am sure that
one feels it in seeing her as Doña Sol.

The tragedy of M. Victor Hugo has always, indeed, stirring
events in plenty; and so long as the human nerves are what
they are, so long will things like the sounding of the horn, in
the famous fifth act of *Hernani*, produce a thrill in us. But so
will Werner's *Twenty-fourth of February*, or Scott's *House of
Aspen*. A thrill of this sort may be raised in us, and yet our
poetic sense may remain profoundly dissatisfied. So it remains
in *Hernani*. M. Sarcey, a critic always acute and intelligent,
and whom one reads with profit and pleasure, says that we
English are fatigued by the long speeches in *Hernani*, and
that we do not appreciate what delights French people in it,
the splendour of the verse, the wondrous beauty of the style,
the poetry. Here recurs the question as to the adequacy of the
French Alexandrine as tragic verse. If this form is vitally in-

adequate for tragedy, then to speak absolutely of splendour of
verse and wondrous beauty of style in it when employed for
tragedy, is misleading. Beyond doubt M. Victor Hugo has an
admirable gift for versification. So had Pope. But to speak
5   absolutely of the splendour of verse and wondrous beauty of
style of the *Essay on Man* would be misleading. Such terms
can be properly used only of verse and style of an altogether
higher and more adequate kind, a verse and style like that of
Dante, Shakspeare, or Milton. Pope's brilliant gift for versifica-
10 tion is exercised within the limits of a form inadequate for true
philosophic poetry, and by its very presence excluding it.
M. Victor Hugo's brilliant gift for versification is exercised
within the limits of a form inadequate for true tragic poetry,
and by its very presence excluding it.

15   But, if we are called upon to prove this from the poetry itself,
instead of inferring it from the form, our task, in the case of
Hernani, is really only too easy. What is the poetical value of
this famous fifth act of *Hernani?* What poetical truth, or veri-
similitude, or possibility has Ruy Gomez, this chivalrous old
20 Spanish grandee, this venerable nobleman, who, because he
cannot marry his niece, presents himself to her and her husband
upon their wedding night, and insists on the husband performing an old promise to commit suicide if summoned by Ruy
Gomez to do so? Naturally the poor young couple raise dif-
25 ficulties, and the venerable nobleman keeps plying them with:
*Bois! Allons! Le sépulcre est ouvert, et je ne puis attendre! J'ai
hâte! Il faut mourir!* This is a mere character of Surrey melodrama. And Hernani, who, when he is reminded that it is by
his father's head that he has sworn to commit suicide, exclaims:

30   "Mon père! mon père!—Ah! j'en perdrai la raison!"

and who, when Doña Sol gets the poison away from him, en-
treats her to return it—

                    "Par pitié, ce poison,
        Rends-le-moi! Par l'amour, par notre âme immortelle!"

35 because

"Le duc a ma parole, et mon père est là-haut!"

The *poetry!* says M. Sarcey,—and one thinks of the poetry of *Lear!* M. Sarcey must pardon me for saying that in

"Le duc a ma parole, et mon père est là-haut!"

we are not in the world of poetry at all, hardly even in the world of literature, unless it be the literature of *Bombastes Furioso*.

Our sense, then, for what is poetry and what is not, the attractiveness of the French plays and players must not make us unlearn. We may and must retain our old conviction of the fundamental insufficiency, both in substance and in form, of the rhymed tragedy of the French. We are to keep, too, what in the main has always been the English estimate of Molière: that he is a man of creative and splendid power, a dramatist whose work is truly delightful, is edifying and immortal; but that even Molière, in poetic drama, is hampered and has not full swing, and, in consequence, leaves us somewhat dissatisfied. Finally, we poor old people should pluck up courage to stand out yet, for the few years of life which yet remain to us, against that passing illusion of the confident young generation who are newly come out on the war-path, that M. Victor Hugo is a poet of the race and lineage of Shakspeare.

What, now, are we to say of the prose drama of modern life, the drama of which the *Sphinx* and the *Étrangère* and the *Demi-Monde* are types, and which was the most strongly attractive part, probably, of the feast offered to us by the French company? The first thing to be said of these pieces is that they are admirably acted. But then constantly, as I have already said, one has the feeling that the French actors are better than the pieces which they play. What are we to think of this modern prose drama in itself, the drama of M. Octave Feuillet, and M. Alexandre Dumas the younger, and M. Augier? Some of the pieces composing it are better constructed and written than others, and much more effective. But this whole drama has one character common to it all. It may be best described as the theatre of the *homme sensuel moyen*, the average sensual man, whose country is France, and whose city is Paris, and whose

ideal life is the free, gay, pleasurable life of Paris,—an ideal which
our young literary generation, now out on the war-path here
in England, seek to adopt from France, and which they busily
preach and work for. Of course there is in Paris much life of
5   another sort too, as there are in France many men of another
type than that of the *homme sensuel moyen*. But for many
reasons, which I need not enumerate here, the life of the free,
confident, harmonious development of the senses, all round,
has been able to establish itself among the French, and at Paris,
10 as it has established itself nowhere else; and the ideal life of
Paris is this sort of life triumphant. And of this ideal the modern
French drama, works like the *Sphinx* and the *Étrangère* and
the *Demi-Monde*, are the expression. It is the drama, I say, this
drama now in question, of the *homme sensuel moyen*, the
15 average sensual man. It represents the life of the senses developing themselves all round without misgiving; a life confident,
fair and free, with fireworks of fine emotions, grand passions,
and devotedness,—or rather, perhaps, we should say *dévouement*,—lighting it up when necessary.

20 We in England have no modern drama at all. We have our
Elizabethan drama. We have a drama of the last century and
of the latter part of the century preceding, a drama which may
be called our drama of *the town*, when *the town* was an entity
powerful enough, because homogeneous enough, to evoke a
25 drama embodying its notions of life. But we have no modern
drama. Our vast society is not at present homogeneous enough
for this,—not sufficiently united, even any large portion of it,
in a common view of life, a common ideal, capable of serving
as basis for a modern English drama. We have apparitions of
30 poetic and romantic drama (as the French, too, have their
charming *Gringoire*), which are always possible, because man
has always in his nature the poetical fibre. Then we have num-
berless imitations and adaptations from the French. All of these
are at the bottom fantastic. We may truly say of them, that
35 "truth and sense and liberty are flown." And the reason is
evident. They are pages out of a life which the ideal of the
homme sensuel moyen rules, transferred to a life where this
ideal, notwithstanding the fervid adhesion to it of our young

generation, does not reign. For the attentive observer the result
is a sense of incurable falsity in the piece as adapted. Let me give
an example. Everybody remembers *Pink Dominos*. The piece
turns upon an incident possible and natural enough in the life
of Paris. Transferred to the life of London the incident is al-   5
together unreal, and its unreality makes the whole piece, in its
English form, fantastic and absurd.

Still that does not prevent such pieces, and the theatre generally, from now exercising upon us a great attraction. For we
are at the end of a period, and have to deal with the facts and   10
symptoms of a new period on which we are entering; and
prominent among these fresh facts and symptoms is the irresisti-
bility of the theatre. We know how the Elizabethan theatre
had its cause in an ardent zest for life and living, a bold and
large curiosity, a desire for a fuller, richer existence, pervading   15
this nation at large, as they pervaded other nations, after the
long mediæval time of obstruction and restraint. But we know,
too, how the great middle class of this nation, alarmed at grave
symptoms which showed themselves in the new movement,
drew back; made choice for its spirit to live at one point, in-   20
stead of living, or trying to live, at many; entered, as I have so
often said, the prison of Puritanism, and had the key turned
upon its spirit there for two hundred years. Our middle class
forsook the theatre. The English theatre reflected no more the
aspiration of a great community for a fuller and richer sense   25
of human existence.

This theatre came afterwards, however, to reflect the aspirations of "the town." It developed a drama to suit these
aspirations; while it also brought back and re-exhibited the
Elizabethan drama, so far as "the town" wanted it and liked it.   30
Finally, as even "the town" ceased to be homogeneous, the
theatre ceased to develop anything expressive. It still repeated
what was old with more or less of talent. But the mass of our
English community, the mass of the middle class, kept aloof
from the whole thing.   35

I remember how, happening to be at Shrewsbury, twenty
years ago, and finding the whole Haymarket company acting
there, I went to the theatre. Never was there such a scene of

desolation. Scattered at very distant intervals through the boxes
were about half-a-dozen chance-comers like myself; there were
some soldiers and their friends in the pit, and a good many
riff-raff in the upper gallery. The real townspeople, the people
who carried forward the business and life of Shrewsbury, and
who filled its churches and chapels on Sundays, were entirely
absent. I pitied the excellent Haymarket company; it must have
been like acting to oneself upon an iceberg. Here one had a
good example,—as I thought at the time, and as I have often
thought since,—of the complete estrangement of the British
middle class from the theatre.

What is certain is, that a signal change is coming over us, and
that it has already made great progress. It is said that there are
now forty theatres in London. Even in Edinburgh, where in
old times a single theatre maintained itself under protest, there
are now, I believe, over half-a-dozen. The change is not due
only to an increased liking in the upper class and in the working
class for the theatre. Their liking for it has certainly increased,
but this is not enough to account for the change. The attraction of the theatre begins to be felt again, after a long interval
of insensibility, by the middle class also. Our French friends
would say that this class, long petrified in a narrow Protestantism and in a perpetual reading of the Bible, is beginning at last
to grow conscious of the horrible unnaturalness and *ennui* of
its life, and is seeking to escape from it. Undoubtedly the type
of religion to which the British middle class has sacrificed the
theatre, as it has sacrificed so much besides, is defective. But I
prefer to say that this great class, having had the discipline of
its religion, is now awakening to the sure truth that the human
spirit cannot live aright if it lives at one point only, that it can
and ought to live at several points at the same time. The human
spirit has a vital need, as we say, for conduct and religion; but
it has the need also for expansion, for intellect and knowledge,
for beauty, for social life and manners. The revelation of these
additional needs brings the middle class to the theatre.

The revelation was indispensable, the needs are real, the
theatre is one of the mightiest means of satisfying them, and
the theatre, therefore, is irresistible. That conclusion, at any

rate, we may take for certain. We have to unlearn, therefore, our long disregard of the theatre; we have to own that the theatre is irresistible.

But I see our community turning to the theatre with eagerness, and finding the English theatre without organisation, or purpose, or dignity, and no modern English drama at all except a fantastical one. And then I see the French company from the chief theatre of Paris showing themselves to us in London,—a society of actors admirable in organisation, purpose, and dignity, with a modern drama not fantastic at all, but corresponding with fidelity to a very palpable and powerful ideal, the ideal of the life of the *homme sensuel moyen* in Paris, his beautiful city. I see in England a materialised upper class, sensible of the nullity of our own modern drama, impatient of the state of false constraint and of blank to which the Puritanism of our middle class has brought our stage and much of our life, delighting in such drama as the modern drama of Paris. I see the emancipated youth of both sexes delighting in it; the new and clever newspapers, which push on the work of emancipation and serve as devoted missionaries of the gospel of the life of Paris and of the ideal of the average sensual man, delighting in it. And in this condition of affairs I see the middle class beginning to arrive at the theatre again after an abstention of two centuries and more; arriving eager and curious, but a little bewildered.

Now, lest at this critical moment such drama as the *Sphinx* and the *Étrangère* and the *Demi-Monde*, positive as it is, and powerful as it is, and pushed as it is, and played with such prodigious care and talent, should too much rule the situation, let us take heart of grace and say, that as the right conclusion from the unparalleled success of the French company was not that we should reverse our old notions about the tragedy of M. Victor Hugo, or about French classic tragedy, or even about the poetic drama of the great Molière, so neither is it the right conclusion from this success that we should be converted and become believers in the legitimacy of the life-ideal of the *homme sensuel moyen,* and in the sufficiency of his drama. This is not the occasion to deliver a moral discourse. It is enough to revert to what has been

already said, and to remark that the French ideal and its theatre
have the defect of leaving out too much of life, of treating the
soul as if it lived at one point or group of points only, of
ignoring other points, or groups of points, at which it must live
5 as well. And herein the conception of life shown in this French
ideal and in its drama really resembles, different as in other
ways they are, the conception of life prevalent with the British
middle class, and has the like kind of defect. Both conceptions
of life are too narrow. Sooner or later, if we adopt either, our
10 soul and spirit are starved, and go amiss, and suffer.

What then, finally, *are* we to learn from the marvellous
success and attractiveness of the performances at the Gaiety
Theatre? What *is* the consequence which it is right and rational
for us to draw? Surely it is this: "The theatre is irresistible;
15 *organise the theatre.*" Surely, if we wish to stand less in our
own way, and to have clear notions of the consequences of
things, it is to this conclusion that we should come.

The performances of the French company show us plainly,
I think, what is gained,—the theatre being admitted to be an
20 irresistible need for civilised communities,—by organising the
theatre. Some of the drama played by this company is, as we
have seen, questionable. But, in the absence of an organisation
such as that of this company, it would be played even yet more;
it would, with a still lower drama to accompany it, almost if
25 not altogether reign; it would have far less correction and relief
by better things. An older and better drama, containing many
things of high merit, some things of surpassing merit, is kept
before the public by means of this company, is given frequently,
is given to perfection. Pieces of truth and beauty, which emerge
30 here and there among the questionable pieces of the modern
drama, get the benefit of this company's skill, and are given to
perfection. The questionable pieces themselves lose something
of their unprofitableness and vice in their hands; the acting
carries us into the world of correct and pleasing art, if the piece
35 does not. And the type of perfection fixed by these fine actors
influences for good every actor in France.

Moreover, the French company shows us not only what is
gained by organising the theatre, but what is meant by organis-

ing it. The organisation in the example before us is simple and
rational. We have a society of good actors, with a grant from
the State on condition of their giving with frequency the
famous and classic stage-plays of their nation, and with a commissioner of the State attached to the society and taking part in   5
council with it. But the society is to all intents and purposes
self-governing. And in connection with the society is the school
of dramatic elocution of the *Conservatoire*, a school with the
names of Regnier, Monrose, Got and Delaunay on its roll of
professors.   10

The Society of the French Theatre dates from Louis the
Fourteenth and from France's great century. It has, therefore,
traditions, effect, consistency, and a place in the public esteem,
which are not to be won in a day. But its organisation is such
as a judicious man, desiring the results which in France have   15
been by this time won, would naturally have devised; and it is
such a judicious man, desiring in another country to secure like
results, would naturally imitate.

We have in England everything to make us dissatisfied with
the chaotic and ineffective condition into which our theatre   20
has fallen. We have the remembrance of better things in the
past, and the elements for better things in the future. We have
a splendid national drama of the Elizabethan age, and a later
drama of "the town" which has no lack of pieces conspicuous by
their stage-qualities, their vivacity and their talent, and interest-   25
ing by their pictures of manners. We have had great actors.
We have good actors not a few at the present moment. But we
have been unlucky, as we so often are, in the work of organisation. In the essay at organisation which in the patent theatres,
with their exclusive privilege of acting Shakspeare, we formerly   30
had, we find by no means an example, such as we have in the
constitution of the French Theatre, of what a judicious man,
seeking the good of the drama and of the public, would naturally devise. We find rather such a machinery as might be devised
by a man prone to stand in his own way, a man devoid of clear   35
notions of the consequences of things. It was inevitable that the
patent theatres should provoke discontent and attack. They
were attacked, and their privilege fell. Still, to this essay, how-

ever imperfect, of a public organisation for the English theatre, our stage owes the days of power and greatness which it has enjoyed. So far as we have had a school of great actors, so far as our stage has had tradition, effect, consistency, and a hold on public esteem, it had them under the system of the privileged theatres. The system had its faults, and was abandoned; but then, instead of devising a better plan of public organisation for the English theatre, we gladly took refuge in our favourite doctrines of the mischief of State interference, of the blessedness of leaving every man free to do as he likes, of the impertinence of presuming to check any man's natural taste for the bathos and pressing him to relish the sublime. We left the English theatre to take its chance. Its present impotence is the result.

It seems to me that every one of us is concerned to find a remedy for this melancholy state of things; and that the pleasure we have had in the visit of the French company is barren, unless it leaves us with the impulse to mend the condition of our theatre, and with the lesson how alone it can be rationally attempted. "Forget,"—can we not hear these fine artists saying in an undertone to us, amidst their graceful compliments of adieu?—"forget your clap-trap, and believe that the State, the nation in its collective and corporate character, does well to concern itself about an influence so important to national life and manners as the theatre. Form a company out of the materials ready to your hand in your many good actors or actors of promise. Give them a theatre at the West End. Let them have a grant from your Science and Art Department; let some intelligent and accomplished man, like our friend Mr. Pigott, your present Examiner of Plays, be joined to them as Commissioner from the Department, to see that the conditions of the grant are observed. Let the conditions of the grant be that a repertory is agreed upon, taken out of the works of Shakspeare and out of the volumes of the *Modern British Drama*, and that pieces from this repertory are played a certain number of times in each season; as to new pieces, let your company use its discretion. Let a school of dramatic elocution and declamation be instituted in connection with your company. It may surprise you to hear that elocution and declamation are things to be taught and

learnt, and do not come by nature; but it is so. Your best and
most serious actors" (this is added with a smile) "would have
been better, if in their youth they had learnt elocution. These
recommendations, you may think, are not very much; but, as
your divine William says, they are enough; they will serve. Try 5
them. When your institution in the West of London has become a success, plant a second of like kind in the East. The
people *will* have the theatre; then make it a good one. Let your
two or three chief provincial towns institute, with municipal
subsidy and co-operation, theatres such as you institute in the 10
metropolis with State subsidy and co-operation. So you will
restore the English theatre. And then a modern drama of your
own will also, probably, spring up amongst you, and you will
not have to come to us for pieces like *Pink Dominos*."

No, and we will hope, too, that the modern English drama, 15
when it comes, may be something different from even the
Sphinx and the *Demi-Monde*. For my part, I have all confidence,
that if it ever does come, it will be different and better. But let
us not say a word to wound the feelings of those who have
given us so much pleasure, and who leave to us as a parting 20
legacy such excellent advice. For excellent advice it is, and
everything we saw these artists say and do upon the Gaiety
stage inculcates it for us, whether they exactly formulated it
in words or no. And still, even now that they are gone, when
I pass along the Strand and come opposite to the Gaiety Thea- 25
tre, I see a fugitive vision of delicate features under a shower
of hair and a cloud of lace, and hear the voice of Mdlle. Sarah
Bernhardt saying in its most caressing tones to the Londoners:
"The theatre is irresistible; *organise the theatre!*"

Joseph de Maistre on Russia

Lettres et Opuscules inédits du Comte Joseph de Maistre.
6th Edition. 2 vols. Paris, 1873.
'Always,' says Goethe, contradicting a popular modern tenet, 'always it is the individual that works for progress, not the age. It was the age, which made away with Socrates by poison; it was the age, which burnt Huss at the stake; the ages have
5 always been the same.'

We listen to Goethe with respect, yet we cannot help remembering that it has been said, on the other hand: 'There is somebody who is cleverer even than Voltaire, cleverer than any man you can name; this somebody is all the world, *tout le monde.*'
10 Nor is that a bad saying, either. But it is not really at variance with the saying of Goethe. Only we must guard it a little, must explain that the *all the world* which is cleverer than the cleverest individual is not the world of his contemporaries, but the world which comes after him, and which he has contributed
15 to form. He was not perfect, he did not see the whole truth; there were at work other eminent individualities besides his; other aspects of the truth were seen besides the aspect which he saw. There was confrontation and collision, and out of the shock came the next age, an *all the world* clearer and cleverer,
20 in many respects, than even the chief individuals of the age preceding. But to these individuals and to their shock it owes all its advance. Individuals emerging from its own life, again, superior to their age, contradicted by it and contradicting it, dissatisfied with its actual gains, in collision with it and with
25 one another, can alone carry it further and make the future.

We must not forget, then, in laying stress with Goethe upon the individual, that the individual is not perfect, and that he works for a future larger and better than himself. Keeping this well in mind, we may admit, as much as ever Goethe pleases, the interest and significance, the overwhelming interest and significance, in human history, of the individual. As his time recedes, he and his strain of thought grow more distinct; his contemporaries and their thoughts grow fainter. They become more and more to us like hollow shadows, saying they know not what: he alone remains among them a living man, who knows what he is saying, and whose words keep a freshness and power. Burke stands thus to us now, as we look back at him among his contemporaries. In the sphere of thought which was his, in politics in the high sense of the word, in what concerns the general influence to be exercised on man's welfare and progress by the means of government and society, Burke's voice is still for us Englishmen a living voice out of the age preceding our own, it is the one living voice left of innumerable voices, the rest are shadowy. A good deal is wanting to Burke's political philosophy; there are many important things which either he cannot see or does not care to see. Whoever followed his teaching simply and absolutely would make shipwreck. Still, such is his weight and power, that while the chatter of a whole wilderness of friends of 'the ideas of 1789' is dead and cold, the voice of this great enemy of the Revolution lives,—moves us and makes us think to this day.

Joseph de Maistre is another of those men whose word, like that of Burke, has vitality. In imaginative power he is altogether inferior to Burke. On the other hand his thought moves in closer order than Burke's, more rapidly, more directly; he has fewer superfluities. Burke is a great writer, but Joseph de Maistre's use of the French language is more powerful, more thoroughly satisfactory, than Burke's use of the English. It is masterly; it shows us to perfection of what that admirable instrument, the French language, is capable. Finally, Joseph de Maistre is more European than Burke; his place at the great spectacle of the Revolution is more central for seeing; moreover he outlived Burke considerably, and saw how events turned. But the two men are of one family, having in common their high stamp of individuality, and their enduring vitality and instructiveness.

They have in common, too, their fundamental ideas. Their
sense of the slowness of the natural growth of things, of their
gradual evolution out of small beginnings, is perfectly expressed
by Joseph de Maistre's maxim: 'Aucune grande chose n'eut de
5   grands commencements'—'Nothing great ever began great.'
That is entirely in Burke's spirit, and the maxim has its indubitable and profound truth. Things grow slowly, and in a gradual
correspondence with human needs. Phrases are not things, and
a Liberal theorist, some revolutionary M. Cherchemot, striking
10   in with his 'Tout est à refaire'—'Everything is to be made
afresh'—is impertinent and vain. Only, in their aversion to M.
Cherchemot and his shallowness, Burke and Joseph de Maistre
do not enough consider the amount of misformation, hamper,
and stoppage, coming at last to be intolerable, to which human
15   things in their slow process of natural growth are undoubtedly
liable. They do not enough consider it; they banish it out of
their thoughts altogether. Another trenchant and characteristic
maxim of Joseph de Maistre, which Burke, too, might have
uttered, is this: 'Il faut absolument tuer l'esprit du dix-huitième
20   siècle'—'The spirit of the eighteenth century must be stamped
out utterly.' One is reminded of Cardinal Newman's antipathy
to 'Liberalism.' And in a serious man a strong sense of the
insufficiency of Liberal nostrums, of the charlatanism of Liberal
practitioners, as also of the real truth, beauty, power, and con-
25   formity to nature of much in the past of which these practitioners are intolerant, is abundantly permissible. Still, when one
has granted all that serious men like Joseph de Maistre and
Cardinal Newman may fairly say against the eighteenth century
and Liberalism, when one has admired the force, the vigour,
30   the acumen, the sentiment, the grace with which it is all said,
one inquires innocently for that better thing which they themselves have in store for us, and then comes the disappointment.
Joseph de Maistre and Cardinal Newman have nothing but the
old, sterile, impossible assumption of their 'infallible Church;'
35   at which a plain man can only shake his head and say with
Shakspeare, 'There's no such thing!'

It cannot be too often repeated: these eminent individualities,
men like Burke, or Joseph de Maistre, or Cardinal Newman,

are by no means to be taken as guides absolutely. Yet they are
full of stimulus and instruction for us. We may find it impossible
to accept their main positions. But the resoluteness with which
they withstand the prevailing ideas of their time, the certainty
with which they predict the apparition of something different, 5
are often a proof of their insight. Whatever we may think of
Ritualism, its growth and power prove Cardinal Newman's insight in perceiving that what he called Liberalism, but what we
may perhaps better describe to ourselves as the mind of Lord
Brougham, was in general, and in the sphere of religion more 10
particularly, quite inadequate, and was not destined to have
things for ever its own way. In like manner, whatever we may
think of Ultramontanism, its growth and power signally prove
Joseph de Maistre's insight. Continental Protestantism, he declared, was going to pieces, Gallicanism was doomed, 'the 15
Sovereign Pontiff and the French priesthood will embrace one
another, and will stifle in that sacred embrace the Gallican
maxims.' Rome would become a power again; by no other
power could the French Revolution, 'satanic in its principle,'
be effectually resisted. 'If England grants, as she probably will, 20
Catholic emancipation, and if the Catholic religion in Europe
comes to speak both French and English, remember what I say,
my good hearer, there is nothing which you may not expect.'
It is enough to make Mr. Whalley turn in his grave. 'A great
revolution is preparing, to which that which is just ended (as 25
people say) was only the preface. The world is in fermentation,
and there will be strange sights seen; the spectacle, it is true,
will be neither for you nor for me, but we may well say to one
another in taking leave of this insane planet (if it is allowable
to recal one's Horace at such a moment): "Spem bonam cer- 30
tamque domum reporto." ' Ultramontanism is but a stage in this
new revolution prophesied by Joseph de Maistre, it is not, as
he imagined, the end; but steadily and confidently, all through
the first twenty years of our century, to have foreseen and
predicted this stage, is no mean proof of insight and originality. 35
   This remarkable man is far less known in England than he
deserves to be. We know him chiefly by one of his publications,
the 'Soirées de Saint-Pétersbourg,' in which the Baconian phi-

losophy is vigorously attacked. Most of us are no further acquainted with the man or his work. Let us run quickly over the
main points in their history. He was born at Chambéry in 1754,
the eldest of ten children, of a family of ancient descent and
austere manners. His father was president of the Senate of
Savoy. The young Joseph-Marie de Maistre was educated by
the Jesuits, and took vigorously to his studies. As a young man
he knew five languages, French, Latin, English, Italian, and
Spanish; to which in later life he added two more, Greek and
German. He entered the magistrature like his father, and in
1786, at the age of thirty-two, he married. In the fermentation
of mind which preceded the French Revolution, he became a
member of the Reformed Lodge of Chambéry, avowed himself an enemy of abuses, and was even accused of Jacobinism.
But from the moment of the French invasion and occupation of
Savoy in 1793, his fidelity to his own sovereign, his hostility to
the French Revolution, never faltered. He quitted Savoy in
January 1794, the day after the birth of his third and youngest
child, his daughter Constance; he never saw her again until 1814.
His property was confiscated. For two years he was employed
at Lausanne on the business of the Sardinian government, and
it was during his stay at Lausanne that he published his 'Considérations sur la France,' a work in which his power and his
characteristic ideas first revealed themselves. In 1797 he was
moved to Turin; Turin was occupied by the French in 1798,
the royal family of Sardinia lost all its possessions on the main-
land, and the Court of Turin became the Court of Cagliari.
Joseph de Maistre was at first employed as chief magistrate of
the island of Sardinia, but in 1802 his government sent him as
minister plenipotentiary to Russia. At St. Petersburg he remained
fifteen years, all through the great struggle with Napoleon.
Ill-paid and ill-understood by the petty government of Cagliari,
he was esteemed and admired by the Emperor Alexander, by
Russian society, and by his diplomatic colleagues; a still better
alleviation of the pressure of embarrassment and anxiety he
found in study. During his stay at St. Petersburg his principal
works were written, but they remained for the time in his
portfolio. He was joined in 1806 by his son Rodolphe, then just

sixteen years old, to whom the Emperor Alexander gave a commission in the Russian Guards. His wife and his two daughters rejoined him in 1814. In 1817 he left Russia and proceeded by way of Paris to Turin, where he was made Chancellor and Minister of State. He now published the works on which he had been long busy in Russia, his 'Du Pape,' his 'De l'Église Gallicane,' and the 'Soirées de Saint-Pétersbourg.' He died at Turin in February 1821, at the age of sixty-seven.

His Correspondence was published in two volumes by his son, a quarter of a century after his death, and has passed through six or seven editions. Striking and suggestive as are works like his 'Considérations' and his 'Soirées de Saint-Pétersbourg,' it is his Correspondence which best makes us feel his variety, his attractiveness, his superiority. These two volumes of his Correspondence will live, and will take their place not merely in Catholic libraries, and as part of the polemics of a great Catholic champion, but in general literature. The literary talent of this Savoyard, whose letters, of far weightier contents than the letters of Madame de Sévigné, are not surpassed by even hers in felicity and vivacity, may well make the French adopt him with pride as one of their classics. But for us, for the world at large, what will preserve his letters is the impression given by them of admirable vigour of mind in union with admirable force and purity of character. We should read them; but alas! we do not even read Burke. Our days go by, and the hour with Mr. Yates in the 'World' is followed by the hour with Mr. Labouchere in 'Truth;' and this fascinating course of reading leaves us with little leisure or taste for anything else. Yet what a pity to be so absorbed by our enchanters as to be unable to feel also the beauty of things like the following, a cry coming from Joseph de Maistre at the end of his hard day, his life of strenuous and grievous travail:—

'I know not what the life of a rogue may be—I have never been one—but the life of an honest man is abominable. How few are those whose passage upon this foolish planet' [we had '*insane* planet' a little way back] 'has been marked by actions really good and useful! I bow myself to the earth before him of whom it can be said, "*Pertransivit benefaciendo;*" who has succeeded in instructing,

consoling, relieving his fellow-creatures; who has made real sacrifices for the sake of doing good; those heroes of silent charity who
hide themselves and expect nothing in this world. But what are the
common run of men like? and how many of us are there in a
thousand who can ask themselves without terror: "What have I
done in this world, *wherein have I advanced the general work*, and
what is there left of me for good or for evil?" '

The great Napoleon, who ill observed his own maxim, was
fond of saying: One must know how to set bounds to oneself—
'Il faut savoir se borner.' The advice is particularly good when
one has to speak of a personage so rich in matter of interest, and
at the same time so little known to the generality of one's
readers, as Joseph de Maistre. The public is prone to demand
grand review-articles, but there are subjects which are too large
for the limits of a single review-article, even a grand one.
Joseph de Maistre is such a subject. He ought to be treated by
instalments. And now, when Russia and the Russian people are
objects of so much importance to us in this country, we propose
to take that portion of Joseph de Maistre's Correspondence
which deals with Russia and things Russian; to observe the
impression made by Russia and the Russians, during his fifteen
years' experience of them, on this independent and powerful
spirit, one of those minds which stand out from the crowd, and
of which the thoughts are still fresh and living as on the day
when they were uttered.

Joseph de Maistre had every reason to speak well of Russia.
In spite of his poverty, in spite of the insignificance of his
Sovereign, he was received there from the first with kindness;
he inspired, as time went on, the most cordial liking and esteem,
and was treated with the most flattering distinction. Not only
did the Emperor Alexander, as has been already mentioned,
give a commission in the guards to the young Rodolphe de
Maistre, but he placed Joseph de Maistre's brother Xavier, the
well-known writer, at the head of the library and museum of
the Russian Admiralty. The society of St. Petersburg was as
favourable as the Czar. Joseph de Maistre had in his character,

had even in his demeanour and conversation, something impetu-
ous and trenchant. He knew it himself:—

'I have said and done in my life,' he writes to Madame de Pont,
'things sufficient to ruin a public man five or six times over. People
have been provoked; they have talked of me in the way you may 5
have heard; and yet here I am, still on my legs—nay, in spite of all
obstacles, I have gone on mounting higher and higher. Every
character has its inconveniences. Do you suppose me not to be
aware that I yawn when I am bored; that a sort of mechanical smile
says sometimes, "*You talk like a fool!*" that in my way of speaking 10
there is something original, something *vibrante*, as the Italians say,
something trenchant, which seems, and particularly in moments of
heat or inadvertence, to announce a certain imperiousness of
opinion to which I have no more right than any other man? I know
it perfectly well, madame: *Chassez le naturel, il revient au galop.*' 15

In spite of this impetuosity, this imperiousness, he pleased.
A diplomatist said of him:—'Count de Maistre is a most fortunate person; he says just what he likes, and yet he never comes
to grief.' Not only did he inspire respect, he inspired warm
liking also, he pleased. He was original, full of knowledge, of 20
high honour and integrity; but at the same time he was entirely
free from peevishness, narrowness or littleness; he was not in
the least a prig or a pedant. 'I am very bookish in my own
study,' he said, 'but in the world I try to be as little bookish as
possible.' Accompanied by simplicity, integrity, good temper, 25
and largeness of mind, his vivacity in conversation warmed and
charmed people without offending them, and in the society of
St. Petersburg he was a signal success.
His life in Russia had its drawbacks, indeed. The first July
after his arrival showed him what the Russian climate was. The 30
warm season is supposed to begin in May, and in July every
one who can get out of St. Petersburg is enjoying the
country:—

'I spent yesterday with the English ambassador, who is in the
country in the direction of Cronstadt. We never left the fire but 35

for a minute or two, to look through his telescope at some vessels in the Gulf. To-day, too, I am obliged to sit by the fire; how long this queer state of things will go on I don't know. People in the country here pave the ground with gold in order to overcome the difficulties of all kinds which nature puts in their way; for climate has to be overcome, and soil also. I have just seen a man spend 10,000 roubles in digging a ditch round a piece of ground which cost 25 roubles. And all this for three months in the very finest years, and for six weeks at the outside in bad years. No outlay seems too great if it will purchase any enjoyment. As I look at all this magnificence, I think of what kind nature does for us by her own unaided power.'

Not only of landscape-gardening and of luxuries was the expense in Russia, to a man of moderate means, prohibitory, but of other and more necessary things also:—

'A foreigner here who has a daughter cannot possibly get her educated (I mean so far as accomplishments are concerned) unless he be the English ambassador or something of that sort. A young lady's education costs ten thousand francs; you can have no idea what it is. People thus go without masters for their children because they cannot afford them.'

Finally even the kindness and hospitality which he met with at St. Petersburg, a capital offering such a contrast to his own 'capitale peu fraternelle,' as he called Turin, were good so far as they went, and were gratifying, but they were something altogether distinct from the friendship of congenial minds, from the intimacies which elsewhere Joseph de Maistre had formed and enjoyed. In a delightful letter to one of his old friends, Madame Huber, of Lausanne, he says:—

'I meet with all manner of kindness in society and at Court, but I stay at home as much as my position will allow me. I have plenty of good books, and I study with might and main; for really one is in duty bound to learn something. As for the supreme pleasures of friendship and of confidential intimacy—a blank. You have often heard people talk of the hospitality of this country, and in one sense what they say is quite true; you are asked to dinner and supper all round, but the foreigner never gets at the heart. I never find myself in full dress amid all the Asiatic pomp here, without thinking of my grey stockings at Lausanne, and of that lantern with which I used to go and visit you at Cour. Oh the delightful drawing-room at Cour! that is what is lacking to me here! After tiring out my horses along these fine streets, if I could but find Friendship in slippers and sit in slippers myself arguing with her, I should be perfectly content. When you have the goodness to say, with your worthy husband, *Quels souvenirs! quels regrets!* listen, and you will hear the echo of the Neva repeating, *Quels souvenirs! quels regrets!*'

The touch of Madame de Sévigné herself, in letter-writing, has not more spirit and grace. But we are to concern ourselves with Russia, not with Joseph de Maistre's gifts as a letter-writer. When he had been four or five years in Russia, he describes to the King of Sardinia the state of things there as follows:—

'The want of money is extreme; nevertheless luxury runs its course without troubling itself about anything, although its extravagances and its utter thoughtlessness are conducting this country to an inevitable revolution. The nobility throws its money away, but this money falls into the hands of the business class, who have only to cut off their beards and to obtain government posts to become masters of Russia. The town of St. Petersburg will soon belong to trade and commerce entirely. In general the impoverishment and the moral decay of the nobility are the true causes of the revolution which we see in France. That revolution will be repeated here, but with peculiar circumstances. I can venture to assure your Majesty that Russia affords to the observer most abundant matter for interesting reflexion, for it brings back before our eyes the Middle Age, and enables us to see in reality what we had only seen in history. But the native Russian revolution, which may be called natural, combining itself with our eighteenth-century revolution, which is abominable, produces such a complication of things as is not to be understood without the most careful attention.'

The Emperor Alexander had his head full of generous projects and reforms for his people:—

'There can be no mistake at present about the intentions of his Imperial Majesty. The emperor is tired of his power as handed

down to him by his predecessors; and, his youth allowing him to
undertake great enterprises, he really means to constitute his people
and to raise them to the European level.'

Joseph de Maistre, with his distrust of written constitutions,
5   his sense of the slow movement of things and of the extreme
actual unripeness of the Russian people, regarded with disfavour
these projects of reform from above. The Russians were unripe
for them, he said; and he was convinced that a law, though
excellent in itself, must prove useless and even mischievous unless
10 the nation were worthy of it and made for it. How else could
a law, he asked, have any real sanction? Bestowed by one emperor upon unripe and passive subjects, it might be revoked by
another. Had not Paul the First established with every solemnity
the Salic Law in Russia? A day or two afterwards, his son abol-
15 ished it. 'Toute nation a le gouvernement qu'elle mérite;' 'every
nation has the government which it is fit for.' As Georgia is to
Russia, so is Russia to Western Europe; and as it fared with the
introduction of the Russian procedure into Georgia, so it will
fare with the introduction of Western constitutionalism into
20 Russia:—

'Formerly the Czar of Georgia used to ride out every morning on
horseback to do justice; at a slow pace, he made a progress through
the streets of Tiflis. Litigants came to him and stated their case.
The Czar administered the stick to the party who seemed to de-
25 serve it. A Georgian said the other day to my brother, quite seriously: "Well, Sir, it was found that these princes very seldom made
a mistake." The Georgians most sincerely regret this bygone street-
procedure; and as to the new procedure which the Russians have
brought amongst them, with its formalities, its delays, its written
30 documents, they cannot abide it, they are sick of it; whoever would
give them back their old stick-law would be hailed as a benefactor.
There are a thousand subtleties in use amongst our old European
nations which I consider to be clean over the heads of the Russians
—the Russians as I know them at this moment, at any rate.'

35 Again and again he returns to this actual unripeness of the
Russian nation, in every one of the great lines along which the
growth of a nation's mental life proceeds:—

'People make a mistake when in this country they put 1815; they ought to put 1515, for we are in the sixteenth century. . . . The kind of moral vegetation which gradually leads nations forward out of barbarism into civilization has been suspended in Russia, and, as it were, cut in two, by two great events: the schism of the tenth 5 century and the invasion of the Tartars.'

The clergy, which in Western Europe has done so much for knowledge and civilization, has done nothing in Russia:—

'Between a Russian pope and an organ-pipe, I see no great differ- ence; both emit sound, and that is all. I have repeatedly asked 10 intelligent Russians whether means might not be found to civilize the clergy, to introduce it into society, to get rid of that dis- favour which now more than ever attaches to it, and to make it of use for education, public morality, &c. All people unite with me in desiring this, but they give me no hope of its being accomplished.' 15

The religious knowledge and ideas of the Russian people in general are what might be expected with such a clergy:—

'On the matter of religion the Russian knows nothing. His abso- lute ignorance of the Latin language shuts him out from all the sources of discussion. Of wits he has plenty; but even the best wits 20 can only know what they have learnt, and the Russian has not looked in this direction (I am speaking of the laity). Now that the light of science is beginning to dawn here, it produces its usual effect—that of unsettling the religion of the country; for no sect can hold out against science. The vulgar and unlearned clergy is 25 nothing and counts for nothing; those who have any mind, and who know Latin and French, are all more or less Protestants. In society you hear this denied, either from ignorance, or from inattention, or because people had rather deny it than set it right; but nothing is more certainly true.' 30

In philosophy Russia was as backward as in religion:—

'I can hear of no good work on jurisprudence or on philosophy. In these two matters, again, as in that of religion, Russia is delivered over, bound hand and foot, to the Germans. The persons who have

influence being either art and part in the thing, or else being led by
the nose, I see no remedy for it.'

The actual demand in Russia for serious reading of any kind
was well shown by the state of the book-trade in St. Peters-
5   burg:—

'A serious work, were it only a hundred pages long, can count
here upon but a hundred and fifty purchasers, of whom ten will
read it and two will understand it. A publisher, it may well be conceived, prints nothing at his own risk.'

10   And again:—

'Pluchart (a bookseller) has assured me, to my great astonishment, that a publisher in this capital, who brings out a philosophical
work, however short, can only reckon upon about a hundred and
fifty buyers. I quite understand that books are often lent; still, a
15   hundred and fifty is a small number for a town of this size.'

Accordingly, Joseph de Maistre was of opinion that the rulers
of Russia had better proceed very gradually with their plans of
reform and constitution. He doubted whether the Russian people
could understand any government except the autocracy of the
20   Czar, or could be held together by it. He prophesied that 'those
who called for the enfranchisement of the serfs would be found
to have been calling for the division of the empire.' For the
present, he thought, 'the reforms of his Imperial Majesty will
end in his putting his people back again into the state where he
25   found them, and no great harm either.' But what if the Russian
nation, unripe as it was, should suddenly shake off its indifference and should take the Emperor's reforms seriously? What if
this nation, at its actual stage of development, a nation neither
sanguinary nor turbulent by nature (he always did it this jus-
30   tice), but which had suffered enormous losses in money and
men from the great war, and was more and more being drawn
into contact with the agitations of Western Europe, 'should be
seized by one of those fits on the brain which have attacked
other nations, not more reasonable than Russia is, but more

raisonneuses?' In this case, Joseph de Maistre foresaw nothing but additional danger and embarrassment from the course now pursued by the emperor:—

'If this nation, arriving at the comprehension of our perfidious novelties and acquiring a taste for them, were to conceive the idea of resisting all revocation or alteration of what it might call its *constitutional privileges;* if some university Pougatscheff were to put himself at the head of a party; if once the people got unsettled, and instead of Asiatic expeditions, began a revolution in the European line, I have no words to express the alarm which might well be felt.

> "Bella, horrida bella!
> Et multo *Nevam* spumantem sanguine cerno." '

Pougatscheff was a personage who figured in a revolt against the government of Catherine the Second.

For the present, however, Joseph de Maistre thought that all offers of code and constitution were likely to fall through, by reason of the indifference of the mass of the Russian people to them. In a letter written in October 1815 to Prince Koslowski, he thus sums up the data presented by the actual situation:—

'In general I incline to think that you have not sufficiently prepared the people for the code before making the code for the people. I have a grudge against your Peter the Great, who appears to me to have committed the greatest of faults, that of failing in proper respect for his own nation. I never read that Numa made his Romans drop their toga, that he treated them as barbarians, and so on. The Decemvirs certainly went to Greece for laws, but they did not bring Greeks to Rome to make them. At present, the national pride is waking up and feeling indignant; but Peter has placed you in a false position with the foreigner. "*Nec tecum possum vivere, nec sine te*"—that is the motto for you. I do not think that there is to be found at this moment, for the man who knows how to observe, a greater and a finer field than your country, my dear Prince. The good side in you every one can see. You are kind, humane, hospitable, quick, intrepid, enterprising, clever at imitating, not in the least pedantic, with a dislike to all restraint, preferring a pitched battle to a lesson in drill. But on this fine body of yours are

established two fistulas which impoverish it—instability and dishonesty. Everything with you is changeable: your laws change like
the ribbons in vogue; your opinions like the waistcoats in wear; systems of every kind like the fashions. A man sells his house just as
readily as his horse; nothing is constant with you except inconstancy,
and nothing is respected, because nothing is ancient—there is your
first mischief. Your second is not less serious. Highway robbery is
less common here than elsewhere, because you are by nature gentle
in as high a degree as you are brave; but the robbery of dishonesty
is chronic with you. If one buys a diamond, it is sure to have a flaw;
if one buys a match, the brimstone is sure to be bad. This spirit,
traversing the channels of business from the highest to the lowest,
makes endless ravages. It is against these enemies that your legislators should employ all their wisdom and all their strength. I could
go on till to-morrow talking on this subject, *sed de his coram.* All I
can now say is, that my interest in you and in all that concerns
you is unbounded; your people have treated me with so much kindness, that they have won my heart, and I have no longer any wish
to leave you.'

To these considerations of the faults, virtues, and condition
of the Russian people are to be added considerations of the
circumstances of the moment, and of the probable influences of
the future:—

'Your great country, involved in this enormous shock of the
French Revolution, on the point at one time of perishing by it, has,
by a rapid turn of events, been saved itself and been made the
saviour of others. What will become of it, God only knows! What
is certain is, that it cannot remain as it is now. It has had its part in
the general commotion; the invasion, in the first place, has not failed
to produce a very perceptible effect on the mental state of your
peasants; the soldiers who have been in France will be inoculators
of a still stronger kind. May God take care of you!'

Not codes and constitutions, but the deeper-working and
gradual agencies of education and religion, were what Joseph
de Maistre placed first in importance for Russia, as he saw and
knew Russia. But neither of them was taking a direction which
he approved, or which he could witness without disquietude.
Of popular education there was no question, the time for it had

not yet come. The only education, of which at that time there was any question in Russia, was the education of the middle and upper classes. The Jesuits, expelled in the eighteenth century from the chief Catholic states of Europe, had found a refuge in Russia, and education had come very much into their hands. Simply as schoolmasters, the Jesuits have great merits; an Englishman should never forget Bacon's testimony to the goodness and success of their methods. 'Talis cum sis,' he says to their Society, applying the words addressed by Agesilaus to Pharnabazus, 'talis cum sis, utinam noster esses!' But in the Jesuit schools, letters and literature were preponderant; the cry of the day was already for science, for more of science and less of letters. The Russians, with their appetite for novelty and fresh fashions, joined in the cry eagerly. The worship of science took forms which were not always judicious, the professors who administered its bread of life were often personages whose walk and conversation left much to be desired:—

'You mention science and the universities. What a chapter, my dear Prince, do we open there! At Wilna they have just been maintaining a thesis that God is caloric at the highest stage (*per perfectionem*), that the human spirit is caloric at a lower stage, the sun a caloric which organizes, the plant a caloric which is organized, &c. An apostate Catholic priest, who has worried two wives to death, and is at present the happy owner of a third, is professor of moral philosophy in one of your universities. Instruction, with you, is planted the wrong end upwards, and bears corruption for you before bearing science.'

In a series of letters written in 1810, at the request of Count Rasoumowsky, the Russian Minister of Public Instruction, Joseph de Maistre examines with his usual acuteness the ideas of educational reform which were prevalent, and discusses their application to the actual state of Russia. He starts from his favourite, fundamental principle. Just as every plan of government is a baneful dream, unless it be in harmony with the character and circumstances of the nation, so it is with education. Before establishing a scheme of education, the habits, inclinations, and state of ripeness of the nation for which it is to be designed, are to be considered. The eighteenth century had promulgated the doctrine that education in the so-called sciences is the whole of education, whereas it is really, says Joseph de Maistre, but a part of it; it is also by far the less interesting part, and one which has no worth at all unless it rests upon moral education. The generation trained according to the new doctrine had made the French Revolution. Still, in Western Europe education had for centuries been in the hands of the clergy, and it still remained to a great extent in their hands. The clergy assign to moral training its proper and prominent place in education. In Western Europe, in spite of the revolutionary propaganda, the schools bear deep traces of the character impressed on them by the clergy, and theories of education are largely influenced by it. In Russia the clergy, 'unhappily cut off from society and deprived of all civil functions,' has never kept school, has created and sustained no tradition of the indispensableness of moral training as a part of education. The Russians, lovers of novelty, and peculiarly liable to be blown about by every breath of vain doctrine, take up with the new theories of scientific education as if they were a revelation, as if they were going to do for Russia just what Russia needed. No error could be greater. The Russians expect from the sciences far more than the sciences can ever give them, but in the meanwhile Russia is not even ripe for the sciences at all. The government might found scientific establishments, but until the nation was ripe for them, and really needed them, they would get no pupils. They would be like the School of Law, not long ago instituted by the emperor, which offered to every student board and lodging free, 300 roubles a year, and a degree; but no students came, and the School had to be closed. And yet, in the times which we call barbarous, the University of Paris could show 4000 students, drawn there from all parts of Europe, and living at their own cost. Everything depends, not on what the government may found, but on what the nation can use:—

'Figure to yourself a government which should go to huge expense for the sake of covering with grand inns a country where nobody travelled; there you have the true image of a government

which makes a great outlay on scientific establishments before the
national genius has shown any turn for the sciences. Learned bodies
of European fame, such as the Academy of Paris, the Royal Society
of London, the Academy *del Cimento* of Florence, began as free
associations of a certain number of individuals united together by   5
their love for the sciences. After a certain time the sovereign,
prompted by the public esteem for them, bestowed on them a civil
existence by means of letters patent; so arose these great academic
bodies. Everywhere they have been established because of the men
of science who were there already, not in the hope of getting men   10
of science by their means. It is a silly business to spend immense
sums on making a cage for the phœnix, before you know whether
the phœnix will come.

‘ "Time," says the Persian proverb, "is the father of miracles."
He is the prime minister of all sovereigns: with him they do every-   15
thing; without him they can do nothing. And yet the Russians hold
him in contempt, and will never wait. Time is affronted, and makes
sport of them. It is a great misfortune that this famous nation
should add to its first error of esteeming the sciences too highly the
second error of wanting to become possessed of them all at once,   20
and of feeling humiliated because Russia is more backward than
other nations in this respect. Never was there a prejudice more false
and more dangerous. The Russians might be the first nation in the
universe, and yet have no talent for the natural sciences.’

Even if the Russians have no turn for the sciences, they may   25
console themselves, says Joseph de Maistre, by remembering
that the Romans, who had none either, nevertheless managed to
cut a considerable figure in the world. But the Poles, a Slav
people like the Russians, produced three centuries ago a man of
science who is one of the ornaments of the human race, the   30
illustrious Copernicus. It is not likely that the water of the
Dwina should have some magical property which prevents science from passing. If nature, then, has, as is probable, endowed
the Russians with an aptitude for the sciences, a spark will at
some favourable moment awaken it, as it has awakened it else-   35
where. Public attention will be turned that way, scientific
societies and establishments will spring up of themselves, and
the Government will only have to give them form and acknowl-

edgment. Until this time of natural fermentation arrives, the
mania for teaching science can lead to no good result, and can
only do mischief. One kind of mischief Joseph de Maistre
points out with especial force:—

5   'A terrible inconvenience springing out of this scientific mania is
that the government, having no professors of their own to satisfy it,
are obliged to have recourse to foreign nations; and, as men of real
attainments and character are not often disposed to leave their own
country, where they are recompensed and honoured, it is always
10   merely second-rate men, often it is vicious and damaged adventurers, who come out here to the North Pole offering their pre-
tended science for money. Russia is at the present day covered with
a scum of this kind, which political storms have driven from other
countries. These runaways bring little with them here except im-
15   pudence and vices. With no affection or esteem for this country,
with no domestic ties civil or religious, they laugh at the undis-
cerning Russians who entrust them with the most precious of their
belongings—their children; their only desire is to make money
enough to enable them to go and live as they please elsewhere; and
20   after trying to take in public opinion by performances which in the
eyes of all good judges prove their gross ignorance, they depart back
again to their own country, and turn Russia into ridicule in worthless
books, which Russia is even good enough to buy of these creatures;
nay, not unfrequently she translates them.'

25   A nation's beginnings of intellectual activity are naturally in
imaginative production and in poetry, and here Joseph de
Maistre observed a genuine movement, as genuine as the scientific movement was factitious. Language and letters a nation
must begin with; above all, the first stage in its mental progress
30   is the respect for its own language and the employment of it.
The predominance of the French language was a real obstacle,
in Russia, to the development of the national genius. Joseph
de Maistre talks sarcastically of 'the St. Petersburg savants who
know French perfectly and Russian a little.' He speaks of the
35   suppression of the French Theatre, in 1816, as favourable to the
improvement of the native drama. In the chief theatre of St.
Petersburg the performances were no longer to be in French,
but in Russian. We do not know whether this theatrical prec-

edence of the Russian tongue is still perfectly kept up at St. Petersburg. But Dr. Neubauer reported the other day a symptom which is full of promise for Russian literature and life; namely, that in the transactions of the Philosophical Society of St. Petersburg, which used always to be in French and German, the Russian language is now adopted.

Religion, however, was the great agency on which Joseph de Maistre relied for expelling evil where it had reigned and made havoc, and for preventing its entrance into communities hitherto unravaged by it. 'The French Revolution is satanic,' he used to say; 'if the counter-revolution is not divine, it is null.' And by this divine counter-revolution he meant 'a moral and religious revolution, without which chaos cannot cease and creation begin.' But he found in the religious fermentation which surrounded him in Russia a mixture of philosophism, Germanism, Protestantism, and illuminism, which seemed to him to announce a dark future for religion, except so far as this darkness was relieved by numerous conversions to Roman Catholicism. But we ought to let him speak for himself:—

'Science, newly arrived here, is commencing its first exploit, which is to take religion by the throat. The conquests of the Protestant spirit, throughout all that portion of the clergy which is acquainted with French and Latin, are incredible. People talk about the Greek Church; the Russian Church is no more Greek than it is Syrian or Armenian; it is an isolated church under a civil head, just like the Church of England. If the patriarch of Constantinople were to dream of giving an order here he would be thought mad; and mad he would indeed be to attempt it. In this state of things, the London Bible Society has come fishing in Russia. This society spent last year 42,000*l.* It was proposed to open a branch here, and the offer was at once accepted, for the Russian is even more greedy of novelties than the Frenchman, with whom he has many points of resemblance. Persons of the highest respectability have become members, and amongst them the Russian and the Catholic archbishops.'

To the plan of 'sowing Bibles broadcast in the vulgar tongue, without distinction of persons and without explanation,' the

Catholic Church has always, as is well known, been resolutely opposed. In Russia, says Joseph de Maistre,—

'A single ancient version—nay, a few lines only of this version—wrongly interpreted by popular fanaticism, have sufficed to create the Russian *rascolnics* (sectaries), that vast ulcer which eats into the national religion and spreads further every day. What will it be when a simple people, taking things absolutely by the letter, shall possess the Bible in the vulgar tongue in all the variety of the Bible versions?'

But it was as 'a Protestant enterprise' conducting men towards '*le* riénisme *Protestant*,' Protestant nothingism, that the Bible Society called forth Joseph de Maistre's deepest enmity. The Society was in his eyes, respectable as might be many of its members and excellent as might be their intentions, in real truth nothing more nor less than 'a Socinian machine for the over-throw of all ecclesiastical authority.' As a Protestant enterprise, he maintained, it moved infallibly towards the sure goal of Protestantism, towards Socinianism or Deism, as people then called it;—in other words, dogmatic decay. With penetrating eye, with the acuteness of a trained observer and the joy of a bitter enemy, Joseph de Maistre saw the ruin, the certain and ever-increasing ruin, upon the Continent, of dogmatic and or-thodox Protestantism. Protestantism was no longer a religion, he said, it was become a mere negation:—

'There is not a point of Christian faith which Protestantism has not attacked and destroyed in the minds of its partizans. What was sure to happen has happened; this unblessed system has allied itself with philosophism, which is indebted to it for its most dangerous weapons; and these two enemies of all religious belief have exer-cised so fatal an influence, that those fair regions of Europe where they prevail may be said to have no longer any religion at all.'

And therefore the Russian Church, which was fast imbibing 'the venom of Germanism and Protestantism,' and bidding fair to become professedly Protestant, would probably announce itself Protestant at a time when there were no Protestants left anywhere else.

In his keen, bold, unsparing criticism of continental Protestantism Joseph de Maistre is wonderfully successful. What
we must never forget is that his own Catholicism, by virtue of
which he thinks himself entitled to treat Protestantism thus
disdainfully, and on which he affects to stand as on a rock,
is an hypothesis arbitrary, artificial, and unavailing. Always
therefore, in watching Joseph de Maistre attack and rout his
adversaries, a good critic will have the feeling, that the ultimate
fate of the day is not yet by any means fully visible, that the
battle is not really won. It is as with Joseph de Maistre's haughty
airs of defiance and contempt of middle-class and popular
opinion. 'What is a nation, my good friend? The sovereign and
the aristocracy. We must weigh voices, not count them. A
hundred shopkeepers of Genoa would go for less with me, as
to what is to be judged expedient or inexpedient for the community, than the family of Brignola alone.' The mind of the
hundred shopkeepers may be indeed but, as Bacon says, 'a poor
and shrunken thing'; but whoever shall imperiously substitute
for it the mind of the House of Brignola, will find the resource
artificial and insufficient.

The tendency to Protestantism was favoured in Russia by
another tendency, also Germanic in its origin, and which was
powerfully influential in the highest quarters—illuminism.
Illuminism, says Joseph de Maistre, has for its ideal a kind of
transcendental and universal Christianity; it conceives Christianity to have been transformed and disfigured by priests, and
is extremely unfavourable to hierarchies and their claims; it
looks upon Christendom as a collection of sects differing on
many points, but all of them united at bottom in something
good, which is fundamental Chritianity. The adherents of this
illuminism were very numerous at St. Petersburg and Moscow.
The Emperor Alexander himself was profoundly imbued with
it. The extraordinary Convention of Paris, in which Austria,
Prussia, and Russia, after the defeat of Napoleon, solemnly
declared their adherence to a universal Christianity, was a concession to the enthusiasm of Alexander for this ideal. 'The
Emperor Alexander,' writes Joseph de Maistre, 'with his universal Christianity, his fundamental dogmas, and his Bible

Society, may be sure that he is on the high road to the destruction of Christianity.' But the Emperor's subjects seemed much inclined to accompany him, and even the Catholic Archbishop joined, as we have already seen, the Bible Society, and when
5 Rome expressed disapprobation and insisted on his leaving it, he took no notice. The picture of this Catholic dignitary, the Archbishop of Mohileff, who must indeed have been a curiosity, is in Joseph de Maistre's raciest manner. 'The Archbishop of Mohileff is Sestrintzewitz, a man eighty years old; formerly
10 a Protestant, then an officer of hussars, finally a Catholic bishop. It was he who said one day, as he saw the Emperor pass: "That is *my* Pope!" '

In illuminism, however, and also in the dogmatic decay of Protestantism, there was much out of which Catholicism could
15 make its profit:—

'The friends of illuminism swarm at St. Petersburg and Moscow; I know an immense number of them. And you are not to think that everything which they say and write is bad; on the contrary, they have some very sound notions, and,—what will surprise you, per-
20 haps,—they tend towards us Catholics in two ways. First, their own clergy has no influence over their minds; they hold their clergy in utter contempt, and accordingly no longer listen to it; if they do not yet listen to our clergy, at any rate they respect it, and even go so far as to own that it has better retained the primitive spirit.
25 Secondly, the Catholic mystics having much that is in agreement with the ideas which these illuminati have formed concerning internal religion, they have plunged head over ears into the reading of this class of authors. They will read nothing but St. Theresa, St. Francis of Sales, Fénelon, Madame Guyon, &c. Now it is impossible
30 they should steep themselves in influences of this kind without being drawn considerably nearer to us; and in fact a great enemy of the Catholic religion said the other day, "What annoys me is, that all this illuminism will end in Catholicism." '

The secret societies, therefore, the centres of illuminism,
35 which in Catholic countries are objectionable, are in non-Catholic countries useful:—

'Let them be. They are coming our way, all of them, but by a spiral line resulting from an invincible attraction towards the centre, modified by a strong though less potent action of pride, which continually draws them all it can from their direct course. These societies, besides, are detestable in Catholic communities, because they attack our fundamental principle of authority; but in non-Catholic nations I consider them to be of infinite use, because they keep fresh 5 and alive the religious fibre in man, and preserve his spirit from Protestant nothingism."

Philosophism and Protestantism, on their part, too, serve the Catholic Church:—

'From the moment that science makes its entry into a non-Catho- 10 lic country, there is a division in the community; the mass will roll towards Deism, whilst a certain body draw near to us. In all Protestant countries, there is not a man of real intelligence left who is a Protestant; all are Socinians, except that band of persons, more or less numerous, whose conversion to Catholicism makes so much 15 noise at present.'

So much noise did it make that Joseph de Maistre quitted Russia in consequence. Amidst the ferment of the new religious movement came a crop of sudden and unexpected conversions to Roman Catholicism. The multiplicity and rapidity of these 20 conversions, principally in the highest rank of society, was, says Joseph de Maistre, 'an admirable spectacle.' They enraged the Minister of Public Worship, Prince Alexander Gallitzin; they greatly disturbed the Emperor himself, to whose autocracy the unbending attitude of the Church of Rome was unfamiliar and 25 unpleasant, while its high doctrine of 'Extra ecclesiam nulla salus' went clean contrary to his notions of a universal Christianity. The Jesuits, whose connection with these conversions was evident, were in 1816 by imperial ukase expelled from St. Petersburg, and their schools were closed. Joseph de Maistre's 30 intimacy with the Jesuits made him suspected of complicity, and the Emperor commissioned one of his ministers to request an explanation from him upon the subject. Joseph de Maistre replied that he had never induced one of his Imperial Majesty's subjects to change his religion, but that, if any of them had 35 happened to confide to him their intention to change it, he could not in honour and conscience have told them that they

were wrong. The Emperor received the explanation with acquiescence, and continued to treat the Sardinian Envoy with the
same courtesy and distinction as before. But Joseph de Maistre
felt that his position at St. Petersburg could no longer be quite
5   what it had been—perfectly free from all constraint and perfectly agreeable; and he made up his mind to quit a place which
had become dear to him, and where he at one time thought of
ending his days. He requested his government to recal him, and
in 1817 he returned, as has been mentioned, to pass the last years
10 of his life at Turin.

He left amongst his papers the sketch of a conclusion to be
added to his 'Soirées de Saint-Pétersbourg,' and with a passage
from this conclusion we may fitly end our record of his comments on Russia and the Russian people:—

15 'To my dying day I shall never cease to bear Russia in memory
and to pray for her welfare. Her welfare will be a constant object
of my thoughts. What will become of you amidst the general un-
settlement of men's minds? and how will you manage to blend so
many diverse elements which within a short space of time have
20 collected amongst you? Blind faith, grossly superstitious ceremonies,
philosophical doctrines, illuminism, the spirit of liberty, passive
obedience, the hut and the palace, the refinements of luxury and the
rudeness of savage life—what will come out of all these elements
set in motion by that turn for novelty which is perhaps the most
25 striking trait in your character, and which, urging you incessantly
in the pursuit of new objects, makes you disgusted with what you
possess? You dislike living in any house but one that you have just
bought. From laws down to ribbons, everything has to follow the
untiring wheel of your changes. Nevertheless consider the nations
30 which cover the globe; it is the contrary system which has made
them famous. In the tenacious Englishman you have a proof of it; his
sovereigns still take pride in bearing the titles which they received
from the Popes, so hard is it to detach this people from its old
institutions. And yet what people surpasses the English in might, in
35 unity, in national glory? Do you wish to be as great as you are
powerful? follow, then, this example given you by England, set
yourselves steadily against the rage you have for novelty and
change, alike in the smallest things and in the greatest. You say,
"My father died in this house, therefore I must sell it." Say rather:

"He died here, therefore sell it I cannot." Have done with all your ignoble lath and plaster; God has given you granite and iron; use these gifts of God, and build for eternity. One looks in vain for monuments amongst you; one would say that you had an aversion to them. If you do nothing for time, what is time likely to do for   5
you? As for the sciences, they will come if they are to come; are you made for them? we shall see. Meanwhile, you start, like all the nations of the world, with poetry and letters; your fine language is capable of anything; let your talents ripen without impatience. Your case is but that of all other nations; your warriors and statesmen   10
have come before your scientific era. Strogonoff, who gave you Siberia; Suwarow, who made your arms famous throughout the world, were of no academy; better have no academy than have to fill it with foreigners. Your time, if it is really to come, will come naturally and without efforts." '   15

   If only, until the time of Russia is fully come, we could have relays of note-takers like Joseph de Maistre, to report progress every quarter or half century!

Cost of Elementary Schools

To the EDITOR *of the* TIMES.

SIR,—I am afraid that nothing is more tiresome to the public than statistics, except the defence of statistics when they are attacked. But I receive so many inquiries respecting the contradiction given to mine that I most unwillingly ask you to admit into *The Times* my reply.

The date of my report is January. That part of it where a comparison is drawn between the cost of French and English schools was written even earlier. When I wrote it I had before me simply a statement of the total cost of elementary education in France according to a volume of statistics just issued, the heads of expense and the sources of contribution, and finally the general rate of cost per child. It was evident that this rate would not be the same in every locality; so evident that the writer, Sir, of your leading article, noticing my comparison between Paris and London schools, at once made the remark of himself. But I had not the variations before me, and, therefore, could not give them; while my object was to bring out the height of the London rate, assuming what, of course, could not be exact, that the general rate for France was the universal rate there.

More than two months afterwards my report went to the printer and the volume of statistics itself had then come into my hands. I therefore corrected my mention of having "statistics before me" by saying that I had "a volume of statistics before me." But I made no change in that part of my report which drew a rough comparison between the cost of schools in France and in England. A close comparison was not my object; the

circumstances of the two countries, as I expressly said in my
report, are widely different.

"Teacher," in his letter to *The Times,* says that the average
cost per child in the secular schools of Paris is 40½f. But the
schools kept by the religious are (or were when I knew them)   5
adopted as communal schools as well as the secular schools.
"Teacher" quotes some scornful language about *ignorantins,*
but the schools of the Christian Brothers are, many of them,
not bad schools at all, they are good schools. I knew the Frère
Philippe, their Superior-General in 1859; only a Jacobin (if we   10
are to bandy these odious terms of reproach) would have called
him an *ignorantin.* What is the average rate for Paris when the
schools kept by the religious are included I cannot say, for I
have not now the statistics in my possession. But I do not care
to inquire, for the Paris rate, even as "Teacher" gives it, is still   15
23s. 6d. per child below the London School Board rate. As for
the cost of French schools in the future, we will talk of that
when we see what it is.

I do not "regard with complacency" the French rate of
expenditure on schools. I think it too low for efficiency, and   20
out of the question in the circumstances of our country. But
it is possible to have a rate unduly high as well as unduly low.

I am, Sir, your obedient servant,
MATTHEW ARNOLD.

Copyright

George Sand died in 1876, and her publisher, Michel Lévy, died
the year before, in 1875. In May 1875, just after Michel Lévy's
death, Madame Sand wrote a letter in which she renders a tribute of praise and gratitude to the memory of that enterprising,
5   sagacious, and successful man. She describes his character, his
habits, his treatment of his authors, his way of doing business,
his conception of the book-trade and of its prospects. It was by
this conception and by the line which he boldly took in pursu-
ance of it that he was original and remarkable; a main creator,
10   says Madame Sand, of our new *modus vivendi* in literature; one
whose disappearance is not the disappearance of a rich man
merely, but of an intellectual force.

The industrial and literary revolution, for which Michel Lévy
did so much, may be summed up in two words: *cheap books.*
15   But by cheap books we are not to understand the hideous and
ignoble things with which, under this name, England and
America have made us familiar. Cheap books, in the revolution
of Michel Lévy, were books in the *format Charpentier* or the
format Lévy, books in duodecimo instead of octavo; and costing,
20   in general, two-and-sixpence or three shillings a volume instead
of eight shillings or nine shillings. But they were still books of
such an outward form and fashion as to satisfy a decent taste,
not to revolt it; books shapely, well printed, well margined;
agreeable to look upon and clear to read.

25   Such as it was, however, the cheapening of their books threw,
at first, French authors into alarm. They thought that it threatened their interests. "I remember the time, not so very long
ago," says Madame Sand, "when we replied to the publishers
who were demonstrating to us what the results of the future

would be: 'Yes, if you succeed, it will be all very well; but if you fail, if, after an immense issue of books, you do not diffuse the taste for reading, then you are lost, and we along with you.' And I urged upon Michel Lévy," she continues, "this objection among others, that frivolous or unhealthy books attracted the masses, to the exclusion of works which are useful and conscientious. He replied to me with that practical intelligence which he possessed in so eminent a degree: 'Possibly, and even probably, it may be so at first. But consider this: that the reading of bad books has inevitably one good result. It inspires a man with the curiosity to read, it gives him the habit of reading, and the habit becomes a necessity. I intend that before ten years are over people shall ask for their book as impatiently as if it were a question of dinner when one is hungry. Food and books, we have to create a state of things when both shall alike be felt as needs; and you will confess then, you writers and artists, that we have solved your problem: *Man does not live by bread alone.*' "

The ten years were not ended before Michel Lévy's authors had to own, says Madame Sand, that their publisher was right. Madame Sand adds that this led her to reflect on the value of the mediocre in art and literature. Illustrious friends and fellow-authors of hers had been in despair at seeing works of the third order obtain a success far beyond any that they could expect for their own works, and they were disposed to think that with cheap books an era of literary decadence was opening. You are misled, she tells them, by the passing disturbance which important innovations always create at first. It was thought, when railways came, that we had seen the last of conveyance by horses and carriages, and that the providers of it must all be ruined; but it turns out that railways have created a business for horses and carriages greater than there ever was before. In the same way, the abundant consumption of middling literature has stimulated the appetite for trying to know and to judge books. Second-rate, commonplace literature is what the ignorant require for catching the first desire for books, the first gleam of light; the day will presently dawn for them as it does for the child, who by degrees, as he learns to read, learns to understand also; and, in fifty years from this time, the bad and the middling

in literature will be unable to find a publisher, because they will
be unable to find a market.

So prophesied George Sand, and the prophecy was certainly
a bold one. May we really hope, that towards the year 1930 the
5   bad and the middling in literature will, either in Paris or in
London, be unable to find a publisher because it will be unable
to find a market? Let us all do our best to bring about such a
consummation, without, however, too confidently counting
upon it.

10   But that on which I at present wish to dwell, in this relation
by Madame Sand of her debate with her energetic publisher
and of her own reflections on it, is the view presented of the
book-trade and of its future. That view I believe to be in the
main sound, and to show the course which things do naturally
15   and properly tend to take, in England as well as in France. I do
not say that I quite adopt the theory offered by Michel Lévy,
and accepted by George Sand, to explain the course which
things are thus taking. I do not think it safe to say, that the consumption of the bad and middling in literature does of itself
20   necessarily engender a taste for the good, and that out of the
multiplication of second-rate books for the million the multiplication of first-rate books does as a natural consequence spring.
But the facts themselves, I think, are as Michel Lévy laid them
down, though one may dispute his explanation and filiation for
25   the facts. It is a fact that there is a need for cheaper books, and
that authors and publishers may comply with it and yet not be
losers. It is a fact that the masses, when they first take to reading,
will probably read a great deal of rubbish, and yet that the
victory will be with good books in the end. In part we can see
30   that this is the course which things are actually taking; in part
we can predict, from knowing the deepest and strongest instincts which govern mankind in its development,—the instinct
of expansion, the instinct of self-preservation,—that it is the
course which things will take in the future.

35   The practical mode by which Michel Lévy revolutionised
the book-trade was this. He brought out in the *format Lévy*, at
three francs or three francs and a half a volume, new works
such as, for example, those of George Sand herself, which form-

erly would have come out at seven francs and a half a volume. Nay, such works would very often have taken two volumes, costing fifteen francs, to give no more than what is given in one volume of the *format Lévy* for three francs and a half. New books in octavo were cheapened likewise. The two octavo volumes, in French, of Prince Metternich's Memoirs and Correspondence, which have lately come out in Paris, cost but eighteen francs. The two octavo volumes of the English version of Prince Metternich's Memoirs and Correspondence cost thirty-six shillings. But in general we may say that the important reform accomplished in the French book-trade by Michel Lévy and by other publishers of like mind with him was this: to give to the public, in the *format Lévy*, new books at half-a-crown or three shillings, instead of at from six to twelve shillings.

And now to apply this, where it seems to me to be of very useful application, to various points which emerge in discussing the copyright of English authors and the conditions of the English book-trade. I leave on one side all questions of copyright in acted plays, music, and pictures. I confine myself to copyright in books, and to the chief questions raised on it. My point of view will be neither an author's point of view, nor a publisher's point of view, nor yet the point of view of one contending against authors or publishers, but the point of view of one whose sole wish is to let things appear to him fairly and naturally, and as they really are.

A Royal Commission on Copyright has lately been sitting, and has made its report. "We have arrived at a conclusion," the report declares, "that copyright should continue to be treated by law as a proprietary right, and that it is not expedient to substitute for this a right to a royalty, or any other of a similar kind."

This opening sentence of the report refers to a great battle. The Commissioners have come, they say, to a conclusion that "copyright should continue to be treated as a *proprietary right*." Here has been the point of conflict,—as to the proprietary right of the author, as to his right of property in his production.

Never perhaps do men show themselves so earnest, so pertina-
cious, so untiringly ingenious, as when they have under discussion the right and idea of property. One is reminded of Pascal:
"This dog is *mine*, said these poor children; behold *my* place in
5 the sun!" It is disputed whether an author has the right of
property in his production after he has once published it. Professor Huxley and Mr. Herbert Spencer contended with indefatigable ingenuity before the Royal Commission on Copyright that he has; and Mr. Farrer, of the Board of Trade, and
10 Sir Louis Mallet maintained resolutely that he has not. There
is no question that a man can have a right of property in his
productions so far as the law may choose to create one for him.
But the first point at issue between many distinguished and
powerful disputants is, whether he has a natural right.

15   Now, for me the matter is simplified by my believing that
men, if they go down into their own minds and deal quite freely
with their own consciousness, will find that they have not any
natural rights at all. And as it so often happens with a difficult
matter of dispute, so it happens here; the difficulty, the embar-
20 rassment, the need for drawing subtle distinctions and for devising subtle means of escape from them, when the right of
property is under discussion, arises from one's having first built
up the idea of natural right as a wall to run one's head against.
An author has no natural right to a property in his production.
25 But then neither has he a natural right to anything whatever
which he may produce or acquire.

        What is true is, that a man has a strong instinct making him
seek to possess what he has produced or acquired, to have it at
his own disposal; that he finds pleasure in so having it, and finds
30 profit. The instinct is natural and salutary, although it may be
over-stimulated and indulged to excess. One of the first objects
of men, in combining themselves in society, has been to afford
to the individual, in his pursuit of this instinct, the sanction and
assistance of the laws, so far as may be consistent with the
35 general advantage of the community.

        The author, like other people, seeks the pleasure and the
profit of having at his own disposal what he produces. Literary
production, wherever it is sound, is its own exceeding great

reward. But that does not destroy or diminish the author's desire and claim to be allowed to have at his disposal, like other people, that which he produces, and to be free to turn it to account. It happens that the thing which he produces is a thing hard for him to keep at his own disposal, easy for other people to appropriate. But then, on the other hand, he is an interesting producer, giving often a great deal of pleasure by what he produces, and not provoking Nemesis by any huge and immoderate profits on his production, even when it is suffered to be at his own disposal.

So society has taken the author under its protection, and has sanctioned, to a certain extent, his property in his work, and enabled him to have it at his own disposal. In England our laws give him the property in his work for forty-two years, or for his own life and seven years afterwards, whichever period is longest. In France, the law gives him the property in his work for his own life, and his widow's life, and for twenty years afterwards if he leave children; for ten years if he have other heirs. In Germany, the property in his work is for his life and thirty years afterwards. In Italy, for his life and forty years afterwards, with a further period during which a royalty has to be paid upon it to his heirs. In the United States, the author's property in his work is guaranteed for twenty-eight years from publication, with the right of renewal to himself, his wife, or his children, for fourteen years more. And this, though the author's production is a thing confessedly difficult to protect, and easy to appropriate. But it is possible to protect it; and so the author is suffered to enjoy the property in his production, to have it at his own disposal.

But is the author's production really property, ask some people; has he any natural right to it? Mr. Farrer, like so many other people, seems to be haunted by a metaphysical conception of *property in itself*,—a conception distinguishing between certain things, as belonging to the class of that which is property in itself, and certain other things, as belonging to the class of that which is not property in itself. Mr. Farrer's *dog,* his *place in the sun* at Abinger, are of the class of property in itself; his *book*, if he produces one, is of the class of that which

is not property in itself. Sir Louis Mallet is in the same order
of ideas, when he insists that "property arises from limitation
of supply." Property according to its essential nature, Sir Louis
Mallet means, property in itself.

5   Let us beware of this metaphysical phantom of property in
itself, which, like other metaphysical phantoms, is hollow and
leads us to delusion. Property is the creation of law. It is effect
given, by society and its laws, to that natural instinct in man
which makes him seek to enjoy ownership in what he produces,
10   acquires or has. The effect is given because the instinct is natural, and because society, which makes the laws, is itself composed of men who feel the instinct. The instinct is natural, and
in general society will comply with it. But there are certain
cases in which society will not comply with it, or will comply
15   with it in a very limited degree only. And what has determined
society, in these cases, to refuse or greatly limit its compliance
with the instinct of ownership, is the difficulty of giving effect
to it, the disadvantage of trying to give effect to it in spite of
such difficulty.

20   There is no property, people often say, in ideas uttered in
conversation, in spoken words; and it is inferred that there ought
to be no property in ideas and words when they are embodied
in a book. But why is there no property in ideas uttered in
conversation, and in spoken words, while there is property in
25   ideas and words when they come in a book? A brilliant talker
may very well have the instinct of ownership in his good sayings, and all the more if he must and can only talk them and not
write them. He might be glad of power to prevent the appropriation of them by other people, to fix the conditions on
30   which alone the appropriation should be allowed, and to de-
rive profit from allowing it. Society, again, may well feel
sympathy with his instinct of ownership, feel a disposition to
assist and favour a production which gives it so much pleasure.
But we are met by the *difficulty*, the insuperable difficulty, of
35   giving effect to the producer's instinct of ownership in this
case, of securing to him the disposal of his spoken ideas and
words. Accordingly, effect is not given to it, and in such
spoken ideas and words there is no property.

In other cases there is a partial and limited property given, and from the same reason,—from the difficulty of giving complete ownership. Game is an instance in point. A man breeds pheasants, rears them and feeds them, and he has a natural instinct to keep them in his entire possession, and at his own disposal. But the law will allow but a partial satisfaction to this instinct of his, and the moment his pheasants leave his land they may be taken by the person to whose ground they go. Of his chickens, meanwhile, a man retains ownership, even though they may pass over to his neighbour's field. Yet very likely he has bought the eggs of the pheasants and of the chickens alike, reared them both, fed them both, and feels the instinct and desire to claim them both alike as his property. But the law gives effect to this desire fully as regards the chickens, only partially as regards the pheasants. Why? Because of the far greater difficulty of giving full effect to it as regards the pheasants, and of the disadvantage which may arise from persisting in giving effect to it in spite of the difficulty. The law denies to a man the complete ownership of his pheasants, because they are difficult to keep at his own disposal, easy for other people to appropriate. And other people are more prone to appropriate them than the chickens, and more inclined to dispute his ownership of them, because of this very difficulty in maintaining it and facility in violating it. Even the partial ownership of his pheasants which the law does allow to a man, it has to fortify by special measures for its support; by making trespass in pursuit of game a different and more serious offence than common trespass. To gratify his instinct of ownership fully, to let a man have his pheasants at his entire disposal, the law would have to take more stringent and exceptional measures in his favour than it takes now; and this every one feels to be out of the question. The law will certainly not do more for him than it does now; the only question is, whether it ought to do so much. To give even as much ownership in game as a man enjoys now, special measures in his favour are required, because his ownership meets with such great natural difficulties. So great are these difficulties, that the special measures to counteract them are far less likely to be reinforced than to be withdrawn.

And now to apply this to the question of copyright. The instinct of an author to desire ownership in his production, and advantage of that ownership, is natural. The author is an interesting person, and society may, and probably will, be even
5   more ready, rather than less ready, to aid in giving effect to the instinct in his case than in the case of others, if it can be done without grave inconvenience. But there is difficulty in securing his ownership. The author's production is a production difficult to keep at his own disposal, easy for others to appropriate. His
10 claim to some benefit of ownership, however, is generally admitted, and he has ownership given to him for a limited term of years. He finds a publisher, and in concert with him he exercises his ownership; and the result in England of this concert between author and publisher is, that English books are
15 exceedingly dear. A strong desire for cheaper books begins to be felt. Here is the real importance of Sir Louis Mallet's contention and of Mr. Farrer's. "To Englishmen," says Sir Louis Mallet, "easy access to the contemporary literature of their own language is only possible on the condition of exile; England is
20 the only country in which English books are scarce or dear." "Nothing can be more intolerable," says Mr. Farrer, "than a system of copyright-law under which the inhabitants of the mother-country in which the books are produced are the only persons in the world who are prevented from obtaining cheap
25 editions of them." An impatience, to which Mr. Farrer and Sir Louis Mallet here give utterance, an impatience at the dearness of English books, a desire to have them cheaper, has therefore to be added to the original difficulty of securing the author's ownership in a kind of production which is by nature hard to
30 keep at his disposal, easy for others to appropriate. An increased difficulty of securing his ownership is the result.

The ingenious reasoning of many advocates of the rights of authors, and even the line taken by Mr. Froude in that instructive and interesting article on Copyright which he published
35 in the *Edinburgh Review*, fail, it seems to me, to touch the point where the strength of their adversaries' case lies. Like their adversaries, they lodge themselves, stark and stiff, in the idea of "property in itself." Only, for them, an author's work

is "property in itself" just as much as his horse or his field; while, for their adversaries, his horse or his field is "property in itself," but his work is not. Let us grant that the adversaries are wrong, and that an author's work is "property in itself" (whatever that may mean), just as much as his horse or his field. He has at any rate, we will suppose, the same instinct making him seek to have the ownership and profit of his work, as to have the ownership and profit of his horse or field. But what makes the law give him such full ownership as it does of his horse or field is not that the horse or field is "property in itself;" it is, that to comply with his natural desire, and to secure him in his ownership, is in the case of the horse or field comparatively easy. And what makes the law give him a more limited ownership of his literary work is not that this work fails to prove its claim to be considered "property in itself;" it is that, in the case of his literary work, to secure him in his ownership is much more difficult. And suppose we add sufficiently to the difficulty by the rise of a general impatience at the dearness of new books in England; of general irritation at seeing that a work like Lord Macaulay's Life comes out at thirty-six shillings in England, while in France it would come out at eighteen francs, that a new novel by George Eliot costs a guinea and a half, while a new novel by George Sand costs three shillings; of general complaints that "the inhabitants of the mother-country in which the books are produced are the only persons in the world who are prevented from obtaining cheap editions of them,"—suppose we add, I say, to the difficulty by all this, and you endanger the retention of even the right of ownership which the law secures to the author now. The advantage of complying with the author's instinct of ownership might be outweighed by the disadvantage of complying with it under such accumulated and immense difficulty.

But yet to secure, so far as without intolerable inconvenience it can be done, the benefits of ownership in his production to the author, every one, or almost every one, professes to desire. And in general, those who profess to desire this do really mean, I think, what they say; and there is no disposition in their minds to put the author off with benefits which are illusory. But Mr.

Farrer and others propose,—no doubt without intending the poor author any harm,—a mode of benefit to him from his productions which does seem quite illusory. The proposal is to set all the world free to print and sell his work as soon as it appears, on condition of paying him a royalty of ten per cent. But both authors and publishers, and all who have the most experience in the matter and the nearest interest, unite in saying that the author's benefit under this plan would be precarious and illusory. The poor man pursuing his ten per cent over Great Britain and Ireland would be pitiable enough. But what shall we say of him pursuing his ten per cent over all the British Dominions? What shall we say of him pursuing it, under an international copyright on this plan between all English-speaking people, over the United States of America? There are many objections to this plan of a royalty; but the decisive objection is, that whereas every one professes the wish not to take away from the author all substantial benefit from the sale of his work, this plan, in the opinion of those best able to judge, would take it away entirely.

The Royal Commission reported against this plan of a royalty, and in favour of continuing the present plan of securing by law to the author an ownership in his work for a limited term of years. The Commissioners have proposed what would, in my opinion, be a very great improvement upon the present arrangement. Instead of a copyright for forty-two years, or for life and seven years after, whichever period is longest, they propose to give, as in Germany, a copyright for the author's life and for thirty years after. But the principle is the same as in the arrangement of 1842, and there is no danger at present, in spite of Mr. Farrer's efforts, of the principle being departed from. Mr. Froude says truly that the course recommended by Mr. Farrer,—the withdrawal from the author, in effect, of the benefits of ownership in his work,—is a course which every single person practically connected with literature consents in condemning. He says truly that there is no agitation for it. He says truly that the press is silent about it, and that no complaints are heard from the public.

And yet the natural facts, in England as in France, are as

Michel Lévy states them in his conversation with Madame Sand: there is a need for cheap books, the need will have to be satisfied, and it may be satisfied without loss to either author or publisher. What gives gravity to the dissatisfaction of Sir Louis Mallet and of Mr. Farrer with the actual course of the book-trade in England is, that the course of our book-trade goes counter to those natural facts. Sooner or later it will have to adjust itself to them, or there will be an explosion of discontent likely enough to sweep away copyright, and to destroy the author's benefit from his work by reducing it to some such illusory benefit as that offered by the royalty plan of Mr. Farrer. As our nation grows more civilised, as a real love of reading comes to prevail more widely, the system which keeps up the present exorbitant price of new books in England, the system of lending-libraries from which books are hired, will be seen to be, as it is, eccentric, artificial, and unsatisfactory in the highest degree. It is a machinery for the multiplication and protection of bad literature, and for keeping good books dear. In general, a book which is worth a man's reading is worth his possessing. The plan of having one's books from a lending-library leads to reading imperfectly and without discrimination, to glancing at books and not going through them, or rather to going through, for the most part, a quantity of the least profitable sort of books only,—novels,—and of but glancing at whatever is more serious. Every genuine reader will feel that the book he cares to read he cares to possess, and the number of genuine readers amongst us, in spite of all our shortcomings, is on the increase.

Mr. Froude, indeed, says, having the experience of an editor's shelves before his eyes, that instead of desiring the possession of more books than one has, one might rather desire not to possess half of those which one has now. But the books he means are just those which a genuine reader would never think of buying, and which yet are shot upon us now in profusion by the lending-libraries. Mr. Froude says, again, that new books are not the best books, and that old books, which are best, are to be bought cheap. True, old books of surpassing value are to be bought cheap; but there are good new books, too, and good

new books have a stimulus and an interest peculiar to themselves, and the reader will not be content to forego them. Mr.
Herbert Spencer may tell him, that to desire the possession of
good new books, when he is not rich, is merely the common
case of the poor desiring to possess what is accessible to the rich
only; that it is as if he wanted fine horses, and the best champagne, and hothouse flowers, and strawberries at Christmas.
But the answer is that the good new books, unlike the horses
and champagne, may be brought within his reach without loss
to the vendor, and that it is only the eccentric, artificial,
and highly unsatisfactory system of our book-trade which
prevents it.

The three-shilling book is our great want,—the book at
three shillings or half-a-crown, like the books of the *format
Lévy*, shapely and seemly, and as acceptable to the eye as the
far dearer books which we have now. The price proposed will
perfectly allow of this. The French books of the *format Lévy*,
and the French books in octavo, are as shapely and seemly, as
acceptable to the eye, as the corresponding English books at
double and treble their price. The two octavo volumes of
Madame de Rémusat's Memoirs, in French, cost but twelve
shillings, yet they make a handsomer book than the two octavo
volumes of the same work in English, which cost thirty-two.
A cheap literature, hideous and ignoble of aspect, like the taw-
dry novels which flare in the book-shelves of our railway
stations, and which seem designed, as so much else that is produced for the use of our middle class seems designed, for people
with a low standard of life, is not what is wanted. A sense of
beauty and fitness ought to be satisfied in the form and aspect
of the books we read, as well as by their contents. To have the
contents offered one for next to nothing, but in hideous and
ignoble form and aspect, is not what one desires. A man would
willingly pay higher, but in the measure of his means, for what
he values, in order to have it in worthy form. But our present
prices are prohibitive. The taste for beautiful books is a charming and humane taste for a rich man, though really, as has been
already said, our ordinary dear books gratify this taste not a
bit better than the French cheaper ones. However, the taste

for beautiful books requires expense, no doubt, to be fully gratified; and in large paper copies and exquisite bindings the rich man may gratify it still, as he still gratifies it in France, even when we have reformed our book-trade as the French have reformed theirs. For reforming ours, the signal innovation necessary, as in France, is the three-shilling book; although, of course, the price of our new works in octavo at sixteen or eighteen shillings a volume would also have to be reduced in proportion. If nothing of this kind is done, if the system of our book-trade remains as it is, dissatisfaction, not loud and active at present,—I grant that to Mr. Froude,—will grow and stir more and more, and will certainly end by menacing, in spite of whatever conclusion the Royal Commission may now adopt and proclaim, the proprietary right of the author.

The doctrine of M. Michel Lévy respecting the book-trade, and what I have been now saying about our book-trade at home, have their application in America also, and I must end with a few words concerning the book-trade of the United States. Indeed, one is invited by the Americans themselves to do so, for the famous publishers in New York, the Messrs. Harper, have addressed to the authors and publishers of this country a proposal for an International Conference on Copyright. Mr. Conant, who is understood to be connected with the publishing house of the Messrs. Harper, has given in an English magazine an exposition of American opinion on the matter; and an Englishman of legal training and great acuteness, who signs himself "C.," but whom we may, I believe, without indiscretion, name as Mr. Leonard Courtney, has commented on Mr. Conant's exposition.

The Americans, as is well known, have at present (to quote the words of an American, Mr. George Putnam, who has published on this question of copyright a pamphlet very temperate and, in general, very judicious) "no regulation to prevent the use, without remuneration, of the literary property of foreign authors." Mr. Putnam adds: "The United States is, therefore, at present the only country, itself possessing a literature of importance, and making a large use of the literature of the world, which has done nothing to recognise and protect

by law the rights of foreign authors of whose property it is
enjoying the benefit, or to obtain a similar recognition and protection for its own authors abroad."

The Americans, some of them, as is also well known, defend
this state of things by adopting the cry of "free books for free
men." A Conference held at Philadelphia, in 1872, passed resolutions declaring that "thought, when given to the world, is,
as light, free to all;" and, moreover, that "the good of the
whole people, and the safety of our republican institutions, demand that books shall not be made too costly for the multitude
by giving the power to foreign authors to fix their price here
as well as abroad."

Mr. Conant, in his representation to the English public of the
case of the American public, adopts these Philadelphian ideas
in principle. But he maintains that in practice the American
publishers have generously waived their right to act on them,
and he carries the war into the enemy's country. He says for
himself and his countrymen: "We are keenly alive to the necessity of the general diffusion of intelligence. Upon it depends
the perpetuity of our republican form of government. Europe
is constantly pouring upon our shores a mighty deluge of
ignorance and superstition. We welcome here the poor, the
outcasts of every land. There is a widespread feeling that the
Old World, which contributes this mass of ignorance and superstition to our population, should also contribute to the alleviation of the resulting ills." Mr. Conant alleges that the
concession in past times of a copyright to English authors
"would have retarded the progress of American culture at least
half a century, and delayed that widespread intellectual development from which English authors reap so large a benefit."

And yet nevertheless, says this good Mr. Conant, "the course
of American publishers, pursued for many years, towards foreign men of letters, shows that they have no disposition to take
advantage of the absence of international copyright." He declares: "As for English authors, they have already learned that
their interests are quite safe in the hands of 'Yankee pirates,'
as some of your writers still persist in calling the men who for
years have conducted the publishing business of this country

with the most scrupulous regard for the rights of foreign authors. Few English people, I think, have any notion of the amount of money paid to British authors by American publishers. Those authors whose books have been reprinted here without compensation to the author, may rest assured that this was owing to the fact that the sale was not remunerative here, and that international copyright will not make it larger." On the other hand: "While for twenty-five years past British authors have enjoyed all the material advantages of copyright in this country, American books have been reprinted in England by the thousand, without compensation to the authors." And therefore, adds Mr. Conant, "in view of these facts, an American may be pardoned for indulging in a quiet laugh at the lofty tone which the Royal Commissioners on Copyright assume in their solemn arraignment of the United States for refusing to grant protection to English authors."

And so the tables are fairly turned upon us. Not only have English authors no reason to complain of America, but American authors have great reason to complain of England.

An English author, as he reads Mr. Conant, will by turns be inclined to laugh and to be indignant. Mr. Leonard Courtney handles Mr. Conant's statement very scornfully and severely. For myself, I am of a gentle disposition, and I am disposed, in reading Mr. Conant in *Macmillan's Magazine*, to ask him before all things Figaro's question:—*Qui est-ce qu'on trompe ici?* —Who is it that is being taken in here? At the Philadelphia Conference Mr. Conant's statement would have been quite in place; but why he should address it to the British public passes my comprehension. Our British middle class, no doubt, like the great middle-class public of the United States, likes to have its defective practice covered by an exhibition of fine sentiments. But it is our own defective practice that we seek to cover by the exhibition of fine sentiments;—as, for instance, when we left Denmark in the lurch after all our admonitions and threatenings to Germany, we assured one another that the whole world admired our moral attitude. But it gives us no pleasure or comfort to see other people's defective practice, by which we are smarting, covered with an exhibition of fine sentiments. And so, as I peruse Mr. Conant, with Figaro I inquire in bewilderment: "Who is it that is being taken in here?" We know perfectly well the real facts of the case, and that they are not as Mr. Conant puts them; and we have no interest in getting them dressed up to look otherwise than as they are. Our interest is to see them as they really are; for as they really are, they are in our favour.

If American authors have not copyright here in England, whose fault is that? It is the fault of America herself, who again and again has refused to entertain the question of international copyright. Again and again, in Mr. Conant's own statement of facts, appears the proposal, on the part of England, of an international copyright; and again and again the end of it is, "the report was adverse," "no action was taken," "shelved," "more pressing matters crowded it out of sight." If Englishmen suffer by having no copyright in America, they have the American government and people to thank for it. If Americans suffer by having no copyright in England, they have only to thank themselves.

But is it true that American authors have no copyright in England? It is so far from being true, that an American has only to visit England when he publishes his book here,—or even, I believe, has only to cross the border into Canada,—in order to have copyright in his work in England. Mr. Motley told me himself that in this way he had acquired copyright in England for his valuable histories. Mr. Henry James gets it in the same way at this moment for those charming novels of his which we are all reading. But no English author can acquire copyright in the United States.

As to the liberal payment given at present, without copyright, by American publishers to English authors, it is more difficult to speak securely. Certainly it is far too much to say of British authors in general, that they "for at least twenty-five years past have enjoyed all the material advantages of copyright in America;" or that they "have learned that their interests are quite safe in the hands of American publishers." Considerable sums have, no doubt, been paid. Men of science, such as Professor Huxley and Professor Tyndall, are especially mentioned as satisfied with the remuneration voluntarily accorded to them by the American publishers; and indeed, to judge by the success of their American dealings, it seems that these inheritors of the future, the men of science, besides having their hold upon the world which is to come, have their hold likewise, lucky fellows, upon the world which now is! Men of letters have not been so fortunate; and the list, given by Mr. Conant, of those to whom a surprising amount of money is paid from America, is to be received with caution. Mr. Tennyson is mentioned; but I hear from the best authority that in truth Mr. Tennyson has received little or nothing from the sale of his works in America. One can at least speak for oneself; and certainly I have never received, from first to last, a hundred pounds from America, though my books have been, I believe, much reprinted there. Mr. Conant will probably say that I am one of those authors "whose sale is not remunerative," and does not come to much either there or here. And perhaps according to the grand scale by which he weighs things, this may very well be true. Only, if I had not received more than a hundred pounds here or in America either during the quarter of a century that I have gone up and down, as the mockers say, preaching sweetness and light, one could never have managed to drag on, even in Grub Street, for all these years.

The truth is, the interests of British authors in general cannot well be safe in America, so long as the publishers there are free to reprint whom they please, and to pay, of the authors they reprint, whom they please, and at what rate they please. The interests of English authors will never be safe in America until the community, as a community, gets the sense, in a higher degree than it has it now, for acting with delicacy. It is the sense of delicacy which has to be appealed to, not the sense of honesty. Englishmen are fond of making the American appropriation of their books a question of honesty. They call the appropriation stealing. If an English author drops his handkerchief in Massachusetts, they say, the natives may not go off with it; but if he drops his poem, they may. This style of talking is exaggerated and false. There is a breach of delicacy in reprinting the foreigner's poem without his consent, there is no breach of honesty. But a finely touched nature, in men or nations, will respect in itself the sense of delicacy not less than the sense of honesty. The Latin nations, the French and Italians, have that instinctive recognition of the charm of art and letters, which 5 disposes them, as a community, to care for the interests of artists and authors, and to treat them with delicacy. In Germany learning is very highly esteemed, and both the government and the community are inclined to treat the interests of authors considerately and delicately. Aristocracies, again, are brought 10 up in elegance and refinement, and are taught to believe that art and letters go for much in making the beauty and grace of human life, and perhaps they do believe it. At any rate, they feel bound to show the disposition to treat the interests of artists and authors with delicacy; and shown it the aristocratic 15 government and parliament of England have. We must not indeed expect them to take the trouble for art and letters which the government of France will take. We must not expect of them the zeal that procured for French authors the Belgian Copyright Treaty of 1854, and stopped those Brussels reprints 20 which drove poor Balzac to despair. Neither in India, nor in Canada, nor yet in the United States, has our aristocratic government interposed on behalf of the author with this energy. They do not think him and his concerns of importance enough to deserve it. Still, they feel a disposition to treat his interests 25 with consideration and with delicacy; and, so far as the thing depends on themselves, they show them.

The United States are a great middle-class community of our own race,—free from many obstructions which cramp the middle class in our own country, and with a supply of humane 30 individuals sown over the land, who keep increasing their numbers and gaining in courage and in strength, and more and more make themselves felt in the press and periodical literature of America. Still, on the whole, the spirit of the American community and government is the spirit, I suppose, of a middle- 35 class society of our race; and this is not a spirit of delicacy. One could not say that in their public acts the United States showed, in general, a spirit of delicacy. Certainly they have not shown that spirit in dealing with authors,—even with their own. They deal with authors, domestic and foreign, much as Manchester, perhaps, might be disposed, if left to itself, to deal with them; as if, provided a sharp bargain was made, and *a good thing*, as the phrase is, was got out of it, that was all which could be desired, and the community might exult. The worship of sharp bar- 5 gains is fatal to delicacy. Nor is the missing grace restored by accompanying the sharp bargain with an exhibition of fine sentiments.

As the great American community becomes more truly and thoroughly civilised, it will certainly learn to add to its many 10 and great virtues the spirit of delicacy. And English authors will be gainers by it. At present they are gainers from another cause. It appears that till lately there was an understanding amongst American publishers, that, when one publisher had made terms with an English author for the republication of his 15 work in America, the rest should respect the agreement, and should leave their colleague in possession of the work. But about two years and a half ago, says Mr. Conant, certain parties began to set at naught this law of trade-courtesy. Certain firms "began to republish the works of foreign authors, paying nothing for 20 the privilege, and bringing out absurdly cheap editions right on the heels of the authorised reprint, which had cost a large outlay for priority and expense of publication." The ruinous competition thus produced has had the effect, Mr. Putnam tells us in his pamphlet, of "pointing out the absurdity of the present 25 condition of literary property, and emphasising the need of an international copyright." It has had the effect, he says, of "influ- encing a material modification of opinion on the part of pub- lishers who have in years past opposed an international copyright as either inexpedient or unnecessary, but who are 30 now quoted as ready to give their support to any practicable and equitable measure that may be proposed." Nothing could be more satisfactory.

Accordingly, it is now suggested from America that an inter- national copyright treaty should be proposed by the United 35 States to Great Britain, and, as a first step, that "a Commission or Conference of American citizens and British subjects, in which the United States and Great Britain shall be equally represented, be appointed respectively by the American Secretary of State and by the British Secretary of State for Foreign Affairs, who shall be invited jointly to consider and present the details of a treaty."

5   The details are reserved for the Conference; but it is no secret what the main lines of such a treaty, if it is to be accepted in America, must be. The American author will be allowed, on registering his work, to have copyright in England, and the English author to have copyright in the United States. But the
10 foreigner's work must be manufactured and published in the country, and by a subject or citizen of the country, in which it is registered. The English author's book, therefore, to be protected in America, must be manufactured and published in America as well as in England. He will not be allowed to print
15 and publish his book in England only, and to send his copies over to the United States for sale. The main object, I think, of Mr. Conant's exposition, is to make it clear to us on the English side of the water that from this condition the Americans will not suffer themselves to be moved.

20 English publishers and authors seem inclined to cry out that such a condition is an interference with the author's "freedom of contract." But then they take their stand on the ground that an author's production is "property in itself," and that one of the incidents of "property in itself" is to confer on its possessor
25 the right to "freedom of contract" respecting it. I, however, who recognise natural difficulty as setting bounds to ownership, must ask whether, supposing the English author's need for copyright in America to be pressing, he can reasonably expect to be admitted to copyright there without this condition.

30 Mr. Froude and Mr. Leonard Courtney both of them seem to think that the question of international copyright is not at all pressing. They say that opinion in America is slowly ripening for some better and more favourable settlement of copyright than any settlement which America is now likely to accept; and
35 that, meanwhile, English authors may be well enough content with their present receipts from American publishers, and had better let things stay as they are.

A few English authors may, perhaps, be content enough with

their present receipts from America, but to suppose that English authors in general may well be so content, is, I think, a very hazardous supposition. That, however, is of little importance. The important question is, whether American opinion, if we give it time, is likely to cease insisting on the condition that 5 English books, in order to acquire copyright in America, must be manufactured and published there; is likely to recognise the English author and publisher as Siamese twins, one of whom is not to be imported without importing the other. Is there any chance, in short, of the Americans, accustomed to cheap English 10 books, submitting to that dearness of English books which is brought about in England by what, in spite of all my attachment to certain English publishers, I must call our highly eccentric, artificial, and unsatisfactory system of book-trade? I confess I see no chance of it whatever. There is a mountain of 15 natural difficulty in the way, there is the irresistible opposition of things.

Here, then, where lies the real gist of his contention, I am after all at one with Mr. Conant. The Americans ought not to submit to our absurd system of dear books. I am sure they will 20 not; and, as a lover of civilisation, I should be sorry, though I am an author, if they did. I hope the Americans will give us copyright. But I hope, also, that they will stick to Michel Lévy's excellent doctrine: "Cheap books are a necessity, and a necessity which need bring, moreover, no loss to either authors or 25 publishers."

The Future of Liberalism

A public man, whose word was once of great power and is now
too much forgotten by us, William Cobbett, had a humorous
way of expressing his contempt for the two great political
parties that between them govern our country, the Whigs and
5   Tories, or Liberals and Conservatives, and who, as we all know,
are fond of invoking their principles. Cobbett used to call these
principles, contemptuously, *the principles of Pratt, the principles of Yorke.* Instead of taking, in the orthodox style, the
divinised heroes of each party, and saying *the principles of Mr.
10 Pitt, the principles of Mr. Fox,* he took a Whig and a Tory
Chancellor, Lord Camden and Lord Hardwicke, who were
more of lawyers than of politicians, and upon them he fathered
the principles of the two great parties in the State. It is as if a
man were now to talk of Liberals and Conservatives adhering,
15 not to *the principles of Mr. Gladstone, the principles of Lord
Beaconsfield,* but to *the principles of Roundell Palmer, the principles of Cairns.* Eminent as are these personages, the effect of
the profession of faith would be somewhat attenuated; and this
is just what Cobbett intended. He meant to throw scorn on both
20 of the rival parties in the State, and on their profession of principles; and so this great master of effect took a couple of lawyers, whose names lent themselves happily to his purpose, and
called the principles contending for mastery in Parliament, *the
principles of Pratt, the principles of Yorke!*
25   Cobbett's politics were at bottom always governed by one
master-thought,—the thought of the evil condition of the English labourer. He saw the two great parties in the State inattentive, as he thought, to that evil condition of the labourer,—
inattentive to it, or ignorantly aggravating it by mismanagement.

Hence his contempt for Whigs and Tories alike. And perhaps I may be allowed to compare myself with Cobbett so far as this: that whereas his politics were governed by a master-thought, the thought of the bad condition of the English labourer, so mine, too, are governed by a master-thought, but by a different one from Cobbett's. The master-thought by which my politics are governed is rather this,—the thought of the bad civilisation of the English middle class. But to this object of my concern I see the two great parties in the State as inattentive as, in Cobbett's regard, they were to the object of his. I see them inattentive to it, or ignorantly aggravating its ill state by mismanagement. And if one were of Cobbett's temper, one might be induced, perhaps, under the circumstances, to speak of our two great political parties as scornfully as he did; and instead of speaking with reverence of the body of Liberal principles which recommend themselves by Mr. Gladstone's name, or of the body of Conservative principles which recommend themselves by Lord Beaconsfield's, to call them gruffly *the principles of Pratt, the principles of Yorke.*

Cobbett's talent any one might well desire to have, but Cobbett's temper is far indeed from being a temper of mildness and sweet reason, and must be eschewed by whoever makes it his study "to liberate," as Plato bids us, "the gentler element in himself." And therefore I will most willingly consent to call the principles of the Liberal and Conservative parties by their regular and handsome title of *the principles of Mr. Gladstone, the principles of Lord Beaconsfield,* instead of disparagingly styling them *the principles of Pratt, the principles of Yorke.* Only, while conceding with all imaginable willingness to Liberals and Conservatives the use of the handsomest title for their principles, I have never been able to see that these principles of theirs, at any rate as they succeed in exhibiting them, have quite the value or solidity which their professors themselves suppose.

It is but the other day that I was remarking to confident Conservatives, at the very most prosperous hour of Conservative rule, how, underneath all external appearances, the country was yet profoundly Liberal. And eight or ten years ago, long before their disaster of 1874 came, I kept assuring confident Liberals that the mind of the country was grown a little weary of their stock performances upon the political stage, and exhorting my young Liberal friends not to be for rushing impetuously upon this stage, but to keep aloof from it for a while, to cultivate a disinterested play of mind upon the stock notions and habits of their party, and to endeavour to promote, with me, an inward working. Without attending to me in the least, they pushed on towards the arena of politics, not at that time very successfully. But they have, I own, been much more fortunate since; and now they stand in the arena of politics, not quite so young as in those days when I last exhorted them, but full of vigour still, and in good numbers. Me they have left staying outside as of old; unconvinced, even yet, of the wisdom of their choice, a Liberal of the future rather than a Liberal of the present, disposed to think that by its actual present words and works the Liberal party, however prosperous it may seem, cannot really succeed, that its practice wants more of simple and sincere thought to direct it, and that our young friends are not taking the surest way to amend this state of things when they cast in their lot with it, but rather are likely to be carried away by the stream themselves.

However, politicians we all of us here in England are and must be, and I too cannot help being a politician; but a politician of that commonwealth of which the pattern, as the philosopher says, exists perhaps somewhere in heaven, but certainly is at present found nowhere on earth,—a Liberal, as I have said, of the future. Still, from time to time Liberals of the future cannot but be stirred up to look and see how their politics relate themselves to the Liberalism which now is, and to test by them the semblances and promises and endeavours of this,—especially at its moments of resurrection and culmination,—and to forecast what its fortunes are likely to be. And this one does for one's own sake first and foremost, and for the sake of the very few who may happen to be likeminded with oneself, to satisfy a natural and irresistible bent for seeing things as they really are, for not being made a dupe of, not being taken in. But partly, also, a Liberal of the future may do it for the sake of his young

Liberal friends, who, though they have committed themselves to the stream of the Liberalism which now is, are yet aware, many of them, of a great need for finding the passage from this Liberalism to the Liberalism of the future. And, although the passage is not easy to find, yet some of them perhaps, as they 5 are men of admirable parts and energy, if only they see clearly the matters with which they have to deal, by a happy and divine inspiration may find it.

Let me begin by making myself as pleasant as I can to our Liberal friends, and by conceding to them that their recent 10 triumph over their adversaries was natural and salutary. They reproach me, sometimes, with having drawn the picture of the Radical and Dissenting Bottles, but left the Tory Bottles unportrayed. Yet he exists, they urge, and is very baneful; and his ignoble Toryism it is, the shoddy Toryism of the City and of 15 the Stock-Exchange, and not, as pompous leading articles say, the intelligence and sober judgment of the educated classes and of mercantile sagacity, which carried the elections in the City of London and in the metropolitan counties for the Conservatives. Profoundly congenial to this shoddy Toryism,—so my 20 Liberal reprovers go on to declare,—were the fashions and policy of Lord Beaconsfield, a policy flashy, insincere, immoral, worshipping material success above everything; profoundly congenial and profoundly demoralising. Now, I will not say that I adopt all these forcible and picturesque expressions of my 25 Liberal friends, but I fully concede to them that although it is with the Radical and Dissenting Bottles that I have occupied myself,—for indeed he interests me far more than the other,— yet the Tory Bottles exists too, exists in great numbers and great force, particularly in London and its neighbourhood; and that, 30 for him, Lord Beaconsfield and Lord Beaconsfield's style of government were at once very attractive and very demoralising. This, however, is but a detail of a great question. In general, the mind of the country is, as I have already said, profoundly Liberal; and it is Liberal by a just instinct. It feels that the 35 Tories have not the secret of life and of the future for us, and it is right in so thinking. It turns to the Tories from time to time, in dissatisfaction at the shortcomings of Liberal statesmanship;

but its reaction and recoil from them, after it has tried them for a little, is natural and salutary. For they cannot really profit the nation, or give it what it needs.

Moreover, we will concede, likewise, that what seems to many people the most dubious part of the Liberal programme, what is blamed as revolutionary and a leap in the dark, what is deprecated even by some of the most intelligent of Liberal statesmen as unnecessary and dangerous,—the proposal to give a vote to the agricultural labourer,—we will concede that this, too, is a thing not to be lamented and blamed, but natural and salutary. Not that there is either any natural right in every man to the possession of a vote, or any gift of wisdom and virtue conferred by such possession. But if experience has established any one thing in this world, it has established this: that it is well for any great class and description of men in society to be able to say for itself what it wants, and not to have other classes, the so-called educated and intelligent classes, acting for it as its proctors, and supposed to understand its wants and to provide for them. They do not really understand its wants, they do not really provide for them. A class of men may often itself not either fully understand its own wants, or adequately express them; but it has a nearer interest and a more sure diligence in the matter than any of its proctors, and therefore a better chance of success. Let the agricultural labourer become articulate, let him speak for himself. In his present case we have the last left of our illusions, that one class is capable of properly speaking for another, answering for another; and it is an illusion like the rest.

All this we may be quite prepared to concede to the Liberalism which now is: the fitness and naturalness of the most disputed article in its programme, the fitness and naturalness of its adversaries' recent defeat. And yet, at the same time, what strikes one fully as much as all this, is the insecureness of the Liberals' hold upon office and upon public favour; the probability of the return, perhaps even more than once, of their adversaries to office, before that final and happy consummation is reached,—the permanent establishment of Liberalism in power.

Many people will tell us that this is because the multitude, by whose votes the elections are now decided, is ignorant and capricious and unstable, and gets tired of those who have been managing its affairs for some time, and likes a change to something new, and then gets tired of this also, and changes back again; and that so we may expect to go on changing from a Conservative government to a Liberal, and from a Liberal government to a Conservative, backwards and forwards for ever. But this is not so. Instinctively, however slowly, the human spirit struggles towards the light; and the adoptions and rejections of its agents by the multitude are never wholly blind and capricious, but have a meaning. And the Liberals of the future are those who preserve themselves from distractions and keep their heads as clear and their tempers as calm as they can, in order that they may discern this meaning; and therefore the Liberals of the present, who are too heated and busy to discern it, cannot do without them altogether, greatly as they are inclined to disregard them, but they have an interest in their cogitations whether they will or no.

What, then, is the meaning of the veerings of public favour from one of the two great parties which administer our affairs to the other, and why is it likely that the gust of favour, by which the Liberals have recently benefited, will not be a steady and permanent wind to bear them for ever prosperously along? Well, the reason of it is very simple, but the simple reason of a thing is often the very last that we will consent to look at. But as the end and aim of all dialectics is, as by the great master of dialectics we have been most truly told, to help us to an answer to the question, how to live; so, beyond all doubt whatever, have politics too to deal with this same question and with the discovery of an answer to it. The true and noble science of politics is even the very chief of the sciences, because it deals with this question for the benefit of man not as an isolated creature, but in that state "without which," as Burke says, "man could not by any possibility arrive at the perfection of which his nature is capable,"—for the benefit of man in society. Now of man in society the capital need is, that the whole body of society should come to live with a life worthy to be called *human,* and corresponding to man's true aspirations and powers. This, the humanisation of man in society, is civilisation. The aim for all of us is to promote it, and to promote it is above all the aim for the true politician.

5   Of these general propositions we none of us, probably, deny or question the truth, although we do not much attend to them in our practice of politics, but are concerned with points of detail. Neither will any man, probably, be disposed to deny that, the aim for all of us, and for the politician more especially,

10   being to make civilisation pervasive and general, the necessary means towards civilisation may be said to be, first and foremost, expansion; and then, the power of expansion being given, these other powers have to follow it and to find their account in it:— the power of conduct, the power of intellect and knowledge,

15   the power of beauty, the power of social life and manners. These are the means towards our end, which is civilisation; and the true politician, who wills the end, cannot but will the means also. And meanwhile, whether the politician wills them or not, there is an instinct in society pushing it to desire them and to

20   tend to them, and making it dissatisfied when nothing is done for them, or when impediment and harm are offered to them; and this instinct we call the instinct of self-preservation in humanity. So long as any of the means to civilisation are neglected, or have impediment and harm offered to them, men are

25   always, whether consciously or no, in want of something which they have not; they can never be really at ease. At times they even get angrily dissatisfied with themselves, their condition, and their government, and seek restlessly for a change.

Expansion we were bound to put first among the means

30   towards civilisation, because it is the basis which man's whole effort to civilise himself requires and presupposes. The instinct for expansion manifests itself conspicuously in the love of liberty, and every one knows how signally this love is exhibited in England. Now, the Liberals are pre-eminently the party

35   appealing to the love of liberty, and therefore to the instinct for expansion. The Conservatives may say that they love liberty as much as the Liberals love it, and that for real liberty they do as much. But it is evident that they do not appeal so principally

as the Liberals to the love of liberty, because their principal appeal is to the love of order, to the respect for what they call "our traditional, existing social arrangements." Order is a most excellent thing, and true liberty is impossible without it; but order is not in itself liberty, and an appeal to the love of order is not a direct appeal to the love of liberty, to the instinct for expansion. The great body of the community, therefore, in which the instinct for expansion works powerfully and spreads more and more, this great body feels that to its primary instinct, its instinct for expansion, the Liberals rather than the Conservatives make appeal. Consequently this great body tends, and must tend, to go with the Liberals. And this is what I meant by saying, even at the time when the late Government seemed strongest, that the country was profoundly Liberal. The instinct for expansion was still, I meant to say, the primary instinct in the great body of our community; and this instinct is in alliance with the Liberals, not with the Conservatives.

To enlarge and secure our existence by the conveniences of life is the object of trade; and the development of trade, like that of liberty, is due to the working in men of the natural instinct of expansion. And the turn for trade our nation has shown as signally as the turn for liberty; and of its instinct for expansion, in this line also, the Liberals, and not the Conservatives, have been the great favourers. The mass of the community, pushed by the instinct for expansion, sees in the Liberals the friends of trade as well as the friends of liberty.

And, in fact, Liberal statesmen like the present Lord Derby (who well deserves, certainly, that among the Liberals, as he himself desires, we should count him), and Liberal orators like Mr. Bright, are continually appealing, when they address the public, either to the love of liberty or to the love of trade, and praising Liberalism for having favoured and helped the one or the other, and blaming Conservatism for having discouraged and checked them. When they make these appeals, when they distribute this praise and this blame, they touch a chord in the public mind which vibrates strongly in answer. What the Liberals have done for liberty, what the Liberals have done for trade, and how under this beneficent impulsion the greatness

of England has arisen, the greatness which comes, as the hearer
is told, from "the cities you have built, the railroads you have
made, the manufactures you have produced, the cargoes which
freight the ships of the greatest mercantile navy the world has
5   ever seen,"—this, together with the virtues of Nonconformity
and of Nonconformists, and the demerits of the Tories, may
be said, as I have often remarked, to be the never-failing theme
of Mr. Bright's speeches; and his treatment of the theme is a
never-failing source of excitement and delight to his hearers.
10 And how skilfully and effectively did Lord Derby the other
day, in a speech in the north of England, treat after his own
fashion the same kind of theme, pitying the wretched Continent
of Europe, given over to "emperors, grand dukes, archdukes,
field-marshals, and tremendous personages of that sort," and
15 extolling Liberal England, free from such incubuses, and enabled
by that freedom to get "its manufacturing industries developed," and to let "our characteristic qualities for industrial
supremacy" have play. Lord Derby here, like Mr. Bright, appeals to the instinct for expansion manifesting itself in our race
20 by the love of liberty and the love of trade; and to such a call,
so effectively made, a popular audience in this country always
responds.

   What a source of strength is this for the Liberals, and how
surely and abundantly do they profit by it! Still, it is not all-
25 sufficient. For we have working in us, as elements towards
civilisation, besides the instinct for expansion, the instinct also,
as was just now said, for conduct, the instinct for intellect and
knowledge, the instinct for beauty, the instinct for a fit and
pleasing form of social life and manners. And Lord Derby will
30 allow, I am sure, when he thinks of St. Helens and of similar
places, that even at his own gate, and amongst a population
developing its manufacturing industries most fully, free from
emperors and archdukes, congratulated by him on its freedom,
and trade, and industrial supremacy, and responding joyfully
35 to his congratulations, there is to be found, indeed, much satisfaction to the instinct in man for expansion, but little satisfaction to his instinct for beauty, and to his instinct for a fit
and pleasing form of social life and manners. I will not at this

moment speak of conduct, or of intellect and knowledge, because I wish to carry Lord Derby unhesitatingly with me in what I say. And certainly he will allow that the instinct of man for beauty, his instinct for fit and pleasing forms of social life and manners, is not well satisfied at St. Helens. Cobbett, whom I have already quoted, used to call places of this kind *Hell-holes*. St. Helens is eminently what Cobbett meant by a *Hell-hole*, but it is only a type, however eminent, of a whole series of places so designated by him, such as Bolton, Wigan, and the like, places developing abundantly their manufacturing industries but in which man's instinct for beauty, and man's instinct for fit and pleasing forms of social life and manners, in which these two instincts, at any rate, to say nothing for the present of others, find little or no satisfaction. Such places certainly must be said to show, in the words of a very different personage from Cobbett, the words of the accomplished President of the Royal Academy, Sir Frederic Leighton, "no love of beauty, no sense of the outward dignity and comeliness of things calling on the part of the public for expression, and, as a corollary, no dignity, no comeliness, for the most part, in their outward aspect."

And not only have the inhabitants of what Cobbett called a Hell-hole, and what Lord Derby and Mr. Bright would call a centre of manufacturing industry, no satisfaction of man's instinct for beauty to make them happy, but even their manufacturing industries they develop in such a manner, that from the exercise of this their instinct for expansion they do not procure the result which they expected, but they find uneasiness and stoppage. For in general they develop their industries in this wise: they produce, not something which it is very difficult to make, and of which people can never have enough, and which they themselves can make far better than anybody else; but they produce that which is not hard to make, and of which there may easily be produced more than is wanted, and which more and more people, in different quarters, fall to making, as times goes on, for themselves, and which they soon make quite as well as the others do. But at a given moment, when there is a demand, or a chance of demand, for

their manufacture, the capitalists in the *Hell-holes,* as Cobbett
would say, or the leaders of industrial enterprise, as Lord Derby
and Mr. Bright would call them, set themselves to produce as
much as ever they can, without asking themselves how long the
5   demand may last, so that it do but last long enough for them
to make their own fortunes by it, or without thinking, in any
way beyond this, about what they are doing, or troubling
themselves any further with the future. And clusters and fresh
clusters of men and women they collect at places like St. Helens
10 and Bolton to manufacture for them, and call them into being
there just as much as if they had begotten them. Then the
demand ceases or slackens, because more has been produced
than was wanted, or because people who used to come to us
for the thing we produced take to producing it for themselves,
15 and think that they can make it (and we have premised that it
is a thing not difficult to make) quite as well as we can; or
even, since some of our heroes of industrial enterprise have been
in too great haste to make their fortunes, and unscrupulous in
their processes, better. And perhaps these capitalists have had
20 time to make their fortunes; but meanwhile they have not made
the fortunes of the clusters of men and women whom they
have called into being to produce for them, and whom they
have, as I said, as good as begotten. But these they leave to the
chances of the future, and of the further development, as Lord
25 Derby says, of great manufacturing industries. And so there
arise periods of depression of trade, there arise complaints of
over-production, uneasiness and distress at our centres of manufacturing industry. People then begin, even although their instinct for expansion, so far as liberty is concerned, may have
30 received every satisfaction, they begin to discover, like those
unionist workmen whose words Mr. John Morley quotes, that
"free political institutions do not guarantee the well-being of
the toiling class."

But we need not go to visit the places which Cobbett called
35 Hell-holes, or travel so far as St. Helens, close by Lord Derby's
gate at Knowsley, or so far as Bolton or Wigan. We Londoners
need not go away from the place where our own daily business
lies, and from London itself, in order to see how insufficient for

man is our way of gratifying his instinct for expansion and this instinct alone, and what comes of trusting too much to what is thus done for us. We have only to take the tramway at King's Cross, and to let ourselves be carried through Camden Town up the slopes towards Highgate and Hampstead, where 5 from the upward-sloping ground, as we ascend, we have a good view all about us, and can survey much of human haunt and habitation. And in the pleasant season of the year, and in this humid and verdure-nursing English climate, we shall see plenty of flowering trees, and grass, and vegetation of all kinds to de- 10 light our eyes; but they will meet with nothing else to delight them. All that man has made there for his habitation and func- tions is singularly dull and mean, and does indeed, as we gradually mount the disfigured slopes and see it clearer and clearer, "reveal the spectacle," as Sir Frederic Leighton says, 15 "of the whole current of human life setting resolutely in a direc- tion opposed to artistic production; no love of beauty, no sense of the outward dignity of things, and, as a corollary, no dignity, no comeliness, for the most part, in their outward aspect." And here, in what we see from the tramway, we have 20 a type, not of life at a centre of manufacturing industry, but of the life in general of the English middle class. We have the life of a class which has been able to follow freely its instinct of expansion, so far as to preserve itself from emperors and archdukes and tremendous personages of that sort, and to enjoy 25 abundance of political liberty and of trade. But man's instinct for beauty has been maltreated and starved, in this class, in the manner we see. And man's instinct, also, for intellect and knowl- edge has been maltreated and starved; because the schools for this class, where it should have called forth and trained this 30 instinct, are the worst of the kind anywhere. And the provision made by this class for the instinct which desires fit and pleasing forms of social life and manners is what might be expected from its provision for the instinct of beauty, and for the in- stinct leading us to intellect and knowledge. 35

But there this class lives, busy and confident; and enjoys the amplest political liberty, and takes what Mr. Bright calls "a commendable interest in politics," and reads, what he says is such admirable reading for all of us, the newspapers. And thus there arises a type of life and opinion which that acute and powerful personage, Prince Bismarck, has described so excellently, that I cannot do better than use his words. "When great numbers of people of this sort," says Prince Bismarck, "live close together, individualities naturally fade out and melt into each other. All sorts of opinions grow out of the air, from hearsays and talk behind people's backs; opinions with little or no foundation in fact, but which get spread abroad through newspapers, popular meetings, and talk, and get themselves established and are ineradicable. People talk themselves into believing the thing that is not; consider it a duty and obligation to adhere to their belief, and excite themselves about prejudices and absurdities." Who does not recognise the truth of this account of *public opinion*,—public opinion in politics, public opinion in religion,—as it forms itself amongst such a description of people as the people through whose seats of habitation the tramway northward from King's Cross takes us; nay, as it forms itself amongst the English middle class in general, amongst the great community which we call that of the Philistines?

Now, this great Philistine community it is, with its liberty, and its publicity, and its trade, and its love of all the three, but with its narrow range of intellect and knowledge, its stunted sense of beauty and dignity, its low standard of social life and manners, and its ignorance of its own deficiencies in respect of all these,—this Philistine middle class it is, to which a Liberal government has especially to make appeal, and on which it relies for support. And where such a government deals with foreign affairs, and addresses foreign nations, this is the force which it is known to have behind it, and to be forced to reckon with; this class trained as we have seen, and with habits of thought and opinion formed as Prince Bismarck describes. It is this Englishman of the middle class, this Philistine with his likes and dislikes, his effusion and confusion, his hot fits and cold fits, his want of dignity and of the steadfastness which comes from dignity, his want of ideas, and of the steadfastness which comes from ideas, on whom a Liberal Foreign Minister must lean for support, and whose dispositions he must in great measure follow. Mr. Grant Duff and others are fond of sketching out a line of foreign policy which they say is the line of Liberal foreign policy, or of insisting on the dignity and ability of this or that Liberal statesman, such as Lord Granville, who may happen to hold the post of Foreign Minister. No one will wish to deny the dignity and ability of Lord Granville; and no one doubts that Mr. Grant Duff and his intelligent friends can easily draw out a striking and able line of foreign policy, and may call it the line of Liberal foreign policy if they please. But the real Liberal Foreign Minister and the real Liberal foreign policy are not to be looked for in Lord Granville left to himself, or in a programme drawn up in Mr. Grant Duff's library by himself and his intelligent friends; they receive a bias from the temper and thoughts, and from the hot fits and cold fits, of that middle class on which a Liberal government leans for support. And so we get such mortifications as those which befell us in the case of Prussia's dealing with Denmark and of Russia's dealing with the Black Sea; and foreign statesmen, knowing how the matter stands with us, say coolly what Dr. Busch reports Prince Bismarck to have said concerning a firm and dignified declaration by our Liberal Foreign Secretary: "What does it matter? Nothing is to be feared, as nothing is to be hoped, from these people."

Thus it happens that we suffer "a loss of prestige," as it is called; and we become aware of it, and then we are vexed and dissatisfied. Just as by following, as we do, our instinct for expansion, and by procuring the amplest political liberty and free trade, and by preserving ourselves from such tremendous personages as emperors, grand dukes, and archdukes, we yet do not preserve ourselves from depression of trade, so neither do we by all these advantages preserve ourselves from loss of prestige. And at this from time to time the public mind, as we all know, gets vexed and dissatisfied.

And other occasions of dissatisfaction, too, there may easily be, and at one or other of them there may be a veering round to the Tories, to see if they, perhaps, can do us any good. Now, we must remember in what case the great body of our community is, when it thus turns to the Tories in the hope of bettering itself. It has so far followed its instinct for expansion,

to which Liberal statesmen make special appeal, as to obtain full political liberty and free trade. How far it has followed its instinct for conduct I will not now enquire; the enquiry might lead us into a discussion of the whole condition of morals and
5   religion in this nation. However, we may certainly say, I think, that in no country has the instinct for conduct been more followed than in our country, in few countries has it been followed so much. But the need of man for intellect and knowledge has not in the great body of our community been much
10 attended to, nor have Liberal statesmen made much appeal to it. For giving the rudiments and instruments of knowledge to the lowest class amongst us they have, indeed, sought of late to make provision, but for the advancement of intellect and knowledge among the middle classes they have made little or
15 none. The need of man for beauty, again, has been by the great body of our community scarcely at all heeded, neither have Liberal statesmen sought to appeal to it. Of the need of man for fit and pleasing forms of social life and manners we may say the same.
20   In this position are things, when from time to time the great body of our community turns to the Conservatives, or, as they are now beginning to be called again, the Tories, in the hope of bettering itself. Now, the need of man for expansion we are all agreed that Liberal statesmen, and not Tory statesmen, make
25 appeal to, and that the great body of the community feels this need powerfully. But the other needs which it feels so little, and to which Liberal statesmen so little make appeal, are yet working obscurely in the community all the time, and craving for some notice and help, and begetting dissatisfaction with the
30 sort of life which is the lot of man when they are utterly neglected.
        So to the Tories, in some such moment of dissatisfaction, the community turns. Now, to the need in man for conduct we will not say that Tory statesmen make much appeal, for the upper
35 class, to which they belong, is now, we know, in great measure materialised; and probably Mr. Jowett, who, though he is a man of integrity and a most honest translator, has yet his strokes of malice, had this in his mind, where he brings in his philos-

opher saying that "the young men of the governing class are as indifferent as the pauper to the cultivation of virtue." Yet so far as dignity is a part of conduct, an aristocratic class, trained to be sensitive on the point of honour, and to think much of the grandeur and dignity of their country, do appeal to the instinct in man for conduct; but perhaps dignity may more conveniently be considered here as a part of beauty than as a part of conduct. Therefore to the need for beauty, starved by those who,—following the hot and cold fits of the opinion of a middle class testy, ignorant, a little ignoble, unapt to perceive when it is making itself ridiculous,—may have brought about for our country a loss of *prestige*, as it is called, and of the respect of foreign nations, to this need Tory statesmen, leaning upon the opinion of an aristocratic class by nature more firm, reticent, dignified, sensitive on the point of honour, do, I think, give some satisfaction. And the aristocratic class, of which they are the agents, give some satisfaction, moreover, to this baffled and starved instinct for beauty, by the spectacle of a splendour, and grace, and elegance of life, due to inherited wealth and to traditional refinement; and to the instinct for fit and seemly forms of social intercourse and manners they give some satisfaction too.

To the instinct for intellect and knowledge, however, the aristocratic class and its agents, the Tory statesmen, give no satisfaction at all. To large and clear ideas of the future and of its requirements, whether at home or abroad, aristocracies are by nature inaccessible; and though the firmness and dignity of their carriage, in foreign affairs, may inspire respect and give satisfaction, yet even here, as they do not see how the world is really going, they can found nothing. By the possession of what is beautiful in outward life, and of what is seemly in manners, they do, as we have seen, attract; but for the active communication and propagation, all through the community, of what is beautiful in outward life, and of what is seemly in manners, they do next to nothing. And, finally, to the instinct in the great body of the community for expansion they are justly felt to be even adverse, in so far as the very first consideration with them as a class,—a few humane individuals

amongst them, lovers of perfection, being left out of account,
—is always the maintenance of "our traditional, existing social
arrangements."

Consequently, however public favour may have veered
round to them for a time, it soon appears that they cannot
satisfy the needs of the community, and the turn of the Liberal
statesmen comes again. Such a turn came to them not long ago.
And the danger is, that the Liberal statesmen should again do
only what it is easy and natural to them to do, because they
have done it so often and so successfully already,—appeal
vigorously to the love of political liberty and to the love of
trade, and lean mainly upon the opinion of the middle class, as
this class now is, and do nothing to make it sounder and better
by appealing to the sense, in the body of the community, for
intellect and knowledge, and striving to call it forth, and by
appealing to the sense for beauty and to the sense for manners;
and by appealing, moreover, to the sense for expansion more
wisely and fruitfully than they do now. But if they do nothing
of this kind, and simply return to their old courses, then there
will inevitably be, after a while, pressure and stoppage and re-
proaches and dissatisfaction, and the turn of the Tories will
come round again. Who knows?—some day, perhaps, even
the Liberal panacea of sheer political liberty may be for a time
discredited, and the fears of "Verax" about personal government may come true, and the last scene in the wonderful career
of Lord Beaconsfield may be that we shall see him, in a field-
marshal's uniform, entering the House of Commons, and
pointing to the mace, and commanding Lord Rowton, in an octogenarian voice, to "take away that bauble." But still the rule
of the Tories, even after such a masterstroke as that, will never
last in our community; such strangers are the Tory statesmen
to the secret of our community's life, to the secret of the future.

Only let Liberal statesmen, at their returns to power, instead
of losing themselves in the petty bustle and schemes of the moment, bethink themselves what that aim of the community's life
really is, and that secret of the life of the future: that it is
civilisation, and civilisation made pervasive and general. Hitherto our Liberal statesmen themselves have conceived that aim

very imperfectly, and very imperfectly worked for it, and this although they are called the leaders of progress. Hence the instability of their government, and the veerings round of public favour, now and again, to their adversaries. I have said that with one great element of civilisation, the instinct in the community for expansion, Liberal statesmen are in alliance, and that their strength is due to that cause. Of the instinct for conduct I have said that we will not here speak; it might lead us too far, and into the midst of matters of which I have spoken enough formerly, and of which I wish, as far as possible, to renounce the discussion. But for the other means of civilisation Liberal statesmen really do little or nothing: and this explains their instability. Let us not cover up their shortcomings, but rather draw them into light. For the need of intellect and knowledge what do they do? They will point to elementary education. But elementary education goes so little way, that in giving it one hardly does more than satisfy man's instinct for expansion, one scarcely satisfies his need of intellect and knowledge at all; any more than the achievement of primitive man in providing himself with his simple working tools is a satisfying of the human need for intellect and knowledge. For the need of beauty Liberal statesmen do nothing, for the need of manners nothing. And they lean especially upon the opinion of one great class,— the middle class,—with virtues of its own, indeed, but at the same time full of narrowness, full of prejudices; with a defective type of religion, a narrow range of intellect and knowledge, a stunted sense of beauty, a low standard of manners; and averse, moreover, to whatever may disturb it in its vulgarity. How can such statesmen be said, any more than the Tories, to grasp that idea of civilisation which is the secret of the life of our community and of the life of the future?—to grasp the idea fully, and with potent effect to work for it?

We who now talk of these things shall be in our graves long before Liberal statesmen can have entirely mended their ways, and set themselves steadily to bring about the reign of a civilisation pervasive and general. But a beginning towards it they may make even now, and perhaps they are making it. Perhaps Liberal statesmen are beginning to see what they have lost by following too submissively middle-class opinion hitherto, our middle class being such as it is now; and they may be resolving to avoid for the future this cause of mischief to them. Perhaps Lord Granville is bent on planning and maintaining a line of foreign policy, such as a man of his means of information and of his insight and high feeling can well devise, and such as Mr. Grant Duff is always telling us that the real line of Liberal foreign policy is; perhaps Lord Granville is even now ready with a policy of this sort, and resolved to adhere to it whatever may be in the meanwhile the hot fits and the cold fits, the effusion and confusion, of the British Philistine of the middle class. Perhaps Liberal statesmen have made up their minds no longer to govern Ireland in deference to the narrow prejudices and antipathies of this class. And perhaps, as time goes on, they will even turn resolutely round and look their middle-class friends full in the face, and tell them of their imperfections, and try to cure them.

And then Lord Derby, when he speaks at St. Helens or at some other place like it, will not extol his hearers as "an intelligent, keen-witted, critical, and well-to-do population such as our northern towns in England show," but he will point out to them that they have a defective type of religion, a narrow range of intellect and knowledge, a stunted sense of beauty, a low standard of manners; and that they prove it by having made St. Helens, and by the life which they lead there; and that they ought to do better. And Mr. Bright, instead of telling his Islington Nonconformists "how much of what there is free and good and great in England, and constantly growing in what is good, is owing to Nonconformist action," will rather admonish them that the Puritan type of life exhibits a religion not true, the claims of intellect and knowledge not satisfied, the claim of beauty not satisfied, the claim of manners not satisfied; and that if, as he says, the lower classes in this country have utterly abandoned the dogmas of Christianity, and the upper classes its practice, the cause lies very much in the impossible and unlovely presentment of Christian dogmas and practice which is offered by the most important part of this nation, the serious middle class, and above all by its Nonconforming portion. And, since the failure here in civilisation comes not from an insufficient care for political liberty and for trade, nor yet from an insufficient care for conduct, but from an insufficient care for intellect and knowledge and beauty and a humane life, let Liberal statesmen despise and neglect for 5 the cure of our present imperfection no means, whether of public schools, now wanting, or of the theatre, now left to itself and to chance, or of anything else which may powerfully conduce to the communication and propagation of real intelligence, and of real beauty, and of a life really humane. 10

Objects which Liberal statesmen pursue now, and which are not in themselves ends of civilisation, they may possibly have to pursue still; but let them pursue them in a different spirit. For instance, there are those well-known Liberal objects, that of legalising marriage with a deceased wife's sister, that of per- 15 mitting Dissenters to use what burial services they like in the parish churchyard, and that of granting what is termed Local Option. Every one of these objects may be attained, and it may even be necessary to attain them, and yet, after they are attained, the imperfections of our civilisation will stand just as 20 they did before, and the real work of Liberal statesmen will have yet to begin.

Some Liberals misconceive the character of these objects strangely. Mr. Bright urges Parliament to pass the Bill legalising marriage with a deceased wife's sister, in order that Parliament 25 may "affirm by an emphatic vote the principle of personal liberty for the men and women of this country in the chief concern of their lives." But the whole institution and sacredness of marriage is an abridgment of the principle of personal liberty in the concern in question. When Herod the tetrarch wanted 30 to marry Herodias, his brother Philip's wife, he was seeking to affirm emphatically the principle of personal liberty in the concern of his marriage; and we all know him to have been doing wrong. Every limitation of choice in marriage is an abridgment of the principle of personal liberty; but there needs more del- 35 icacy of perception, more civilisation, to understand and accept the abridgment in some cases than in others. Very many in the lower class in this country, and many in the middle class,—

the civilisation and the capacity for delicate perception in these classes being what they are,—fail to understand and accept the prohibition to marry their deceased wife's sister. That they ought not to marry their brother's wife they can perceive; that they ought not to marry their wife's sister they cannot. And so they contract these marriages freely, and the evil of their freely committing a breach of the law may be more than the good of imposing on them a restriction, which in their present state they have not perception enough to understand and obey. Therefore it may be expedient to legalise, amongst our people, marriage with a deceased wife's sister. Still, our civilisation, which it is the end of the true and noble science of politics to perfect, gains thereby hardly anything; and of its continued imperfection, indeed, the very call for the Bill in question is a proof.

So, again, with measures like that for granting Local Option, as it is called, for doing away the addiction of our lower class to their porter and their gin. It is necessary to do away their addiction to these; and, for that end, to receive at the hands of the friends of temperance some such measure as the Bill for granting Local Option. Yet the alimentary secret of the life of civilised man is by no means possessed by the friends of temperance as we now see them either here or in America; and whoever has been amongst the population of the Médoc district, in France, will surely feel, if he is not a fanatic, that the civilised man of the future is more likely to adopt their beverage than to eat and drink like Dr. Richardson.

And so too, again, with the Burials Bill. It is a Bill for enabling the Dissenters to use their own burial services in the parish churchyard. Now, we all know what the services of many of the Protestant Dissenters are; and that whereas the burial service of the Church of England may be compared, as I have said somewhere or other, to a reading from Milton, so a burial service, such as pleases many of the Protestant Dissenters, may be likened to a reading from Eliza Cook. But fractious clergymen could refuse, as is well known, to give their reading from Milton, or any reading at all, over the children of Baptists; and the remedy for this was to abolish the rubric giving them the power of such refusal. The clergy, however, as if to prove the truth of Clarendon's sentence on them, a sentence which should be written up over the portal of the Lower House of Convocation: *"Clergymen, who under-stand the least, and take the worst measure of human affairs, of all mankind that can write and read!"*—the clergy, it seems, had rather the world should go to pieces than that this rubric should be abolished. And so Liberal statesmen must pass the Burials Bill;—for it is better even to have readings from Eliza Cook in the parish churchyard than to have fractious clergy-men armed with the power of refusing to bury the children of Baptists. Still, our civilisation is not really advanced by any such measure as the Burials Bill; nay, in so far as readings from Eliza Cook are encouraged to produce themselves in public, and to pass themselves off as equivalent to readings from Milton, it is retarded.

Therefore do not let Liberal statesmen estimate the so-called Liberal measures, many of them, which they may be called upon to recommend now, at more than they are worth, or sup-pose that by recommending them they at all remedy their shortcomings in the past;—shortcomings which consist in their having taken an incomplete view of the life of the com-munity and of its needs, and in having done little or nothing for the need of intellect and knowledge, and for the need of beauty, and for the need of manners, but having thought it enough to work for political liberty and free trade, for the need of expansion.

Nay, but even for the need of expansion our Liberal statesmen have not worked adequately. Doubtless the need of expansion in men suffers a defeat when they are over-tutored, over-governed, *sat upon*, as we say, by authority military or civil. From such a defeat of our instinct for expansion, political liberty saves us Englishmen; and Liberal statesmen have worked for political liberty. But the need of expansion suffers a defeat, also, wherever there is an immense inequality of conditions and property; such inequality inevitably depresses and degrades the inferior masses. And whenever any great need of human nature suffers defeat, then the nation in which the defeat hap-

pens finds difficulties befalling it from that cause; nay, and the
victories of other great needs do not compensate for the defeat
of one. Germany, where the need for intellect and science is
well cared for, where the sense of conduct is strong, has neither
liberty nor equality; the instinct for expansion suffers there
signal defeat. Hence the difficulties of Germany. France has
liberty and equality, the instinct for expansion is victorious
there; but how greatly does the need for conduct suffer defeat!
and hence the difficulties of France. We English people have,
deep and strong, the sense of conduct, and we have half of the
instinct for expansion fully satisfied;—that is to say, we have
admirable political liberty, and we have free trade. But we have
inequality rampant, and hence arise many of our difficulties.

For in honest truth our present state, as I have elsewhere
said, may without any great injustice be summed up thus: that
we have an upper class materialised, a middle class vulgarised,
a lower class brutalised. And this we owe to our inequality.
For, if Lord Derby would think of it, he is himself at Knowsley
quite as tremendous a personage, over against St. Helens, as
the emperors and grand dukes and archdukes who fill him with
horror. And though he himself may be one of the humane few
who emerge in all classes, and may have escaped being materialised, yet still, owing to his tremendousness, the middle
class of St. Helens is thrown in upon itself, and not civilised;
and the lower class, again, is thrown in upon itself, and not
civilised. And some who fill the place which he now fills are
certain to be, some of them, materialised;—like his great-grandfather, for instance, whose cock-fights, as it is said, are still
remembered with gratitude and love by old men in Preston.
And he himself, being so able and acute as he is, would never,
if he were not in a false position and compelled by it to use
unreal language, he would never talk so much to his hearers,
in the towns of the north, about their being "an intelligent,
keen-witted, critical, and well-to-do population;" but he would
reproach them, though kindly and mildly, for having made
St. Helens and places like it, and he would exhort them to
civilise themselves.

But of inequality, as a defeat to the instinct in the community

for expansion, and as a sure cause of trouble, Liberal statesmen
are very shy to speak. And in Ireland, where inequality and the
system of great estates produces, owing to differences of religion, and to absenteeism, and to the ways of personages such
as the late Lord Leitrim, even more tremendous, perhaps, than
an emperor or an archduke, and to the whole history of the
country and character of the people,—in Ireland, I say, where
inequality produces, owing to all these, more pressing and
evident troubles than in England, and is the second cause of our
difficulties with the Irish, as the habit of governing them in
deference to British middle-class prejudices is the first,—in
Ireland Liberal statesmen never look the thing fairly in the
face, or apply a real remedy, but invent palliatives like the Irish
Land Act, which do not go to the root of the evil, but which
unsettle men's notions as to the constitutive characters of property, making these characters something quite different in one
place from what they are in another. And in England, where
inequality and the system of great estates produces trouble too,
though not trouble so glaring as in Ireland, in England Liberal
statesmen shrink even more from looking the thing in the face,
and apply little palliatives; and even for these little palliatives
they allege reasons which are extremely questionable, such as
that each child has a natural right to his equal share of his
father's property, or that land in the hands of many owners
will certainly produce more than in the hands of few. And the
true and simple reason against inequality they avert their eyes
from, as if it were a Medusa;—the reason, namely, that inequality, in a society like ours, sooner or later inevitably materialises the upper class, vulgarises the middle class, brutalises
the lower class.

Not until this need to which they appeal, the need in man for
expansion, is better understood by Liberal statesmen, is understood to include equality as well as political liberty and free
trade,—and is cared for by them, yet cared for not singly and
exorbitantly, but in union and proportion with the progress of
man in conduct, and his growth in intellect and knowledge,
and his nearer approach to beauty and manners,—will Liberal
governments be secure. But when Liberal statesmen have

learned to care for all these together, and to go on unto perfection or true civilisation, then at last they will be professing
and practising the true and noble science of politics and the
true and noble science of economics, instead of, as now, semblances only of these sciences, or at best fragments of them.
And then will come at last the extinction or the conversion of
the Tories, the restitution of all things, the reign of the Liberal
saints. But meanwhile, so long as the Liberals do only as they
have done hitherto, they will not permanently satisfy the community; but the Tories will again, from time to time, be tried,—
tried and found wanting. And we, who study to be quiet, and
to keep our temper and our tongue under control, shall continue to speak of the prinicples of our two great political parties
much as we do now; while clear-headed, but rough, impatient,
and angry men, like Cobbett, will call them *the principles of
Pratt, the principles of Yorke.*

The Study of Poetry[1]

'The future of poetry is immense, because in poetry, where it is worthy of its high destinies, our race, as time goes on, will find an ever surer and surer stay. There is not a creed which is not shaken, not an accredited dogma which is not shown to be questionable, not a received tradition which does not threaten   5
to dissolve. Our religion has materialised itself in the fact, in the supposed fact; it has attached its emotion to the fact, and now the fact is failing it. But for poetry the idea is everything; the rest is a world of illusion, of divine illusion. Poetry attaches its emotion to the idea; the idea *is* the fact. The strongest part   10
of our religion to-day is its unconscious poetry.'

Let me be permitted to quote these words of my own, as uttering the thought which should, in my opinion, go with us and govern us in all our study of poetry. In the present work it is the course of one great contributory stream to the world-   15
river of poetry that we are invited to follow. We are here invited to trace the stream of English poetry. But whether we set ourselves, as here, to follow only one of the several streams that make the mighty river of poetry, or whether we seek to know them all, our governing thought should be the same. We   20
should conceive of poetry worthily, and more highly than it has been the custom to conceive of it. We should conceive of it as capable of higher uses, and called to higher destinies, than those which in general men have assigned to it hitherto. More and more mankind will discover that we have to turn to poetry   25
to interpret life for us, to console us, to sustain us. Without poetry, our science will appear incomplete; and most of what

[1] Published in 1880 as the General Introduction to *The English Poets*, edited by T. H. Ward.

now passes with us for religion and philosophy will be replaced
by poetry. Science, I say, will appear incomplete without it.
For finely and truly does Wordsworth call poetry 'the impassioned expression which is in the countenance of all science';
and what is a countenance without its expression? Again,
Wordsworth finely and truly calls poetry 'the breath and finer
spirit of all knowledge': our religion, parading evidences such
as those on which the popular mind relies now; our philosophy,
pluming itself on its reasonings about causation and finite and
infinite being; what are they but the shadows and dreams and
false shows of knowledge? The day will come when we shall
wonder at ourselves for having trusted to them, for having
taken them seriously; and the more we perceive their hollow-
ness, the more we shall prize 'the breath and finer spirit of
knowledge' offered to us by poetry.

But if we conceive thus highly of the destinies of poetry, we
must also set our standard for poetry high, since poetry, to be
capable of fulfilling such high destinies, must be poetry of a
high order of excellence. We must accustom ourselves to a
high standard and to a strict judgment. Sainte-Beuve relates that
Napoleon one day said, when somebody was spoken of in his
presence as a charlatan: 'Charlatan as much as you please; but
where is there *not* charlatanism?'—'Yes,' answers Sainte-Beuve,
'in politics, in the art of governing mankind, that is perhaps true.
But in the order of thought, in art, the glory, the eternal honour
is that charlatanism shall find no entrance; herein lies the in-
violableness of that noble portion of man's being.' It is admirably said, and let us hold fast to it. In poetry, which is thought
and art in one, it is the glory, the eternal honour, that charlatanism shall find no entrance; that this noble sphere be kept
inviolate and inviolable. Charlatanism is for confusing or oblit-
erating the distinctions between excellent and inferior, sound
and unsound or only half-sound, true and untrue or only half-
true. It is charlatanism, conscious or unconscious, whenever
we confuse or obliterate these. And in poetry, more than anywhere else, it is unpermissible to confuse or obliterate them.
For in poetry the distinction between excellent and inferior,
sound and unsound or only half-sound, true and untrue or only

half-true, is of paramount importance. It is of paramount importance because of the high destinies of poetry. In poetry, as a criticism of life under the conditions fixed for such a criticism by the laws of poetic truth and poetic beauty, the spirit of our race will find, we have said, as time goes on and as other helps fail, its consolation and stay. But the consolation and stay will be of power in proportion to the power of the criticism of life. And the criticism of life will be of power in proportion as the poetry conveying it is excellent rather than inferior, sound rather than unsound or half-sound, true rather than untrue or half-true.

The best poetry is what we want; the best poetry will be found to have a power of forming, sustaining, and delighting us, as nothing else can. A clearer, deeper sense of the best in poetry, and of the strength and joy to be drawn from it, is the most precious benefit which we can gather from a poetical collection such as the present. And yet in the very nature and conduct of such a collection there is inevitably something which tends to obscure in us the consciousness of what our benefit should be, and to distract us from the pursuit of it. We should therefore steadily set it before our minds at the outset, and should compel ourselves to revert constantly to the thought of it as we proceed.

Yes; constantly, in reading poetry, a sense for the best, the really excellent, and of the strength and joy to be drawn from it, should be present in our minds and should govern our estimate of what we read. But this real estimate, the only true one, is liable to be superseded, if we are not watchful, by two other kinds of estimate, the historic estimate and the personal estimate, both of which are fallacious. A poet or a poem may count to us historically, they may count to us on grounds personal to ourselves, and they may count to us really. They may count to us historically. The course of development of a nation's language, thought, and poetry, is profoundly interesting; and by regarding a poet's work as a stage in this course of development we may easily bring ourselves to make it of more importance as poetry than in itself it really is, we may come to use a language of quite exaggerated praise in criticising it;

in short, to over-rate it. So arises in our poetic judgments the
fallacy caused by the estimate which we may call historic.
Then, again, a poet or a poem may count to us on grounds
personal to ourselves. Our personal affinities, likings, and cir-
5   cumstances, have great power to sway our estimate of this or
that poet's work, and to make us attach more importance to
it as poetry than in itself it really possesses, because to us it is,
or has been, of high importance. Here also we over-rate the
object of our interest, and apply to it a language of praise which
10   is quite exaggerated. And thus we get the source of a second
fallacy in our poetic judgments—the fallacy caused by an
estimate which we may call personal.

Both fallacies are natural. It is evident how naturally the
study of the history and development of a poetry may incline
15   a man to pause over reputations and works once conspicuous
but now obscure, and to quarrel with a careless public for
skipping, in obedience to mere tradition and habit, from one
famous name or work in its national poetry to another, ignorant
of what it misses, and of the reason for keeping what it keeps,
20   and of the whole process of growth in its poetry. The French
have become diligent students of their own early poetry, which
they long neglected; the study makes many of them dissatisfied
with their so-called classical poetry, the court-tragedy of the
seventeenth century, a poetry which Pellisson long ago re-
25   proached with its want of the true poetic stamp, with its *po-
litesse stérile et rampante*, but which nevertheless has reigned
in France as absolutely as if it had been the perfection of classical poetry indeed. The dissatisfaction is natural; yet a lively
and accomplished critic, M. Charles d'Héricault, the editor of
30   Clément Marot, goes too far when he says that 'the cloud of
glory playing round a classic is a mist as dangerous to the
future of a literature as it is intolerable for the purposes of
history.' 'It hinders,' he goes on, 'it hinders us from seeing more
than one single point, the culminating and exceptional point; the
35   summary, fictitious and arbitrary, of a thought and of a work.
It substitutes a halo for a physiognomy, it puts a statue where
there was once a man, and hiding from us all trace of the labour,
the attempts, the weaknesses, the failures, it claims not study
but veneration; it does not show us how the thing is done, it

imposes upon us a model. Above all, for the historian this creation of classic personages is inadmissible; for it withdraws the
poet from his time, from his proper life, it breaks historical
relationships, it blinds criticism by conventional admiration,
and renders the investigation of literary origins unacceptable. 5
It gives us a human personage no longer, but a God seated im-
movable amidst His perfect work, like Jupiter on Olympus;
and hardly will it be possible for the young student, to whom
such work is exhibited at such a distance from him, to believe
that it did not issue ready made from that divine head.' 10
All this is brilliantly and tellingly said, but we must plead
for a distinction. Everything depends on the reality of a poet's
classic character. If he is a dubious classic, let us sift him; if he
is a false classic, let us explode him. But if he is a real classic,
if his work belongs to the class of the very best (for this is 15
the true and right meaning of the word *classic, classical*), then
the great thing for us is to feel and enjoy his work as deeply
as ever we can, and to appreciate the wide difference between
it and all work which has not the same high character. This
is what is salutary, this is what is formative; this is the great 20
benefit to be got from the study of poetry. Everything which
interferes with it, which hinders it, is injurious. True, we must
read our classic with open eyes, and not with eyes blinded with
superstition; we must perceive when his work comes short,
when it drops out of the class of the very best, and we must 25
rate it, in such cases, at its proper value. But the use of this
negative criticism is not in itself, it is entirely in its enabling
us to have a clearer sense and a deeper enjoyment of what is
truly excellent. To trace the labour, the attempts, the weaknesses, the failures of a genuine classic, to acquaint oneself with 30
his time and his life and his historical relationships, is mere
literary dilettantism unless it has that clear sense and deeper
enjoyment for its end. It may be said that the more we know
about a classic the better we shall enjoy him; and, if we lived
as long as Methuselah and had all of us heads of perfect clear- 35
ness and wills of perfect steadfastness, this might be true in fact
as it is plausible in theory. But the case here is much the same
as the case with the Greek and Latin studies of our schoolboys.
The elaborate philological groundwork which we require them

to lay is in theory an admirable preparation for appreciating
the Greek and Latin authors worthily. The more thoroughly
we lay the groundwork, the better we shall be able, it may be
said, to enjoy the authors. True, if time were not so short, and
5   schoolboys' wits not so soon tired and their power of attention
exhausted; only, as it is, the elaborate philological preparation
goes on, but the authors are little known and less enjoyed. So
with the investigator of 'historic origins' in poetry. He ought
to enjoy the true classic all the better for his investigations; he
10   often is distracted from the enjoyment of the best, and with
the less good he overbusies himself, and is prone to over-rate
it in proportion to the trouble which it has cost him.

The idea of tracing historic origins and historical relationships
cannot be absent from a compilation like the present. And na-
15   turally the poets to be exhibited in it will be assigned to those
persons for exhibition who are known to prize them highly,
rather than to those who have no special inclination towards
them. Moreover the very occupation with an author, and the
business of exhibiting him, disposes us to affirm and amplify
20   his importance. In the present work, therefore, we are sure of
frequent temptation to adopt the historic estimate, or the personal estimate, and to forget the real estimate; which latter,
nevertheless, we must employ if we are to make poetry yield
us its full benefit. So high is that benefit, the benefit of clearly
25   feeling and of deeply enjoying the really excellent, the truly
classic in poetry, that we do well, I say, to set it fixedly before
our minds as our object in studying poets and poetry, and to
make the desire of attaining it the one principle to which, as
the *Imitation* says, whatever we may read or come to know, we
30   always return. *Cum multa legeris et cognoveris, ad unum sem-
per oportet redire principium.*

The historic estimate is likely in especial to affect our judgment and our language when we are dealing with ancient poets;
the personal estimate when we are dealing with poets our con-
35   temporaries, or at any rate modern. The exaggerations due to
the historic estimate are not in themselves, perhaps, of very
much gravity. Their report hardly enters the general ear; probably they do not always impose even on the literary men who

adopt them. But they lead to a dangerous abuse of language. So we hear Cædmon, amongst our own poets, compared to Milton. I have already noticed the enthusiasm of one accomplished French critic for 'historic origins.' Another eminent French critic, M. Vitet, comments upon that famous document of the early poetry of his nation, the *Chanson de Roland*. It is indeed a most interesting document. The *joculator* or *jongleur* Taillefer, who was with William the Conqueror's army at Hastings, marched before the Norman troops, so said the tradition, singing 'of Charlemagne and of Roland and of Oliver, and of the vassals who died at Roncevaux'; and it is suggested that in the *Chanson de Roland* by one Turoldus or Théroulde, a poem preserved in a manuscript of the twelfth century in the Bodleian Library at Oxford, we have certainly the matter, perhaps even some of the words, of the chaunt which Taillefer sang. The poem has vigour and freshness; it is not without pathos. But M. Vitet is not satisfied with seeing in it a document of some poetic value, and of very high historic and linguistic value; he sees in it a grand and beautiful work, a monument of epic genius. In its general design he finds the grandiose conception, in its details he finds the constant union of simplicity with greatness, which are the marks, he truly says, of the genuine epic, and distinguish it from the artificial epic of literary ages. One thinks of Homer; this is the sort of praise which is given to Homer, and justly given. Higher praise there cannot well be, and it is the praise due to epic poetry of the highest order only, and to no other. Let us try, then, the *Chanson de Roland* at its best. Roland, mortally wounded, lays himself down under a pine-tree, with his face turned towards Spain and the enemy—

> 'De plusurs choses à remembrer li prist,
> De tantes teres cume li bers cunquist,
> De dulce France, des humes de sun lign,
> De Carlemagne sun seignor ki l'nurrit.'[1]

[1] Then began he to call many things to remembrance,—all the lands which his valour conquered, and pleasant France, and the men of his lineage, and Charlemagne his liege lord who nourished him.'—*Chanson de Roland*, iii. 939–942.

That is primitive work, I repeat, with an undeniable poetic quality of its own. It deserves such praise, and such praise is sufficient for it. But now turn to Homer—

5
"Ὣς φάτο· τοὺς δ᾽ ἤδη κάτεχεν φυσίζοος αἶα
ἐν Λακεδαίμονι αὖθι, φίλῃ ἐν πατρίδι γαίῃ.[1]

We are here in another world, another order of poetry altogether; here is rightly due such supreme praise as that which M. Vitet gives to the *Chanson de Roland*. If our words are to have any meaning, if our judgments are to have any solidity, we
10 must not heap that supreme praise upon poetry of an order immeasurably inferior.

Indeed there can be no more useful help for discovering what poetry belongs to the class of the truly excellent, and can therefore do us most good, than to have always in one's mind
15 lines and expressions of the great masters, and to apply them as a touchstone to other poetry. Of course we are not to require this other poetry to resemble them; it may be very dissimilar. But if we have any tact we shall find them, when we have lodged them well in our minds, an infallible touchstone
20 for detecting the presence or absence of high poetic quality, and also the degree of this quality, in all other poetry which we may place beside them. Short passages, even single lines, will serve our turn quite sufficiently. Take the two lines which I have just quoted from Homer, the poet's comment on Helen's
25 mention of her brothers;—or take his

Ἆ δειλώ, τί σφῶϊ δόμεν Πηλῆϊ ἄνακτι
θνητῷ; ὑμεῖς δ᾽ ἐστὸν ἀγήρω τ᾽ ἀθανάτω τε.
ἦ ἵνα δυστήνοισι μετ᾽ ἀνδράσιν ἄλγε᾽ ἔχητον ;[2]

[1] So said she; they long since in Earth's soft arms were reposing,
30   There, in their own dear land, their fatherland, Lacedæmon.'
                    Iliad, iii. 243, 244 (translated by Dr. Hawtrey).

[2] 'Ah, unhappy pair, why gave we you to King Peleus, to a mortal? but ye are without old age, and immortal. Was it that with men born to misery ye might have sorrow?'—*Iliad*, xvii. 443–445.

the address of Zeus to the horses of Peleus;—or take finally his

$$\text{Καὶ σέ, γέρον, τὸ πρὶν μὲν ἀκούομεν ὄλβιον εἶναι·}^1$$

the words of Achilles to Priam, a suppliant before him. Take that incomparable line and a half of Dante, Ugolino's tremendous words—

> 'Io non piangeva; sì dentro impietrai.
> Piangevan elli . . .'[2]

take the lovely words of Beatrice to Virgil—

> 'Io son fatta da Dio, sua mercè, tale,
> Che la vostra miseria non mi tange,
> Nè fiamma d'esto incendio non m'assale . . .'[3]

take the simple, but perfect, single line—

> 'In la sua volontade è nostra pace.'[4]

Take of Shakespeare a line or two of Henry the Fourth's expostulation with sleep—

> 'Wilt thou upon the high and giddy mast
> Seal up the ship-boy's eyes, and rock his brains
> In cradle of the rude imperious surge . . .'

and take, as well, Hamlet's dying request to Horatio—

> 'If thou didst ever hold me in thy heart,
> Absent thee from felicity awhile,

[1] 'Nay, and thou too, old man, in former days wast, as we hear, happy.'—*Iliad*, xxiv. 543.

[2] 'I wailed not, so of stone grew I within;—*they* wailed.'—*Inferno*, xxxiii. 49, 50.

[3] 'Of such sort hath God, thanked be His mercy, made me, that your misery toucheth me not, neither doth the flame of this fire strike me.'—*Inferno*, ii. 91–93.

[4] 'In His will is our peace.'—*Paradiso*, iii. 85.

> And in this harsh world draw thy breath in pain
> To tell my story . . .'

Take of Milton that Miltonic passage—

>   'Darken'd so, yet shone
> Above them all the archangel; but his face
> Deep scars of thunder had intrench'd, and care
> Sat on his faded cheek . . .'

add two such lines as—

> 'And courage never to submit or yield
> And what is else not to be overcome . . .'

and finish with the exquisite close to the loss of Proserpine, the loss

> ' . . . which cost Ceres all that pain
> To seek her through the world.'

These few lines, if we have tact and can use them, are enough even of themselves to keep clear and sound our judgments about poetry, to save us from fallacious estimates of it, to conduct us to a real estimate.

The specimens I have quoted differ widely from one another, but they have in common this: the possession of the very highest poetical quality. If we are thoroughly penetrated by their power, we shall find that we have acquired a sense enabling us, whatever poetry may be laid before us, to feel the degree in which a high poetical quality is present or wanting there. Critics give themselves great labour to draw out what in the abstract constitutes the characters of a high quality of poetry. It is much better simply to have recourse to concrete examples;—to take specimens of poetry of the high, the very highest quality, and to say: The characters of a high quality of poetry are what is expressed *there*. They are far better recognised by being felt in the verse of the master, than by being perused in the prose of the critic. Nevertheless if we are urgently pressed to give some critical account of them, we may safely, perhaps, venture on laying down, not indeed how and why the characters arise, but where and in what they arise. They are in the matter and substance of the poetry, and they are in its manner and style. Both of these, the substance and matter on the one hand, the style and manner on the other, have a mark, an accent, of high beauty, worth, and power. But if we are asked to define this mark and accent in the abstract, our answer must be: No, for we should thereby be darkening the question, not clearing it. The mark and accent are as given by the substance and matter of that poetry, by the style and manner of that poetry, and of all other poetry which is akin to it in quality.

Only one thing we may add as to the substance and matter of poetry, guiding ourselves by Aristotle's profound observation that the superiority of poetry over history consists in its possessing a higher truth and a higher seriousness ($\phi\iota\lambda o\sigma o$-$\phi\acute{\omega}\tau\epsilon\rho o\nu$ $\kappa\alpha\grave{\iota}$ $\sigma\pi o\upsilon\delta\alpha\iota\acute{o}\tau\epsilon\rho o\nu$). Let us add, therefore, to what we have said, this: that the substance and matter of the best poetry acquire their special character from possessing, in an eminent degree, truth and seriousness. We may add yet further, what is in itself evident, that to the style and manner of the best poetry their special character, their accent, is given by their diction, and, even yet more, by their movement. And though we distinguish between the two characters, the two accents, of superiority, yet they are nevertheless vitally connected one with the other. The superior character of truth and seriousness, in the matter and substance of the best poetry, is inseparable from the superiority of diction and movement marking its style and manner. The two superiorities are closely related, and are in steadfast proportion one to the other. So far as high poetic truth and seriousness are wanting to a poet's matter and substance, so far also, we may be sure, will a high poetic stamp of diction and movement be wanting to his style and manner. In proportion as this high stamp of diction and movement, again, is absent from a poet's style and manner, we shall find, also, that high poetic truth and seriousness are absent from his substance and matter.

So stated, these are but dry generalities; their whole force
lies in their application. And I could wish every student of
poetry to make the application of them for himself. Made by
himself, the application would impress itself upon his mind far
5   more deeply than made by me. Neither will my limits allow
me to make any full application of the generalities above pro-
pounded; but in the hope of bringing out, at any rate, some
significance in them, and of establishing an important principle
more firmly by their means, I will, in the space which remains
10   to me, follow rapidly from the commencement the course of
our English poetry with them in my view.

Once more I return to the early poetry of France, with
which our own poetry, in its origins, is indissolubly connected.
In the twelfth and thirteenth centuries, that seed-time of all
15   modern language and literature, the poetry of France had a
clear predominance in Europe. Of the two divisions of that
poetry, its productions in the *langue d'oil* and its productions
in the *langue d'oc*, the poetry of the *langue d'oc*, of southern
France, of the troubadours, is of importance because of its
20   effect on Italian literature;—the first literature of modern
Europe to strike the true and grand note, and to bring forth, as
in Dante and Petrarch it brought forth, classics. But the predominance of French poetry in Europe, during the twelfth
and thirteenth centuries, is due to its poetry of the *langue d'oil*,
25   the poetry of northern France and of the tongue which is now
the French language. In the twelfth century the bloom of this
romance-poetry was earlier and stronger in England, at the
court of our Anglo-Norman kings, than in France itself. But it
was a bloom of French poetry; and as our native poetry formed
30   itself, it formed itself out of this. The romance-poems which
took possession of the heart and imagination of Europe in the
twelfth and thirteenth centuries are French; 'they are,' as
Southey justly says, 'the pride of French literature, nor have
we anything which can be placed in competition with them.'
35   Themes were supplied from all quarters; but the romance-
setting which was common to them all, and which gained the
ear of Europe, was French. This constituted for the French
poetry, literature, and language, at the height of the Middle

Age, an unchallenged predominance. The Italian Brunetto Latini, the master of Dante, wrote his *Treasure* in French because, he says, 'la parleure en est plus délitable et plus commune à toutes gens.' In the same century, the thirteenth, the French romance-writer, Christian of Troyes, formulates the claims, in chivalry and letters, of France, his native country, as follows:—

> 'Or vous ert par ce livre apris,
> Que Gresse ot de chevalerie
> Le premier los et de clergie;
> Puis vint chevalerie à Rome,
> Et de la clergie la some,
> Qui ore est en France venue.
> Diex doinst qu'ele i soit retenue,
> Et que li lius li abelisse
> Tant que ja meis de France n'isse
> L'onor qui s'i est arestée!'

'Now by this book you will learn that first Greece had the renown for chivalry and letters; then chivalry and the primacy in letters passed to Rome, and now it is come to France. God grant it may be kept there; and that the place may please it so well, that the honour which has come to make stay in France may never depart thence!'

Yet it is now all gone, this French romance-poetry, of which the weight of substance and the power of style are not unfairly represented by this extract from Christian of Troyes. Only by means of the historic estimate can we persuade ourselves now to think that any of it is of poetical importance.

But in the fourteenth century there comes an Englishman nourished on this poetry, taught his trade by this poetry, getting words, rhyme, metre from this poetry; for even of that stanza which the Italians used, and which Chaucer derived immediately from the Italians, the basis and suggestion was probably given in France. Chaucer (I have already named him) fascinated his contemporaries, but so too did Christian of Troyes and Wolfram of Eschenbach. Chaucer's power of fascination, however, is enduring; his poetical importance does not need the assistance of the historic estimate; it is real. He is a genuine source of joy and strength, which is flowing still for us and will flow always. He will be read, as times goes on, far more generally than he is read now. His language is a cause of difficulty for us; but so also, and I think in quite as great a degree, is the language of Burns. In Chaucer's case, as in that of Burns, it is a difficulty to be unhesitatingly accepted and overcome.

If we ask ourselves wherein consists the immense superiority of Chaucer's poetry over the romance-poetry—why it is that in passing from this to Chaucer we suddenly feel ourselves to be in another world, we shall find that his superiority is both in the substance of his poetry and in the style of his poetry. His superiority in substance is given by his large, free, simple, clear yet kindly view of human life,—so unlike the total want, in the romance-poets, of all intelligent command of it. Chaucer has not their helplessness; he has gained the power to survey the world from a central, a truly human point of view. We have only to call to mind the Prologue to *The Canterbury Tales*. The right comment upon it is Dryden's: 'It is sufficient to say, according to the proverb, that *here is God's plenty*.' And again: 'He is a perpetual fountain of good sense.' It is by a large, free, sound representation of things, that poetry, this high criticism of life, has truth of substance; and Chaucer's poetry has truth of substance.

Of his style and manner, if we think first of the romance-poetry and then of Chaucer's divine liquidness of diction, his divine fluidity of movement, it is difficult to speak temperately. They are irresistible, and justify all the rapture with which his successors speak of his 'gold dew-drops of speech.' Johnson misses the point entirely when he finds fault with Dryden for ascribing to Chaucer the first refinement of our numbers, and says that Gower also can show smooth numbers and easy rhymes. The refinement of our numbers means something far more than this. A nation may have versifiers with smooth numbers and easy rhymes, and yet may have no real poetry at all. Chaucer is the father of our splendid English poetry; he is our 'well of English undefiled,' because by the lovely charm of his diction, the lovely charm of his movement, he makes an epoch and founds a tradition. In Spenser, Shakespeare, Milton, Keats, we can follow the tradition of the liquid diction, the fluid movement, of Chaucer; at one time it is his liquid diction of which in these poets we feel the virtue, and at another time it is his fluid movement. And the virtue is irresistible.

Bounded as is my space, I must yet find room for an example of Chaucer's virtue, as I have given examples to show the virtue of the great classics. I feel disposed to say that a single line is enough to show the charm of Chaucer's verse; that merely one line like this—

       'O martyr souded[1] to virginitee!'

has a virtue of manner and movement such as we shall not find in all the verse of romance-poetry;—but this is saying nothing. The virtue is such as we shall not find, perhaps, in all English poetry, outside the poets whom I have named as the special inheritors of Chaucer's tradition. A single line, however, is too little if we have not the strain of Chaucer's verse well in our memory; let us take a stanza. It is from *The Prioress's Tale*, the story of the Christian child murdered in a Jewry—

    'My throte is cut unto my nekke-bone
    Saidè this child, and as by way of kinde
    I should have deyd, yea, longè time agone;
    But Jesu Christ, as ye in bookès finde,
    Will that his glory last and be in minde,
    And for the worship of his mother dere
    Yet may I sing *O Alma* loud and clere.'

Wordsworth has modernised this Tale, and to feel how delicate and evanescent is the charm of verse, we have only to read Wordsworth's first three lines of this stanza after Chaucer's—

    'My throat is cut unto the bone, I trow,
    Said this young child, and by the law of kind
    I should have died, yea, many hours ago.'

    [1] The French *soudé;* soldered, fixed fast.

The charm is departed. It is often said that the power of liquidness and fluidity in Chaucer's verse was dependent upon a free,
a licentious dealing with language, such as is now impossible;
upon a liberty, such as Burns too enjoyed, of making words like
5   *neck*, *bird*, into a dissyllable by adding to them, and words like
cause, *rhyme*, into a dissyllable by sounding the *e* mute. It is
true that Chaucer's fluidity is conjoined with this liberty, and
is admirably served by it; but we ought not to say that it was
dependent upon it. It was dependent upon his talent. Other
10 poets with a like liberty do not attain to the fluidity of Chaucer;
Burns himself does not attain to it. Poets, again, who have a
talent akin to Chaucer's, such as Shakespeare or Keats, have
known how to attain to his fluidity without the like liberty.

And yet Chaucer is not one of the great classics. His poetry
15 transcends and effaces, easily and without effort, all the romance-poetry of Catholic Christendom; it transcends and effaces
all the English poetry contemporary with it, it transcends and
effaces all the English poetry subsequent to it down to the
age of Elizabeth. Of such avail is poetic truth of substance, in
20 its natural and necessary union with poetic truth of style. And
yet, I say, Chaucer is not one of the great classics. He has not
their accent. What is wanting to him is suggested by the mere
mention of the name of the first great classic of Christendom,
the immortal poet who died eighty years before Chaucer,—
25 Dante. The accent of such verse as

'In la sua volontade è nostra pace . . .'

is altogether beyond Chaucer's reach; we praise him, but we
feel that this accent is out of the question for him. It may be
said that it was necessarily out of the reach of any poet in the
30 England of that stage of growth. Possibly; but we are to adopt
a real, not a historic, estimate of poetry. However we may account for its absence, something is wanting, then, to the poetry
of Chaucer, which poetry must have before it can be placed
in the glorious class of the best. And there is no doubt what
35 that something is. It is the σπουδαιότης, the high and excellent
seriousness, which Aristotle assigns as one of the grand virtues
of poetry. The substance of Chaucer's poetry, his view of

things and his criticism of life, has largeness, freedom, shrewdness, benignity; but it has not this high seriousness. Homer's criticism of life has it, Dante's has it, Shakespeare's has it. It is this chiefly which gives to our spirits what they can rest upon; and with the increasing demands of our modern ages upon poetry, this virtue of giving us what we can rest upon will be more and more highly esteemed. A voice from the slums of Paris, fifty or sixty years after Chaucer, the voice of poor Villon out of his life of riot and crime, has at its happy moments (as, for instance, in the last stanza of *La Belle Heaulmière*[1]) more of this important poetic virtue of seriousness than all the productions of Chaucer. But its apparition in Villon, and in men like Villon, is fitful; the greatness of the great poets, the power of their criticism of life, is that their virtue is sustained.

To our praise, therefore, of Chaucer as a poet there must be this limitation; he lacks the high seriousness of the great classics, and therewith an important part of their virtue. Still, the main fact for us to bear in mind about Chaucer is his sterling value according to that real estimate which we firmly adopt for all poets. He has poetic truth of substance, though he has not high poetic seriousness, and corresponding to his truth of substance he has an exquisite virtue of style and manner. With him is born our real poetry.

[1] The name *Heaulmière* is said to be derived from a head-dress (helm) worn as a mark by courtesans. In Villon's ballad, a poor old creature of this class laments her days of youth and beauty. The last stanza of the ballad runs thus—

> 'Ainsi le bon temps regretons
> Entre nous, pauvres vieilles sottes,
> Assises bas, à croppetons,
> Tout en ung tas comme pelottes;
> A petit feu de chenevottes
> Tost allumées, tost estainctes.
> Et jadis fusmes si mignottes!
> Ainsi en prend à maintz et maintes.'

'Thus amongst ourselves we regret the good time, poor silly old things. low-seated on our heels, all in a heap like so many balls; by a little fire of hemp-stalks, soon lighted, soon spent. And once we were such darlings! So fares it with many and many a one.'

For my present purpose I need not dwell on our Elizabethan poetry, or on the continuation and close of this poetry in Milton. We all of us profess to be agreed in the estimate of this poetry; we all of us recognise it as great poetry, our greatest, and Shakespeare and Milton as our poetical classics. The real estimate, here, has universal currency. With the next age of our poetry divergency and difficulty begin. An historic estimate of that poetry has established itself; and the question is, whether it will be found to coincide with the real estimate.

The age of Dryden, together with our whole eighteenth century which followed it, sincerely believed itself to have produced poetical classics of its own, and even to have made advance, in poetry, beyond all its predecessors. Dryden regards as not seriously disputable the opinion 'that the sweetness of English verse was never understood or practised by our fathers.' Cowley could see nothing at all in Chaucer's poetry. Dryden heartily admired it, and, as we have seen, praised its matter admirably; but of its exquisite manner and movement all he can find to say is that 'there is the rude sweetness of a Scotch tune in it, which is natural and pleasing, though not perfect.' Addison, wishing to praise Chaucer's numbers, compares them with Dryden's own. And all through the eighteenth century, and down even into our own times, the stereotyped phrase of approbation for good verse found in our early poetry has been, that it even approached the verse of Dryden, Addison, Pope, and Johnson.

Are Dryden and Pope poetical classics? Is the historic estimate, which represents them as such, and which has been so long established that it cannot easily give way, the real estimate? Wordsworth and Coleridge, as is well known, denied it; but the authority of Wordsworth and Coleridge does not weigh much with the young generation, and there are many signs to show that the eighteenth century and its judgments are coming into favour again. Are the favourite poets of the eighteenth century classics?

It is impossible within my present limits to discuss the question fully. And what man of letters would not shrink from seeming to dispose dictatorially of the claims of two men who are, at any rate, such masters in letters as Dryden and Pope;

two men of such admirable talent, both of them, and one of them, Dryden, a man, on all sides, of such energetic and genial power? And yet, if we are to gain the full benefit from poetry, we must have the real estimate of it. I cast about for some mode of arriving, in the present case, at such an estimate without offence. And perhaps the best way is to begin, as it is easy to begin, with cordial praise.

When we find Chapman, the Elizabethan translator of Homer, expressing himself in his preface thus: 'Though truth in her very nakedness sits in so deep a pit, that from Gades to Aurora and Ganges few eyes can sound her, I hope yet those few here will so discover and confirm her that, the date being out of her darkness in this morning of our poet, he shall now gird his temples with the sun,'—we pronounce that such a prose is intolerable. When we find Milton writing: 'And long it was not after, when I was confirmed in this opinion, that he, who would not be frustrate of his hope to write well hereafter in laudable things, ought himself to be a true poem,'—we pronounce that such a prose has its own grandeur, but that it is obsolete and inconvenient. But when we find Dryden telling us: 'What Virgil wrote in the vigour of his age, in plenty and at ease, I have undertaken to translate in my declining years; struggling with wants, oppressed with sickness, curbed in my genius, liable to be misconstrued in all I write,'—then we exclaim that here at last we have the true English prose, a prose such as we would all gladly use if we only knew how. Yet Dryden was Milton's contemporary.

But after the Restoration the time had come when our nation felt the imperious need of a fit prose. So, too, the time had likewise come when our nation felt the imperious need of freeing itself from the absorbing preoccupation which religion in the Puritan age had exercised. It was impossible that this freedom should be brought about without some negative excess, without some neglect and impairment of the religious life of the soul; and the spiritual history of the eighteenth century shows us that the freedom was not achieved without them. Still, the freedom was achieved; the preoccupation, an undoubtedly baneful and retarding one if it had continued, was got rid of. And as with religion amongst us at that period, so

it was also with letters. A fit prose was a necessity; but it was
impossible that a fit prose should establish itself amongst us
without some touch of frost to the imaginative life of the soul.
The needful qualities for a fit prose are regularity, uniformity,
5   precision, balance. The men of letters, whose destiny it may be
to bring their nation to the attainment of a fit prose, must of
necessity, whether they work in prose or in verse, give a predominating, an almost exclusive attention to the qualities of
regularity, uniformity, precision, balance. But an almost ex-
10 clusive attention to these qualities involves some repression and
silencing of poetry.

   We are to regard Dryden as the puissant and glorious
founder, Pope as the splendid high priest, of our age of prose
and reason, of our excellent and indispensable eighteenth cen-
15 tury. For the purposes of their mission and destiny their poetry,
like their prose, is admirable. Do you ask me whether Dryden's
verse, take it almost where you will, is not good?

> 'A milk-white Hind, immortal and unchanged,
> Fed on the lawns and in the forest ranged.'

20 I answer: Admirable for the purposes of the inaugurator of an
age of prose and reason. Do you ask me whether Pope's verse,
take it almost where you will, is not good?

> 'To Hounslow Heath I point, and Banstead Down;
> Thence comes your mutton, and these chicks my own.'

25 I answer: Admirable for the purposes of the high priest of an
age of prose and reason. But do you ask me whether such verse
proceeds from men with an adequate poetic criticism of life,
from men whose criticism of life has a high seriousness, or even,
without that high seriousness, has poetic largeness, freedom,
30 insight, benignity? Do you ask me whether the application of
ideas to life in the verse of these men, often a powerful application, no doubt, is a powerful *poetic* application? Do you ask
me whether the poetry of these men has either the matter or
the inseparable manner of such an adequate poetic criticism;
35 whether it has the accent of

> 'Absent thee from felicity awhile . . .'

or of

> 'And what is else not to be overcome . . .'

or of

> 'O martyr souded to viginitee!'

I answer: It has not and cannot have them; it is the poetry of   5
the builders of an age of prose and reason. Though they may
write in verse, though they may in a certain sense be masters
of the art of versification, Dryden and Pope are not classics
of our poetry, they are classics of our prose.

Gray is our poetical classic of that literature and age; the   10
position of Gray is singular, and demands a word of notice
here. He has not the volume or the power of poets who, coming
in times more favourable, have attained to an independent criticism of life. But he lived with the great poets, he lived, above
all, with the Greeks, through perpetually studying and enjoy-   15
ing them; and he caught their poetic point of view for regarding life, caught their poetic manner. The point of view and
the manner are not self-sprung in him, he caught them of
others; and he had not the free and abundant use of them. But
whereas Addison and Pope never had the use of them, Gray   20
had the use of them at times. He is the scantiest and frailest of
classics in our poetry, but he is a classic.

And now, after Gray, we are met, as we draw towards the
end of the eighteenth century, we are met by the great name
of Burns. We enter now on times where the personal estimate   25
of poets begins to be rife, and where the real estimate of them
is not reached without difficulty. But in spite of the disturbing
pressures of personal partiality, of national partiality, let us try
to reach a real estimate of the poetry of Burns.

By his English poetry Burns in general belongs to the eigh-   30
teenth century, and has little importance for us.

> 'Mark ruffian Violence, distain'd with crimes,
> Rousing elate in these degenerate times;
> View unsuspecting Innocence a prey,
> As guileful Fraud points out the erring way;   35

> While subtle Litigation's pliant tongue
> The life-blood equal sucks of Right and Wrong!'

Evidently this is not the real Burns, or his name and fame would have disappeared long ago. Nor is Clarinda's love-poet, Sylvander, the real Burns either. But he tells us himself: 'These English songs gravel me to death. I have not the command of the language that I have of my native tongue. In fact, I think that my ideas are more barren in English than in Scotch. I have been at *Duncan Gray* to dress it in English, but all I can do is desperately stupid.' We English turn naturally, in Burns, to the poems in our own language, because we can read them easily; but in those poems we have not the real Burns.

The real Burns is of course in his Scotch poems. Let us boldly say that of much of this poetry, a poetry dealing perpetually with Scotch drink, Scotch religion, and Scotch manners, a Scotchman's estimate is apt to be personal. A Scotchman is used to this world of Scotch drink, Scotch religion, and Scotch manners; he has a tenderness for it; he meets its poet half way. In this tender mood he reads pieces like the *Holy Fair* or *Halloween*. But this world of Scotch drink, Scotch religion, and Scotch manners is against a poet, not for him, when it is not a partial countryman who reads him; for in itself it is not a beautiful world, and no one can deny that it is of advantage to a poet to deal with a beautiful world. Burns's world of Scotch drink, Scotch religion, and Scotch manners, is often a harsh, a sordid, a repulsive world; even the world of his *Cotter's Saturday Night* is not a beautiful world. No doubt a poet's criticism of life may have such truth and power that it triumphs over its world and delights us. Burns may triumph over his world, often he does triumph over his world, but let us observe how and where. Burns is the first case we have had where the bias of the personal estimate tends to mislead; let us look at him closely, he can bear it.

Many of his admirers will tell us that we have Burns, convivial, genuine, delightful, here—

> 'Leeze me on drink! it gies us mair
> Than either school or college;

It kindles wit, it waukens lair,
　　It pangs us fou o' knowledge.
Be't whisky gill or penny wheep
　　Or ony stronger potion,
It never fails, on drinking deep,   5
　　To kittle up our notion
　　　　　　By night or day.'

There is a great deal of that sort of thing in Burns, and it is
unsatisfactory, not because it is bacchanalian poetry, but because it has not that accent of sincerity which bacchanalian   10
poetry, to do it justice, very often has. There is something in
it of bravado, something which makes us feel that we have not
the man speaking to us with his real voice; something, therefore, poetically unsound.

　　With still more confidence will his admirers tell us that we   15
have the genuine Burns, the great poet, when his strain asserts
the independence, equality, dignity, of men, as in the famous
song *For a' that and a' that*—

'A prince can mak' a belted knight,
　　A marquis, duke, and a' that;
But an honest man's aboon his might,   20
　　Guid faith he mauna fa' that!
　　　For a' that, and a' that,
　　　　Their dignities, and a' that,
　　　　The pith o' sense, and pride o' worth,   25
　　　　　Are higher rank than a' that.'

Here they find his grand, genuine touches; and still more, when
this puissant genius, who so often set morality at defiance, falls
moralising—

'The sacred lowe o' weel-placed love   30
　　Luxuriantly indulge it;
But never tempt th' illicit rove,
　　Tho' naething should divulge it.
I waive the quantum o' the sin,
　　The hazard o' concealing,   35

> But och! it hardens a' within,
>   And petrifies the feeling.'

Or in a higher strain—

> 'Who made the heart, 'tis He alone
>   Decidedly can try us;
> He knows each chord, its various tone;
>   Each spring, its various bias.
> Then at the balance let's be mute,
>   We never can adjust it;
> What's *done* we partly may compute,
>   But know not what's resisted.'

Or in a better strain yet, a strain, his admirers will say, unsurpassable—

> 'To make a happy fire-side clime
>   To weans and wife,
> That's the true pathos and sublime
>   Of human life.'

There is criticism of life for you, the admirers of Burns will say to us; there is the application of ideas to life! There is, undoubtedly. The doctrine of the last-quoted lines coincides almost exactly with what was the aim and end, Xenophon tells us, of all the teaching of Socrates. And the application is a powerful one; made by a man of vigorous understanding, and (need I say?) a master of language.

But for supreme poetical success more is required than the powerful application of ideas to life; it must be an application under the conditions fixed by the laws of poetic truth and poetic beauty. Those laws fix as an essential condition, in the poet's treatment of such matters as are here in question, high seriousness;—the high seriousness which comes from absolute sincerity. The accent of high seriousness, born of absolute sincerity, is what gives to such verse as

> 'In la sua volontade è nostra pace . . .'

to such criticism of life as Dante's, its power. Is this accent felt in the passages which I have been quoting from Burns? Surely not; surely, if our sense is quick, we must perceive that we have not in those passages a voice from the very inmost soul of the genuine Burns; he is not speaking to us from these depths, he 5 is more or less preaching. And the compensation for admiring such passages less, from missing the perfect poetic accent in them, will be that we shall admire more the poetry where that accent is found.

No; Burns, like Chaucer, comes short of the high seriousness 10 of the great classics, and the virtue of matter and manner which goes with that high seriousness is wanting to his work. At moments he touches it in a profound and passionate melancholy, as in those four immortal lines taken by Byron as a motto for *The Bride of Abydos*, but which have in them a depth of poetic 15 quality such as resides in no verse of Byron's own—

> 'Had we never loved sae kindly,
> Had we never loved sae blindly,
> Never met, or never parted,
> We had ne'er been broken-hearted.' 20

But a whole poem of that quality Burns cannot make; the rest, in the *Farewell to Nancy*, is verbiage.

We arrive best at the real estimate of Burns, I think, by conceiving his work as having truth of matter and truth of manner, but not the accent or the poetic virtue of the highest 25 masters. His genuine criticism of life, when the sheer poet in him speaks, is ironic; it is not—

> 'Thou Power Supreme, whose mighty scheme
>   These woes of mine fulfil,
> Here firm I rest, they must be best 30
>   Because they are Thy will!'

It is far rather: *Whistle owre the lave o't!* Yet we may say of him as of Chaucer, that of life and the world, as they come before him, his view is large, free, shrewd, benignant,—truly poetic, therefore; and his manner of rendering what he sees is 35

to match. But we must note, at the same time, his great difference from Chaucer. The freedom of Chaucer is heightened, in
Burns, by a fiery, reckless energy; the benignity of Chaucer
deepens, in Burns, into an overwhelming sense of the pathos
5   of things;—of the pathos of human nature, the pathos, also, of
non-human nature. Instead of the fluidity of Chaucer's manner,
the manner of Burns has spring, bounding swiftness. Burns is
by far the greater force, though he has perhaps less charm. The
world of Chaucer is fairer, richer, more significant than that
10   of Burns; but when the largeness and freedom of Burns get full
sweep, as in *Tam o' Shanter*, or still more in that puissant and
splendid production, *The Jolly Beggars*, his world may be what
it will, his poetic genius triumphs over it. In the world of *The
Jolly Beggars* there is more than hideousness and squalor, there
15   is bestiality; yet the piece is a superb poetic success. It has a
breadth, truth, and power which make the famous scene in
Auerbach's Cellar, of Goethe's *Faust*, seem artificial and tame
beside it, and which are only matched by Shakespeare and
Aristophanes.

20   Here, where his largeness and freedom serve him so admirably, and also in those poems and songs where to shrewdness
he adds infinite archness and wit, and to benignity infinite
pathos, where his manner is flawless, and a perfect poetic whole
is the result,—in things like the address to the mouse whose
25   home he had ruined, in things like *Duncan Gray*, *Tam Glen*,
O Whistle and I'll come to you, my Lad, *Auld Lang Syne* (this
list might be made much longer),—here we have the genuine
Burns, of whom the real estimate must be high indeed. Not a
classic, nor with the excellent σπουδαιότης of the great classics,
30   nor with a verse rising to a criticism of life and a virtue like
theirs; but a poet with thorough truth of substance and an
answering truth of style, giving us a poetry sound to the core.
We all of us have a leaning towards the pathetic, and may be
inclined perhaps to prize Burns most for his touches of piercing,
35   sometimes almost intolerable, pathos; for verse like—

'We twa hae paidl't i' the burn
From mornin' sun till dine;

> But seas between us braid hae roar'd
> Sin auld lang syne . . .'

where he is as lovely as he is sound. But perhaps it is by the
perfection of soundness of his lighter and archer masterpieces
that he is poetically most wholesome for us. For the votary   5
misled by a personal estimate of Shelley, as so many of us have
been, are, and will be,—of that beautiful spirit building his
many-coloured haze of words and images

> 'Pinnacled dim in the intense inane'—

no contact can be wholesomer than the contact with Burns at   10
his archest and soundest. Side by side with the

> 'On the brink of the night and the morning
>   My coursers are wont to respire,
> But the Earth has just whispered a warning
>   That their flight must be swifter than fire . . .'   15

of *Prometheus Unbound*, how salutary, how very salutary, to
place this from *Tam Glen*—

> 'My minnie does constantly deave me
>   And bids me beware o' young men;
> They flatter, she says, to deceive me;   20
>   But wha can think sae o' Tam Glen?'

But we enter on burning ground as we approach the poetry
of times so near to us—poetry like that of Byron, Shelley, and
Wordsworth—of which the estimates are so often not only
personal, but personal with passion. For my purpose, it is   25
enough to have taken the single case of Burns, the first poet we
come to of whose work the estimate formed is evidently apt to
be personal, and to have suggested how we may proceed, using
the poetry of the great classics as a sort of touchstone, to correct
this estimate, as we had previously corrected by the same means   30
the historic estimate where we met with it. A collection like
the present, with its succession of celebrated names and cele-

brated poems, offers a good opportunity to us for resolutely endeavouring to make our estimates of poetry real. I have sought to point out a method which will help us in making them so, and to exhibit it in use so far as to put any one who likes in
5   a way of applying it for himself.

At any rate the end to which the method and the estimate are designed to lead, and from leading to which, if they do lead to it, they get their whole value,—the benefit of being able clearly to feel and deeply to enjoy the best, the truly classic,
10 in poetry,—is an end, let me say it once more at parting, of supreme importance. We are often told that an era is opening in which we are to see multitudes of a common sort of readers, and masses of a common sort of literature; that such readers do not want and could not relish anything better than such litera-
15 ture, and that to provide it is becoming a vast and profitable industry. Even if good literature entirely lost currency with the world, it would still be abundantly worth while to continue to enjoy it by oneself. But it never will lose currency with the world, in spite of momentary appearances; it never will lose
20 supremacy. Currency and supremacy are insured to it, not indeed by the world's deliberate and conscious choice, but by something far deeper,—by the instinct of self-preservation in humanity.

Thomas Gray[1]

James Brown, Master of Pembroke Hall at Cambridge, Gray's friend and executor, in a letter written a fortnight after Gray's death to another of his friends, Dr. Wharton of Old Park, Durham, has the following passage:—

'Everything is now dark and melancholy in Mr. Gray's room, not a trace of him remains there; it looks as if it had been for some time uninhabited, and the room bespoke for another inhabitant. The thoughts I have of him will last, and will be useful to me the few years I can expect to live. He never spoke out, but I believe from some little expressions I now remember to have dropped from him, that for some time past he thought himself nearer his end than those about him apprehended.'

He never spoke out. In these four words is contained the whole history of Gray, both as a man and as a poet. The words fell naturally, and as it were by chance, from their writer's pen; but let us dwell upon them, and press into their meaning, for in following it we shall come to understand Gray.

He was in his fifty-fifth year when he died, and he lived in ease and leisure, yet a few pages hold all his poetry; *he never spoke out* in poetry. Still, the reputation which he has achieved by his few pages is extremely high. True, Johnson speaks of him with coldness and disparagement. Gray disliked Johnson, and refused to make his acquaintance; one might fancy that Johnson wrote with some irritation from this cause. But Johnson was not by nature fitted to do justice to Gray and to his poetry; this by itself is a sufficient explanation of the deficiencies of his criticism of Gray. We may add a further explanation of them

[1] Prefixed to the Selection from Gray in Ward's *English Poets*, vol. iii. 1880.

which is supplied by Mr. Cole's papers. 'When Johnson was
publishing his Life of Gray,' says Mr. Cole, 'I gave him several
anecdotes, *but he was very anxious as soon as possible to get to
the end of his labours.*' Johnson was not naturally in sympathy
5   with Gray, whose life he had to write, and when he wrote it
he was in a hurry besides. He did Gray injustice, but even
Johnson's authority failed to make injustice, in this case, prevail.
Lord Macaulay calls the Life of Gray the worst of Johnson's
Lives, and it had found many censurers before Macaulay. Gray's
10   poetical reputation grew and flourished in spite of it. The poet
Mason, his first biographer, in his epitaph equalled him with
Pindar. Britain has known, says Mason,

> ' . . . a Homer's fire in Milton's strains,
> A Pindar's rapture in the lyre of Gray.'

15   The immense vogue of Pope and of his style of versification had
at first prevented the frank reception of Gray by the readers
of poetry. The *Elegy* pleased; it could not but please: but
Gray's poetry, on the whole, astonished his contemporaries at
first more than it pleased them; it was so unfamiliar, so unlike
20   the sort of poetry in vogue. It made its way, however, after
his death, with the public as well as with the few; and Gray's
second biographer, Mitford, remarks that 'the works which
were either neglected or ridiculed by their contemporaries have
now raised Gray and Collins to the rank of our two greatest
25   lyric poets.' Their reputation was established, at any rate, and
stood extremely high, even if they were not popularly read.
Johnson's disparagement of Gray was called 'petulant,' and
severely blamed. Beattie, at the end of the eighteenth century,
writing to Sir William Forbes, says: 'Of all the English poets
30   of this age Mr. Gray is most admired, and I think with justice.'
Cowper writes: 'I have been reading Gray's works, and think
him the only poet since Shakespeare entitled to the character
of sublime. Perhaps you will remember that I once had a different opinion of him. I was prejudiced.' Adam Smith says: 'Gray
35   joins to the sublimity of Milton the elegance and harmony of

Pope; and nothing is wanting to render him, perhaps, the first poet in the English language, but to have written a little more.' And, to come nearer to our own times, Sir James Mackintosh speaks of Gray thus: 'Of all English poets he was the most finished artist. He attained the highest degree of splendour of 5 which poetical style seemed to be capable.'

In a poet of such magnitude, how shall we explain his scantiness of production? Shall we explain it by saying that to make of Gray a poet of this magnitude is absurd; that his genius and resources were small, and that his production, therefore, was 10 small also, but that the popularity of a single piece, the *Elegy*, —a popularity due in great measure to the subject,—created for Gray a reputation to which he has really no right? He himself was not deceived by the favour shown to the *Elegy*. 'Gray told me with a good deal of acrimony,' writes Dr. Gregory, 15 'that the *Elegy* owed its popularity entirely to the subject, and that the public would have received it as well if it had been written in prose.' This is too much to say; the *Elegy* is a beautiful poem, and in admiring it the public showed a true feeling for poetry. But it is true that the *Elegy* owed much of its success 20 to its subject, and that it has received a too unmeasured and unbounded praise.

Gray himself, however, maintained that the *Elegy* was not his best work in poetry, and he was right. High as is the praise due to the *Elegy*, it is yet true that in other productions of Gray 25 he exhibits poetical qualities even higher than those exhibited in the *Elegy*. He deserves, therefore, his extremely high reputation as a poet, although his critics and the public may not always have praised him with perfect judgment. We are brought back, then, to the question: How, in a poet so really considerable, 30 are we to explain his scantiness of production?

Scanty Gray's production, indeed, is; so scanty that to supplement our knowledge of it by a knowledge of the man is in this case of peculiar interest and service. Gray's letters and the records of him by his friends have happily made it possible for 35 us thus to know him, and to appreciate his high qualities of mind and soul. Let us see these in the man first, and then observe

how they appear in his poetry; and why they cannot enter into
it more freely and inspire it with more strength, render it more
abundant.

We will begin with his acquirements. 'Mr. Gray was,' writes
his friend Temple, 'perhaps the most learned man in Europe. He
knew every branch of history both natural and civil; had read
all the original historians of England, France, and Italy; and was
a great antiquarian. Criticism, metaphysics, morals, politics,
made a principal part of his study. Voyages and travels of all
sorts were his favourite amusements; and he had a fine taste in
painting, prints, architecture, and gardening.' The notes in his
interleaved copy of Linnæus remained to show the extent and
accuracy of his knowledge in the natural sciences, particularly
in botany, zoology, and entomology. Entomologists testified
that his account of English insects was more perfect than any
that had then appeared. His notes and papers, of which some
have been published, others remain still in manuscript, give
evidence, besides, of his knowledge of literature ancient and
modern, geography and topography, painting, architecture and
antiquities, and of his curious researches in heraldry. He was
an excellent musician. Sir James Mackintosh reminds us, moreover, that to all the other accomplishments and merits of Gray
we are to add this: 'That he was the first discoverer of the
beauties of nature in England, and has marked out the course
of every picturesque journey that can be made in it.'

Acquirements take all their value and character from the
power of the individual storing them. Let us take, from amongst
Gray's observations on what he read, enough to show us his
power. Here are criticisms on three very different authors, criticisms without any study or pretension, but just thrown out in
chance letters to his friends. First, on Aristotle:—

'In the first place he is the hardest author by far I ever meddled
with. Then he has a dry conciseness that makes one imagine one is
perusing a table of contents rather than a book; it tastes for all the
world like chopped hay, or rather like chopped logic; for he has
a violent affection to that art, being in some sort his own invention;
so that he often loses himself in little trifling distinctions and verbal

niceties, and what is worse, leaves you to extricate yourself as you can. Thirdly, he has suffered vastly by his transcribers, as all authors of great brevity necessarily must. Fourthly and lastly, he has abundance of fine, uncommon things, which make him well worth the pains he gives one. You see what you have to expect.'   5

Next, on Isocrates:—

'It would be strange if I should find fault with you for reading Isocrates; I did so myself twenty years ago, and in an edition at least as bad as yours. The Panegyric, the De Pace, Areopagitic, and Advice to Philip, are by far the noblest remains we have of this   10
writer, and equal to most things extant in the Greek tongue; but it depends on your judgment to distinguish between his real and occasional opinion of things, as he directly contradicts in one place what he has advanced in another; for example, in the Panathenaic and the De Pace, on the naval power of Athens; the latter of the two is   15
undoubtedly his own undisguised sentiment.'

After hearing Gray on Isocrates and Aristotle, let us hear him on Froissart:—

'I rejoice you have met with Froissart, he is the Herodotus of a barbarous age; had he but had the luck of writing in as good a   20
language, he might have been immortal. His locomotive disposition (for then there was no other way of learning things), his simple curiosity, his religious credulity, were much like those of the old Grecian. When you have *tant chevauché* as to get to the end of him, there is Monstrelet waits to take you up, and will set you down at   25
Philip de Commines; but previous to all these, you should have read Villehardouin and Joinville.'

Those judgments, with their true and clear ring, evince the high quality of Gray's mind, his power to command and use his learning. But Gray was a poet; let us hear him on a poet, on   30
Shakespeare. We must place ourselves in the full midst of the eighteenth century and of its criticism; Gray's friend, West, had praised Racine for using in his dramas 'the language of the times and that of the purest sort'; and he had added: 'I will not decide what style is fit for our English stage, but I should rather   35

choose one that bordered upon Cato, than upon Shakespeare.'
Gray replies:—

'As to matter of style, I have this to say: The language of the age
is never the language of poetry; except among the French, whose
verse, where the thought does not support it, differs in nothing from
prose. Our poetry, on the contrary, has a language peculiar to itself,
to which almost every one that has written has added something. In
truth, Shakespeare's language is one of his principal beauties; and he
has no less advantage over your Addisons and Rowes in this, than
in those other great excellences you mention. Every word in him is
a picture. Pray put me the following lines into the tongue of our
modern dramatics—

"But I, that am not shaped for sportive tricks,
    Nor made to court an amorous looking-glass"—

and what follows. To me they appear untranslatable; and if this be
the case, our language is greatly degenerated.'

It is impossible for a poet to lay down the rules of his own
art with more insight, soundness, and certainty. Yet at that
moment in England there was perhaps not one other man,
besides Gray, capable of writing the passage just quoted.

Gray's quality of mind, then, we see; his quality of soul will
no less bear inspection. His reserve, his delicacy, his distaste for
many of the persons and things surrounding him in the Cambridge of that day,—'this silly, dirty place,' as he calls it,—have
produced an impression of Gray as being a man falsely fastidious, finical, effeminate. But we have already had that grave
testimony to him from the Master of Pembroke Hall: 'The
thoughts I have of him will last, and will be useful to me the
few years I can expect to live.' And here is another to the same
effect from a younger man, from Gray's friend Nicholls:—

'You know,' he writes to his mother, from abroad, when he heard
of Gray's death, 'that I considered Mr. Gray as a second parent,
that I thought only of him, built all my happiness on him, talked of
him for ever, wished him with me whenever I partook of any
pleasure, and flew to him for refuge whenever I felt any uneasiness.
To whom now shall I talk of all I have seen here? Who will teach

me to read, to think, to feel? I protest to you, that whatever I did or thought had a reference to him. If I met with any chagrins, I comforted myself that I had a treasure at home; if all the world had despised and hated me, I should have thought myself perfectly recompensed in his friendship. There remains only one loss more; 5 if I lose you, I am left alone in the world. At present I feel that I have lost half of myself.'

Testimonies such as these are not called forth by a fastidious effeminate weakling; they are not called forth, even, by mere qualities of mind; they are called forth by qualities of soul. And 10 of Gray's high qualities of soul, of his σπουδαιότης, his excellent seriousness, we may gather abundant proof from his letters. Writing to Mason who had just lost his father, he says:—

'I have seen the scene you describe, and know how dreadful it is; I know too I am the better for it. We are all idle and thoughtless 15 things, and have no sense, no use in the world any longer than that sad impression lasts; the deeper it is engraved the better.'

And again, on a like occasion to another friend:—

'He who best knows our nature (for he made us what we are) by such afflictions recalls us from our wandering thoughts and idle 20 merriment, from the insolence of youth and prosperity, to serious reflection, to our duty, and to himself; nor need we hasten to get rid of these impressions. Time (by appointment of the same Power) will cure the smart and in some hearts soon blot out all the traces of sorrow; but such as preserve them longest (for it is left partly in 25 our own power) do perhaps best acquiesce in the will of the chastiser.'

And once more to Mason, in the very hour of his wife's death; Gray was not sure whether or not his letter would reach Mason before the end:— 30

'If the worst be not yet past, you will neglect and pardon me; but if the last struggle be over, if the poor object of your long anxieties be no longer sensible to your kindness or to her own sufferings, allow me, at least in idea (for what could I do, were I present, more

than this?) to sit by you in silence and pity from my heart not her,
who is at rest, but you, who lose her. May he, who made us, the
Master of our pleasures and of our pains, support you! Adieu.'

5   Seriousness, character, was the foundation of things with him;
where this was lacking he was always severe, whatever might
be offered to him in its stead. Voltaire's literary genius charmed
him, but the faults of Voltaire's nature he felt so strongly that
when his young friend Nicholls was going abroad in 1771, just
before Gray's death, he said to him: 'I have one thing to beg of
10   you which you must not refuse.' Nicholls answered: 'You know
you have only to command; what is it?'—'Do not go to see
Voltaire,' said Gray; and then added: 'No one knows the mischief that man will do.' Nicholls promised compliance with
Gray's injunction; 'But what,' he asked, 'could a visit from me
15   signify?'—'Every tribute to such a man signifies,' Gray answered. He admired Dryden, admired him, even, too much; had
too much felt his influence as a poet. He told Beattie 'that if
there was any excellence in his own numbers he had learned
it wholly from the great poet'; and writing to Beattie afterwards
20   he recurs to Dryden, whom Beattie, he thought, did not honour
enough as a poet: 'Remember Dryden,' he writes, 'and be blind
to all his faults.' Yes, his faults as a poet; but on the man Dryden,
nevertheless, his sentence is stern. Speaking of the Poet-Laure-
ateship, 'Dryden,' he writes to Mason, 'was as disgraceful to the
25   office from his character, as the poorest scribbler could have
been from his verses.' Even where crying blemishes were absent,
the want of weight and depth of character in a man deprived
him, in Gray's judgment, of serious significance. He says of
Hume: 'Is not that *naïveté* and good-humour, which his admir-
30   ers celebrate in him, owing to this, that he has continued all his
days an infant, but one that unhappily has been taught to read
and write?'
     And with all this strenuous seriousness, a pathetic sentiment,
and an element, likewise, of sportive and charming humour. At
35   Keswick, by the lakeside on an autumn evening, he has the
accent of the *Rêveries*, or of Obermann, or Wordsworth:—

'In the evening walked alone down to the lake by the side of Crow Park after sunset and saw the solemn colouring of night draw on, the last gleam of sunshine fading away on the hill-tops, the deep serene of the waters, and the long shadows of the mountains thrown across them, till they nearly touched the hithermost shore. At distance heard the murmur of many waterfalls, not audible in the daytime. Wished for the Moon, but she was *dark to me and silent, hid in her vacant interlunar cave.*'

Of his humour and sportiveness his delightful letters are full; his humour appears in his poetry too, and is by no means to be passed over there. Horace Walpole said that 'Gray never wrote anything easily but things of humour; humour was his natural and original turn.'

Knowledge, penetration, seriousness, sentiment, humour, Gray had them all; he had the equipment and endowment for the office of poet. But very soon in his life appear traces of something obstructing, something disabling; of spirits failing, and health not sound; and the evil increases with years. He writes to West in 1737:—

'Low spirits are my true and faithful companions; they get up with me, go to bed with me, make journeys and returns as I do; nay, and pay visits and will even affect to be jocose and force a feeble laugh with me; but most commonly we sit alone together, and are the prettiest insipid company in the world.'

The tone is playful, Gray was not yet twenty-one. 'Mine,' he tells West four or five years later, 'mine, you are to know, is a white Melancholy, or rather *Leucocholy*, for the most part; which, though it seldom laughs or dances, nor ever amounts to what one calls joy or pleasure, yet is a good easy sort of a state.' But, he adds in this same letter:—

'But there is another sort, black indeed, which I have now and then felt, that has something in it like Tertullian's rule of faith, *Credo quia impossibile est;* for it believes, nay, is sure of everything that is unlikely, so it be but frightful; and on the other hand excludes and shuts its eyes to the most possible hopes, and everything that is pleasurable; from this the Lord deliver us! for none but he and sunshiny weather can do it.'

Six or seven years pass, and we find him writing to Wharton from Cambridge thus:—

'The spirit of laziness (the spirit of this place) begins to possess even me, that have so long declaimed against it. Yet has it not so prevailed, but that I feel that discontent with myself, that *ennui*, that ever accompanies it in its beginnings. Time will settle my conscience, time will reconcile my languid companion to me; we shall smoke, we shall tipple, we shall doze together, we shall have our little jokes, like other people, and our long stories. Brandy will finish what port began; and, a month after the time, you will see in some corner of a London Evening Post, "Yesterday died the Rev. Mr. John Gray, Senior-Fellow of Clare Hall, a facetious companion, and well-respected by all who knew him."'

The humorous advertisement ends, in the original letter, with a Hogarthian touch which I must not quote. Is it Leucocholy or is it Melancholy which predominates here? at any rate, this entry in his diary, six years later, is black enough:—

'*Insomnia crebra, atque expergiscenti surdus quidam doloris sensus; frequens etiam in regione sterni oppressio, et cardialgia gravis, fere sempiterna.*'

And in 1757 he writes to Hurd:—

'To be employed is to be happy. This principle of mine (and I am convinced of its truth) has, as usual, no influence on my practice. I am alone, and *ennuyé* to the last degree, yet do nothing. Indeed I have one excuse; my health (which you have so kindly inquired after) is not extraordinary. It is no great malady, but several little ones, that seem brewing no good to me.'

From thence to the end his languor and depression, though still often relieved by occupation and travel, keep fatally gaining on him. At last the depression became constant, became mechanical. 'Travel I must,' he writes to Dr. Wharton, 'or cease to exist. Till this year I hardly knew what *mechanical* low spirits were; but now I even tremble at an east wind.' Two months afterwards he died.

What wonder, that with this troublous cloud, throughout the whole term of his manhood, brooding over him and weighing him down, Gray, finely endowed though he was, richly stored with knowledge though he was, yet produced so little, found no full and sufficient utterance, '*never*,' as the Master of Pembroke Hall said, '*spoke out*.' He knew well enough, himself, how it was with him.

'My *verve* is at best, you know' (he writes to Mason), 'of so delicate a constitution, and has such weak nerves, as not to stir out of its chamber above three days in a year.' And to Horace Walpole he says: 'As to what you say to me civilly, that I ought to write more, I will be candid, and avow to you, that till fourscore and upward, whenever the humour takes me, I will write; because I like it, and because I like myself better when I do so. If I do not write much, it is because I cannot.' How simply said, and how truly also! Fain would a man like Gray speak out if he could, he 'likes himself better' when he speaks out; if he does not speak out, 'it is because I cannot.'

Bonstetten, that mercurial Swiss who died in 1832 at the age of eighty-seven, having been younger and livelier from his sixtieth year to his eightieth than at any other time in his life, paid a visit in his early days to Cambridge, and saw much of Gray, to whom he attached himself with devotion. Gray, on his part, was charmed with his young friend; 'I never saw such a boy,' he writes; 'our breed is not made on this model.' Long afterwards Bonstetten published his reminiscences of Gray. 'I used to tell Gray,' he says, 'about my life and my native country, but *his* life was a sealed book to me; he never would talk of himself, never would allow me to speak to him of his poetry. If I quoted lines of his to him, he kept silence like an obstinate child. I said to him sometimes: "Will you have the goodness to give me an answer?" But not a word issued from his lips.' *He never spoke out.* Bonstetten thinks that Gray's life was poisoned by an unsatisfied sensibility, was withered by his having never

loved; by his days being passed in the dismal cloisters of Cambridge, in the company of a set of monastic book-worms, 'whose existence no honest woman ever came to cheer.' Sainte-Beuve, who was much attracted and interested by Gray, doubts
5   whether Bonstetten's explanation of him is admissible; the secret of Gray's melancholy he finds rather in the sterility of his poetic talent, 'so distinguished, so rare, but so stinted'; in the poet's despair at his own unproductiveness.

But to explain Gray, we must do more than allege his sterility,
10   as we must look further than to his reclusion at Cambridge. What caused his sterility? Was it his ill-health, his hereditary gout? Certainly we will pay all respect to the powers of hereditary gout for afflicting us poor mortals. But Goethe, after pointing out that Schiller, who was so productive, was 'almost
15   constantly ill,' adds the true remark that it is incredible how much the spirit can do, in these cases, to keep up the body. Pope's animation and activity through all the course of what he pathetically calls 'that long disease, my life,' is an example presenting itself signally, in Gray's own country and time, to
20   confirm what Goethe here says. What gave the power to Gray's reclusion and ill-health to induce his sterility?

The reason, the indubitable reason as I cannot but think it, I have already given elsewhere. Gray, a born poet, fell upon an age of prose. He fell upon an age whose task was such as to
25   call forth in general men's powers of understanding, wit and cleverness, rather than their deepest powers of mind and soul. As regards literary production, the task of the eighteenth century in England was not the poetic interpretation of the world, its task was to create a plain, clear, straightforward, efficient
30   prose. Poetry obeyed the bent of mind requisite for the due fulfilment of this task of the century. It was intellectual, argumentative, ingenious; not seeing things in their truth and beauty, not interpretative. Gray, with the qualities of mind and soul of a genuine poet, was isolated in his century. Maintaining and forti-
35   fying them by lofty studies, he yet could not fully educe and enjoy them; the want of a genial atmosphere, the failure of sympathy in his contemporaries, were too great. Born in the same year with Milton, Gray would have been another man;

born in the same year with Burns, he would have been another man. A man born in 1608 could profit by the larger and more poetic scope of the English spirit in the Elizabethan age; a man born in 1759 could profit by that European renewing of men's minds of which the great historical manifestation is the French Revolution. Gray's alert and brilliant young friend, Bonstetten, who would explain the void in the life of Gray by his having never loved, Bonstetten himself loved, married, and had children. Yet at the age of fifty he was bidding fair to grow old, dismal and torpid like the rest of us, when he was roused and made young again for some thirty years, says M. Sainte-Beuve, by the events of 1789. If Gray, like Burns, had been just thirty years old when the French Revolution broke out, he would have shown, probably, productiveness and animation in plenty. Coming when he did, and endowed as he was, he was a man born out of date, a man whose full spiritual flowering was impossible. The same thing is to be said of his great contemporary, Butler, the author of the *Analogy*. In the sphere of religion, which touches that of poetry, Butler was impelled by the endowment of his nature to strive for a profound and adequate conception of religious things, which was not pursued by his contemporaries, and which at that time, and in that atmosphere of mind, was not fully attainable. Hence, in Butler too, a dissatisfaction, a weariness, as in Gray; 'great labour and weariness, great disappointment, pain and even vexation of mind.' A sort of spiritual east wind was at that time blowing; neither Butler nor Gray could flower. They *never spoke out*.

Gray's poetry was not only stinted in quantity by reason of the age wherein he lived, it suffered somewhat in quality also. We have seen under what obligation to Dryden Gray professed himself to be—'if there was any excellence in his numbers, he had learned it wholly from that great poet.' It was not for nothing that he came when Dryden had lately 'embellished,' as Johnson says, English poetry; had 'found it brick and left it marble.' It was not for nothing that he came just when 'the English ear,' to quote Johnson again, 'had been accustomed to the mellifluence of Pope's numbers, and the diction of poetry had grown more splendid.' Of the intellectualities, ingenuities,

personifications, of the movement and diction of Dryden and
Pope, Gray caught something, caught too much. We have little
of Gray's poetry, and that little is not free from the faults of
his age. Therefore it was important to go for aid, as we did, to
5 Gray's life and letters, to see his mind and soul there, and to
corroborate from thence that high estimate of his quality which
his poetry indeed calls forth, but does not establish so amply
and irresistibly as one could desire.

For a just criticism it does, however, clearly establish it. The
10 difference between genuine poetry and the poetry of Dryden,
Pope, and all their school, is briefly this: their poetry is conceived and composed in their wits, genuine poetry is conceived
and composed in the soul. The difference between the two
kinds of poetry is immense. They differ profoundly in their
15 modes of language, they differ profoundly in their modes of
evolution. The poetic language of our eighteenth century in
general is the language of men composing *without their eye on
the object,* as Wordsworth excellently said of Dryden; language
merely recalling the object, as the common language of prose
20 does, and then dressing it out with a certain smartness and
brilliancy for the fancy and understanding. This is called
'splendid diction.' The evolution of the poetry of our eighteenth
century is likewise intellectual; it proceeds by ratiocination,
antithesis, ingenious turns and conceits. This poetry is often
25 eloquent, and always, in the hands of such masters as Dryden
and Pope, clever; but it does not take us much below the surface
of things, it does not give us the emotion of seeing things in
their truth and beauty. The language of genuine poetry, on the
other hand, is the language of one composing with his eye on
30 the object; its evolution is that of a thing which has been
plunged in the poet's soul until it comes forth naturally and
necessarily. This sort of evolution is infinitely simpler than the
other, and infinitely more satisfying; the same thing is true of
the genuine poetic language likewise. But they are both of them
35 also infinitely harder of attainment; they come only from those
who, as Emerson says, 'live from a great depth of being.'

Goldsmith disparaged Gray who had praised his *Traveller,*
and indeed in the poem on the *Alliance of Education and*

Government had given him hints which he used for it. In retaliation let us take from Goldsmith himself a specimen of the poetic language of the eighteenth century.

'No cheerful murmurs fluctuate in the gale'—

there is exactly the poetic diction of our prose century! rhetorical, ornate,—and, poetically, quite false. Place beside it a line of genuine poetry, such as the

'In cradle of the rude, imperious surge'

of Shakespeare; and all its falseness instantly becomes apparent.

Dryden's poem on the death of Mrs. Killigrew is, says Johnson, 'undoubtedly the noblest ode that our language ever has produced.' In this vigorous performance Dryden has to say, what is interesting enough, that not only in poetry did Mrs. Killigrew excel, but she excelled in painting also. And thus he says it—

'To the next realm she stretch'd her sway,
  For Painture near adjoining lay—
A plenteous province and alluring prey.
A Chamber of Dependences was framed
(As conquerors will never want pretence
  When arm'd, to justify the offence),
And the whole fief, in right of Poetry, she claim'd.'

The intellectual, ingenious, superficial evolution of poetry of this school could not be better illustrated. Place beside it Pindar's

αἰὼν ἀσφαλὴς
οὐκ ἔγεντ' οὔτ' Αἰακίδᾳ παρὰ Πηλεῖ,
οὔτε παρ' ἀντιθέῳ Κάδμῳ . . .

'A secure time fell to the lot neither of Peleus the son of Æacus, nor of the godlike Cadmus; howbeit these are said to have had, of all mortals, the supreme of happiness, who heard the golden-snooded Muses sing,—on the mountain the one heard them, the other in seven-gated Thebes.'

There is the evolution of genuine poetry, and such poetry kills
Dryden's the moment it is put near it.

Gray's production was scanty, and scanty, as we have seen,
it could not but be. Even what he produced is not always pure
in diction, true in evolution. Still, with whatever drawbacks,
he is alone, or almost alone (for Collins has something of the
like merit) in his age. Gray said himself that 'the style he aimed
at was extreme conciseness of expression, yet pure, perspicuous,
and musical.' Compared, not with the work of the great masters
of the golden ages of poetry, but with the poetry of his own
contemporaries in general, Gray's may be said to have reached,
in style, the excellence at which he aimed; while the evolution
also of such a piece as his *Progress of Poesy* must be accounted
not less noble and sound than its style.

John Keats[1]

Poetry, according to Milton's famous saying, should be 'simple, sensuous, impassioned.' No one can question the eminency, in Keats's poetry, of the quality of sensuousness. Keats as a poet is abundantly and enchantingly sensuous; the question with some people will be, whether he is anything else. Many things may be brought forward which seem to show him as under the fascination and sole dominion of sense, and desiring nothing better. There is the exclamation in one of his letters: 'O for a life of sensations rather than of thoughts!' There is the thesis, in another, 'that with a great Poet the sense of Beauty overcomes every other consideration, or rather obliterates all considera- tion.' There is Haydon's story of him, how 'he once covered his tongue and throat as far as he could reach with Cayenne pepper, in order to appreciate the delicious coldness of claret in all its glory—his own expression.' One is not much surprised when Haydon further tells us, of the hero of such a story, that once for six weeks together he was hardly ever sober. 'He had no decision of character,' Haydon adds; 'no object upon which to direct his great powers.'

Character and self-control, the *virtus verusque labor* so necessary for every kind of greatness, and for the great artist, too, indispensable, appear to be wanting, certainly, to this Keats of Haydon's portraiture. They are wanting also to the Keats of the *Letters to Fanny Brawne*. These letters make as unpleasing an impression as Haydon's anecdotes. The editor of Haydon's journals could not well omit what Haydon said of his friend, but for the publication of the *Letters to Fanny*

[1] Prefixed to the Selection from Keats in Ward's *English Poets*, vol. iv. 1880.

Brawne I can see no good reason whatever. Their publication appears to me, I confess, inexcusable; they ought never to have been published. But published they are, and we have to take notice of them. Letters written when Keats was near his end, under the throttling and unmanning grasp of mortal disease, we will not judge. But here is a letter written some months before he was taken ill. It is printed just as Keats wrote it.

'You have absorb'd me. I have a sensation at the present moment as though I was dissolving—I should be exquisitely miserable without the hope of soon seeing you. I should be afraid to separate myself far from you. My sweet Fanny, will your heart never change? My love, will it? I have no limit now to my love.... Your note came in just here. I cannot be happier away from you. 'Tis richer than an Argosy of Pearles. Do not threat me even in jest. I have been astonished that Men could die Martyrs for religion— I have shuddered at it. I shudder no more—I could be martyred for my Religion—Love is my religion—I could die for that. I could die for you. My Creed is Love and you are its only tenet. You have ravished me away by a Power I cannot resist; and yet I could resist till I saw you; and even since I have seen you I have endeavoured often "to reason against the reasons of my Love." I can do that no more—the pain would be too great. My love is selfish. I cannot breathe without you.'

A man who writes love-letters in this strain is probably predestined, one may observe, to misfortune in his love-affairs; but that is nothing. The complete enervation of the writer is the real point for remark. We have the tone, or rather the entire want of tone, the abandonment of all reticence and all dignity, of the merely sensuous man, of the man who 'is passion's slave.' Nay, we have them in such wise that one is tempted to speak even as *Blackwood* or the *Quarterly* were in the old days wont to speak; one is tempted to say that Keats's love-letter is the love-letter of a surgeon's apprentice. It has in its relaxed self-abandonment something underbred and ignoble, as of a youth ill brought up, without the training which teaches us that we must put some constraint upon our feelings and upon the expression of them. It is the sort of love-letter of a surgeon's

apprentice which one might hear read out in a breach of
promise case, or in the Divorce Court. The sensuous man
speaks in it, and the sensuous man of a badly bred and badly
trained sort. That many who are themselves also badly bred and
badly trained should enjoy it, and should even think it a   5
beautiful and characteristic production of him whom they call
their 'lovely and beloved Keats,' does not make it better. These
are the admirers whose pawing and fondness does not good
but harm to the fame of Keats; who concentrate attention upon
what in him is least wholesome and most questionable; who   10
worship him, and would have the world worship him too, as
the poet of

> 'Light feet, dark violet eyes, and parted hair,
> Soft dimpled hands, white neck, and creamy breast.'

This sensuous strain Keats had, and a man of his poetic powers   15
could not, whatever his strain, but show his talent in it. But
he has something more, and something better. We who believe
Keats to have been by his promise, at any rate, if not fully by
his performance, one of the very greatest of English poets, and
who believe also that a merely sensuous man cannot either by   20
promise or by performance be a very great poet, because poetry
interprets life, and so large and noble a part of life is outside of
such a man's ken,—we cannot but look for signs in him of
something more than sensuousness, for signs of character and
virtue. And indeed the elements of high character Keats un-   25
doubtedly has, and the effort to develop them; the effort is
frustrated and cut short by misfortune, and disease, and time,
but for the due understanding of Keats's worth the recognition
of this effort, and of the elements on which it worked, is
necessary.   30
   Lord Houghton, who praises very discriminatingly the
poetry of Keats, has on his character also a remark full of
discrimination. He says: 'The faults of Keats's disposition were
precisely the contrary of those attributed to him by common
opinion.' And he gives a letter written after the death of   35
Keats by his brother George, in which the writer, speaking of

the fantastic *Johnny Keats* invented for common opinion by
Lord Byron and by the reviewers, declares indignantly: 'John
was the very soul of manliness and courage, and as much like
the Holy Ghost as *Johnny Keats*.' It is important to note this
5   testimony, and to look well for whatever illustrates and con-
firms it.

Great weight is laid by Lord Houghton on such a direct
profession of faith as the following: 'That sort of probity and
disinterestedness,' Keats writes to his brothers, 'which such men
10   as Bailey possess, does hold and grasp the tip-top of any
spiritual honours that can be paid to anything in this world.'
Lord Houghton says that 'never have words more effectively
expressed the conviction of the superiority of virtue above
beauty than those.' But merely to make a profession of faith
15   of the kind here made by Keats is not difficult; what we
should rather look for is some evidence of the instinct for
character, for virtue, passing into the man's life, passing into his
work.

Signs of virtue, in the true and large sense of the word, the
20   instinct for virtue passing into the life of Keats and strengthen-
ing it, I find in the admirable wisdom and temper of what he
says to his friend Bailey on the occasion of a quarrel between
Reynolds and Haydon:—

'Things have happened lately of great perplexity; you must have
25   heard of them; Reynolds and Haydon retorting and recriminating,
and parting for ever. The same thing has happened between Haydon and Hunt. It is unfortunate; men should bear with each other;
there lives not the man who may not be cut up, aye, lashed to
pieces, on his weakest side. The best of men have but a portion of
30   good in them.... The sure way, Bailey, is first to know a man's
faults, and then be passive. If, after that, he insensibly draws you
towards him, then you have no power to break the link. Before
I felt interested in either Reynolds or Haydon, I was well read
in their faults; yet, knowing them, I have been cementing grad-
35   ually with both. I have an affection for them both, for reasons
almost opposite; and to both must I of necessity cling, supported
always by the hope that when a little time, a few years, shall have
tried me more fully in their esteem, I may be able to bring them
together.'

Butler has well said that 'endeavouring to enforce upon our own minds a practical sense of virtue, or to beget in others that practical sense of it which a man really has himself, is a virtuous *act.*' And such an 'endeavouring' is that of Keats in those words written to Bailey. It is more than mere words; so justly thought and so discreetly urged as it is, it rises to the height of a virtuous *act*. It is proof of character.

The same thing may be said of some words written to his friend Charles Brown, whose kindness, willingly exerted whenever Keats chose to avail himself of it, seemed to free him from any pressing necessity of earning his own living. Keats felt that he must not allow this state of things to continue. He determined to set himself to 'fag on as others do' at periodical literature, rather than to endanger his independence and his self-respect; and he writes to Brown:—

'I had got into a habit of mind of looking towards you as a help in all difficulties. This very habit would be the parent of idleness and difficulties. You will see it is a duty I owe to myself to break the neck of it. I do nothing for my subsistence—make no exertion. At the end of another year you shall applaud me, not for verses, but for conduct.'

He had not, alas, another year of health before him when he announced that wholesome resolve; it then wanted but six months of the day of his fatal attack. But in the brief time allowed to him he did what he could to keep his word.

What character, again, what strength and clearness of judgment, in his criticism of his own productions, of the public, and of 'the literary circles'! His words after the severe reviews of *Endymion* have often been quoted; they cannot be quoted too often:—

'Praise or blame has but a momentary effect on the man whose love of beauty in the abstract makes him a severe critic on his own works. My own criticism has given me pain without comparison beyond what *Blackwood* or the *Quarterly* could possibly inflict; and also, when I feel I am right, no external praise can give me such a glow as my own solitary reperception and ratification of what is fine. J. S. is perfectly right in regard to the "slip-shod Endymion." That it is so is no fault of mine. No! though it may sound a little paradoxical, it is as good as I had power to make it by myself.'

And again, as if he had foreseen certain of his admirers gushing over him, and was resolved to disengage his responsibility:—

'I have done nothing, except for the amusement of a few people who refine upon their feelings till anything in the un-understandable way will go down with them. I have no cause to complain, because I am certain anything really fine will in these days be felt. I have no doubt that if I had written *Othello* I should have been cheered. I shall go on with patience.'

Young poets almost inevitably over-rate what they call 'the might of poesy,' and its power over the world which now is. Keats is not a dupe on this matter any more than he is a dupe about the merit of his own performances:—

'I have no trust whatever in poetry. I don't wonder at it; the marvel is to me how people read so much of it.'

His attitude towards the public is that of a strong man, not of a weakling avid of praise, and made to 'be snuff'd out by an article':—

'I shall ever consider the public as debtors to me for verses, not myself to them for admiration, which I can do without.'

And again, in a passage where one may perhaps find fault with the capital letters, but surely with nothing else:—

'I have not the slightest feel of humility towards the public or to anything in existence but the Eternal Being, the Principle of Beauty, and the Memory of great Men....I would be subdued before my friends, and thank them for subduing me; but among multitudes of men I have no feel of stooping; I hate the idea of humility to them. I never wrote one single line of poetry with the least shadow of thought about their opinion. Forgive me for vexing you, but it eases me to tell you: I could not live without the love of my friends; I would jump down Etna for any great public good—but I hate a mawkish popularity. I cannot be subdued before them. My glory would be to daunt and dazzle the thousand jabberers about pictures and books.'

Against these artistic and literary 'jabberers,' amongst whom Byron fancied Keats, probably, to be always living, flattering them and flattered by them, he has yet another outburst:—

'Just so much as I am humbled by the genius above my grasp, am I exalted and look with hate and contempt upon the literary world. Who could wish to be among the commonplace crowd of the little famous, who are each individually lost in a throng made up of themselves?'

And he loves Fanny Brawne the more, he tells her, because he believes that she has liked him for his own sake and for nothing else. 'I have met with women who I really think would like to be married to a Poem and to be given away by a Novel.'

There is a tone of too much bitterness and defiance in all this, a tone which he with great propriety subdued and corrected when he wrote his beautiful preface to *Endymion*. But the thing to be seized is, that Keats had flint and iron in him, that he had character; that he was, as his brother George says, 'as much like the Holy Ghost as *Johnny Keats*,'—as that imagined sensuous weakling, the delight of the literary circles of Hampstead.

It is a pity that Byron, who so misconceived Keats, should never have known how shrewdly Keats, on the other hand, had characterised *him*, as 'a fine thing' in the sphere of 'the worldly, theatrical, and pantomimical.' But indeed nothing is more remarkable in Keats than his clear-sightedness, his lucidity; and lucidity is in itself akin to character and to high and severe work. In spite, therefore, of his overpowering feeling for beauty, in spite of his sensuousness, in spite of his facility, in spite of his gift of expression, Keats could say resolutely:—

'I know nothing, I have read nothing; and I mean to follow Solomon's directions: "Get learning, get understanding." There is but one way for me. The road lies through application, study, and thought. I will pursue it.'

And of Milton, instead of resting in Milton's incomparable phrases, Keats could say, although indeed all the while 'looking upon fine phrases,' as he himself tells us, 'like a lover'—

'Milton had an exquisite passion for what is properly, in the
5   sense of ease and pleasure, poetical luxury; and with that, it appears to me, he would fain have been content, if he could, so doing, preserve his self-respect and feeling of duty performed; but there was working in him, as it were, that same sort of thing which operates in the great world to the end of a prophecy's
10 being accomplished. Therefore he devoted himself rather to the ardours than the pleasures of song, solacing himself at intervals with cups of old wine.'

In his own poetry, too, Keats felt that place must be found for 'the ardours rather than the pleasures of song,' although
15 he was aware that he was not yet ripe for it—

'But my flag is not unfurl'd
On the Admiral-staff, and to philosophise
I dare not yet.'

Even in his pursuit of 'the pleasures of song,' however,
20 there is that stamp of high work which is akin to character, which is character passing into intellectual production. '*The best sort of poetry*—that,' he truly says, 'is all I care for, all I live for.' It is curious to observe how this severe addiction of his to the best sort of poetry affects him with a certain
25 coldness, as if the addiction had been to mathematics, towards those prime objects of a sensuous and passionate poet's regard, love and women. He speaks of 'the opinion I have formed of the generality of women, who appear to me as children to whom I would rather give a sugar-plum than my time.' He
30 confesses 'a tendency to class women in my books with roses and sweetmeats—they never see themselves dominant'; and he can understand how the unpopularity of his poems may be in part due to 'the offence which the ladies,' not unnaturally, 'take at him' from this cause. Even to Fanny Brawne he can

write 'a flint-worded letter,' when his 'mind is heaped to the full' with poetry:—

'I know the generality of women would hate me for this; that I should have so unsoftened, so hard a mind as to forget them; forget the brightest realities for the dull imaginations of my own brain.... My heart seems now made of iron—I could not write a proper answer to an invitation to Idalia.'

The truth is that 'the yearning passion for the Beautiful,' which was with Keats, as he himself truly says, the master-passion, is not a passion of the sensuous or sentimental man, is not a passion of the sensuous or sentimental poet. It is an intellectual and spiritual passion. It is 'connected and made one,' as Keats declares that in his case it was, 'with the ambition of the intellect.' It is, as he again says, 'the mighty *abstract idea* of Beauty in all things.' And in his last days Keats wrote: 'If I should die, I have left no immortal work behind me—nothing to make my friends proud of my memory; *but I have loved the principle of beauty in all things*, and if I had had time I would have made myself remembered.' He *has* made himself remembered, and remembered as no merely sensuous poet could be; and he has done it by having 'loved the principle of beauty in all things.'

For to see things in their beauty is to see things in their truth, and Keats knew it. 'What the Imagination seizes as Beauty must be Truth,' he says in prose; and in immortal verse he has said the same thing—

> 'Beauty is truth, truth beauty,—that is all
> Ye know on earth, and all ye need to know.'

No, it is not all; but it is true, deeply true, and we have deep need to know it. And with beauty goes not only truth, joy goes with her also; and this too Keats saw and said, as in the famous first line of his *Endymion* it stands written—

> 'A thing of beauty is a joy for ever.'

It is no small thing to have so loved the principle of beauty as to perceive the necessary relation of beauty with truth, and of both with joy. Keats was a great spirit, and counts for far more than many even of his admirers suppose, because this just and high perception made itself clear to him. Therefore a dignity and a glory shed gleams over his life, and happiness, too, was not a stranger to it. 'Nothing startles me beyond the moment,' he says; 'the setting sun will always set me to rights, or if a sparrow come before my window I take part in its existence and pick about the gravel.' But he had terrible bafflers,—consuming disease and early death. 'I think,' he writes to Reynolds, 'if I had a free and healthy and lasting organisation of heart, and lungs as strong as an ox's, so as to be able to bear unhurt the shock of extreme thought and sensation without weariness, I could pass my life very nearly alone, though it should last eighty years. But I feel my body too weak to support me to the height; I am obliged continually to check myself, and be nothing.' He had against him even more than this; he had against him the blind power which we call Fortune. 'O that something fortunate,' he cries in the closing months of his life, 'had ever happened to me or my brothers!—then I might hope,—but despair is forced upon me as a habit.' So baffled and so sorely tried,—while laden, at the same time, with a mighty formative thought requiring health, and many days, and favouring circumstances, for its adequate manifestation,— what wonder if the achievement of Keats be partial and in- complete?

Nevertheless, let and hindered as he was, and with a short term and imperfect experience,—'young,' as he says of him- self, 'and writing at random, straining after particles of light in the midst of a great darkness, without knowing the bearing of any one assertion, of any one opinion,' —notwithstanding all this, by virtue of his feeling for beauty and of his perception of the vital connection of beauty with truth, Keats accom- plished so much in poetry, that in one of the two great modes by which poetry interprets, in the faculty of naturalistic inter- pretation, in what we call natural magic, he ranks with Shake- speare. 'The tongue of Kean,' he says in an admirable criticism of that great actor and of his enchanting elocution, 'the tongue of Kean must seem to have robbed the Hybla bees and left them honeyless. There is an indescribable *gusto* in his voice;—in *Richard*, "Be stirring with the lark to-morrow, gentle Norfolk!" comes from him as through the morning atmosphere towards which he yearns.' This magic, this 'indescribable *gusto* in the voice,' Keats himself, too, exhibits in his poetic expression. No one else in English poetry, save Shakespeare, has in expression quite the fascinating felicity of Keats, his perfection of loveliness. 'I think,' he said humbly, 'I shall be among the English poets after my death.' He is; he is with Shakespeare.

For the second great half of poetic interpretation, for that faculty of moral interpretation which is in Shakespeare, and is informed by him with the same power of beauty as his naturalistic interpretation, Keats was not ripe. For the architectonics of poetry, the faculty which presides at the evolution of works like the *Agamemnon* or *Lear*, he was not ripe. His *Endymion*, as he himself well saw, is a failure, and his *Hyperion*, fine things as it contains, is not a success. But in shorter things, where the matured power of moral interpretation, and the high architectonics which go with complete poetic development, are not required, he is perfect. The poems which follow prove it,—prove it far better by themselves than anything which can be said about them will prove it. Therefore I have chiefly spoken here of the man, and of the elements in him which explain the production of such work. Shakespearian work it is; not imitative, indeed, of Shakespeare, but Shakespearian, because its expression has that rounded perfection and felicity of loveliness of which Shakespeare is the great master. To show such work is to praise it. Let us now end by delighting ourselves with a fragment of it, too broken to find a place among the pieces which follow, but far too beautiful to be lost. It is a fragment of an ode for May-day. O might I, he cries to May, O might I

> '. . . thy smiles
> Seek as they once were sought, in Grecian isles,
> By bards who died content on pleasant sward,

Leaving great verse unto a little clan!
O, give me their old vigour, and unheard
Save of the quiet primrose, and the span
            Of heaven, and few ears,
5   Rounded by thee, my song should die away,
            Content as theirs,
Rich in the simple worship of a day!'

Byron[1]

When at last I held in my hand the volume of poems which I had chosen from Wordsworth, and began to turn over its pages, there arose in me almost immediately the desire to see beside it, as a companion volume, a like collection of the best poetry of Byron. Alone amongst our poets of the earlier part of this century, Byron and Wordsworth not only furnish material enough for a volume of this kind, but also, as it seems to me, they both of them gain considerably by being thus exhibited. There are poems of Coleridge and of Keats equal, if not superior, to anything of Byron or Wordsworth; but a dozen pages or two will contain them, and the remaining poetry is of a quality much inferior. Scott never, I think, rises as a poet to the level of Byron and Wordsworth at all. On the other hand, he never falls below his own usual level very far; and by a volume of selections from him, therefore, his effectiveness is not increased. As to Shelley there will be more question; and indeed Mr. Stopford Brooke, whose accomplishments, eloquence, and love of poetry we must all recognise and admire, has actually given us Shelley in such a volume. But for my own part I cannot think that Shelley's poetry, except by snatches and fragments, has the value of the good work of Wordsworth and Byron; or that it is possible for even Mr. Stopford Brooke to make up a volume of selections from him which, for real substance, power, and worth, can at all take rank with a like volume from Byron or Wordsworth.

Shelley knew quite well the difference between the achievement of such a poet as Byron and his own. He praises Byron

[1] Preface to *Poetry of Byron*, chosen and arranged by Matthew Arnold, 1881.

too unreservedly, but he sincerely felt, and he was right in feeling, that Byron was a greater poetical power than himself. As a
man, Shelley is at a number of points immeasurably Byron's
superior; he is a beautiful and enchanting spirit, whose vision,
when we call it up, has far more loveliness, more charm for
our soul, than the vision of Byron. But all the personal charm of
Shelley cannot hinder us from at last discovering in his poetry
the incurable want, in general, of a sound subject-matter, and
the incurable fault, in consequence, of unsubstantiality. Those
who extol him as the poet of clouds, the poet of sunsets, are
only saying that he did not, in fact, lay hold upon the poet's
right subject-matter; and in honest truth, with all his charm of
soul and spirit, and with all his gift of musical diction and
movement, he never, or hardly ever, did. Except, as I have said,
for a few short things and single stanzas, his original poetry is
less satisfactory than his translations, for in these the subject-
matter was found for him. Nay, I doubt whether his delightful
Essays and Letters, which deserve to be far more read than they
are now, will not resist the wear and tear of time better, and
finally come to stand higher, than his poetry.

      There remain to be considered Byron and Wordsworth. That
Wordsworth affords good material for a volume of selections,
and that he gains by having his poetry thus presented, is an
old belief of mine which led me lately to make up a volume of
poems chosen out of Wordsworth, and to bring it before the
public. By its kind reception of the volume, the public seems
to show itself a partaker in my belief. Now Byron also supplies plenty of material for a like volume, and he too gains, I
think, by being so presented. Mr. Swinburne urges, indeed, that
'Byron, who rarely wrote anything either worthless or faultless, can only be judged or appreciated in the mass; the greatest
of his works was his whole work taken altogether.' It is quite
true that Byron rarely wrote anything either worthless or
faultless; it is quite true also that in the appreciation of Byron's
power a sense of the amount and variety of his work, defective
though much of his work is, enters justly into our estimate.
But although there may be little in Byron's poetry which can
be pronounced either worthless or faultless, there are portions

of it which are far higher in worth and far more free from fault than others. And although, again, the abundance and variety of his production is undoubtedly a proof of his power, yet I question whether by reading everything which he gives us we are so likely to acquire an admiring sense even of his variety and abundance, as by reading what he gives us at his happier moments. Varied and abundant he amply proves himself even by this taken alone. Receive him absolutely without omission or compression, follow his whole outpouring stanza by stanza and line by line from the very commencement to the very end, and he is capable of being tiresome.

Byron has told us himself that the *Giaour* 'is but a string of passages.' He has made full confession of his own negligence. 'No one,' says he, 'has done more through negligence to corrupt the language.' This accusation brought by himself against his poems is not just; but when he goes on to say of them, that 'their faults, whatever they may be, are those of negligence and not of labour,' he says what is perfectly true. '*Lara*,' he declares, 'I wrote while undressing after coming home from balls and masquerades, in the year of revelry, 1814. The *Bride* was written in four, the *Corsair* in ten days.' He calls this 'a humiliating confession, as it proves my own want of judgment in publishing, and the public's in reading, things which cannot have stamina for permanence.' Again he does his poems injustice; the producer of such poems could not but publish them, the public could not but read them. Nor could Byron have produced his work in any other fashion; his poetic work could not have first grown and matured in his own mind, and then come forth as an organic whole; Byron had not enough of the artist in him for this, nor enough of self-command. He wrote, as he truly tells us, to relieve himself, and he went on writing because he found the relief become indispensable. But it was inevitable that works so produced should be, in general, 'a string of passages,' poured out, as he describes them, with rapidity and excitement, and with new passages constantly suggesting themselves, and added while his work was going through the press. It is evident that we have here neither deliberate scientific construction, nor yet the instinctive artistic creation of poetic

wholes; and that to take passages from work produced as
Byron's was is a very different thing from taking passages out
of the *Œdipus* or the *Tempest*, and deprives the poetry far
less of its advantage.

5   Nay, it gives advantage to the poetry, instead of depriving
it of any. Byron, I said, has not a great artist's profound and
patient skill in combining an action or in developing a character,—a skill which we must watch and follow if we are to
do justice to it. But he has a wonderful power of vividly con-

10   ceiving a single incident, a single situation; of throwing himself
upon it, grasping it as if it were real and he saw and felt it, and
of making us see and feel it too. The *Giaour* is, as he truly called
it, 'a string of passages,' not a work moving by a deep internal
law of development to a necessary end; and our total impression

15   from it cannot but receive from this, its inherent defect, a
certain dimness and indistinctness. But the incidents of the
journey and death of Hassan, in that poem, are conceived and
presented with a vividness not to be surpassed; and our impression from them is correspondingly clear and powerful. In *Lara*,

20   again, there is no adequate development either of the character
of the chief personage or of the action of the poem; our total
impression from the work is a confused one. Yet such an
incident as the disposal of the slain Ezzelin's body passes before
our eyes as if we actually saw it. And in the same way as these

25   bursts of incident, bursts of sentiment also, living and vigorous,
often occur in the midst of poems which must be admitted to
be but weakly-conceived and loosely-combined wholes. Byron
cannot but be a gainer by having attention concentrated upon
what is vivid, powerful, effective in his work, and withdrawn

30   from what is not so.

Byron, I say, cannot but be a gainer by this, just as Wordsworth is a gainer by a like proceeding. I esteem Wordsworth's
poetry so highly, and the world, in my opinion, has done it
such scant justice, that I could not rest satisfied until I had

35   fulfilled, on Wordsworth's behalf, a long-cherished desire;—
had disengaged, to the best of my power, his good work from
the inferior work joined with it, and had placed before the
public the body of his good work by itself. To the poetry of

Byron the world has ardently paid homage; full justice from his contemporaries, perhaps even more than justice, his torrent of poetry received. His poetry was admired, adored, 'with all its imperfections on its head,'—in spite of negligence, in spite of diffuseness, in spite of repetitions, in spite of whatever faults it possessed. His name is still great and brilliant. Nevertheless the hour of irresistible vogue has passed away for him; even for Byron it could not but pass away. The time has come for him, as it comes for all poets, when he must take his real and permanent place, no longer depending upon the vogue of his own day and upon the enthusiasm of his contemporaries. Whatever we may think of him, we shall not be subjugated by him as they were; for, as he cannot be for us what he was for them, we cannot admire him so hotly and indiscriminately as they. His faults of negligence, of diffuseness, of repetition, his faults of whatever kind, we shall abundantly feel and unsparingly criticise; the mere interval of time between us and him makes disillusion of this kind inevitable. But how then will Byron stand, if we relieve him too, so far as we can, of the encumbrance of his inferior and weakest work, and if we bring before us his best and strongest work in one body together? That is the question which I, who can even remember the latter years of Byron's vogue, and have myself felt the expiring wave of that mighty influence, but who certainly also regard him, and have long regarded him, without illusion, cannot but ask myself, cannot but seek to answer. The present volume is an attempt to provide adequate data for answering it.

Byron has been over-praised, no doubt. 'Byron is one of our French superstitions,' says M. Edmond Scherer; but where has Byron not been a superstition? He pays now the penalty of this exaggerated worship. 'Alone among the English poets his contemporaries, Byron,' said M. Taine, '*atteint à la cime*,—gets to the top of the poetic mountain.' But the idol that M. Taine had thus adored M. Scherer is almost for burning. 'In Byron,' he declares, 'there is a remarkable inability ever to lift himself into the region of real poetic art,—art impersonal and disinterested,—at all. He has fecundity, eloquence, wit, but even these qualities themselves are confined within somewhat narrow limits. He has treated hardly any subject but one,—himself; now the man, in Byron, is of a nature even less sincere than the poet. This beautiful and blighted being is at bottom a coxcomb. He posed all his life long.'

Our poet could not well meet with more severe and unsympathetic criticism. However, the praise often given to Byron has been so exaggerated as to provoke, perhaps, a reaction in which he is unduly disparaged. 'As various in composition as Shakespeare himself, Lord Byron has embraced,' says Sir Walter Scott, 'every topic of human life, and sounded every string on the divine harp, from its slightest to its most powerful and heart-astounding tones.' It is not surprising that some one with a cool head should retaliate, on such provocation as this, by saying: 'He has treated hardly any subject but one, *himself*.' 'In the very grand and tremendous drama of *Cain*,' says Scott, 'Lord Byron has certainly matched Milton on his own ground.' And Lord Byron has done all this, Scott adds, 'while managing his pen with the careless and negligent ease of a man of quality.' Alas, 'managing his pen with the careless and negligent ease of a man of quality,' Byron wrote in his *Cain*—

> 'Souls that dare look the Omnipotent tyrant in
> His everlasting face, and tell him that
> His evil is not good;'

or he wrote—

> '. . . And *thou* would'st go on aspiring
> To the great double Mysteries! the *two Principles!*'[1]

One has only to repeat to oneself a line from *Paradise Lost* in order to feel the difference.

Sainte-Beuve, speaking of that exquisite master of language, the Italian poet Leopardi, remarks how often we see the alliance, singular though it may at first sight appear, of the poetical genius with the genius for scholarship and philology. Dante and

[1] The italics are in the original.

Milton are instances which will occur to every one's mind.
Byron is so negligent in his poetical style, he is often, to say
the truth, so slovenly, slipshod, and infelicitous, he is so little
haunted by the true artist's fine passion for the correct use and
consummate management of words, that he may be described   5
as having for this artistic gift the insensibility of the barbarian;
—which is perhaps only another and a less flattering way of
saying, with Scott, that he 'manages his pen with the careless and
negligent ease of a man of quality.' Just of a piece with the
rhythm of   10

> 'Dare you await the event of a few minutes'
> Deliberation?'

or of

> 'All shall be void—
> Destroy'd!'   15

is the diction of

> 'Which now is painful to these eyes,
> Which have not seen the sun to rise;'

or of

> '. . . there let him lay!'   20

or of the famous passage beginning

> 'He who hath bent him o'er the dead;'

with those trailing relatives, that crying grammatical solecism,
that inextricable anacolouthon! To class the work of the author
of such things with the work of the authors of such verse as   25

> 'In the dark backward and abysm of time'—

or as

> 'Presenting Thebes, or Pelops' line,
>   Or the tale of Troy divine'—

is ridiculous. Shakespeare and Milton, with their secret of consummate felicity in diction and movement, are of another and
5   an altogether higher order from Byron, nay, for that matter,
from Wordsworth also; from the author of such verse as

> 'Sol hath dropt into his harbour'—

or (if Mr. Ruskin pleases) as

> 'Parching summer hath no warrant'—

10   as from the author of

> 'All shall be void—
>   Destroy'd!'

With a poetical gift and a poetical performance of the very
highest order, the slovenliness and tunelessness of much of By-
15   ron's production, the pompousness and ponderousness of much
of Wordsworth's, are incompatible. Let us admit this to the full.
    Moreover, while we are hearkening to M. Scherer, and going
along with him in his fault-finding, let us admit, too, that the
man in Byron is in many respects as unsatisfactory as the poet.
20   And, putting aside all direct moral criticism of him,—with
which we need not concern ourselves here,—we shall find that
he is unsatisfactory in the same way. Some of Byron's most
crying faults as a man,—his vulgarity, his affectation,—are
really akin to the faults of commonness, of want of art, in his
25   workmanship as a poet. The ideal nature for the poet and artist
is that of the finely touched and finely gifted man, the εὐφυής of
the Greeks; now, Byron's nature was in substance not that of
the εὐφυής at all, but rather, as I have said, of the barbarian.
The want of fine perception which made it possible for him to
30   formulate either the comparison between himself and Rousseau, or his reason for getting Lord Delawarr excused from a

'licking' at Harrow, is exactly what made possible for him also his terrible dealings in, *An ye wool; I have redde thee; Sunburn me; Oons, and it is excellent well.* It is exactly, again, what made possible for him his precious dictum that Pope is a Greek temple, and a string of other criticisms of the like force; it is exactly, in fine, what deteriorated the quality of his poetic production. If we think of a good representative of that finely touched and exquisitely gifted nature which is the ideal nature for the poet and artist,—if we think of Raphael, for instance, who truly is εὐφυής just as Byron is not,—we shall bring into clearer light the connection in Byron between the faults of the man and the faults of the poet. With Raphael's character Byron's sins of vulgarity and false criticism would have been impossible, just as with Raphael's art Byron's sins of common and bad workmanship.

Yes, all this is true, but it is not the whole truth about Byron nevertheless; very far from it. The severe criticism of M. Scherer by no means gives us the whole truth about Byron, and we have not yet got it in what has been added to that criticism here. The negative part of the true criticism of him we perhaps have; the positive part, by far the more important, we have not. Byron's admirers appeal eagerly to foreign testimonies in his favour. Some of these testimonies do not much move me; but one testimony there is among them which will always carry, with me at any rate, very great weight,—the testimony of Goethe. Goethe's sayings about Byron were uttered, it must however be remembered, at the height of Byron's vogue, when that puissant and splendid personality was exercising its full power of attraction. In Goethe's own household there was an atmosphere of glowing Byron-worship; his daughter-in-law was a passionate admirer of Byron, nay, she enjoyed and prized his poetry, as did Tieck and so many others in Germany at that time, much above the poetry of Goethe himself. Instead of being irritated and rendered jealous by this, a nature like Goethe's was inevitably led by it to heighten, not lower, the note of his praise. The Time-Spirit, or *Zeit-Geist*, he would himself have said, was working just then for Byron. This working of the *Zeit-Geist* in his favour was an advantage

added to Byron's other advantages, an advantage of which he had a right to get the benefit. This is what Goethe would have thought and said to himself; and so he would have been led even to heighten somewhat his estimate of Byron, and to ac-
5   centuate the emphasis of praise. Goethe speaking of Byron at that moment was not and could not be quite the same cool critic as Goethe speaking of Dante, or Molière, or Milton. This, I say, we ought to remember in reading Goethe's judgments on Byron and his poetry. Still, if we are careful to bear this in
10   mind, and if we quote Goethe's praise correctly,—which is not always done by those who in this country quote it,—and if we add to it that great and due qualification added to it by Goethe himself,—which so far as I have seen has never yet been done by his quoters in this country at all,—then we shall have
15   a judgment on Byron, which comes, I think, very near to the truth, and which may well command our adherence.

In his judicious and interesting Life of Byron, Professor Nichol quotes Goethe as saying that Byron 'is undoubtedly to be regarded as the greatest genius of our century.' What Goethe
20   did really say was 'the greatest *talent*,' not 'the greatest *genius*.' The difference is important, because, while talent gives the notion of power in a man's performance, genius gives rather the notion of felicity and perfection in it; and this divine gift of consummate felicity by no means, as we have seen, belongs
25   to Byron and to his poetry. Goethe said that Byron 'must un-questionably be regarded as the greatest talent of the century.'[1] He said of him moreover: 'The English may think of Byron what they please, but it is certain that they can point to no poet who is his like. He is different from all the rest, and in the
30   main greater.' Here, again, Professor Nichol translates: 'They can show no (living) poet who is to be compared to him;'— inserting the word *living*, I suppose, to prevent its being thought that Goethe would have ranked Byron, as a poet, above Shakespeare and Milton. But Goethe did not use, or, I think,
35   mean to imply, any limitation such as is added by Professor Nichol. Goethe said simply, and he meant to say, '*no* poet.'

[1] 'Der ohne Frage als das grösste Talent des Jahrhunderts anzusehen ist.'

Only the words which follow[1] ought not, I think, to be rendered, 'who is to be compared to him,' that is to say, '*who is his equal as a poet.*' They mean rather, 'who may properly be compared with him,' '*who is his parallel.*' And when Goethe said that Byron was 'in the main greater' than all the rest of the English poets, he was not so much thinking of the strict rank, as poetry, of Byron's production; he was thinking of that wonderful personality of Byron which so enters into his poetry, and which Goethe called 'a personality such, for its eminence, as has never been yet, and such as is not likely to come again.' He was thinking of that 'daring, dash, and grandiosity,'[2] of Byron, which are indeed so splendid; and which were, so Goethe maintained, of a character to do good, because 'everything great is formative,' and what is thus formative does us good.

The faults which went with this greatness, and which impaired Byron's poetical work, Goethe saw very well. He saw the constant state of warfare and combat, the 'negative and polemical working,' which makes Byron's poetry a poetry in which we can so little find rest; he saw the *Hang zum Unbegrenzten*, the straining after the unlimited, which made it impossible for Byron to produce poetic wholes such as the *Tempest* or *Lear;* he saw the *zu viel Empirie*, the promiscuous adoption of all the matter offered to the poet by life, just as it was offered, without thought or patience for the mysterious transmutation to be operated on this matter by poetic form. But in a sentence which I cannot, as I say, remember to have yet seen quoted in any English criticism of Byron, Goethe lays his finger on the cause of all these defects in Byron, and on his real source of weakness both as a man and as a poet. 'The moment he reflects, he is a child,' says Goethe;—'*sobald er reflectirt ist er ein Kind.*'

Now if we take the two parts of Goethe's criticism of Byron, the favourable and the unfavourable, and put them together,

---

[1] 'Der ihm zu vergleichen wäre.'

[2] 'Byron's Kühnheit, Keckheit und Grandiosität, ist das nicht alles bildend?—Alles Grosse bildet, sobald wir es gewahr werden.'

we shall have, I think, the truth. On the one hand, a splendid
and puissant personality—a personality 'in eminence such as
has never been yet, and is not likely to come again'; of which
the like, therefore, is not to be found among the poets of our
5   nation, by which Byron 'is different from all the rest, and in
the main greater.' Byron is, moreover, 'the greatest talent of
our century.' On the other hand, this splendid personality and
unmatched talent, this unique Byron, 'is quite too much in the
dark about himself;'[1] nay, 'the moment he begins to reflect, he
10   is a child.' Then we have, I think, Byron complete; and in
estimating him and ranking him we have to strike a balance
between the gain which accrues to his poetry, as compared
with the productions of other poets, from his superiority, and
the loss which accrues to it from his defects.

15   A balance of this kind has to be struck in the case of all poets
except the few supreme masters in whom a profound criticism
of life exhibits itself in indissoluble connection with the laws
of poetic truth and beauty. I have seen it said that I allege
poetry to have for its characteristic this: that it is a criticism
20   of life; and that I make it to be thereby distinguished from
prose, which is something else. So far from it, that when I first
used this expression, *a criticism of life*, now many years ago, it
was to literature in general that I applied it, and not to poetry
in especial. 'The end and aim of all literature,' I said, 'is, if one
25   considers it attentively, nothing but that: *a criticism of life*.'
And so it surely is; the main end and aim of all our utterance,
whether in prose or in verse, is surely a criticism of life. We
are not brought much on our way, I admit, towards an adequate definition of poetry as distinguished from prose by that
30   truth; still a truth it is, and poetry can never prosper if it is
forgotten. In poetry, however, the criticism of life has to be
made conformably to the laws of poetic truth and poetic
beauty. Truth and seriousness of substance and matter, felicity
and perfection of diction and manner, as these are exhibited in
35   the best poets, are what constitute a criticism of life made in
conformity with the laws of poetic truth and poetic beauty;
and it is by knowing and feeling the work of those poets, that

1 'Gar zu dunkel über sich selbst.'

we learn to recognize the fulfilment and non-fulfilment of such conditions.

The moment, however, that we leave the small band of the very best poets, the true classics, and deal with poets of the next rank, we shall find that perfect truth and seriousness of matter, in close alliance with perfect truth and felicity of manner, is the rule no longer. We have now to take what we can get, to forego something here, to admit compensation for it there; to strike a balance, and to see how our poets stand in respect to one another when that balance has been struck. Let us observe how this is so.

We will take three poets, among the most considerable of our century: Leopardi, Byron, Wordsworth. Giacomo Leopardi was ten years younger than Byron, and he died thirteen years after him; both of them, therefore, died young—Byron at the age of thirty-six, Leopardi at the age of thirty-nine. Both of them were of noble birth, both of them suffered from physical defect, both of them were in revolt against the established facts and beliefs of their age; but here the likeness between them ends. The stricken poet of Recanati had no country, for an Italy in his day did not exist; he had no audience, no celebrity. The volume of his poems, published in the very year of Byron's death, hardly sold, I suppose, its tens, while the volumes of Byron's poetry were selling their tens of thousands. And yet Leopardi has the very qualities which we have found wanting to Byron; he has the sense for form and style, the passion for just expression, the sure and firm touch of the true artist. Nay, more, he has a grave fulness of knowledge, an insight into the real bearings of the questions which as a sceptical poet he raises, a power of seizing the real point, a lucidity, with which the author of *Cain* has nothing to compare. I can hardly imagine Leopardi reading the

'. . . And *thou* would'st go on aspiring
To the great double Mysteries! the *two Principles!*'

or following Byron is his theological controversy with Dr. Kennedy, without having his features overspread by a calm

and fine smile, and remarking of his brilliant contemporary, as
Goethe did, that 'the moment he begins to reflect, he is a child.'
But indeed whoever wishes to feel the full superiority of Leopardi over Byron in philosophic thought, and in the expression
of it, has only to read one paragraph of one poem, the paragraph of *La Ginestra* beginning

'Sovente in queste piagge,'

and ending

'Non so se il riso o la pietà prevale.'

In like manner, Leopardi is at many points the poetic superior of Wordsworth too. He has a far wider culture than
Wordsworth, more mental lucidity, more freedom from illusions as to the real character of the established fact and of
reigning conventions; above all, this Italian, with his pure and
sure touch, with his fineness of perception, is far more of the
artist. Such a piece of pompous dulness as

'O for the coming of that glorious time,'

and all the rest of it, or such lumbering verse as Mr. Ruskin's
enemy,

'Parching summer hath no warrant'—

would have been as impossible to Leopardi as to Dante. Where,
then, is Wordsworth's superiority? for the worth of what he
has given us in poetry I hold to be greater, on the whole, than
the worth of what Leopardi has given us. It is in Wordsworth's
sound and profound sense

'Of joy in widest commonalty spread;'

whereas Leopardi remains with his thoughts ever fixed upon
the *essenza insanabile,* upon the *acerbo, indegno mistero delle
cose.* It is in the power with which Wordsworth feels the re-

sources of joy offered to us in nature, offered to us in the primary human affections and duties, and in the power with which, in his moments of inspiration, he renders this joy, and makes us, too, feel it; a force greater than himself seeming to lift him and to prompt his tongue, so that he speaks in a style far above   5
any style of which he has the constant command, and with a truth far beyond any philosophic truth of which he has the conscious and assured possession. Neither Leopardi nor Wordsworth are of the same order with the great poets who made such verse as   10

> Τλητὸν γὰρ Μοῖραι θυμὸν θέσαν ἀνθρώποισιν·

or as

> 'In la sua volontade è nostra pace;

or as

> '... Men must endure   15
> Their going hence, even as their coming hither;
> Ripeness is all.'

But as compared with Leopardi, Wordsworth, though at many points less lucid, though far less a master of style, far less of an artist, gains so much by his criticism of life being, in certain   20
matters of profound importance, healthful and true, whereas Leopardi's pessimism is not, that the value of Wordsworth's poetry, on the whole, stands higher for us than that of Leopardi's, as it stands higher for us, I think, than that of any modern poetry except Goethe's.   25

Byron's poetic value is also greater, on the whole, than Leopardi's; and his superiority turns in the same way upon the surpassing worth of something which he had and was, after all deduction has been made for his shortcomings. We talk of Byron's *personality*, 'a personality in eminence such as has never   30
been yet, and is not likely to come again;' and we say that by this personality Byron is 'different from all the rest of English poets, and in the main greater.' But can we not be a little more

circumstantial, and name that in which the wonderful power
of this personality consisted? We can; with the instinct of a
poet Mr. Swinburne has seized upon it and named it for us.
The power of Byron's personality lies in 'the splendid and im-
5   perishable excellence which covers all his offences and outweighs all his defects: *the excellence of sincerity and strength.*'
        Byron found our nation, after its long and victorious strug-
gle with revolutionary France, fixed in a system of established
facts and dominant ideas which revolted him. The mental bond-
10   age of the most powerful part of our nation, of its strong
middle class, to a narrow and false system of this kind, is what
we call British Philistinism. That bondage is unbroken to this
hour, but in Byron's time it was even far more deep and dark
than it is now. Byron was an aristocrat, and it is not difficult
15   for an aristocrat to look on the prejudices and habits of the
British Philistine with scepticism and disdain. Plenty of young
men of his own class Byron met at Almack's or at Lady Jersey's,
who regarded the established facts and reigning beliefs of the
England of that day with as little reverence as he did. But these
20   men, disbelievers in British Philistinism in private, entered
English public life, the most conventional in the world, and at
once they saluted with respect the habits and ideas of British
Philistinism as if they were a part of the order of creation, and
as if in public no sane man would think of warring against
25   them. With Byron it was different. What he called the *cant*
of the great middle part of the English nation, what we call
its Philistinism, revolted him; but the cant of his own class,
deferring to this Philistinism and profiting by it, while they
disbelieved in it, revolted him even more. 'Come what may,'
30   are his own words, 'I will never flatter the million's canting in
any shape.' His class in general, on the other hand, shrugged
their shoulders at this cant, laughed at it, pandered to it, and
ruled by it. The falsehood, cynicism, insolence, misgovernment,
oppression, with their consequent unfailing crop of human
35   misery, which were produced by this state of things, roused
Byron to irreconcilable revolt and battle. They made him indignant, they infuriated him; they were so strong, so defiant, so
maleficent,—and yet he felt that they were doomed. 'You have

seen every trampler down in turn,' he comforts himself with saying, 'from Buonaparte to the simplest individuals.' The old order, as after 1815 it stood victorious, with its ignorance and misery below, its cant, selfishness, and cynicism above, was at home and abroad equally hateful to him. 'I have simplified my politics,' he writes, 'into an utter detestation of all existing governments.' And again: 'Give me a republic. The king-times are fast finishing; there will be blood shed like water and tears like mist, but the peoples will conquer in the end. I shall not live to see it, but I foresee it.'

Byron himself gave the preference, he tells us, to politicians and doers, far above writers and singers. But the politics of his own day and of his own class,—even of the Liberals of his own class,—were impossible for him. Nature had not formed him for a Liberal peer, proper to move the Address in the House of Lords, to pay compliments to the energy and self-reliance of British middle-class Liberalism, and to adapt his politics to suit it. Unfitted for such politics, he threw himself upon poetry as his organ; and in poetry his topics were not Queen Mab, and the Witch of Atlas, and the Sensitive Plant— they were the upholders of the old order, George the Third and Lord Castlereagh and the Duke of Wellington and Southey, and they were the canters and tramplers of the great world, and they were his enemies and himself.

Such was Byron's personality, by which 'he is different from all the rest of English poets, and in the main greater.' But he posed all his life, says M. Scherer. Let us distinguish. There is the Byron who posed, there is the Byron with his affectations and silliness, the Byron whose weakness Lady Blessington, with a woman's acuteness, so admirably seized: 'His great defect is flippancy and a total want of self-possession.' But when this theatrical and easily criticised personage betook himself to poetry, and when he had fairly warmed to his work, then he became another man; then the theatrical personage passed away; then a higher power took possession of him and filled him; then at last came forth into light that true and puissant personality, with its direct strokes, its ever-welling force, its satire, its energy, and its agony. This is the real Byron; whoever stops

at the theatrical preludings does not know him. And this real
Byron may well be superior to the stricken Leopardi, he may
well be declared 'different from all the rest of English poets, and
in the main greater,' in so far as it is true of him, as M. Taine
well says, that 'all other souls, in comparison with his, seem
inert'; in so far as it is true of him that with superb, exhaustless
energy he maintained, as Professor Nichol well says, 'the struggle that keeps alive, if it does not save, the soul;' in so far,
finally, as he deserves (and he does deserve) the noble praise
of him which I have already quoted from Mr. Swinburne; the
praise for 'the splendid and imperishable excellence which
covers all his offences and outweighs all his defects: *the excellence of sincerity and strength.*'

True, as a man, Byron could not manage himself, could not
guide his ways aright, but was all astray. True, he has no light,
cannot lead us from the past to the future; 'the moment he
reflects, he is a child.' The way out of the false state of things
which enraged him he did not see,—the slow and laborious way
upward; he had not the patience, knowledge, self-discipline,
virtue, requisite for seeing it. True, also, as a poet, he has no fine
and exact sense for word and structure and rhythm; he has not
the artist's nature and gifts. Yet a personality of Byron's force
counts for so much in life, and a rhetorician of Byron's force
counts for so much in literature! But it would be most unjust
to label Byron, as M. Scherer is disposed to label him, as a
rhetorician only. Along with his astounding power and passion
he had a strong and deep sense for what is beautiful in nature,
and for what is beautiful in human action and suffering. When
he warms to his work, when he is inspired, Nature herself
seems to take the pen from him as she took it from Wordsworth,
and to write for him as she wrote for Wordsworth, though in
a different fashion, with her own penetrating simplicity. Goethe
has well observed of Byron, that when he is at his happiest his
representation of things is as easy and real as if he were im-
provising. It is so; and his verse then exhibits quite another and
a higher quality from the rhetorical quality,—admirable as this
also in its own kind of merit is,—of such verse as

'Minions of splendour shrinking from distress,'

and of so much more verse of Byron's of that stamp. Nature, I say, takes the pen for him; and then, assured master of a true poetic style though he is not, any more than Wordsworth, yet as from Wordsworth at his best there will come such verse as

'Will no one tell me what she sings?' 5

so from Byron, too, at his best, there will come such verse as

'He heard it, but he heeded not; his eyes
Were with his heart, and that was far away.'

Of verse of this high quality, Byron has much; of verse of a quality lower than this, of a quality rather rhetorical than truly 10 poetic, yet still of extraordinary power and merit, he has still more. To separate, from the mass of poetry which Byron poured forth, all this higher portion, so superior to the mass, and still so considerable in quantity, and to present it in one body by itself, is to do a service, I believe, to Byron's reputation, 15 and to the poetic glory of our country.

Such a service I have in the present volume attempted to perform. To Byron, after all the tributes which have been paid to him, here is yet one tribute more—

'Among thy mightier offerings here are mine!' 20

not a tribute of boundless homage certainly, but sincere; a tribute which consists not in covering the poet with eloquent eulogy of our own, but in letting him, at his best and greatest, speak for himself. Surely the critic who does most for his author is the critic who gains readers for his author himself, 25 not for any lucubrations on his author;—gains more readers for him, and enables those readers to read him with more admiration.

And in spite of his prodigious vogue, Byron has never yet, perhaps, had the serious admiration which he deserves. Society 30 read him and talked about him, as it reads and talks about *Endymion* to-day; and with the same sort of result. It looked in Byron's glass as it looks in Lord Beaconsfield's, and sees, or fancies that it sees, its own face there; and then it goes its way,

and straightway forgets what manner of man it saw. Even of his passionate admirers, how many never got beyond the theatrical Byron, from whom they caught the fashion of deranging their hair, or of knotting their neck-handkerchief, or of
5 leaving their shirt-collar unbuttoned; how few profoundly felt his vital influence, the influence of his splendid and imperishable excellence of sincerity and strength!

His own aristocratic class, whose cynical make-believe drove him to fury; the great middle class, on whose impregnable
10 Philistinism he shattered himself to pieces,—how little have either of these felt Byron's vital influence! As the inevitable break-up of the old order comes, as the English middle class slowly awakens from its intellectual sleep of two centuries, as our actual present world, to which this sleep has condemned
15 us, shows itself more clearly,—our world of an aristocracy materialised and null, a middle class purblind and hideous, a lower class crude and brutal,—we shall turn our eyes again, and to more purpose, upon this passionate and dauntless soldier of a forlorn hope, who, ignorant of the future and unconsoled by
20 its promises, nevertheless waged against the conservation of the old impossible world so fiery battle; waged it till he fell,— waged it with such splendid and imperishable excellence of sincerity and strength.

Wordsworth's value is of another kind. Wordsworth has an
25 insight into permanent sources of joy and consolation for mankind which Byron has not; his poetry gives us more which we may rest upon than Byron's,—more which we can rest upon now, and which men may rest upon always. I place Wordsworth's poetry, therefore, above Byron's on the whole, al
30 though in some points he was greatly Byron's inferior, and although Byron's poetry will always, probably, find more readers than Wordsworth's, and will give pleasure more easily. But these two, Wordsworth and Byron, stand, it seems to me, first and pre-eminent in actual performance, a glorious pair,
35 among the English poets of this century. Keats had probably, indeed, a more consummate poetic gift than either of them; but he died having produced too little and being as yet too immature to rival them. I for my part can never even think of

equalling with them any other of their contemporaries;— either Coleridge, poet and philosopher wrecked in a mist of opium; or Shelley, beautiful and ineffectual angel, beating in the void his luminous wings in vain. Wordsworth and Byron stand out by themselves. When the year 1900 is turned, and our nation comes to recount her poetic glories in the century which has then just ended, the first names with her will be these.

The Incompatibles

I

The Irish Land Bill has not yet, at the moment when I write this, made its appearance. No one is very eager, I suppose, to read more about the Irish Land Bill while we do not yet know what the Bill will be. Besides, and above all, no one under any circumstances, perhaps, can much care to read what an insignificant person, and one who has no special connection with Ireland, may have to say about the grave and sad affairs of that country.

But even the most insignificant Englishman, and the least connected with Ireland and things Irish, has a deep concern, surely, in the present temper and action of the Irish people towards England, and must be impelled to seek for the real explanation of them. We find ourselves,—though conscious, as we assure one another, of nothing but goodwill to all the world,—we find ourselves the object of a glowing, fierce, unexplained hatred on the part of the Irish people. "The Liberal Ministry resolved," said one of our leading Liberal statesmen a few years ago, when the Irish Church Establishment was abolished, "the Liberal Ministry resolved to knit the hearts of the empire into one harmonious concord, and knitted they were accordingly." "Knitted" indeed! The Irish people send members to our Parliament, whose great recommendation with their constituencies is, says Miss Charlotte O'Brien, that they are wolves ready to fly at the throat of England; and more and more of these wolves, we are told, are likely to be sent over to us. These wolves ravin and destroy in the most savage and mortifying way; they obstruct our business, lacerate our good

name, deface our dignity, make our cherished fashions of government impossible and ridiculous. And then come eloquent
rhetoricians, startling us with the prediction that Ireland will
have either to be governed in future despotically, or to be
given up. Even more alarming are certain grave and serious
observers, who will not leave us even the cold comfort of the
rhetorician's alternative, but declare that Ireland is irresistibly
drifting to a separation from us, and to an unhappy separation;
—a separation which will bring confusion and misery to Ireland,
danger to us.

For my part, I am entirely indisposed to believe the eloquent
rhetoricians who tell us that Ireland must either be governed
for the future as a Crown colony or must be given up. I am
also entirely indisposed to believe the despondent observers
who tell us that Ireland is fatally and irresistibly drifting to a
separation, and a miserable separation, from England. I no more
believe the eloquent rhetoricians than I should believe them if
they prophesied to me that Scotland, Wales, or Cornwall would
have either to be governed as Crown colonies for the future, or
to be given up. I no more believe the despondent observers
than I should believe them if they assured me that Scotland,
Wales, or Cornwall were fatally and irresistibly drifting to a
miserable separation from England. No doubt Ireland presents
many and great difficulties, and England has many and great
faults and shortcomings. But after all the English people, with
"its ancient and inbred piety, integrity, good nature, and good
humour," has considerable merits, and has done considerable
things in the world. In presence of such terrifying predictions
and assurances as those which I have been just quoting, it becomes right and necessary to say so. I refuse to believe that
such a people is unequal to the task of blending Ireland with
itself in the same way that Scotland, Wales, and Cornwall are
blended with us, if it sets about the task seriously.

True, there are difficulties. One of the greatest is to be
found in our English habit of adopting a conventional account
of things, satisfying our own minds with it, and then imagining
that it will satisfy other people's minds also, and may really be
relied on. Goethe, that sagest of critics, and moreover a

great lover and admirer of England, noted this fault in us. "It is good in the English," says he, "that they are always for being practical in their dealings with things, *aber sie sind Pedanten,* —but they are pedants." The pedant is he who is governed 5 by phrases and does not get to the reality of things. Elsewhere Goethe attributes this want of insight in the English, their acceptance of phrase and convention, and their trust in these, —their pedantry in short,—to the habits of our public life, and to the reign amongst us of party spirit and party formulas. 10 Burke supplies a remarkable confirmation of this account of the matter, when he complains of Parliament as being a place where it is "the business of a Minister still further to contract the narrowness of men's ideas, to confirm inveterate prejudices, to inflame vulgar passions, and to abet all sorts of 15 popular absurdities." The true explanation of any matter is therefore seldom come at by us, but we rest in that account of things which it suits our class, our party, our leaders, to adopt and to render current. We adopt a version of things because we choose, not because it really represents them; and we ex-20 pect it to hold good because we wish that it may.

But "it is not your fond desire or mine," says Burke again, "that can alter the nature of things; by contending against which, what have we got, or shall ever get, but defeat and shame?" These words of Burke should be laid to heart by us. 25 We shall solve at last, I hope and believe, the difficulty which the state of Ireland presents to us. But we shall never solve it without first understanding it; and we shall never understand it while we pedantically accept whatever accounts of it happen to pass current with our class, or party, or leaders, and to be 30 recommended by our fond desire and theirs. We must see the matter as it really stands; we must cease to ignore, and to try to set aside, the nature of things; "by contending against which, what have we got, or shall ever get, but defeat and shame?"

Pedantry and conventionality, therefore, are dangerous when 35 we are in difficulties; and our habits of class and party action, and our ways of public discussion, tend to encourage pedantry and conventionality in us. Now there are insignificant people, detached from classes and parties and their great movements, people unclassed and unconsidered, but who yet are lovers of their country, and lovers of the humane life and of civilisation, and therefore grievously distressed at the condition in which they see Ireland and Irish sentiment at the present time, and appalled at the prophecies they hear of the turn which 5 things in Ireland must certainly take. Such persons,—who after all, perhaps, are not so very few in number,—may well desire to talk the case over one to another in their own quiet and simple way, without pedantry and conventionality, admitting unchallenged none of the phrases with which classes and parties 10 are apt to settle matters, resolving to looks things full in the face and let them stand for what they really are; in order that they may ascertain whether there is any chance of comfort in store, or whether things are really as black and hopeless as we are told. Let us perish in the light, at any rate (if perish we 15 must), and not in a cloud of pedantry; let us look fairly into that incompatibility, alleged to be incurable, between us and the Irish nation.

Even to talk of the people inhabiting an island quite near to us, and which we have governed ever since the twelfth century, 20 as a distinct nation from ourselves, ought to seem strange and absurd to us;—as strange and absurd as to talk of the people inhabiting Brittany as a distinct nation from the French. However, we know but too well that the Irish consider themselves a distinct nation from us, and that some of their leaders, upon 25 this ground, claim for them a parliament, and even an army and navy and a diplomacy, separate and distinct from ours. And this, again, ought to seem as strange and absurd as for Scotland or Wales or Cornwall to claim a parliament, an army and navy, and a diplomacy, distinct from ours; or as for Brittany or 30 Provence to claim a parliament, an army and navy, and a diplomacy, distinct from those of France. However, it is a fact that for Ireland such claims are made, while for Scotland, Wales, Cornwall, Brittany, and Provence, they are not. That is because Scotland, Wales, and Cornwall are really blended in national 35 feeling with us, and Brittany and Provence with the rest of France. And it is well that people should come to understand

and feel that it is quite incumbent on a nation to have its parts
blended together in a common national feeling; and that there
is insecurity, there is reason for mortification and humiliation,
if they are not. At last this much, at least, has been borne in
5   upon the mind of the general public in England, which for a
long while troubled itself not at all about the matter,—that it is
a ground of insecurity to us, and a cause of mortification and
humiliation, that we have so completely failed to attach Ireland. I remember when I was visiting schools in Alsace twenty
10 years ago, I noticed a number of points in which questions of
language and religion seemed to me likely to raise irritation
against the French government, and to call forth in the people
of Alsace the sense of their separate nationality. Yet all such
irritating points were smoothed down by the power of a com-
15 mon national feeling with France; and we all know how deeply
German and Protestant Alsace regretted, and still regrets, the
loss of her connection with France Celtic and Catholic. Undoubtedly this does great honour to French civilisation and to
its attractive forces. We, on the other hand, Germanic and
20 Protestant England, we have utterly failed to attach Celtic and
Catholic Ireland, although our language prevails there, and
although we have no great counter-nationality on the borders
of Ireland to compete with us for the possession of her affections, as the French had Germany on the borders of Alsace.
25   England holds Ireland, say the Irish, by means of conquest
and confiscation. But almost all countries have undergone conquest and confiscation; and almost all property, if we go back
far enough, has its source in these violent proceedings. After
such proceedings, however, people go about their daily busi-
30 ness, gradually things settle down, there is well-being and toler-
able justice, prescription arises, and nobody talks about
conquest and confiscation any more. The Frankish conquest
of France, the Norman conquest of England, came in this
way, with time, to be no longer talked of, to be no longer even
35 thought of.
     The seizure of Strasburg by France is an event belonging to
modern history. It was a violent and scandalous act. But it has
long ago ceased to stir resentment in a single Alsatian bosom. On
the other hand, the English conquest of Ireland took place little

more than a century after the Norman conquest of England. But in Ireland it did not happen that people went about their daily business, that their condition improved, that things settled down, that the country became peaceful and prosperous, and that gradually all remembrance of conquest and confiscation died out. On the contrary the conquest had again and again to be renewed; the sense of prescription, the true security of all property, never arose. The angry memory of conquest and confiscation, the ardour for revolt against them, have continued, therefore, to irritate and inflame men's minds. They irritate and inflame them still; the present relations between landlord and tenant in Ireland offer only too much proof of it.

But this is only saying over again that England has failed to attach Ireland. We must ask, then, what it is which makes things, after a conquest, settle peaceably down, what makes a sense of prescription arise, what makes property secure and blends the conquered people into one nation with the conquerors. Certainly we must put, as one of the first and chief causes, general well-being. Never mind how misery arises, whether by the fault of the conquered or by the fault of the conqueror, its very existence prevents the solid settlement of things, prevents the dying out of desires for revolt and change.

Now, let us consult the testimonies from Elizabeth's reign, when the middle age had ended and the modern age had begun, down to the present time. First we have this picture of Irish misery by the poet Spenser:—

"Out of every corner of the woods and glens they came creeping forth upon their hands, for their legs could not bear them; they looked like anatomies of death, they spake like ghosts crying out of their graves; they did eat the dead carrions, happy where they could find them, yea, and one another soon after, insomuch as the very carcases they spared not to scrape out of their graves; and if they found a plot of water-cresses or shamrocks there, they flocked as to a feast for the time, yet not able long to continue these withal; that in short space there were none almost left."

Then, a hundred and forty years later, we have another picture of Irish misery, a picture drawn by the terrible hand of Swift. He describes "the miserable dress and diet and dwelling of the people, the general desolation in most parts of the kingdom." He says:—

"Some persons of a desponding spirit are in great concern about the aged, diseased, or maimed poor; but I am not in the least pain upon that matter, because it is very well known that they are every day dying and rotting by cold and famine, and filth and vermin, as fast as can be reasonably expected."

And again:—

"I confess myself to be touched with a very sensible pleasure when I hear of a mortality in any country parish or village, where the wretches are forced to pay, for a filthy cabin and two ridges of potatoes, treble the worth; brought up to steal or beg, for want of work; to whom death would be the best thing to be wished for, on account both of themselves and the public."

Next and finally, after the lapse of a hundred and fifty years more, coming down to our own day, we have this sentence, strong and short, from Colonel Gordon:—

"The state of our fellow-countrymen in the south-west of Ireland is worse than that of any people in the world,—let alone Europe."

I say, where there is this misery going on for centuries after a conquest, acquiescence in the conquest cannot take place;—a sense of permanent settlement and of the possessors' prescriptive title to their property cannot spring up, the conquered cannot blend themselves into one nation with their conquerors. English opinion, indeed, attributes Irish misery to the faults of the Irish themselves, to their insubordination, to their idleness and improvidence, and to their Popish religion. But however the misery arises, there cannot, as I have already said, be fusion, there cannot be forgetfulness of past violences and confiscations, while the misery lasts. Still, if the misery is due to the faults of the Irish, it is in curing faults on their side that we have to seek the remedy, not in curing faults of our own.

Undoubtedly the native Irish have the faults which we commonly attribute to them. Undoubtedly those Anglo-Irish, who lead them, too often superadd to the passionate unreason of the natives our own domestic hardness and narrow doggedness, and the whole makes a very unpleasant mixture. Undoubtedly it is not agreeable to have people offering to fly like wolves at your throat,—these people knowing, at the same time, that you will not put out your full strength against them, and covering you on that account with all the more menace and contumely. England must often enough be disposed to answer such assailants gruffly, to vow that she will silence them once for all, and to ejaculate, as Cæsar did when he threatened to silence the tribune Metellus: "And when I say this, young man, to say it is more trouble to me than to do it." Were there ever people, indeed, who so aggravated their own difficulties as the Irish people, so increased the labour and sorrow of him who toils to find a remedy for their ills? "Always ready to react against the despotism of fact,"—so their best friend[1] among their French kinsmen describes them. "Poor brainsick creatures!"—a sterner critic[2] among these kinsmen says,—"poor brainsick creatures, distraught with misery and incurable ignorance! by inflaming themselves against the English connection, by refusing to blend their blood, their habits, their hopes, with those of the leading country, they are preparing for themselves a more miserable future than that of any other people in Europe." It seems as if this poor Celtic people were bent on making what one of its own poets has said of its heroes hold good for ever: "They went forth to the war, *but they always fell.*"

All this may be very true. But still we ought to know whether the faults and misery of the Irish are due solely to themselves, and all we can do is to hold down the poor brainsick creatures and punish them, which, to say the truth, we have done freely enough in the past; or whether their state is due, either in whole or in large part, to courses followed by ourselves, and not even yet discontinued by us entirely, in which it may be possible to make a change.

Now, I imagine myself to be at present talking quietly to

[1] M. Henri Martin.   [2] A writer in the *République Française.*

open-minded, unprejudiced, simple people, free from class
spirit and party spirit, resolved to forswear self-delusion and
make-believe, not to be pedants, but to see things as they really
are. Such people will surely be most anxious, just as I too was
anxious, on this question of the rights and the wrongs in England's dealings with Ireland, to put themselves in good hands.
And if they find a guide whom they can thoroughly trust they
will not be restive or perverse with him; they will admit his
authority frankly. Now, Edmund Burke is here a guide whom
we can thus trust. Burke is, it seems to me, the greatest of
English statesmen in this sense, at any rate: that he is the only
one who traces the reason of things in politics and who enables
us to trace it too. Compared with him, Fox is a brilliant and
generous schoolboy, and Pitt is a schoolboy with a gift (such
as even at school not unfrequently comes out) for direction
and government. Burke was, moreover, a great *conservative*
statesman,—conservative in the best sense. On the French Revolution his utterances are not entirely those of the Burke of the
best time, of the Burke of the American War. He was abundantly wise in condemning the crudity and tyrannousness of
the revolutionary spirit. Still, there has to be added to Burke's
picture of the Revolution a side which he himself does not
furnish; we ought to supplement him, as we read him, and
sometimes to correct him. But on Ireland, which he knew
thoroughly, he was always the Burke of the best time; he never
varied; his hatred of Jacobinism did not here make him go back
one hair's-breadth. "I am of the same opinion," he writes in
1797 (the year in which he died), "to my last breath, which I
entertained when my faculties were at the best." Mr. John
Morley's admirable biography has interested all of us afresh
in Burke's life and genius; the Irish questions which now press
upon us should make us seek out and read every essay, letter,
and speech of Burke on the subject of Ireland.

Burke is clear in the opinion that down to the end of his life,
at any rate, Irish misery and discontent have been due more to
English misgovernment and injustice than to Irish faults. "We
found the people heretics and idolaters," he says; "we have,
by way of improving their condition, rendered them slaves and

beggars; they remain in all the misfortune of their old errors, and all the superadded misery of their recent punishment." It is often alleged in England that the repeated confiscations of Irish lands and even the Popery Laws themselves, were necessitated by the rebelliousness and intractableness of the Irish themselves; the country could only be held down for England by a Protestant garrison, and through these severe means. Burke dissipates this flattering illusion. Even the Penal Code itself, he says, even "the laws of that unparalleled code of oppression, were manifestly the effects of national hatred and scorn towards a conquered people, whom the victors delighted to trample upon, and were not at all afraid to provoke. *They were not the effect of their fears, but of their security.* They who carried on this system looked to the irresistible force of Great Britain for their support in their acts of power. They were quite certain that no complaints of the natives would be heard on this side of the water with any other sentiments than those of contempt and indignation. In England, the double name of the complainant, Irish and Papist (it would be hard to say which singly was the most odious), shut up the hearts of every one against them. They were looked upon as a race of bigoted savages, who were a disgrace to human nature itself."

And therefore, although Burke declared that "hitherto the plan for the government of Ireland has been to sacrifice the civil prosperity of the nation to its religious improvement," yet he declared, also, that "*it is injustice, and not a mistaken conscience,* that has been the principle of persecution." That "melancholy and invidious title," he says, "the melancholy and unpleasant title of grantees of confiscation, is a favourite." The grantees do not even wish "to let Time draw his oblivious veil over the unpleasant modes by which lordships and demesnes have been acquired in theirs and almost in all other countries upon earth." On the contrary, "they inform the public of Europe that their estates are made up of forfeitures and confiscations from the natives. They abandon all pretext of the general good of the community." The Popery Laws were but part of a system for enabling the grantees of confiscation to hold Ireland without blending with the natives or reconciling them.

The object of those laws, and their effect, was "to reduce the
Catholics of Ireland to a miserable populace, without property,
without estimation, without education. They divided the nation
into two distinct bodies, without common interest, sympathy,
or connection. One of these branches was to possess *all* the
franchises, *all* the property, *all* the education; the other was to
be composed of drawers of water and cutters of turf for them."

In short, the mass of the Irish people were kept without well-
being and without justice. Now if well-being is a thing needed
to make a conquered people one with its conquerors, so is
justice, and so, also, is good treatment and kindness. Well might
Burke adjure all concerned to "reflect upon the possible consequences of keeping, in the heart of your country, a bank of
discontent every hour accumulating, upon which every description of seditious men may draw at pleasure." Well might
he austerely answer that worthy Philistine at Bristol who re-
monstrated with them against making concessions to the Irish:
"Sir, it is proper to inform you that our measures *must be
healing.*"[1] Well might he add: "Their temper, too, must be
managed, and their good affections cultivated." Burke hated
Jacobinism, the angry and premature destruction of the existing order of things, even more than he hated Protestant ascendency. But this, he remarked, led straight to the other. "If
men are kept as being no better than half citizens for any length
of time, they will be made whole Jacobins."

In 1797 this great man died, without having convinced Parliament or the nation of truths which he himself saw so clearly,
and had seen all his life. In his very last years, while he was
being hailed as the grand defender of thrones and altars, while
George the Third thanked him for his *Reflections on the
French Revolution,* and while that book was lying on the table
of every great house and every parsonage in England, Burke
writes that as regards Ireland he is absolutely without influence,
and that, if any Irish official were known to share his views,
such a man would probably be dismissed. What an illustration
of the truth of Goethe's criticism on us: "Their Parliamentary
parties are great opposing forces which paralyse one another,

[1] The italics are Burke's own.

and where the superior insight of an individual can hardly break through!"

Burke died three years before the Union. He left behind him two warnings, both of them full of truth, full of gravity. One is, that concessions, sufficient if given in good time and at a particular conjuncture of events, become insufficient if deferred. The other is, that concessions, extorted from embarrassment and fear, produce no gratitude, and allay no resentment. "God forbid," he cries, "that our conduct should demonstrate to the world that Great Britain can in no instance whatsoever be brought to a sense of rational and equitable policy, but by coercion and force of arms."

Burke thought, as every sane man must think, "connection between Great Britain and Ireland essential to the welfare of both." He was for a Union. But he doubted whether the particular time of the closing years of the last century was favourable for a Union. Mr. Lecky, in his delightful book, *The Leaders of Public Opinion in Ireland,* expresses a like doubt. The restrictions on Irish trade had given to the Anglo-Irish and to the native Irish a joint interest, adverse to those restrictions; they had acted together in this interest, they had acted together on behalf of Irish independence; the beginnings of a common national feeling between them had sprung up. The Catholics had been admitted to vote for members of Parliament, and it seemed likely that they would soon be declared capable of sitting in Parliament. But the Union came, and imported into the settlement of that matter a new personage, our terrible friend the British Philistine. And for thirty years this personage, of whose ideas George the Third was the faithful mouthpiece, delayed Catholic emancipation, which, without the Union, would probably have been granted much sooner. John Wesley wrote, Mr. Lecky tells us, against the withdrawal of the penal laws. At last, in 1829, the disabilities of Catholics were taken off,—but in dread of an insurrection. A wise man might at that moment well have recalled Burke's two warnings. What was done in 1829 could not have the sufficiency which in 1800 it might have had; what was yielded in dread of insurrection could not produce gratitude.

Meanwhile Irish misery went on; there were loud complaints of the "grantees of confiscation," the landlords. Ministers replied, that the conduct of many landlords was deplorable, and that absenteeism was a great evil, but that nothing could be done against them, and that the sufferers must put their hopes in "general sympathy." The people pullulated in the warm steam of their misery; famine and Fenianism appeared. Great further concessions have since been made;—the abolition of tithes, the abolition of the Irish Church Establishment, the Land Act of 1870. But with respect to every one of them Burke's warnings hold good; they were given too late to produce the effect which they might have produced earlier, and they seemed to be given not from a desire to do justice, but from the apprehension of danger. Finally, we have to-day in parts of Ireland the misery to which Colonel Gordon bears witness; we have the widespread agitation respecting the land; we have the Irish people, if not yet "whole Jacobins," as Burke said we were making them, at least in a fair way to become so. And to meet these things we have coercion and the promised Land Bill.

For my part, I do not object, wherever I see disorder, to see coercion applied to it. And in Ireland there has been, and there is, most serious disorder. I do not agree with the orators of popular meetings, and I do not agree with some Liberals with whom I agree in general, I do not agree with them in objecting to apply coercion to Irish disorder, or to any other. Tumultuously doing what one likes is the ideal of the populace; it is not mine. True, concessions have often been wrung from governments only by the fear of tumults and disturbances, but it is an unsafe way of winning them, and concessions so won, as Burke has shown us, are never lucky. Unswerving firmness in repressing disorder is always a government's duty; so, too, is unswerving firmness in redressing injustice. It will be said that we have often governments firm enough in repressing disorder, who, after repressing it, leave injustice still unredressed. True; but it is our business to train ourselves, and to train public opinion, to make governments do otherwise, and do better. It is our business to bring them, not to be irresolute in repressing disorder, but to be both resolute in repressing disorder, and resolute, also, in redressing injustice.

"Sir, it is proper to inform you that our measures *must be healing*." Ireland has had injustice and ill-treatment from us; measures are wanted which shall redress them and wipe out their memory. I do not yet know what the new Land Bill will be. But we have the Land Act of 1870 before our eyes, and we are told that proceeding a good deal farther upon the lines of that Act is what is intended. Will this be *healing?*—that is the question. I confess that if one has no class or party interests to warp one, and if one is resolved not to be a pedant, but to look at things simply and naturally, it seems difficult to think so.

The truth is, as every one who is honest with himself must perceive,—the truth is, what is most needed, in dealing with the land in Ireland, is to redress our injustice, and to make the Irish see that we are doing so. And the most effective way, surely, to do this is not to confer boons on all tenants, but to execute justice on bad landlords. Property is sacred, will be the instant reply; the landlords, good or bad, have prescription in their favour. Property is sacred when it has prescription in its favour; but the very point is, that in Ireland prescription has never properly arisen. There has been such lack of well-being and justice there, that things have never passed,—at least they have never throughout the whole length and breadth of Ireland passed,—out of their first violent, confiscatory stage. "I shall never praise either confiscations or counter-confiscations," says Burke. A wise man will not approve the violences of a time of confiscation; but, if things settle down, he would never think of proposing counter-confiscation as an atonement for those violences. It is far better that things should settle down, and that the past should be forgotten. But in Ireland things have not settled down; and the harshness, vices, and neglect of many of the grantees of confiscation have been the main cause why they have not. "The law bears, and must bear," says Burke again, "with the vices and follies of men, until they actually strike at the root of order." In general, the vices and follies of individual owners of property are borne with, be-

cause they are scattered, single cases, and do not strike at the
root of order. But in Ireland they represent a system which has
made peace and prosperity impossible, and which strikes at the
root of order. Some good landlords there always were in Ireland; as a class they are said to be now good, certainly there
are some who are excellent. But there are not a few, also, who
are still very bad; and these keep alive in the Irish people the
memory of old wrong, represent and continue to the Irish mind
the old system. A government, by executing justice upon them,
would declare that it breaks with that system, and founds a
state of things in which the good owners of property, now
endangered along with the bad, will be safe, in which a real
sense of prescription can take root, in which general well-being
and a general sense of good and just treatment,—that necessary
condition precedent of Ireland's cheerful acquiescence in the
English connection,—may become possible, and the country
can settle down. Such a measure would be a truly conservative
one, and every landowner who does his duty would find his
security in it and ought to wish for it. A Commission should
draw up a list of offenders, and an Act of Parliament should
expropriate them without scruple.

English landowners start with horror at such a proposal; but
the truth is, in considering these questions of property and land,
they are pedants. They look without horror on the expropriation of the monastic orders by Henry the Eighth's Parliament,
and many of them are at this very day great gainers by that
transaction. Yet there is no reason at all why expropriating
certain religious corporations, to give their lands to individuals,
should not shock a man; but expropriating certain individual
owners, to sell their lands in such manner as the State may
think advisable, should shock him so greatly. The estates of
religious corporations, as such, are not, says the conservative
Burke severely but truly, "in worse hands than estates to the
like amount in the hands of this earl or that squire, although
it may be true that so many dogs and horses are not kept by
the religious." But it was alleged that many monastic establishments, by their irregularities and vices, were a cause of public
harm, struck at the root of order. The same thing may most

certainly be said of too many Irish landlords at this day, with their harshness, vices, and neglect of duty. Reason of State may be alleged for dealing with both. In the mode of dealing, there can be no parallel. The monks were expropriated wholesale, good as well as bad, with little or no compensation. Of the landlords it is proposed to expropriate only the worst, so as to found for the good ones security and prescription; and the compensation assigned to the bad expropriated landlords by the English Parliament is sure to be not insufficient, rather it will be too ample.

For the confiscations of the lands of the native Irish themselves, from Elizabeth's time downwards, the plea of justification has been always this: *the reason of State,* the plea that the faults of the Irish possessor "struck at the root of order." Those confiscations were continuous and severe; they were carried on both by armed force and by legal chicane; they were in excess of what the reason of State, even at the time, seemed to fair men to require. "By English Acts of Parliament," says Burke, "forced upon two reluctant kings, the lands of Ireland were put up to a mean and scandalous auction in every goldsmith's shop in London; or chopped to pieces and cut into rations, to pay the soldiery of Cromwell." However, the justification was this, as I have said: the reason of State. The faults of the Irish possessor struck at the root of order. And if order and happiness had arisen under the new possessors, not a word more would ever have been heard about past confiscations. But order and happiness have not arisen under them; a great part of the Irish people is in a chronic state of misery, discontent, and smouldering insurrection. To reconquer and chastise them is easy; but after you have chastised them, your eternal difficulty with them recommences. I pass by the suggestion that the Irish people should be entirely extirpated; no one can make it seriously. They must be brought to order when they are disorderly; but they must be brought, also, to acquiescence in the English connection by good and just treatment. Their acquiescence has been prevented by the vices, harshness, and neglect of the grantees of confiscation; and it never will arise, so long as there are many of these who prevent it by their

vices, harshness, and neglect still. Order will never strike root.
The very same reason of State holds good, therefore, for
expropriating bad landlords, which held good in their predecessors' eyes, and in the eyes of English Parliaments, for ex-
5   propriating the native Irish possessors.

However, the expropriation of English or Anglo-Irish landlords is a thing from which English ministers will always avert
their thoughts as long as they can, and so another remedy for
Irish discontent has been hit upon. It has been suggested, as
10   every one knows, by the Ulster custom. In Ireland, the landlord has not been in the habit of doing for his farms what a
landlord does for his farms in England; and this, too, undoubtedly sprang out of the old system of rule on the part of
the grantees of confiscation as if they were lords and masters
15   simply, and not men having a joint interest with the tenant.
"In Ireland," says Burke, "the farms have neither dwelling-
houses nor good offices; nor are the lands almost anywhere provided with fences and communications. The landowner there
never takes upon him, as it is usual in this kingdom, to supply all
20   these conveniences, and to set down his tenant in what may be
called a completely furnished farm. If the tenant will not do it,
it is never done." And if the tenant did it, what was done was
still the property of the landlord, and the tenant lost the benefit
of it by losing his farm. But in Ulster, where the tenants were a
25   strong race and Protestants, there arose a custom of compensa-
ting them for their improvements, and letting them sell the
value which by their improvements they had added to the
property. But a bad landlord could set the custom at defiance;
so the Land Act of 1870 regulated the custom, and gave the
30   force of law to what had before possessed the force of custom
only. And many people think that what ministers intend, is
to develop considerably the principles and provisions of that
Act,—so considerably, indeed, as to guarantee to the tenants
fair rents, fixity of tenure, and free sale; and to extend the
35   operation of the Act, so developed, to the whole of Ireland.

The new Bill is not yet before us; and I speak besides, as I
well know and frankly avow, without special local knowledge
of Irish affairs. But a scheme such as that which has been

indicated has inconveniences which must be manifest, surely, to every one who uses his common sense, and is not hindered from using it freely by the obligation not to do what would be really effective, but still to do something. Landowners hate parting with their land, it is true; but it may be doubted whether 5 for the landlord to assign a portion of land in absolute property to the tenant, in recompense for the improvements hitherto effected, and in future himself to undertake necessary improvements, as an English landlord does, would not be a better, safer, and more pacifying solution of tenant-right claims, than 10 either the Act of 1870, or any Act proceeding upon the lines there laid down. For it is evident that, by such an Act, ownership and tenure will be made quite a different thing in Ireland from that which they are in England, and in countries of our sort of civilisation generally; and this is surely a disadvantage. 15 It is surely well to have plain, deep, common marks recognised everywhere, at least in all countries possessing a common civilisation, as characterising ownership and as characterising tenancy, and to introduce as little of novel and fanciful complication here as possible. Above all this is desirable, one would think, 20 with a people like the Irish, sanguine and imaginative, who, if they are told that tenancy means with them more than it means elsewhere, will be prone to make it mean yet more than you intend. It is surely a disadvantage, again, to put a formal compulsion on good landlords to do what they were accustomed 25 to do willingly, and to deprive them of all freedom and credit in the transaction. And the bad landlord, the real creator of our difficulties, remains on the spot still, but partially tied and entirely irritated; it will be strange indeed, if plenty of occasions of war do not still arise between him and his tenant, and 30 prevent the growth of a sense of reconcilement, pacification, and prescription.

However, there are many people who put their faith in the Land Act of 1870, properly developed, and extended to the whole of Ireland. Other people, again, put their faith in emigra- 35 tion, as the means of relieving the distressed districts, and that, they say, is all that is wanted. And if these remedies, either the Land Act singly, or emigration singly, or both of them together, prove to be sufficient, there is not a word more to be said. If Ireland settles down, if its present state of smothered revolt ceases, if misery goes out and well-being comes in, if a sense of the prescriptive right of the legal owner of land springs up, and a sense of acquiescence in the English connection, there is not a word more to be said. What abstracted people may devise in their study, or may say in their little companies when they come together, will not be regarded. Attention it will then, indeed, not require; and it is never easy to procure attention for it, even when it requires attention. English people live in classes and parties, English statesmen think of classes and parties in whatever they do. Burke himself, as I have said, on this question of Ireland which he had so made his own, Burke at the height of his fame, when men went to consult him, we are told, "as an oracle of God," Burke himself, detached from party and class, had no influence in directing Irish matters, could effect nothing. "You have formed," he writes to a friend in Ireland who was unwilling to believe this, "you have formed to my person a flattering, yet in truth a very erroneous opinion of my power with those who direct the public measures. I never have been directly or indirectly consulted about anything that is done."

No, *the English are pedants*, and will proceed in the ways of pedantry as long as they possibly can. They will not ask themselves what really meets the wants of a case, but they will ask what may be done without offending the prejudices of their classes and parties, and then they will agree to say to one another and to the world that this is what really meets the wants of the case, and that it is the only thing to be done. And ministers will always be prone to avoid facing difficulty seriously, and yet to do something and to put the best colour possible on that something; and so "still further to contract," as Burke says, "the narrowness of men's ideas, to confirm inveterate prejudices, and to abet all sorts of popular absurdities." But if a Land Act on the lines of that of 1870 fails to appease Ireland, or if emigration fails to prove a sufficient remedy, then quiet people who have accustomed themselves to consider the thing without pedantry and prejudice, may have the consolation of knowing

that there is still something in reserve, still a resource which
has not been tried, and which may be tried and may perhaps
succeed. Not only do we not exceed our duty towards Ireland
in trying this resource, if necessary, but, until we try it, we have
not even gone to the extent of our duty. And when rhetoricians 5
who seek to startle us, or despondent persons who seek to
lighten their despondency by making us share it with them,
when these come and tell us that in regard to Ireland we have
only a choice between two desperate alternatives before us, or
that we have nothing before us except ruin and confusion, then 10
simple people, who have divested themselves of pedantry, may
answer: "You forget that there is one remedy which you have
never mentioned, and apparently never thought of. It has not
occurred to you to try breaking visibly, and by a striking and
solemn act,—the expropriation of bad landlords,—with your 15
evil and oppressive past in Ireland. Perhaps your other remedies
may succeed if you add this remedy to them, even though
without it they cannot." And surely we insignificant people,
in our retirement, may solace our minds with the imagination
of right-minded and equitable Englishmen, men like the Lord 20
Chief Justice of England, and Mr. Samuel Morley, and others
whom one could easily name, acting as a Commission to draw
up a list of the thoroughly bad landlords, representatives of the
old evil system, and then bringing their list back to London
and saying: "Expropriate these, as the monks were expropriated, 25
by Act of Parliament." And since nothing is so exasperating as
pedantry when people are in serious troubles, it may console
the poor Irish, too, when official personages insist on assuring
them that certain insufficient remedies are sufficient, and are
also the only remedies possible, it may console them to know, 30
that there are a number of quiet people, over here, who feel
that this sort of thing is pedantry and make-believe, and who
dislike and distrust our common use of it, and think it dangerous. These quiet people know that it must go on being used
for a long time yet, but they condemn and disown it; and they 35
do their best to prepare opinion for banishing it.

But the truth is, in regard to Ireland, the prejudices of our
two most influential classes, the upper class and the middle

class, tend always to make a compromise together, and to be
tender to one another's weaknesses; and this is unfortunate for
Ireland. It prevents the truth, on the two matters where English
wrong-doing has been deepest,—the land and religion,—from
being ever strongly spoken out and fairly acted upon, even by
those who might naturally have been expected to go right in the
matter in question. The English middle class, who have not
the prejudices and passions of a landowning class, might have
been expected to sympathise with the Irish in their ill-usage by
the grantees of confiscation, and to interfere in order to relieve
them from it. The English upper class, who have not the prejudices and passions of our middle class, might have been expected
to sympathise with the Irish in the ill-treatment of their religion,
and to interfere in order to relieve them from it. But nothing
clouds men's minds and impairs their honesty like prejudice.
Each class forbears to touch the other's prejudice too roughly,
for fear of provoking a like rough treatment of its own. Our
aristocratic class does not firmly protest against the unfair
treatment of Irish Catholicism, because it is nervous about the
land. Our middle class does not firmly insist on breaking with
the old evil system of Irish landlordism, because it is nervous
about Popery.

And even if the middle class were to insist on doing right
with the land, it would be of no use, it would not reconcile
Ireland, unless they can also be brought to do right, when the
occasion comes, with religion. It is very important to keep this
in full view. The land question is the question of the moment.
Liberals are fond of saying that Mr. Gladstone's concessions
will remove Irish discontent. Even the *Pall Mall Gazette*, the
most serious and clear-minded of the exponents of Liberal ideas,
talks sometimes as if a good Land Bill would settle everything.
It will not; and it is deceiving ourselves to hope that it will. The
thing is to bring Ireland to acquiesce cordially in the English
connection. This can be brought about only by doing perfect
justice to Ireland, not in one particular matter only, but in all
the matters where she has suffered great wrong. Miss O'Brien
quotes an excellent saying of Fox's: "We ought not to presume
to legislate for a nation in whose feelings and affections, wants

and interests, opinions and prejudices, we have no sympathy."
It is most true; and it is of general application. Mr. Bright is
said to be desirous of dealing thoroughly with the Irish Land
Question. With the wants and interests of the Irish people in
this matter, even with their feelings and affections, opinions 5
and prejudices, he is capable of sympathy. But how as to their
wants and interests, feelings and affections, opinions and prejudices, in the matter of their religion? When they ask to have
their Catholicism treated as Anglicanism is treated in England,
and Presbyterianism is treated in Scotland, is Mr. Bright capable 10
of sympathy with them? If he is, would he venture to show it
if they made their request? I think one may pretty well antici-
pate what would happen. Mr. Carvell Williams would begin to
stir, Mr. Jesse Collings would trot out that spavined, vicious-
eyed Liberal hobby, expressly bred to do duty against the 15
Irish Catholics: *The Liberal party has emphatically condemned
religious endowment;*—and I greatly fear that Mr. Bright would
pat it approvingly.

"Sir, it is proper to inform you, that our measures *must be
healing.*" Who but a pedant could imagine that our disestab- 20
lishment of the Irish Church was a satisfaction of the equitable
claims of Irish Catholicism upon us? that it was *healing?* By this
policy, in 1868, "the Liberal Ministry resolved to knit the hearts
of the empire into one harmonious concord; and knitted they
were accordingly." Parliament and public of pedants! they were 25
nothing of the kind, and you know it. Ministers could disestablish
the Irish Church, because there is among the Nonconformists
of England and Scotland an antipathy to religious establishments; but justice to Irish Catholicism, and equal treatment with
Anglicanism in England and with Presbyterianism in Scotland, 30
your Government could not give, because of the bigotry of the
English and Scotch of the middle class. Do you suppose that
the Irish Catholics feel any particular gratitude to a Liberal
Ministry for gratifying its Nonconformist supporters, and giving itself the air of achieving "a grand and genial policy of con- 35
ciliation," without doing them real justice? They do not, and
cannot; and your measure was not healing. I think I was the
only person who said so, in print at any rate, at the time.

Plenty of people saw it, but *the English are pedants*, and it was
thought that if we all agreed to call what we had done "a grand
and genial policy of conciliation," perhaps it would pass for
being so. But "it is not your fond desire nor mine that can alter
5   the nature of things." At present I hear on all sides that the
Irish Catholics, who to do them justice are quick enough, see
our "grand and genial" act of 1868 in simply its true light, and
are not grateful for it in the least.

    Do I say that a Liberal Ministry could, in 1868, have done
10 justice to Irish Catholicism, or that it could do justice to it now?
"Go to the Surrey Tabernacle," say my Liberal friends to me;
"regard that forest of firm, serious, unintelligent faces uplifted
towards Mr. Spurgeon, and then ask yourself what would be
the effect produced on all that force of hard and narrow preju-
15 dice by a proposal of Mr. Gladstone to pay the Catholic priests
in Ireland, or to give them money for their houses and churches,
or to establish schools and universities suited to Catholics, as
England has public schools and universities suited to Anglicans,
and Scotland such as are suited to Presbyterians. What would
20 be Mr. Gladstone's chance of carrying such a measure?" I know
quite well, of course, that he would have no chance at all of
carrying it. But the English people are improvable, I hope.
Slowly this powerful race works its way out of its confining
ruts and its clouded vision of things, to the manifestation of
25 those great qualities which it has at bottom,—piety, integrity,
good-nature, and good-humour. Our serious middle class, which
has so turned a religion full of grace and truth into a religion
full of hardness and misapprehension, is not doomed to lie in
its present dark obstruction for ever, it is improvable. And we
30 insignificant quiet people, as we had our consolation from perceiving what might yet be done about the land, when rhetoricians were startling us out of our senses, and despondent persons
were telling us that there was no hope left, so we have our
consolation, too, from perceiving what may yet be done about
35 Catholicism. There is still something in reserve, still a resource
which we have not yet tried, and which all classes and parties
amongst us have agreed never to mention, but which in quiet
circles, where pedantry is laid aside and things are allowed to be

what they are, presents itself to our minds and is a great comfort to us. And the Irish too, when they are exasperated by the pedantry and unreality of the agreement, in England, to pass off as "a great and genial policy of conciliation" what is nothing of the kind, may be more patient if they know that there is an increasing number of persons, over here, who abhor this make-believe and try to explode it, though keeping quite in the background at present, and seeking to work on men's minds quietly rather than to bustle in Parliament and at public meetings.

Before, then, we adopt the tremendous alternative of either governing Ireland as a Crown colony or casting her adrift, before we afflict ourselves with the despairing thought that Ireland is going inevitably to confusion and ruin, there is still something left for us. As we pleased ourselves with the imagination of Lord Coleridge and Mr. Samuel Morley, and other like men of truth and equity, going as a Commission to Ireland, and enabling us to break with the old evil system as to the land by expropriating the worst landlords, and as we were comforted by thinking that though this might be out of the question at present, yet perhaps, if everything else failed, it might be tried and succeed,—so we may do in regard to Catholicism. We may please ourselves with the imagination of Lord Coleridge and the other Mr. Morley,—Mr. John Morley,—and men of like freedom with them from bigotry and prejudice, going as a Commission to Ireland, and putting us in the right way to do justice to the religion of the mass of the Irish people, and to make amends for our abominable treatment of it under the long reign of the Penal Code,—a treatment much worse than Louis the Fourteenth's treatment of French Protestantism, much worse, even, than the planters' treatment of their slaves, and yet maintained without scruple by our religious people while they were invoking the vengeance of heaven on Louis the Fourteenth, and were turning up their eyes in anguish at the ill-usage of the distant negro. And here, too, though to carry a measure really *healing* may be out of the question at present, yet perhaps, if everything else fails, such a measure may at last be tried and succeed.

But it is not yet enough, even, that our measures should be healing. "The temper, too, of the Irish must be managed, and their good affections cultivated." If we want to bring the Irish to acquiesce cordially in the English connection, it is not enough
5   even to do justice and to make well-being general; we and our civilisation must also be attractive to them. And this opens a great question, on which I must proceed to say something.

[II]

Since the foregoing remarks were written, the Irish Land Bill has been brought into Parliament. It is much what was antici-
10   pated. And it is easy enough, no doubt, to pick holes in the claim of such a measure to be called *healing*.

For let us recapitulate how the matter stands. It stands thus. The Irish chafe against the connection with this country. They are exasperated with us; they are, we are told, like wolves ready
15   to fly at the throat of England. And their quarrel with us, so far as it proceeds from causes which can be dealt with by a Land Act,—their quarrel with us is for maintaining the actual land-system and landlords of Ireland by the irresistible might of Great Britain. Now, the grievance which they allege against
20   the land-system and landlords is twofold; it is both moral and material. The moral grievance is, that the system and the men represent a hateful history of conquest, confiscation, ill-usage, misgovernment, and tyranny. The material grievance is, that it never having been usual with the landowner in Ireland, as it is in
25   England, to set down his tenant in what may be called a completely furnished farm, the Irish tenant had himself to do what was requisite; but when he had done it, it was the landlord's property, and the tenant lost the benefit of it by losing his farm.

As to the material grievance there is no dispute. As to the
30   moral grievance, it is urged on our side that "the confiscations, the public auctions, the private grants, the plantations, the transplantations, which animated," says Burke, "so many adventurers to Irish expeditions," are things of the past, and of a distant past; that they are things which have happened in all
35   countries, and have been forgiven and forgotten with the course

of time. True; but in Ireland they have not been forgiven and forgotten. And a fair man will find himself brought to the conservative Burke's conclusion, that this is mainly due to the proceedings of the English in-comers, with whom their "melancholy and invidious title" of grantees of confiscation was for so long time a favourite, and who so long looked upon the native Irish as a race of bigoted savages, to be treated with contempt and tyranny at their pleasure. Instead of putting these disagreeable facts out of sight, as we are so apt to do when we think and speak of the state of Ireland, we ought resolutely to keep them before us. "Even the harsh laws against popery were the product," says Burke, "of contempt and tyranny, rather than of religious zeal. From what I have observed, it is pride, arrogance, and a spirit of domination, and not a bigoted spirit of religion, that has caused and kept up these oppressive statutes." The memory of the original "terrible confiscatory and exterminatory periods" was thus kept alive, and the country never settled down.

However, it is urged, again, that the possessors of the soil are now quite changed in spirit towards the native Irish, and changed in their way of acting towards them. It is urged that some good landlords there always were, and that now, as a class, they are good, while there are many of them who are excellent. But the memory of an odious and cruel past is not so easily blotted out. And there are still in Ireland landlords, both old and new, both large and small, who are very bad, and who by their hardness and oppressiveness, or by their contempt and neglect, keep awake the sense of ancient, intolerable wrong. So stands the case with the moral grievance; it exists, it has cause for existing, and it calls for remedy.

The best remedy, one would have thought, would be a direct one. The grievance is moral, and is best to be met and wiped out by a direct moral satisfaction. Every one who considers the thing fairly will see that the Irish have a moral grievance, that it is the chief source of their restlessness and resentment, that by indirect satisfactions it is not easy to touch it, but that by such an act as the expropriation of bad landlords it would have been met directly. Such an act would be a moral expiation and satisfaction for a moral wrong; it would be a visible breaking,

on the part of this country and its Government, with the odious
and oppressive system long upheld by their power. "The
law bears with the vices and follies of men until they actually strike at the root of order." The vices and follies of
5   the bad landlords in Ireland have struck at the root of
order. Things have gone on without real and searching cure
there, until the country is in a revolutionary state. Expropriation is, say objectors, a revolutionary measure. But when
a country is in a revolutionary state you must sometimes have
10 the courage to apply revolutionary measures. The revolution
is there already; you must have the courage to apply the
measures which really cope with it. Coercion, imprisonment of
men without trial, is a revolutionary measure. But it may be
very right to apply coercion to a country in Ireland's present
15 state; perhaps even to apply a coercion far more stringent and
effectual than that which we apply now. It would be a revolutionary measure to have the bad landlords of Ireland scheduled
in three classes by a Commission, and, taking twenty-five years'
purchase as the ordinary selling-price of an Irish estate, to
20 expropriate the least bad of the three classes of scheduled
landlords at twenty years' purchase, the next class at fifteen
years' purchase, the worst at ten years' purchase. But it would
be an act justified by the revolutionary state into which the
misdoing of landlords of this sort, preventing prescription and
25 a secure settlement of things from arising, has brought Ireland.
It would fall upon those who represent the ill-doers of the past,
and who are actually ill-doers themselves. And finally, it would
be a moral reparation and satisfaction, made for a great and
passionately felt moral wrong, and would, as such, undoubtedly
30 have its full effect upon the heart and imagination of the Irish
people. To have commuted the partial ownership, which the
Irish tenant has in equity acquired by his improvements of the
land cultivated by him, for absolute ownership of a certain
portion of the land, as Stein commuted the peasant's partial
35 ownership in Prussia; to have given facilities, as is now proposed, for emigration, and for the purchase of land and its
distribution amongst a greater number of proprietors than at
present;—this, joined to the expropriation of bad landlords, is
what might naturally occur to one as the simple and direct way

of remedying Irish agrarian discontent, and as likely to have been effective and sufficient for the purpose.

The Land Bill of the Government has provisions for furthering emigration, and provisions to facilitate the purchase of land. But the moral grievance of the Irish occupier it does not deal with at all; it gives no satisfaction to it and attempts to give none. It directs itself exclusively to his material grievance. It makes no distinction between good and bad landlords,—it treats them all as alike. But to the partial ownership which the occupier has in equity acquired in the land by his improvements, it gives the force of law, establishes a tribunal for regulating and enforcing it, and does its best to make this sort of partial ownership perpetual. The desirable thing, if it could but be done, is, on the contrary, as every one who weighs the matter calmly must surely admit, to sweep away this partial ownership,— to sweep away tenant-right altogether. It is said that tenant-right is an Irish invention, a remedy by which the Irish people themselves have in some degree met the wants of their own case, and that it is dear to them on that account. In legislating for them we ought studiously to adopt, we are told, their inventions, and not to impose upon them ours. Such reasoners forget that tenant-right was a mere palliative, used in a state of things where thorough relief was out of the question. Tenant-right was better than nothing, but ownership is better still. The absolute ownership of a part, by a process of commutation like Stein's in Prussia, engages a man's affections far more than any tenant-right, or divided and disputable ownership in a whole. Such absolute ownership was out of the question when the Irish occupier invented tenant-right; but it would in itself please him better than tenant-right, and commutation might have now given it to him.

The Land Bill, on the other hand, adopts, legalises, formulates tenant-right, a description of ownership unfamiliar to countries of our sort of civilisation, and very inconvenient. It establishes it throughout Ireland, and, by a scheme which is a miracle of intricacy and complication, it invites the most contentious and litigious people in the world to try conclusions with their landlords as to the ownership divided between them.

I cannot think such a measure naturally healing. A divided

ownership of this kind will probably, however, no more be able to establish itself permanently in Ireland than it has established itself in France or Prussia. One has the comfort of thinking that the many and new proprietors who will, it is to be hoped,

5   be called into being by the Purchase Clauses, will indubitably find the plan of divided ownership intolerable, and will sooner or later get rid of it.

I had recourse to Burke in the early part of these remarks, and I wish to keep him with me, as far as possible, to the end.

10 Burke writes to Windham: "Our politics want directness and simplicity. A spirit of chicane predominates in all that is done; we proceed more like lawyers than statesmen. All our misfortunes have arisen from this intricacy and ambiguity of our politics." It is wonderful how great men agree. For really Burke

15 is here telling us, in another way, only what we found Goethe telling us when we began to discuss these Irish matters: *the English are pedants.* The pedant, the man of routine, loves the movement and bustle of politics, but by no means wants to have to rummage and plough up his mind; he shrinks from simplicity,

20 therefore, he abhors it; for simplicity cannot be had without thinking, without considerable searchings of spirit. He abhors simplicity, and therefore of course his governments do not often give it to him. He has his formula, his catchword, which saves him from thinking, and which he is always ready to apply;

25 and anything simple is, from its very simplicity, more likely to give him an opening to apply his formula. If you propose to him the expropriation of bad landlords, he has his formula ready, that *the Englishman has a respect for the eighth commandment.* If you propose to him to do justice to the Irish

30 Catholics, he has his formula, at one time, that *the sovereign must not violate his coronation oath*, at another, that *the Protestants of Great Britain are implacably hostile to the endowment of Catholicism in any shape or form*, or else, that *the Liberal party has emphatically condemned religious endow-*

35 *ment.* A complicated intricate measure is the very thing for governments to offer him, because, while it gives him the gratifying sense of taking in hand something considerable, it does not bring him face to face with a principle, does not pro-

voke him to the exhibition of one of those formulas which, in presence of a principle, he has always at hand in order to save himself the trouble of thinking. And having this personage to deal with, governments are not much to be blamed, perhaps, for approaching their object in an indirect manner, for eschewing simplicity and for choosing complication. 5

The Irish Land Bill, then, does not meet the moral grievance of the Irish occupier at all, and it meets his material grievance in a roundabout, complicated manner, and by means that are somewhat hard upon good landlords. But it does meet it after a 10 fashion. And, in meeting it, it does not challenge the exhibition of any of the pedantic Englishman's stock formulas; while it effects, at the same time, some very useful things by the way.

And, certainly, governments which seek to compass their ends in this kind of manner do not incur that severe condemna- 15 tion which Burke passes upon ministers who make it their business "still further to contract the narrowness of men's ideas, to confirm inveterate prejudices, to inflame vulgar passions, and to abet all sorts of popular absurdities." No, not by any means do they deserve this formidable blame. But when Burke 20 writes to the Duke of Richmond of that day, that, without censuring his political friends, he must say that he perceives in them no regular or steady endeavour of any kind to bestow the same pains which they bestow on carrying a measure, or winning an election, or keeping up family interest in a county, "on 25 that which is the end and object of all elections, namely, *the disposing our people to a better sense of their condition,*"— when Burke says this, then he says what does touch, it seems to me, both the present government, and almost all governments which come and go in this country;—touches them very nearly. 30 Governments acquiesce too easily in the mass of us English people being, as Goethe says, pedants; they are too apprehensive of coming into conflict with our pedantry; they show too much respect to its formulas and catchwords. They make no regular or sustained endeavours of any kind to dispose us poor 35 creatures to a better sense of our condition. If they acquiesce so submissively in our being pedants in politics, pedants we shall always be. We want guidance from those who are placed

in a condition to see. "God and nature never made them," says
Burke of all the pedantic rank and file of us in politics, "to
think or to act without guidance or direction." But we hardly
ever get it from our government.

5   And I suppose it was despair at this sort of thing, in his own
time and commonwealth, which made Socrates say, when he
was reproached for standing aloof from politics, that in his own
opinion, by taking the line he did, he was the only true politician of men then living. Socrates saw that the thing most
10   needful was "*to dispose the people to a better sense of their
condition*," and that the actual politicians never did it. And
serious people at the present day may well be inclined, though
they have no Socrates to help them, at any rate to stand aside,
as he did, from the movement of our prominent politicians and
15   journalists, and of the rank and file who appear to follow, but
who really do oftenest direct them;—to stand aside, and to try
whether they cannot bring *themselves*, at all events, to a better
sense of their own condition and of the condition of the people
and things around them.

20   The problem is, to get Ireland to acquiesce in the English
connection as cordially as Scotland, Wales, or Cornwall acquiesce in it. We quiet people pretend to no lights which are
not at the disposal of all the world. Possibly, if we were mixed
up in the game of politics, we should play it much as other
25   people do, according to the laws of that routine. Meanwhile,
not playing it, and being in the safe and easy position of lookers-
on and critics, we ought assuredly to be very careful to treat the
practical endeavours and plans of other people without pedantry
and without prejudice, only remembering that our one business
30   is to see things as they really are. Ireland, then, is to be brought,
if possible, to acquiesce cordially in the English connection; and
to this end our measures must be *healing*. Now, the Land Bill
of the Government does not seem to deserve thoroughly the
name of a *healing* measure. We have given our reasons for
35   thinking so. But the question is, whether that Bill proposes so
defective a settlement as to make, of itself, Ireland's cordial
acquiescence in the English connection impossible, and to
compel us to resign ourselves a prey to the alarmists. One cannot

without unfairness and exaggeration say this of it. It is offered with the best intentions, it deals with the material grievance of the Irish occupier if not with his moral grievance, and it proposes to do certain unquestionably good and useful things, besides redressing this grievance. It will not of itself make the Irish acquiesce cordially in the English connection. But then neither would a thoroughly good Land Bill suffice to do this. The partisans of the Government are fond of saying, indeed: "A good Land Bill will take the political bread out of Mr. Parnell's mouth." Mr. Parnell maintains that he and his friends "have the forces of nature, the forces of nationality, and the forces of patriotism" working for the separation of Ireland from England: and so they have, up to the present time. Now, a good Land Bill will not suffice to stay and annul the working of these forces, though politicians who are busy over a Land Bill will always be prone to talk as if it would suffice to do whatever may be required. But it will not. Much more than a good Land Bill is necessary in order to annul the forces which are working for separation. The best Land Bill will not reduce to impotence the partisans of separation, unless other things are accomplished too. On the other hand, the present Land Bill is not so defective as that it need prevent cordial union, if these other things are accomplished.

One of them has been mentioned already in the former part of these remarks. I mean the equitable treatment of Catholicism. To many of the Liberal party it is a great deal easier to offer to Ireland a fair Land Bill, than to offer to her a fair treatment of Catholicism. You may offer as fair a Land Bill as you please; but nevertheless if, presently, when the Irish ask to have public schools and universities suited to Catholics, as England has public schools and universities suited to Anglicans, and Scotland such as are suited to Presbyterians, you fall back in embarrassment upon your formula of pedants, *The Liberal party has emphatically condemned religious endowment,* then you give to the advocates of separation a new lease of power and influence. You enable them still to keep saying with truth, that they have "the forces of nature, the forces of nationality, and the forces of patriotism," on their side. "Our measures *must be healing,"* and it is not only as to Irish land that healing measures are necessary; they are necessary as to the Irish people's religion also.

If this were in any good measure accomplished, if, even, we offered the Land Bill which Mr. Gladstone brings forward now, and if we offered a treatment of Catholicism as well intentioned and as fair in its way, then indeed things would have a look of cheerful promise, and politicians would probably think that the grand consummation had been reached, and that the millennium was going to begin. But a quiet bystander might still be cool-headed enough to suspect, that for winning and attaching a people so alienated from us as the Irish, something more, even, is required than fair measures in redress of actual misusage and wrong. "Their temper, too, must be managed, and their good affections cultivated."

Many of us talk as if the mere calculation of their interest, of the advantage to their commerce, industry, and security from the English connection, must induce the Irish to blend readily with us, if they were but treated justly. But with a people such as the Irish, and when once such a feeling of repulsion has been excited in them as we have managed to excite, the mere redress of injustice and the calculation of their interest is not alone sufficient to win them. They must find in us something that in general suits them and attracts them; they must feel an attractive force, drawing and binding them to us, in what is called our civilisation. This is what blends Scotland and Wales with us; not alone their interest, but that our civilisation in general suits them and they like it. This is what so strongly attached to France the Germanic Alsace, and keeps it attached in spirit to France still: the wonderfully attractive power of French civilisation.

Some say, that what we have in Ireland is a lower civilisation, hating the advent of a higher civilisation from England, and rebelling against it. And it is quite true, that certain obvious merits of the English, and by which they have much prospered, —such as their exactness and neatness, for instance (to say no more than what everybody must admit),—are disagreeable to Irish laxity and slovenliness, and are resisted by them. Still, a high civilisation is naturally attractive. The turn and habits of the French have much that is irksome and provoking to Germans, yet French civilisation attracted Alsace powerfully. It behoves us to make quite sure, before we talk of Ireland's lower civilisation resisting the higher civilisation of England, that our civilisation is really high,—high enough to exercise attraction.

Business is civilisation, think many of us; it creates and implies it. The general diffusion of material well-being is civilisation, thought Mr. Cobden, as that eminent man's biographer has just informed us; it creates and implies it. Not always. And for fear we should forget what business and what material well-being have to create, before they do really imply civilisation, let us, at the risk of being thought tiresome, repeat here what we have said often of old. Business and material well-being are signs of expansion and parts of it; but civilisation, that great and complex force, includes much more than even that power of expansion of which they are parts. It includes also the power of conduct, the power of intellect and knowledge, the power of beauty, the power of social life and manners. To the building up of human life all these powers belong. If business is civilisation, then business must manage to evolve all these powers; if a widely-spread material well-being is civilisation, then that well-being must manage to evolve all of them. It is written: *Man doth not live by bread alone.*

Now, one of the above-mentioned factors of civilisation is, without doubt, singularly absent from ours,—the power of social life and manners. "The English are just, but not amiable," was a sentence which, as we know, even those who had benefited by our rule felt themselves moved to pass on us. We underrate the strength of this particular element of civilisation, underrate its attractive influence, its power. *Mansueti possidebunt terram;*—the gentle shall possess the earth. We are apt to account amiability weak and hardness strong. But, even if it were so, "there are forces," as George Sand says truly and beautifully, "there are forces of weakness, of docility, of attractiveness, or of suavity, which are quite as real as the forces of vigour, of encroachment, of violence, or of brutality." And to those softer but not less real forces the Irish people are pecu-

liarly susceptible. They are full of sentiment. They have by
nature excellent manners themselves, and they feel the charm of
manners instinctively.

"Courtesy," says Vauvenargues, "is the bond of all society,
and there is no society which can last without it." But if
courtesy is required to cement society, no wonder the Irish are
estranged from us. For we must remember who it is of us that
they mostly see, who and what it is that in the main represent
our civilisation to them. The power of social life and manners,
so far as we have it, is in Great Britain displayed above all in
our aristocratic class. Mr. Carlyle's tribute to the manners and
merits of this class will be fresh in our minds. "With due
limitation of the grossly worthless, I should vote at present that,
of classes known to me in England, the aristocracy (with its
perfection of human politeness, its continual grace of bearing
and of acting, steadfast 'honour,' light address, and cheery
stoicism), if you see well into it, is actually yet the best of
English classes." But our aristocracy, who have, on Mr. Carlyle's
showing, this power of manners so attractive to the Irish nature,
and who in England fill so large a place, and do really produce
so much effect upon people's minds and imaginations, the Irish
see almost nothing of. Their members who are connected with
Ireland are generally absentees. Mr. Lecky is disposed to regret
very much this want in Ireland of a resident aristocracy, and
says that the Irish people are by nature profoundly aristocratical. At any rate, the Irish people are capable of feeling strongly
the attraction of the power of manners in an aristocracy; and
with an aristocracy filling the place there which it fills in
Great Britain, Ireland would no doubt have been something
very different from what it is now.

While I admit, however, the merits of our aristocracy, while
I admit the effect it produces in England and the important
place it fills, while I admit that if a good body of it were resident
in Ireland we should probably have Ireland in another and a
more settled state, yet I do not think that a real solution would
have been thus reached there any more than it has been
reached, I think, here. I mean, if Ireland had had the same
social system as we have, she would have been different from

her present self indeed, but sooner or later she would have found herself confronting the same difficulty which we in England are beginning to feel now: the difficulty, namely, that the social system in question ends by landing modern communities in the possessorship of an upper class materialised, a middle class vulgarised, a lower class brutalised. But I am not going to discuss these matters now. What I want now to point out is, that the Irish do not much come across our aristocracy, exhibiting that factor of civilisation, the power of manners, which has undoubtedly a strong attraction for them. What they do come across, and what gives them the idea they have of our civilisation and of its promise, is our middle class.

I have said so much about this class at divers times, and what I have said about it has made me so many enemies, that I prefer to take the words of anybody rather than myself for showing the impression which this class is likely to make, and which it does make, upon the Irish, and the sort of idea which the Irish and others may be apt to form of the attractions of its civilisation for themselves, or for mankind in general, or for any one except us natives of Great Britain. There is a book familiar to us all, and the more familiar now, probably, to many of us, because Mr. Gladstone solaced himself with it after his illness, and so set all good Liberals (of whom I wish to be considered one) upon reading it over again. I mean *David Copperfield.* Much as I have published, I do not think it has ever yet happened to me to comment in print upon any production of Charles Dickens.What a pleasure to have the opportunity of praising a work so sound, a work so rich in merit, as *David Copperfield!* "Man lese nicht die mit-strebende, mit-wirkende!" says Goethe: "do not read your fellow-strivers, your fellow-workers!" Of the contemporary rubbish which is shot so plentifully all round us, we can, indeed, hardly read too little. But to contemporary work so good as *David Copperfield*, we are in danger of perhaps not paying respect enough, of reading it (for who could help reading it?) too hastily, and then putting it aside for something else and forgetting it. What treasures of gaiety, invention, life, are in that book! what alertness and resource! what a soul of good nature and kindness governing the whole! Such is the admirable work which I am now going to call in evidence.

Intimately, indeed, did Dickens know the middle class; he was bone of its bone and flesh of its flesh. Intimately he knew its bringing up. With the hand of a master he has drawn for us a type of the teachers and trainers of its youth, a type of its places of education. Mr. Creakle and Salem House are immortal. The type itself, it is to be hoped, will perish; but the drawing of it which Dickens has given cannot die. Mr. Creakle, the "stout gentleman with a bunch of watch-chain and seals, in an arm chair," with the fiery face and the thick veins in his forehead; Mr. Creakle sitting at his breakfast with the cane, and a newspaper, and the buttered toast before him, will sit on, like Theseus, for ever. For ever will last the recollection of Salem House, and of "the daily strife and struggle" there; the recollection

"of the frosty mornings when we were rung out of bed, and the cold, cold smell of the dark nights when we were rung into bed again; of the evening schoolroom dimly lighted and indifferently warmed, and the morning schoolroom which was nothing but a great shivering machine; of the alternation of boiled beef with roast beef, and boiled mutton with roast mutton; of clods of bread and butter, dog's-eared lesson-books, cracked slates, tear-blotted copy-books, canings, rulerings, hair-cuttings, rainy Sundays, suet-puddings, and a dirty atmosphere of ink surrounding all."

A man of much knowledge and much intelligence, Mr. Baring Gould, published not long ago a book about Germany, in which he adduced testimony which, in a curious manner, proves how true and to the life this picture of Salem House and of Mr. Creakle is. The public schools of Germany come to be spoken of in that book, and the training which the whole middle class of Germans gets in them; and Mr. Gould mentions what is reported by young Germans trained in their own German schools, who have afterwards served as teachers of foreign languages and ushers in the ordinary private schools for the middle class in England. With one voice they tell us of estab-

lishments like Salem House and principals like Mr. Creakle. They are astonished, disgusted. They cannot understand how such things can be, and how a great and well-to-do class can be content with such an ignoble bringing up. But so things are, and they report their experience of them, and their experi-   5
ence brings before us, over and over again, Mr. Creakle and Salem House.

A critic in the *World* newspaper says, what is very true, that in this country the middle class has no naturally defined limits, that it is difficult to say who properly belong to it and who do   10
not, and that the term, *middle class,* is taken in different senses by different people. This is most true. And therefore, for my part, to prevent ambiguity and confusion, I always have adopted an educational test, and by the middle class I understand those who are brought up at establishments which are more or less   15
like Salem House, and by educators who are more or less like Mr. Creakle. And the great mass of the middle part of our community, the part which comes between those who labour with their hands, on the one side, and people of fortune, on the other, is brought up at establishments of the kind, although   20
there is a certain portion broken off at the top which is educated at better. But the great mass are both badly taught, and are also brought up on a lower plane than is right, brought up ignobly. And this deteriorates their standard of life, their civilisation.   25

True, they have at the same time great merits, of which they are fully conscious themselves, and of which all who are in any way akin to them, and disposed to judge them fairly and kindly, cannot but be conscious also. True, too, there are exceptions to the common rule among the establishments and educators that   30
bring them up; there are good schools and good schoolmasters scattered among them. True, moreover, amongst the thousands who undergo Salem House and Mr. Creakle there are some born lovers of the humane life, who emerge from the training with natures unscathed, or who at any rate recover from it. But,   35
on the mass, the training produces with fatal sureness the effect of lowering their standard of life and impairing their

civilisation. It helps to produce in them, and it perpetuates, a
defective type of religion, a narrow range of intellect and knowledge, a stunted sense of beauty, a low standard of manners.

And this is what those who are not akin to them, who are
not at all disposed to be friendly observers of them, this is what
such people see in them;—this, and nothing more. This is what
the Celtic and Catholic Irish see in them. The Scotch, the
Scotch of the Lowlands, of by far the most populous and
powerful part of Scotland, are men of just the same stock as
ourselves, they breed the same sort of middle class as we do,
and naturally do not see their own faults. Wales is Celtic, but
the Welsh have adopted with ardour our middle-class religion,
and this at once puts them in sympathy with our middle-class
civilisation. With the Irish it is different. English civilisation
means to the Irish the civilisation of our middle class; and few
indeed are the attractions which to the Irish, with their quickness, sentiment, fine manners, and indisposition to be pleased
with things English, that civilisation seems, or can seem, to
have. They do not see the exceptions in our middle class; they
do not see the good which is present even in the mis-trained
mass of it. All its members seem of one type of civilisation to an
Irish eye, and that type a repulsive one. They are all tarred with
one brush, and that brush is Creakle's.

We may even go further still in our use of that charming
and instructive book, the *History of David Copperfield*. We
may lay our finger there on the very types in adult life
which are the natural product of Salem House and of Mr.
Creakle; the very types of our middle class, nay of Englishmen
and the English nature in general, as to the Irish imagination
they appear. We have only to recall, on the one hand, Mr.
Murdstone. Mr. Murdstone may be called the natural product
of a course of Salem House and of Mr. Creakle, acting upon
hard, stern, and narrow natures. Let us recall, then, Mr. Murdstone; Mr. Murdstone with his firmness and severity, with his
austere religion and his tremendous visage in church; with his
view of the world as "a place for action, and not for moping and
droning in;" his view of young Copperfield's disposition as
"requiring a great deal of correcting, and to which no greater

service can be done than to force it to conform to the ways of the working world, and to bend it and break it." We may recall, too, Miss Murdstone, his sister, with the same religion, the same tremendous visage in church, the same firmness; Miss Murdstone with her "hard steel purse," and her "uncompromising hard black boxes with her initials on the lids in hard brass nails;" severe and formidable like her brother, "whom she greatly resembled in face and voice." These two people, with their hardness, their narrowness, their want of consideration for other people's feelings, their inability to enter into them, are just the type of the Englishman and his civilisation as he presents himself to the Irish mind by his serious side. His energy, firmness, industry, religion, exhibit themselves with these unpleasant features; his bad qualities exhibit themselves without mitigation or relief.

Now, a disposition to hardness is perhaps the special fault and danger of our English race in general, going along with our merits of energy and honesty. It is apt even to appear in all kinds and classes of us, when the circumstances are such as to call it forth. One can understand Cromwell himself, whom we earnest English Liberals reverentially name "the great Puritan leader," standing before the Irish imagination as a glorified Murdstone; and the late Lord Leitrim, again, as an aristocratical Murdstone. Mr. Bence Jones, again, improver and benefactor as he undoubtedly is, yet takes a tone with the Irish which may not unnaturally, perhaps, affect them much as Murdstone's tone affected little Copperfield. But the genuine, unmitigated Murdstone is the common middle-class Englishman, who has come forth from Salem House and Mr. Creakle. He is seen in full force, of course, in the Protestant north; but throughout Ireland he is a prominent figure of the English garrison. Him the Irish see, see him only too much and too often. And he represents to them the promise of English civilisation on its serious side; what this civilisation accomplishes for that great middle part of the community towards which the masses below are to look up and to ascend, what it invites those who blend themselves with us to become and to be.

The thing has no power of attraction. The Irish quick-witted-

ness, sentiment, keen feeling for social life and manners, demand
something which this hard and imperfect civilisation cannot
give them. Its social form seems to them unpleasant, its energy
and industry to lead to no happiness, its religion to be false and
repulsive. A friend of mine who lately had to pursue his avoca-
tions in Lancashire, in the parts about St. Helens, and who has
lately been transferred to the west of Ireland, writes to me that
he finds with astonishment, how "even in the farthest *ultima
Thule* of the west, amongst literally the most abjectly poverty-
stricken cottiers, life appears to be more enjoyed than by a
Lancashire factory-hand and family who are in the receipt of
five pounds a week, father, mother, and children together, from
the mill." He writes that he finds "all the country people here
so full of courtesy and graciousness!" That is just why our
civilisation has no attractions for them. So far as it is possessed
by any great body in our own community, and capable of being
imparted to any great body in another community, our civilisation has no courtesy and graciousness, it has no enjoyment of
life, it has the curse of hardness upon it.

The penalty nature makes us pay for hardness is dulness. If
we are hard, our life becomes dull and dismal. Our hardness
grows at last weary of itself. In Ireland, where we have been
so hard, this has been strikingly exemplified. Again and again,
upon the English conqueror in his hardness and harshness, the
ways and nature of the down-trodden, hated, despised Irish,
came to exercise a strange, an irresistible magnetism. "Is it
possible," asks Eudoxus, in Spenser's *View of the State of Ireland*, "is it possible that an Englishman, brought up in such
sweet civility as England affords, should find such liking in
that barbarous rudeness that he should forget his own nature
and forego his own nation?" And Spenser, speaking under the
name of Irenæus, answers that unhappily it did, indeed, often
happen so. The Protestant Archbishop Boulter tells us, in like
manner, that under the iron sway of the penal laws against
Popery, and in the time of their severest exercise, the conversions from Protestantism to Popery were nevertheless a good
deal more numerous than the conversions from Popery to
Protestantism. Such, I say, is nature's penalty upon hardness.

Hardness grows irksome to its very own self, it ends by wearying those who have it. If our hardness is capable of wearying
ourselves, can we wonder that a civilisation stamped with it
has no attractions for the Irish; that Murdstone, the product of
Salem House and of Mr. Creakle, is a type of humanity which
repels them, and that they do not at all wish to be like him?

But in Murdstone we see English middle-class civilisation
by its severe and serious side only. That civilisation has undoubtedly also its gayer and lighter side. And this gayer and lighter
side, as well as the other, we shall find, wonderful to relate, in
that all-containing treasure-house of ours, the *History of David
Copperfield*. Mr. Quinion, with his gaiety, his chaff, his rough
coat, his incessant smoking, his brandy and water, is the
jovial, genial man of our middle-class civilisation, prepared
by Salem House and Mr. Creakle, as Mr. Murdstone is its
severe man. Quinion, we are told in our *History*, was the
manager of Murdstone's business, and he is truly his pendant.
He is the answer of our middle-class civilisation to the demand
in man for beauty and enjoyment, as Murdstone is its answer
to the demand for temper and manners. But to a quick, sentimental race, Quinion can be hardly more attractive than Murdstone. Quinion produces our towns considered as seats of
pleasure, as Murdstone produces them considered as seats of
business and religion. As it is Murdstone, the serious man, whose
view of life and demands on life have made our *Hell-holes*, as
Cobbett calls our manufacturing towns, have made the dissidence of dissent and the Protestantism of the Protestant religion,
and the refusal to let Irish Catholics have schools and universities suited to them because their religion is *a lie and heathenish
superstition*, so it is Quinion, the jovial man, whose view of
life and demands on it have made our popular songs, comedy,
art, pleasure,—made the City Companies and their feasts, made
the London streets, made the Griffin. Nay, Quinion has been
busy in Dublin, too, for have we not conquered Ireland? The
streets and buildings of Dublin are full of traces of him; his
sense of beauty governed the erection of Dublin Castle itself.
As the civilisation of the French middle class is the maker of the
streets and buildings of modern Paris, so the civilisation of the

English middle class is the maker of the streets and buildings of modern London and Dublin.

Once more. Logic and lucidity in the organising and administering of public business are attractive to many; they are satisfactions to that instinct of intelligence in man which is one of the great powers in his civilisation. The immense, homogeneous, and (comparatively with ours) clear-thinking French middle class prides itself on logic and lucidity in its public business. In our public business logic and lucidity are conspicuous by their absence. Our public business is governed by the wants of our middle class, and is in the hands of public men who anxiously watch those wants. Now, our middle class cares for liberty; it does not care for logic and lucidity. Murdstone and Quinion do not care for logic and lucidity. Salem House and Mr. Creakle have not prepared them for it. Accordingly, we see the proceedings of our chief seat of public business, the House of Commons, governed by rules of which one may, I hope, at least say, without risk of being committed for contempt, that logic and lucidity have nothing to do with them. Mr. Chamberlain, again, was telling us only the other day, that "England, the greatest commercial nation in the world, has in its bankruptcy law the worst commercial legislation of any civilised country." To be sure, Mr. Chamberlain has also said, that "if in England we fall behind other nations in the intelligent appreciation of art, we minister to a hundred wants of which the other nations have no suspicion." As we are a commercial people, one would have thought that logic and lucidity in commercial legislation was one of these wants to which we minister; however, it seems that we do not. But, outside our own immediate circle, logic and lucidity are felt by many people to be attractive; they inspire respect, their absence provokes ridicule. It is a plea for Home Rule if we inflict the privation of them, in public concerns, upon people of quicker minds, who would by nature be disposed to relish them. Probably the Irish themselves, though they are gainers by the thing, yet laugh in their sleeves at the pedantries and formalities with which our love of liberty, Murdstone and Quinion's love of liberty, and our total want of instinct for logic and lucidity, embarrass our attempts to coerce them. Certainly they must have laughed outright, being people with a keen sense of the ridiculous, when in the information to which the traversers had to plead at the late trials, it was set forth that the traversers "did conspire, combine, confederate, and agree together, to solicit, incite, and procure," and so on. We must be Englishmen, countrymen of Murdstone and Quinion, loving liberty and a "freedom broadening slowly down from precedent to precedent,"—not fastidious about modern and rational forms of speech, about logic and lucidity, or much comprehending how other people can be fastidious about them, —to take such a jargon with proper seriousness.

The dislike of Ireland for England the resistance of a lower civilisation to a higher one! Why, everywhere the attractions of this middle-class civilisation of ours, which is what we have really to offer in the way of civilisation, seem to fail of their effect. "The puzzle seems to be," says the *Times* mournfully, "where we are to look for our friends." But there is no great puzzle in the matter if we will consider it without pedantry. Our civilisation, as it looks to outsiders, and in so far as it is a thing broadly communicable, seems to consist very much in the Murdstonian drive in business and the Murdstonian religion, on the one hand, and in the Quinionian joviality and geniality, on the other. Wherever we go, we put forward Murdstone and Quinion, and call their ways civilisation. Our governing class nervously watch the ways and wishes of Murdstone and Quinion, and back up their civilisation all they can. But do what we will, this civilisation does not prove attractive.

The English in South Africa "will all be commercial gentlemen," says Lady Barker,—commercial gentlemen like Murdstone and Quinion. Their wives will be the ladies of commercial gentlemen, they will not even tend poultry. The English in the Transvaal, we hear again, contain a wonderful proportion of attorneys, speculators, land-jobbers, and persons whose antecedents will not well bear inspection. Their recent antecedents we will not meddle with, but one thing is certain: their early antecedents were those of the English middle class in general, those of Murdstone and Quinion. They have almost all, we may

be very sure, passed through the halls of a Salem House and
the hands of a Mr. Creakle. They have the stamp of either
Murdstone or Quinion. Indeed we are so prolific, so enterprising, so world-covering, and our middle class and its civilisation
so entirely take the lead wherever we go, that there is now, one
may say, a kind of odour of Salem House all round the globe. It
is almost inevitable that Mr. Sprigg should have been reared in
some such establishment; it is ten to one that Mr. Berry is an old
pupil of Mr. Creakle. And when they visit Europe, no doubt
they go and see Mr. Creakle, where he is passing the evening of
his days in honourable retirement,—a Middlesex magistrate, a
philanthropist, and a member of the Society of Arts. And Mr.
Berry can tell his old master of a happy country all peopled by
ourselves, where the Murdstone and Quinion civilisation seems
to men the most natural thing in the world and the only right
civilisation, and where it gives entire satisfaction. But poor Mr.
Sprigg has to report of a land plagued with a large intermixture
of foreigners, to whom our unique middle-class civilisation does
not seem attractive at all, but they find it entirely disagreeable.
And so, too, to come back much nearer home, do the Irish.

So that if we, who are in consternation at the dismal prophecies we hear concerning what is in store for Ireland and England, if we determine, as I say, to perish in the light at any rate,
to abjure all self-deception, and to see things as they really are,
we shall see that our civilisation, in its present state, will not
help us much with the Irish. Now, even though we gave them
really healing measures, yet still, estranged as the Irish at present
are, it would be further necessary to manage their tempers and
cultivate their good affections by the gift of a common civilisation congenial to them. But our civilisation is not congenial to
them. To talk of it, therefore, as a substitute for perfectly healing measures is ridiculous. Indeed, the pedantry, bigotry, and
narrowness of our middle class, which disfigure the civilisation
we have to offer, are also the chief obstacle to our offering
measures perfectly healing. And the conclusion is, that our
middle class and its civilisation require to be transformed. With
all their merits, which I have not here much insisted upon,
because the question was, how their demerits make them to be

judged by unfriendly observers,—with all their merits, they require, as I have so often said, to be transformed. And for my part I see no way so promising for setting about it as the abolishment of Salem House and of Mr. Creakle. This initiatory stage governs for them in a great degree all the rest, and with this initiatory stage we should above all deal.

I think I hear people saying: *There! he has got on his old hobby again!* Really, people ought rather to commend the strictly and humbly practical character of my writings. It was very well for Mr. Carlyle to bid us have recourse, in our doubts and miseries, to earnestness and reality, and veracity and the everlasting yea, and generalities of that kind; Mr. Carlyle was a man of genius. But when one is not a man of genius, and yet attempts to give counsel in times of difficulty, one should be above all things practical. Now, our relations with Ireland will not in any case be easily and soon made satisfactory; but while our middle class is what it is now, they never will. And our middle class, again, will not be easily and soon transformed; but while it gets its initiation to life through Salem House and Mr. Creakle, it never will.

The great thing is to initiate it to life by means of public schools. Public schools for the middle classes are not a panacea for our ills. No, but they are the indispensable preliminary to our real improvement on almost all the lines where as a nation we now move with embarrassment. If the consideration of our difficulties with Ireland had not, like so much else, brought me at last full upon this want,—which is capital, but far too little remarked,—I should probably not have ventured to intrude into the discussion of them. However terrified and dejected by the alarmists, I should have been inclined to bear my burden silently in that upper chamber in Grub Street, where I have borne in silence so many sorrows. I know that the professional people find the intervention of outsiders very trying in politics, and I have no wish to provoke their resentment. But when the discussion of any matter tends inevitably to show the crying need which there is for transforming our middle-class education, I cannot forbear from striking in; for if I do not speak of the need shown, nobody else will.

Yet the need is, certainly, great and urgent enough to attract
notice. But then our middle class is very strong and self-satisfied,
and every one flatters it. It is like that strong and enormous
creature described by Plato, surrounded by obsequious people
5   seeking to understand what its noises mean, and to make in their
turn the noises which may please it. At best, palliatives are now
and then attempted; as there is a company, I believe, at this
moment projected to provide better schools for the middle
classes. Alas, I should not be astonished to find presently Mr.
10 Creakle himself among the directors of a company to provide
better schools for the middle classes, and the guiding spirit of
its proceedings! so far, at least, as his magisterial functions, and
his duties on philanthropical committees, and on committees of
the Society of Arts, permit him to take part in them. But oftener
15 our chief people take the bull by the horns, and actually congratulate the middle class on the character and conditions of its
education. And so they play the part of a sort of spiritual
pander to its defects and weaknesses, and do what in them lies
to perpetuate them. Lord Frederick Cavendish goes down to
20 Sheffield, to address an audience almost entirely trained by
Salem House and by Mr. Creakle, and the most suitable thing he
can find to say to them is, he thinks, to congratulate them on
their energy and self-reliance in being so trained, and to give
them to understand that he himself, if he were not Lord
25 Frederick Cavendish, brought up at Cambridge, would gladly
be Murdstone or Quinion, brought up by Mr. Creakle. But this
is an old story, a familiar proceeding, for which the formula
has long since been given: namely, that the upper class do not
want to be disturbed in their preponderance, nor the middle
30 class in their vulgarity. But if we wish cordially to attach Ireland
to the English connection, not only must we offer healing
political measures, we must also, and that as speedily as we can,
transform our middle class and its social civilisation.

I perceive that I have said little of faults on the side of the
35 Irish, as I have said little of the merits which accompany, in our
middle class, their failure in social civilisation. And for the same
reason,—because the matter in hand was the failure on our
part to do all in our power to attach Ireland, and how to set

about remedying that failure. But as I have spoken with so much frankness of my own people and kindred, the Irish will allow me, perhaps, to end with quoting three queries of Bishop Berkeley's, and with recommending these to their attention:—

"1. Whether it be not the true interest of both nations to become one people, and whether either be sufficiently apprised of this?

"2. Whether Ireland can propose to thrive so long as she entertains a wrong-headed distrust of England?

"3. Whether in every instance by which the Irish prejudice England, they do not in a greater degree prejudice themselves?"

Perhaps, our Irish friends might do well also to perpend the good bishop's caution against "a general parturiency in Ireland with respect to politics and public counsel;" a parturiency which in clever young Irishmen does often, certainly, seem to be excessive. But, after all, my present business is not with the Irish but with the English;—to exhort my countrymen to healing measures and an attractive form of civilisation. And if one's countrymen insist upon it, that found to be sweet and attractive their form of civilisation is, or, if not, ought to be, then we who think differently must labour diligently to follow Burke's injunctions, and to "dispose people to a better sense of their condition."

Preface

[to Burke's *Letters, Speeches and Tracts on Irish Affairs*]

Who now reads Bolingbroke? Burke once asked; and if the same question were at this day asked in respect to Burke himself, what would be the answer? Certainly not that he is read anything like as much as he deserves to be read. We English make
5   far too little use of our prose classics,—far less than the French make of theirs. The place which a writer like Pascal, for instance, fills in French education, and in the minds of cultivated Frenchmen in general, how different is it from the place which Burke fills in our reading and thoughts, and how much larger!
10   Shakespeare and Milton we are all supposed to know something of; but of none of our prose classics, I think, if we leave stories out of the account, such as are the *Pilgrim's Progress* and the *Vicar of Wakefield*, are we expected to have a like knowledge. Perhaps an exception is to be made for Bacon's *Essays*, but even
15   of this I do not feel sure. Our grandfathers were bound to know their Addison, but for us the obligation has ceased; nor is that loss, indeed, a very serious matter. But to lose Swift and Burke out of our mind's circle of acquaintance is a loss indeed, and a loss for which no conversance with contemporary prose
20   literature can make up, any more than conversance with contemporary poetry could make up to us for unacquaintance with Shakespeare and Milton. In both cases the unacquaintance shuts us out from great sources of English life, thought, and language, and from the capital records of its history and development,
25   and leaves us in consequence very imperfect and fragmentary Englishmen. It can hardly be said that this inattention to our prose classics is due to their being contained in collections made up of many volumes,—collections dear and inaccessible. Their remaining buried in such collections,—a fate so unlike that

which has been Rousseau's in France, or Lessing's in Germany, —is rather the result of our inattention than its cause. While they are so buried, however, they are in truth almost inaccessible to the general public, and all occasions for rescuing and exhibiting representative specimens of them should be welcomed and used.

Such an occasion offers itself, for Burke, in the interest about Ireland which the present state of that country compels even the most unwilling Englishman to feel. Our neglected classic is by birth an Irishman; he knows Ireland and its history thoroughly. "I have studied it," he most truly says, "with more care than is common." He is the greatest of our political thinkers and writers. But his political thinking and writing has more value on some subjects than on others; the value is at its highest when the subject is Ireland. The writings collected in this volume cover a period of more than thirty years of Irish history, and show at work all the causes which have brought Ireland to its present state. The tyranny of the grantees of confiscation; of the English garrison; Protestant ascendency; the reliance of the English Government upon this ascendency and its instruments as their means of government; the yielding to menaces of danger and insurrection what was never yielded to considerations of equity and reason; the recurrence to the old perversity of mismanagement as soon as ever the danger was passed,—all these are shown in this volume; the evils, and Burke's constant sense of their gravity, his constant struggle to cure them. The volume begins with the *Tracts on the Popery Laws,* written probably between 1760 and 1765, when that penal code, of which the monstrosity is not half known to Englishmen, and may be studied by them with profit in the *Tracts,* was still in force, and when Irish trade was restricted, almost annulled, from jealousy lest it should interfere with the trade of England. Then comes the American war. In the pressure of difficulty and danger, as that war proceeded, Lord North's Government proposed, in 1778, to conciliate Ireland by partly withdrawing the restrictions on her trade. The commercial middle class,—the class with which a certain school of politicians supposes virtue, abhorring nobles and squires, to have taken refuge,—the men

of Liverpool, Manchester, Glasgow, and Bristol, were instantly
in angry movement, and forced the Minister to abandon his
propositions. The danger deepened; Spain joined herself with
France and America; the Irish volunteers appeared in arms.
5 Then, in 1779, the restrictions on Irish trade, of which the
partial withdrawal had been refused the year before, were
withdrawn altogether. But the irritation of his constituents at
his supporting this withdrawal, and at his supporting a measure
of relief to Catholics, cost Burke his seat at Bristol. Meanwhile,
10 the Irish Parliament proceeded in establishing its independence
of that of Great Britain. Irish affairs were controlled by Irish
legislators; the penal laws were relaxed, the Catholics admitted
to the franchise, though not to Parliament. The English Government had to govern Ireland through the Irish Legislature.
15 But it persisted on leaning upon that party in the Irish Legislature,—a Protestant Legislature, no doubt, but containing such
patriotic and liberal Protestants as Grattan,—it persisted on
leaning upon that party which represented Protestant ascendency and the rule of the grantees of confiscation in its worst
20 form. In 1789 came the French Revolution. To remove the
disabilities under which the Catholics of Ireland still lay was a
measure which commended itself to all the best politicians at
that time. The English Government sent, in 1795, Burke's
friend, Lord Fitzwilliam, as Viceroy to Ireland. Lord Fitz-
25 william was the declared friend of Catholic emancipation. It
seemed on the point of being granted, when the Irish Protestant
junto, as Burke calls it, prevailed with Mr. Pitt, and Lord Fitzwilliam was the declared friend of Catholic emancipation. It
apprehensions for the future; in 1798 came the Irish Rebellion.
30 But with the Rebellion we pass beyond the life of Burke, and
beyond the period of Irish history covered by this volume.
      The rapid summary just given of that history, from 1760 to
1797, will afford a sufficient clue to the writings and speeches
which follow. Burke, let me observe in passing, greatly needs
35 to be re-edited; indeed, he has never yet been properly edited
at all. But all that I have attempted to do in the present volume
is to arrange chronologically the writings and speeches on Irish
affairs, which, in Burke's collected works, are now scattered

promiscuously; and to subjoin the most important of his private
letters on the same subject, taken from the correspondence
published in 1844 by the late Lord Fitzwilliam, the son of
Burke's friend, the Irish Viceroy.[1] In my opinion, the importance of Burke's thoughts on the policy pursued in Ireland is   5
as great now as when he uttered them, and when they were
received, as he himself tells us, with *contempt*. "You do not
suppose," said Mr. Bright the other day in the City,—"you do
not suppose that the fourteen members of the Government
spend days and weeks in the consideration of a measure such   10
as the Irish Land Bill without ascertaining in connexion with
it everything everybody else can know." Alas! how many
English Governments have been confident that they had as-
certained in connexion with their Irish policy "everything
everybody else could know!" Burke writes to Mrs. Crewe that   15
a work of his has, he is told, "put people in a mood a little
unusual to them—*it has set them on thinking*." "One might have
imagined," he adds, "that the train of events, as they passed before their eyes, might have done that!" Nevertheless, it does
not; and so, he concludes, "Let them think now who never   20
thought before!" In general, our Governments, however well
informed, feel bound, it would seem, to adapt their policy to
our normal mental condition, which is, as Burke says, a non-
thinking one. Burke's paramount and undying merit as a politician is, that instead of accepting as fatal and necessary this   25
non-thinking condition of ours, he battles with it, mends and
changes it; he will not rest until he has "put people in a mood a
little unusual with them," until he has "set them on thinking."

---

[1] The copyright of these Letters belongs to Messrs. Rivington, and I
have to thank them for their kindness in permitting me to print such as I   30
needed for my purpose.

A Genevese Judge[1]

On the 10th of May, 1800, Mallet du Pan died of consumption
at Richmond. He and Joseph de Maistre are the chief intellectual figures of the emigration. Both of them have intellectual
and spiritual affinities with Burke—Mallet du Pan with Burke
5 at his best, Joseph de Maistre with Burke, brilliant, indeed, but
warped, yielding himself to exaggeration, paradox, self-will.
M. Taine, in his history of the Revolution, recalls attention
to Mallet du Pan and to his thoughts; it would be well if
he and they were better known to us in England. At present,
10 however, it is not of Mallet du Pan that we wish to speak, but
of Mallet du Pan's grandson, Eugène Colladon, who died last
year at the age of seventy-five. For forty-one years M. Colladon was a member of the magistrature of the republic of
Geneva—he became Procureur-Général, and afterwards the
15 President of the High Court. He was an excellent magistrate,
an excellent citizen, and socially he was delightful. He was also
a lover of letters, and a contributor to the well-known Swiss
review, the *Bibliothèque Universelle de Genève*. Since his death
his family have published a small volume of extracts and frag-
20 ments from these review articles. Sainte-Beuve would not unfrequently ask, when a new work of literature appeared, "Qu'en
pense M. Eugène Colladon?" and the memorial volume of him
well deserves a word of notice. One might desire more variety
in the extracts; and to us, at any rate, the discretion which
25 withholds M. Colladon's criticisms on the poetry of M. Victor
Hugo because they contain "des pages dont plus d'une pour-

[1] "Eugène Colladon, Études et Fragments littéraires." (Genève: Jules
Sandoz.)

rait paraître assez mordante aux lecteurs de 1881"—in other words, because they are at variance with the deification since effected and the legend now dominant—appears excessive. Still, the extracts as they stand are remarkable—remarkable both for their own merit and also as bringing before us a type of culture which is probably passing away, but which will not easily find a successor of equal value to replace it.

Eugène Colladon's training was obtained from the Greek and Latin classics—the Latin very much more than the Greek— and from the French literature of the seventeenth and eigh- teenth centuries. For a man of intelligence, character, and practical occupations in life, this training appears to have had an extraordinary value. Eugène Colladon was neither a genius nor a professional author. He was a magistrate and a judge, with the intelligence and integrity which are the due outfit for that honourable position. From the ancient classics he drew the elevation which they have been so generally found to give; from the French literature of the seventeenth century he drew the sense for style, and for style not in a remote and dead language, but in his mother tongue; from that of the eighteenth century he drew its quick and strong mental movement, its straightforwardness and lucidity of thinking. This combination produced, as its result, a stamp of something widely human, European and central, in comparison with which the intellectual modes of other nations appeared provincial and arbitrary, and in which lies the secret of the strong attraction exercised by the French language and culture. Its characteristic is that it is impressed on society rather than that it is impressed on isolated thinkers and men of letters. Colladon, a functionary and a man of affairs, is strikingly marked with it, and it is better studied in such a man than in Voltaire.

Many of us remember Châtelard near Montreux. Colladon speaks of a visit to its owner, M. Marquis, and of a conversa- tion "by the fireside of the immense salon." He says:—"I remember that I was struck by the turn that Marquis speedily gave, without effort and without the least pedantry, to a con- versation that would otherwise have very cheerfully been allowed to stop at vineyard prospects and family gossip. In his

busy solitude he thought much, he loved ideas, and he had
ideas of his own."

There is one of the signs of the culture we have been
speaking of, its ardour! It presses its possessor to extend his
interest beyond his vines and his crops, to "love ideas," and to
"have them of his own." But *ideas* is a wide term; to love what
sort of ideas, to have what sort of ideas of his own? Well,
Colladon writes to a friend that he has been reading Quinet's
"History of the Revolution," in which he finds much to admire;
we have not space for the whole of the letter, but here is the
conclusion of it:—

No doubt Quinet's general point of view is chimerical; for he
thinks that, in order to be profitable to the advent and the durabil-
ity of freedom, the political revolution which came to pass at the
end of the last century ought to have been accompanied by a
religious revolution that should have been equally profound and
equally destructive of the past; in a word, that, in order to remain
a free, liberal, strong, and great republic, France ought before all
else to become Protestant. This is perhaps true; but as nobody
thought of it, as the need has been nowhere felt, and as France
would rather have gone over to Mahommedanism than have
dreamed for an instant of turning Protestant, it is only a sort of
retrospective romance, a play of imagination, to summon from
the bowels of fiction a Protestant France, for the sake of endowing
it with every kind of virtue, of greatness, and of liberties.

If Lord Selborne and Lord Cairns will allow us to use them
as an illustration, we will say that we can perfectly imagine
their occupying themselves in their leisure with other things
than their vines and their crops; can imagine them reading
with interest a grave history and writing letters about it,
but that we cannot by any possibility imagine either of them
writing such a letter about it as Colladon's. What distinguishes
Colladon's letter is the central point of view, the lucidity, what
our neighbours call the *coup d'oeil;* it is the letter of a man
who has, in Sainte-Beuve's words, "une intelligence ouverte et
traversée." And yet Colladon is not a philosopher by profession,
not a Niebuhr or Burke, neither historical philosopher nor

political philosopher; he is a man in the daily exercise of a profession full of practical detail, full of routine. But he has had a culture which keeps his thinking quick and large and fresh and lucid, and which makes thinking of this sort a necessity to him. It is not for nothing that his spirit, nourished first 5 on the Latin classics and on the French classics of the seventeenth century, has then felt the electric shock of the French genius of the eighteenth century, of its free thought, its bold and clear literature, its incomparable *art de causer.*

How charming an art, how worthy of our liveliest regrets—the 10 art of conversation! Its tradition grows weaker every day, perhaps because we have become more serious, perhaps because family life has taken so great a place in the interests of all of us, but perhaps, too, because egotism has grown stronger, because the love of money and of material pleasures has been so lamentably developed. 15 And then, especially, politics, having fallen into the domain of everybody, people fling themselves on that easy food for talk, accessible as it is to every sort of intelligence; for on this ground nobody is without ability enough to contribute to conversation his contingent of commonplaces, of insipid stalenesses, of inane 20 conjectures, and futile hypotheses. Whereas real *causerie*, made up of ideas, the stimulation of mind by mind, the study in common of the historic and literary past, the spontaneous association of various intelligences for the purpose of analyzing some work of thought, of art, of poetry, of philosophy, and all this with life, 25 with pleasant eagerness, without pretention, among people of subtle and delicate minds—is it not a fine and a lawful source of enjoyment? And especially when this intellectual tournament is directed by the hand of a woman who to all the grace of her sex joins a real depth of thought, surely it doubles in value. 30

The extract is long, and in the columns of a newspaper we ought to pay due regard to the claims of politics, and of readers anxious to "se ruer sur cette facile pâture." Still, though long, it describes so finely and accurately a phase of culture never to be forgotten that we have not the heart to abridge it. It is 35 worthy of Mdlle. de Lespinasse herself, or of some other heroine of the "art charmant et vivement regrettable—celui de causer." The France of the present day, the France of M. Zola, is in its

intellectual habits and aims very far removed from the France
of Mdlle. de Lespinasse, which so much influenced M. Colladon.
M. Colladon has noted the actual tendencies of the French
literature of to-day, tendencies with which he was by no means
in sympathy. "Real life in our time is so full of events, so full of
storms, that the public will have nothing to say to a book in
which there are not to be found ferocious passions and
sanguinary crimes—all that the imagination can contain of
horror and delirium. But a man of genius would soar above this
passing extravagance of humour, and, instead of giving way
before the torrent, he would do his best, by force of talent,
to restore his generation to nature and good taste."

Pending the arrival of this man of genius, we will remark
that the old French culture, with all its limitations, bore excellent fruits, and that in M. Colladon they are exhibited in
singular perfection. We may say of him what Voltaire said of
one of his visitors: that there are few people to be met with
"qui aient l'esprit plus juste, plus net, plus cultivé, et plus
éclairé."

An Unregarded Irish Grievance

In 1796, the very year before his death, when the political prospect for the people of Ireland seemed desperate, and all political struggle on their part useless and impotent, Burke wrote to an Irishman as follows:—

"I should recommend to the middle ranks, in which I include   5
not only all merchants, but all farmers and tradesmen, that they
would change as much as possible those expensive modes of living
and that dissipation to which our countrymen in general are so
much addicted. It does not at all become men in a state of persecution. They ought to conform themselves to the circumstances   10
of a people whom Government is resolved not to consider as upon
a par with their fellow-subjects. Favour they will have none. They
must aim at other resources, and to make themselves independent
in fact before they aim at a *nominal* independence. Depend upon
it, that with half the privileges of the others, joined to a different   15
system of manners, they would grow to a degree of importance to
which, without it, no privileges could raise them, much less any
intrigues or factious practices. I know very well that such a discipline, among so numerous a people, is not easily introduced, but I
am sure it is not impossible. If I had youth and strength, I would   20
go myself over to Ireland to work on that plan; so certain I am
that the well-being of all descriptions in the kingdom, as well as
of themselves, depends upon a reformation amongst the Catholics.
The work will be new, and slow in its operation, but it is certain
in its effect. There is nothing which will not yield to perseverance   25
and method."

Whether a sumptuary reform in the habits of the middle
classes in Ireland is a crying need of the present hour, I have
no sufficient means of judging. If it is, it is not a reform which

we can well isolate from other needs, can well pursue by itself alone, and directly. It is a reform which must depend upon enlarging the minds and raising the aims of those classes; upon humanising and civilising them. Expense in living, dissipation,
5   are the first and nearest dangers, perhaps, to the Irish middle class, while its civilisation is low, because they are its first and nearest pleasures. They can only cease to be its first and nearest pleasures, if now they are so, by a rise in its standard of life, by an extending and deepening of its civilisation.
10   True, this greatly needs to be done. True, the improvement of Ireland, the self-government of Ireland, must come mainly through the middle class, and yet this class, defective in civilisation as it now is, is not ripe for the functions required of it. Its members have indeed to learn, as Burke says, "to make
15   themselves independent *in fact* before they aim at a *nominal* independence." But not Ireland alone needs, alas, the lesson; we in England need it too. In England, too, power is passing away from the now governing class. The part to be taken in English life by the middle class is different from the part which
20   the middle class has had to take hitherto,—different, more public, more important. Other and greater functions devolve upon this class than of old; but its defective civilisation makes it unfit to discharge them. It comes to the new time and to its new duties, it comes to them, as its flatterers will never tell it,
25   but as it must nevertheless bear to be told and well to consider, —it comes to them with a defective type of religion, a narrow range of intellect and knowledge, a stunted sense of beauty, a low standard of manners.
       The characters of defective civilisation in the Irish middle
30   class are not precisely the same as in the English. But for the faults of the middle class in Ireland, as in England, the same remedy presents itself to start with; not a panacea by any means, not all-sufficient, not capable of working miracles of change in a moment, but yet a remedy sure to do good; the first and
35   simplest and most natural remedy to apply, although it is left singularly out of sight, and thought, and mention. The middle class in both England and Ireland is the worst schooled middle class in Western Europe. Surely this may well have something

to do with defects of civilisation! Surely it must make a difference to the civilisation of a middle class, whether it is brought up in ignoble schools where the instruction is nearly worthless, or in schools of high standing where the boy is carried through a well-chosen course of the best that has been known and said 5 in the world! I, at any rate, have long been of opinion that the most beneficent reform possible in England, at present, is a reform about which hardly anybody seems to think or care,— the establishment of good public schools for the middle classes.

Most salutary for Ireland also would be the establishment of 10 such schools there. In what state is the actual supply of schools for the middle classes in Ireland, we learn from a report lately published by a very acute observer, Professor Mahaffy, of Trinity College, Dublin. I propose to give here a short account of what he tells us, and to add a few thoughts which suggest 15 themselves after reading him.

Professor Mahaffy was appointed by the Endowed Schools Commission in 1879 to visit and report upon the Grammar Schools of Ireland. He inspected the buildings and accommodations, attended the classes, examined the pupils; and he also 20 visited some of the principal Grammar Schools in England, such as Winchester, Marlborough, Uppingham, and the City of London School, to provide himself with a definite standard of comparison. Professor Mahaffy is a man, as is well known, of brilliant attainments; he has had, also, great practical experience 25 in teaching, and he writes with a freshness, plainness, and point which make his report very easy and agreeable reading.

The secondary schools of Ireland are classified by Professor Mahaffy as follows: the Royal Schools, the lesser schools managed by the Commissioners of Education, the Erasmus 30 Smith's schools, the Incorporated Society's schools, the Protestant diocesan schools, the schools with private endowments, the Roman Catholic colleges, and the unendowed schools. He visited schools of each class. In all or almost all of them he found the instruction profoundly affected by the rules of the Inter- 35 mediate Schools Commissioners. His report is full of remarks on the evil working of the examinations of this Intermediate Board, and he appears to consider the most important part of his business, as reporter, to be the delivering of his testimony against them. The Board arose, as is well known, out of the desire to do something for intermediate education in Ireland without encountering what is called the religious difficulty.

5   "The Liberal party has emphatically condemned religious endowment; the Protestants of Great Britain are emphatically hostile to the endowment of Catholicism in any shape or form." We have all heard these parrot cries till one is sick of them. Schools, therefore, were not to be founded or directly aided, be-

10   cause this might be an endowment of Catholicism; but a system of examinations and prizes was established, whereby Catholic schools may be indeed aided indirectly, but so indirectly, it seems, as to suffer the consciences of the Protestants of Great Britain to remain at peace. Only this system of examinations

15   and prizes, while good for the consciences of the Protestants of Great Britain, is very bad, in Professor Mahaffy's opinion, for the Irish schools. He insists on its evil effects in the very first page of his report, in speaking of the Royal School of Armagh, the chief of the Royal Schools, and the school with which he

20   begins. He says:—

"Under the rules of the Intermediate Commissioners it is found more advantageous to answer in a number of unimportant subjects, of which a hastily learned smattering suffices, than to study with earnestness the great subjects of education,—classics and mathe-

25   matics. Hence, boys spend every leisure moment, and even part of their proper school-time, in learning little text-books on natural science, music, and even Irish, to the detriment of their solid progress. This is not all. Owing to the appointing of fixed texts in classics and the paucity of new passages in the examination, the

30   boys are merely crammed in the appointed texts without being taught real scholarship. When examining a senior division in classics, I observed that they all brought up annotated texts, in fact so fully annotated that every second clause was translated for them; and upon observing this to the master, he replied that he

35   knew the evil, but that he could not get them through the intermediate course in any other way."

All through the report this is Professor Mahaffy's great and ever-recurring complaint: "The multiplication of subjects supported by the Intermediate Board, which suit inaccurate and

ill-taught pupils far better than those who learn the great
subjects thoroughly." Everywhere it struck him, that "the boys,
even when not over-worked, were addled with a quantity of
subjects. They are taught a great many valuable truths; but they
have not assimilated them, and only answer by accident. I have
found this mental condition all over the country." He calls
the intermediate examinations "the lowest and poorest of all
public competitions." The more intelligent of the schoolmasters,
he says, condemn them:—

"The principal (of the French college at Blackrock) has very
large and independent views about education, which are well
worthy of serious attention. He objects altogether to the intermediate examinations, and says that his profession is ruined by the
complete subjugation of all school-work to the fixed programme,
which is quite insufficient to occupy the better boys for a year,
and which thus seriously impairs their progress. He also protests
against the variety of unimportant subjects which produce fees
for results, and thinks that a minimum of at least thirty-five per
cent should be struck off the answering, if these subjects are retained."

However, "the false stimulus now supplied in the system of
intermediate examinations established by Government" is too
strong to be resisted:—

"So strong a mercenary spirit has been excited both in masters
and parents by this system, that all the schools in Ireland with
one exception (the Friends' School in Waterford) have been
forced into the competition; every boy is being taught the intermediate course, every error in the management of that course is
affecting the whole country, and the best educator is unable to
stem the tide, or do more than protest against any of the defects."

Professor Mahaffy is a hearty admirer of the great English
public schools. He is of opinion, "that what distinguishes the
Englishman, all over the world, above men of equal breeding
and fortune in other nations, is the training of those peculiar
commonwealths, in which boys form a sort of constitution, and
govern themselves under the direction of a higher authority."
But he thinks that the over-use of prize-competitions and ex-

aminations is doing harm in the great English schools too,
though they are not yet enslaved by it as the Irish schools are:—

"I find that by the spirit of the age, and the various requirements
of many competitions, both English and Irish Schools have been
driven into the great vice of multiplying subjects of instruction,
and so crowding together hours of diverse teaching that the worst
results must inevitably ensue. There is, in the first place, that
enervating mental fatigue and consequent ill-health which is beginning to attract attention. When I visited Winchester it was easy
to distinguish in a large class the boys who had won their way into
the foundation by competition; they were remarkable for their
worn and unhealthy looks. This evil, however, the evil of over-
work at examination-courses, has already excited public attention,
and is, I trust, in a fair way of being remedied. Nor did it strike
me as at all so frequent, in Irish schools, as another mischief arising
from the same cause. It rather appeared to me all over Ireland, and
in England also, that the majority of boys, without being over-
worked, were *addled by the multiplicity* of their subjects, and
instead of increasing their knowledge had utterly confused it.
Whenever I asked the masters to point me out a brilliant boy,
they replied that the race had died out. Is it conceivable that this
arises from any inherent failing of the stock, and not rather from
some great blundering in the system of our education? The great
majority of thoughtful educators with whom I conferred agreed
that it was due to this constant addition of new subjects;—to the
cry after English grammar and English literature, and French and
German, and natural science; to the subdivision of the wretched
boy's time into two hours in the week for this, two hours for that,
alternate days for this, alternate days for that; in fact, to an injurious system of so teaching him everything that he can reason
intelligently in nothing. I cannot speak too strongly of the melancholy impression forced upon me by the examination of many
hundred boys in various schools through England and Ireland. I
sought in vain for bright promise, for quick intelligence, for keen
sympathy with their studies. It was not, I am sure, the boys' fault
nor the masters'. It is the result of the present boa-constrictor system of competitive examination which is strangling our youth in
its fatal embrace."

Professor Mahaffy finds fault with the Irish secondary schools
as too often dirty and untidy, and ill-provided with proper

accommodations. "Whitewashing, painting, and scouring of floors are urgently needed; indeed an additional supply of soap to the boys would not come amiss." He notices the Jesuit College of St. Stanislaus, and a school at Portarlington, as signal exceptions. In general "the floors are so filthy as to give a grimy and disgusting appearance to the whole room; people are so accustomed to this in all Irish schools that they wonder at my remarking it." At the chief of the Erasmus Smith's Schools, the high school in Dublin, "I was detained," he tells us, "some time at the door, owing to the deafness of the porter, and thus having ample leisure to inspect the front of the house found that the exceeding dirt of the windows made it pre-eminent, even among its shabbiest neighbours. I learned, on inquiry, that most of the window-sashes are not movable. It is surprising that the members of the Board are not offended by this aspect of squalor and decay. I found the playground a mass of mud, which was carried on the boys' boots all through the stairs and school-rooms, thus making the inside of the house correspond with the outside." Professor Mahaffy finds fault with the "wretched system of management" which prevails in the Endowed Schools,—a system which prevents needful re-forms, which perpetuates inefficient arrangements and perpetu-ates the employment of incompetent teachers, "old and wearied men." Those who elect the master, he says of the Clonmel School, "are two absent lords; and I suppose a more unlikely Board to select a good schoolmaster could not easily be found. In the present case a rule has been followed the very opposite of that which prevails in England. There a schoolmaster retires upon a living; here a clergyman has retired from a living upon a school." In another school, where the head-master is well qualified, Professor Mahaffy finds the assistant-master stopping the way:—

"But when we come to the assistant-master we find things in a deplorable condition. He holds his place by appointment of the patron, and is not removable by the head-master or Commissioners, or perhaps by any one. The present usher is a man of about eighty or ninety years of age, indeed he may possibly be one hundred; he is so dull and shrivelled with age that he only comes in late and is unable to teach anything. I do not think he comprehended who I was or what I wanted. His appointment dates from the remote past, and when I asked what his qualifications were or had once been, I could learn nothing but some vague legends about his great severity in early youth; in fact, I was told *he had once pult the ear off a boy*. But these were venerable traditions."

Finally, Professor Mahaffy finds fault with that which is our signal deficiency in England also, the want of all general organisation of the service of secondary instruction, of all co-ordination of the existing resources scattered over the country:—

"The general impression produced by a survey of the Irish Grammar Schools is this, that while there are many earnest and able men engaged in teaching and in improving the condition of education, all these efforts are individual efforts or scattered efforts, and the results produced are vastly inferior to those which might be expected from the existing national endowments both of money and of talent. For the Irish nation, with all its patent faults, is a clever nation; Irish boys are above the average in smartness and versatility. If the system of education were at all perfect, great intellectual results might fairly be expected."

Still, the tyranny of the intermediate course, and the bad effects it is producing on the Irish schools, are so completely the governing idea in our reporter's mind, that after enumerating all other hindrances to secondary instruction in Ireland, he cannot but return to this chief hindrance and conclude with it. He laments that the better endowed schools, at any rate, were not excluded by the Act from competing, and from ruining their school-course accordingly:—

"For my own part, I feel constrained to recommend (to Irish parents for their sons) schools in England or elsewhere, where this enslaving system has not penetrated. It may no doubt act as a great stimulus to bad schools, and to a low type of scholars, who had otherwise been subject to no test whatever. To all higher schools, and to the higher class of boys who desire and deserve a real education in literature and science, this competition is an almost unmixed evil. To the real schoolmaster, who desires to develop the nature of his boys after his own fashion and by his own methods, such a system is a death-blow. The day will yet come, when men will look back on the mania in our legislation for competition as the anxious blundering of honest reformers,   5 who tried to cure the occasional abuses of favouritism by substituting universal hardships, and to raise the tone of lower education by levelling down the higher, by substituting diversity for depth, and by destroying all that freedom and leisure in learning which are the true conditions of solid and lasting culture."   10

Professor Mahaffy admires, as I have said, the public schools in England, and envies us them greatly. "The English public school," he says, "remains and will remain a kind of training place to which no nation in Europe, not to say the Irish, can show a parallel." I agree with him in admiring our great public   15 schools; still, the capital failure of Ireland, in regard to secondary instruction, is exhibited by us also. We have indeed good schools in England, expensive but good, for the boys of the aristocratic and landed class, and of the higher professional classes, and for the sons of wealthy merchants and manufac-   20 turers. But it is not difficult to provide good schools for people who can and will, in considerable numbers, pay highly for them. Irish parents who belong to the aristocratic and landed class, or to the higher professional classes, or to the class of wealthy merchants and manufacturers, can and do send their   25 sons to our English public schools, and get them well trained and taught there. Professor Mahaffy approves of their doing so. "It is not the least surprising that Irish parents who can afford it should choose this system for the education of their boys. No foolish talk about patriotism, no idle rant about ab-   30 senteeism, can turn any conscientious parent from studying, above all, his children's welfare, and if he visits the great public schools of England he will certainly be impressed with their enormous advantages."

I cannot myself see any disadvantage, or anything but ad-   35 vantage, to an Irish boy in being trained at one of the English public schools. If, therefore, the middle class in Ireland could as a whole afford to use these schools, I should not bemoan its

condition, or busy myself about reforming the state of secondary instruction in Ireland. But it cannot. The bulk of the middle
class in Ireland cannot, and the bulk of the middle class in
England cannot either. The real weak point in the secondary
5   instruction of both countries is the same. M. Gambetta is the
son, I am told, of a tradesman at Cahors, and he was brought
up in the *lycée* of Cahors; a school not so delightful and historic
as Eton, certainly, but with a status as honourable as that of
Eton, and with a teaching on the whole as good. In what kind
10 of schools are the sons of tradesmen in England and Ireland
brought up? They are brought up in the worst and most ignoble
secondary schools in Western Europe. Ireland has nothing to
envy us here. For the great bulk of our middle class, no less
than for the great bulk of hers, the school-provision is miser-
15 ably inadequate.

It can only become adequate by being treated as a public
service, as a service for which the State, the nation in its collective and corporate character, is responsible. This proposition
I have often advanced and sufficiently expounded. To me its
20 truth seems self-evident, and the practice of other countries is
present, besides, to speak for it. I am not going to enlarge upon
this theme now. I want rather to point out how it comes to pass,
that in England and Ireland the truth is not accepted and acted
upon, and what difference there is, in this respect, between the
25 case of England and that of Ireland.

In England, secondary instruction is not a public service,
popular politicians and speakers at public meetings would tell
us, because of the individual energy and self-reliance of the
Englishman, and his dislike to State-interference. No doubt
30 there is in the Englishman a repugnance to being meddled with,
a desire to be let alone. No doubt he likes to act individually
whenever he can, and not to have recourse to action of a collective and corporate character. To make even popular education a public service was very difficult. It is only a few years
35 since one might hear State-aided elementary schools described
as schools with the *State-taint* upon them. However, the ex-
pediency and necessity of making popular education a public
service grew to appear so manifest, that the repugnance was

overcome. So far as our popular education is concerned, the reproach of *State-taint* has disappeared from people's mouths and minds.

Now, to make middle-class education a public service is only less expedient and necessary than to make popular education a public service. But, as to popular education, the light has dawned upon the community here in England; as to middle-class education, it has not. To talk of the *State-taint* in this case is still popular; and a prominent member of the governing class, such as Lord Frederick Cavendish, will go and extol a middle-class audience, composed of people with a defective type of religion, a narrow range of intellect and knowledge, a stunted sense of beauty, a low standard of manners,—he will positively go and extol them for their energy and self-reliance in not adopting the means most naturally and directly fitted to lift them out of this imperfect state of civilisation, and will win their delighted applause by doing so.

This is a phenomenon of our social politics which receives its explanation, as I have often said, only when we consider that the upper class amongst us does not wish to be disturbed in its preponderance, or the middle class in its vulgarity. Not that Lord Frederick Cavendish does not speak in perfect good faith. He takes as a general rule the native English conviction that to act individually is a wholesome thing, and thinks that he cannot be wrong in applying it in any novel case that may arise. Still, at the bottom of the mind of our governing class is an instinct, on this matter of education, telling it that a really good and public education of the middle class is the surest means of removing, in the end, those inferiorities which at present make our middle class impossible as a governing class, and our upper class indispensable:—and this removal it is not every one in a governing class who can desire, though every one ought to desire it.

That the middle class should seek not to be disturbed in its vulgarity may seem more strange. But here, too, is at bottom the native English instinct for following one's individual course, for not being meddled with. Then, also, what most strongly moves and attaches, or has most strongly moved and attached

hitherto, the strongest part of our middle class, the Puritan part, is the type of religion to which their nature and circumstances have since the Reformation led them. Now, to this type of religion, the State, or the nation acting as a whole in its col-
5 lective and corporate character, has in general not been favourable. They are apprehensive, then, that to their religion a training in the schools of the State might not be favourable. Indeed, to the whole narrow system of life, arising out of the peculiar conjunction of the second great interest of their lives,
10 business, with the first great interest of their lives, religion,— a system of life now become a second nature to them and greatly endeared to their hearts,— they are apprehensive that the wider ideas and larger habits of public schools might not be favourable. And so they are, on their part, as little forward to
15 make middle-class education a public service as the governing class, on their part, are little forward to do so. And although the necessities of the future, and a pressing sense of the defects of its actual civilisation, will in the end force the middle class to change its line and to demand what it now shrinks from, yet
20 this has not happened yet, and perhaps may not happen for some years to come, may not happen in our life-time.

   If, therefore, secondary instruction remains in a very faulty and incoherent state in England, at least it is by the English nation's own doing that it remains so. The governing class
25 here is not seriously concerned to make it adequate and coherent; it is, on the contrary, indisposed to do so. That governing class will do what is actually desired and demanded of it by the middle class, by the class on whose favour political power depends; but it will do no more. The middle class, again, the
30 class immediately concerned, has not yet acquired sufficient lucidity of mind to desire public schools, and to demand the resolute investigation and appliance of the best means for making them good. It has no such simple and logical aims governing its mind in this matter. A coherent system of public middle-
35 class schools it does not at present want at all. Aims of quite another sort govern our middle class whenever anything has to be done in regard to education. Its Protestant feelings must

be respected, openings must be provided as far as possible for its children, and whatever is done must be plausible. And the governing class will always take good care to meet its wishes.

Professor Mahaffy will find that the things which so disturb his peace as a lover of education are all due to this cause: that the English middle class has aims quite other than the direct aim of making education efficient, and that the governing class, in whatever it does, respects and consults these aims of the middle class. He complains of the Intermediate Board and its system of prizes and examinations. But what would he have? Something had to be done for Irish secondary instruction. But the English public was by no means simply bent on doing what was best for this; alas! it is not even bent on doing what is best for its own! Something, I say, had to be done in Ireland for secondary instruction; but, in doing it, the Protestant feelings of the public of Great Britain must before all things be respected. "The Liberal party has emphatically condemned religious endowment; the Protestants of Great Britain are implacably hostile to the endowment of Catholicism in any shape or form." And the Government paid all due respect to these Liberal and Protestant feelings. Hence the Intermediate Board.

The whole system of perpetual competitive examinations everywhere, which Professor Mahaffy thinks so fatal, and which he attributes to the anxious blundering of honest reformers trying to cure the occasional abuses of favouritism, is he right in so attributing it? Surely not; there was no such blundering as he speaks of, because there was no desire to discover and do what was positively best in the matter. But the great British middle-class public had a desire to procure as many openings as possible for its children, and the Government could gratify this desire, and also relieve itself of responsibility. Hence our competitive examinations. The composition of the Boards and Commissions for Education, again, on which so much depends when studies have to be organised and programmes laid down, Professor Mahaffy is dissatisfied with them. He wants, he says, "one responsible body, not made up altogether of lords

and bishops and judges who give their spare moments to such
duties, but mainly of practical educators. No one is so likely to
be led away by novelties as the elderly amateur in education,
who knows nothing of its practical working, and legislates on
specious theories. So long as Boards in Ireland are chiefly made
up of people of social or political importance only, education
will not prosper." But does Professor Mahaffy imagine that the
British public has a fancy for a lucid and logical-minded Board,
simply bent on perfecting education? Not at all! it wants a
Board that is plausible; and the Government, whenever it institutes a Board, at least does its best to make a plausible one.
Hence the "lords and bishops and judges;" hence the "elderly
amateur." Professor Mahaffy anticipates that the new Irish
University will probably be arranged like the Intermediate
Board, and not as a lover of education would desire. On that
point I will give no opinion; all I am sure of is that it will be
arranged plausibly. That is what our middle-class public want,
and the Government will certainly accomplish it.

No, the great English middle-class public is at present by no
means bent seriously on making education efficient all round.
It prefers its routine and its claptrap to even its own education.
It is and must be free to do so if it likes. We who lament its
doing so, we who see what it loses by doing so, we can only
resolve not to be dupes of its claptrap ourselves, and not to help
in duping others with it, but to work with patience and perseverance for the evocation of that better spirit which will
surely arise in this great class at last.

Meanwhile, however, the English middle class sacrifices to
its routine and claptrap not only its own education, but the
education of the Irish middle class also. And this is certainly
hard. It is hard, that is, if the Irish middle class is not of one
mind with it in the matter, does not share in its routine and
claptrap and prefer them to its own education. I suppose no
one will dispute that the type of secondary instruction in the
Intermediate Board, the type of superior instruction in the new
Irish University, is determined by that maxim regnant, as we
are told, in the middle-class electorate of Great Britain: "The
Liberal party has emphatically condemned religious endow-

ment." And this when we have, in Great Britain, Oxford and Cambridge, and Eton and Winchester, and the Scotch universities! And one of the organs of the British Philistine expresses astonishment at my thinking it worth while at the present day to collect Burke's Irish writings,—says that the state of things with which Burke had to deal is now utterly gone, that he had to deal with Protestant ascendency, and that "the Catholics have now not a single cause of complaint." As if the Intermediate Board, as if the new Irish University, determined in the manner they are, and from the motives they are, were not in themselves evidences of the continued reign of Protestant ascendency!

But not only has Ireland a just claim not to have her education determined by the "Protestant feelings" of Great Britain. She has a just claim not to have it determined by other feelings, also, of our British public, which go to determine it now. She has a just claim, in short, to have it determined as she herself likes. It is a plea, as I have elsewhere said, for Home Rule, if the way of dealing with education, and with other like things, which satisfies our Murdstones and Quinions, but does not satisfy people of quicker minds, is imposed on these people when they desire something better, because it is the way which our Murdstones and Quinions know and like. The Murdstones and Quinions of our middle class, with their strong individuality and their peculiar habits of life, do not want things instituted by the State, by the nation acting in its collective and corporate character. They do not want State schools, or State festivals, or State theatres. They prefer their Salem House, and their meeting, and their music-hall, and to be congratulated by Lord Frederick Cavendish upon their energy and self-reliance. And this is all very well for the Murdstones and Quinions, since they like to have it so. But it is hard that they should insist on the Irishman, too, acting as if he had the same peculiar taste, if he have not.

With other nations, the idea of the State, of the nation in its collective and corporate character, instituting means for developing and dignifying the national life, has great power. Such a disposition of mind is also more congenial, perhaps, to the Irish people likewise, than the disposition of mind of our middle class in Great Britain. The executive Government in Ireland is a very different thing from the executive Government in England, and has a much more stringent operation. But it does little, nevertheless, in this sense of giving effect to aspirations of the national life for developing and raising itself. Dublin Castle is rather a bureau of management for governing the country in compliance, as far as possible, with English ideas.

If the Irish desire to make the State do otherwise and better in Ireland than it does in England, if they wish their middle-class education, for instance, to be a public service with the organisation and guarantees of a public service, they may fairly claim to have these wishes listened to. And listened to, if they are clearly formed, rationally conceived, and steadily persisted in, such wishes ultimately must be. It would be too monstrous that Ireland should be refused an advantage which she desires, and which all our civilised neighbours on the Continent find indispensable, because the middle class in England does not care to claim for itself the advantage in question. The great thing is for the Irish to make up their own minds clearly on the matter. Do they earnestly desire to make their middle-class education adequate and efficient; to leave it no longer dependent on "individual efforts, scattered efforts;" to rescue it from its dirt and dilapidation, and from such functionaries as the aged assistant *who once pult the ear off a boy?* Then let them make it a public service. Does Professor Mahaffy wish to relieve Irish boys from the unintelligent tyranny of endless examinations and competitions, and from being "stupefied by a multiplicity of subjects?" Let him, then, get his countrymen to demand that their secondary instruction shall be made a public service, with the honest, single-minded, logically-pursued aim of efficiency.

Then these questions as to studies, competitions, and examinations will come,—as with us at present, whether in England or in Ireland, they never come,—under responsible review by a competent mind; and this is what is wanted. The "personages of high social standing," the "lords and bishops and judges," the "elderly amateur," of whom Professor Mahaffy complains, will cease to potter; and we shall have, instead, the responsible review of a competent mind. Ireland will not only be doing good to herself by demanding this, by obtaining this; she will also be teaching England and the English middle class how to live.

5

Preface to *Irish Essays*

The Essays which make the chief part of this volume have all appeared during the last year or two in well-known periodicals. The Prefaces which follow at the end were published in 1853 and 1854 as prefaces to my *Poems,* and have not been reprinted
5 since. Some of the readers of my poetry have expressed a wish for their reappearance, and with that wish I here comply. Exactly as they stand, I should not have written them now; but perhaps they are none the worse on that account.

The three essays regarding Ireland which commence the
10 present volume, and which give it its title, were received with no great favour when they appeared, and will probably be received with no great favour now. Practical politicians and men of the world are apt rather to resent the incursion of a man of letters into the field of politics; he is, in truth, not on his own
15 ground there, and is in peculiar danger of talking at random. No one feels this more than I do. Nevertheless I have set in the front of this volume the essays on Irish affairs. If I am asked why, I should be disposed to answer that I am curious to know how they will look ten years hence, if anyone hap-
20 pens then to turn to them.

English people keep asking themselves what we ought to do about Ireland. The great contention of these essays is, that in order to attach Ireland to us solidly, English people have not only to *do* something different from what they have done
25 hitherto, they have also to *be* something different from what they have been hitherto. As a whole, as a community, they have to acquire a larger and sweeter temper, a larger and more lucid mind. And this is indeed no light task, yet it is the capital task now appointed to us, and our safety depends on our accom-

312

plishing it: to *be* something different, much more, even, than
to *do* something different.

I have enquired how far the Irish Land Act seemed likely, to
a fair and dispassionate observer, to attach Ireland to us, to
prove *healing*. It was easy to see reasons for thinking beforehand   5
that it would not prove healing. Now that it is in operation, it
is easy to see reasons for thinking so still. At the present moment
one especial aspect of the matter can hardly fail to catch any
clear-sighted man's attention. No one can deny that the Act
seems likely to have a very large and far-reaching effect. But   10
neither can it be denied, on the other hand, that leading Ministers declared their belief, which of course was entirely sincere,
that the number of extortionate landlords in Ireland was inconsiderable, and that the general reduction of rents in Ireland
would be inconsiderable. But it turns out that probably the   15
general reduction of rents in Ireland, through the operation of
the Land Courts fixing a judicial rent, will, on the contrary, be
very considerable. Most certainly the inference of the people
of Ireland will be that the number of extortionate landlords,
also, was in fact very considerable. But this was just the con-   20
tention of the people of Ireland. The Government, however,
did not admit its truth, and instituted the Land Courts without
expecting that they would bring about any radical and universal
change. If, therefore, they do bring about such a change, what,
even though the Irish tenants profit by it, will be their gratitude   25
to the Government? They will say that the English Government has done them a service without intending it, and without
understanding and acknowledging the justice of their case. But
so strong was the justice of their case, they will say, that it
victoriously established itself as soon as the English Govern-   30
ment, not dreaming of any such result, gave them a tribunal for
determining a fair rent.

It seems to me impossible not to see this, if one does not either
shut one's eyes or turn them another way. We shall have
brought about a radical change, we shall have established by law   35
a divided ownership full of critical consequences, we shall have
disturbed the accepted and ordinary constitutive characters of
property,—and we shall get little or no gratitude for it; we

shall be said to have done it without intending it. Our measure
is not likely, therefore, of itself to avail to win the affections of
the Irish people to us and to heal their estrangement. Yet to
make a radical change without doing this, opens no good pros-
5   pect for the future. To break down the landlords in Ireland,
as we have already broken down the Protestant Church there,
is merely to complete the destruction of the *modus vivendi*
hitherto existing for society in that country; a most imperfect
modus vivendi indeed, but the only one practically attained
10 there up to this time as a substitute for anarchy. Simply to
leave to the Irish people the free and entire disposal of their
own affairs is recommended by some counsellors as the one
safe solution of the Irish difficulty. But the safety of this solution depends upon the state and dispositions of the people to
15 whom we apply it. May not a people be in such a state that
Shakespeare's words hold true of it—

> ". . . Your affections are
> A sick man's appetite, who desires most that
> Which would increase his evil?"

20 And may it not be affirmed, that if ever those words seemed
true of any people, they seem true of the Irish at this hour?
To heal the estrangement between Ireland and England is
what is needed above all things, and I cannot say that the Land
Act appears to me to have in itself the elements for healing it.
25 Nor can I see the use of pretending to find them in it if they
are not really there. Nothing, indeed, could be more absurd
than for irresponsible people to press seriously their fancy solu-
tions, though they may properly enough throw them out, on
a suitable occasion, for purposes of discussion and illustration.
30 Nothing, moreover, is further from my thoughts, in what is
here said, than to find fault with the responsible Government,
which has to provide not a fancy solution for difficulties, but a
solution which may be put in practice. I know that it was as
impossible to go on governing Ireland by means of the land-
35 lords as by means of the Protestant Church. I am ready to admit
that the Government, the *power* and *purchase* at their disposal
being what it is, could not well but have had recourse to some

such measure as the Land Act. I think, even, as I have said in the following pages, that the Land Act of the Government, with what it does and what it gives the power of doing, is probably quite capable of satisfying the Irish people as a Land Act, if a certain other indispensable condition is complied with. But this condition the Land Act will not of itself realise. The indispensable condition is, that England and English civilisation shall become more attractive; or, as I began by saying, that we should not only *do* to Ireland something different from what we have done hitherto, but should also *be* something different. On this need of a changed and more attractive power in English civilisation almost all the essays in the present volume, and not alone those dealing directly with Ireland, will be found to insist.

The barren logomachies of Plato's *Theætetus* are relieved by half-a-dozen immortal pages, and among them are those in which is described the helplessness of the philosopher in the ways of the world, the helplessness of the man of the world in a spiritual crisis. The philosopher Thales in the ditch had been an easy and a frequent subject for merriment; it was reserved for Plato to amuse himself with the practical politician and man of the world in a spiritual crisis. Mr. Jowett is uncommonly happy in his translation of Plato's account of the man of the world, at such a crisis, "drawn into the upper air," having to "get himself out of his commonplaces to the consideration of government and of human happiness and misery in general,—what they are, and how a man is to attain the one and avoid the other." "Then, indeed," says Plato, "when that narrow, vain, little practical mind is called to account about all this, he gives the philosopher his revenge. For, dizzied by the height at which he is hanging, whence he looks into space, which is a strange experience to him, he being dismayed and lost and stammering out broken words is laughed at, not by Thracian handmaidens such as laughed at Thales, or by any other uneducated persons, for they have no eye for the situation, but by every man who has been brought up as a true freeman."

Our practical politicians and men of the world, carried up by the course of time and change into a new air, and still ruefully trying there to gasp out their formulas, such as "Freedom

of contract," or "The Liberal party has emphatically condemned religious endowment," or "Our traditional, existing,
social arrangements," could not be better hit off. The man of
the world, with his utter astonishment that the Irish tenants
should stop the hunting, when the hunting "caused the noble
master of the hounds to spend among them ten thousand a
year!" the man of the world, with his mournful and incessant
cries of "Revolution!" Yes, we are in a revolution; "a revolution," as the late Duke of Wellington said, "by due course of
law." And one of the features of it is, that the Irish tenants prefer to stop the hunting of those whom they regard as a set of
aliens encamped amongst them for sporting purposes, who
have in the past treated them and spoken to them as if they were
slaves, and who are disposed, many of them, to treat them and
speak to them as if they were slaves still,—the Irish people had
rather stop this hunting, than profit by an expenditure upon it
to the tune of ten thousand a year. The man of the world has
had and has one formula for attaching neighbours and tenants
to us, and one only,—expenditure. And now he is "drawn into
upper air," and has to hear such new and strange formulas as
this, for example, of the most charming of French moralists:—
*Pour gagner l'humanité, il faut lui plaire; pour lui plaire, il faut
être aimable.* Or, if the man of the world can stand Holy Writ,
let him hear the Psalmist:—"*Mansueti possidebunt terram*, the
gentle shall possess the earth."

Indeed we are at the end of a period, and always at the end
of a period the word goes forth: "Now is the judgment of this
world." The "traditional, existing, social arrangements," which
satisfied before, satisfy no longer; the conventions and phrases,
which once passed without question, are challenged. That saying of the saints comes to be fulfilled: *Peribit totum quod non
est ex Deo ortum.* Each people has its own periods of national
life, with their own characters. The period which is now ending for England is that which began, when, after the sensuous
tumult of the Renascence, Catholicism being discredited and
gone, our serious nation desired, as had been foretold, "to see
one of the days of the Son of Man and did not see it;" but men
said to them, *See here* or *See there*, and they went after the

blind guides and followed the false direction; and the actual civilisation of England and of America is the result. A civilisation with many virtues! but without lucidity of mind, and without largeness of temper. And now we English, at any rate, have to acquire them, and to learn the necessity for us "to live,"   5 as Emerson says, "from a greater depth of being." The sages and the saints alike have always preached this necessity; the so-called practical people and men of the world have always derided it. In the present collapse of their wisdom, we ought to find it less hard to rate their stock ideas and stock phrases,   10 their claptrap and their catchwords, at their proper value, and to cast in our lot boldly with the sages and with the saints. *Sine ut mortui sepeliant mortuos suos, sed tu vade adnuntia regnum Dei.*

Appendix

1. Arnold's Selection from Wordsworth's Poems.

Poems of Ballad Form

We are Seven; Lucy Gray; Ancedote for Fathers; Alice Fell; The Pet Lamb; The Childless Father; The Reverie of Poor Susan; Power of Music; Star-Gazers.

Narrative Poems

Ruth; Simon Lee; Fidelity; Incident Characteristic of a Favourite Dog; Hart-Leap Well; The Force of Prayer; The Affliction of Margaret; The Complaint of a Forsaken Indian Woman; Song at the Feast of Brougham Castle; The Leech-Gatherer, or, Resolution and Independence; The Brothers; Michael; Margaret [*The Excursion*, I, 1—37, 443—933, 939—70].

Lyrical Poems

"My Heart leaps up"; To a Butterfly ["Stay near me—"]; The Sparrow's Nest; To a Butterfly ["I've watched you"]; The Redbreast and Butterfly; "The Cock is crowing"; To the Daisy ["Bright flower"]; To the Small Celandine ["Pansies, Lilies"]; To the same Flower ["Pleasures newly found"]; "I wandered lonely as a Cloud"; To a Sky-Lark ["Up with me!"]; Stray Pleasures; To my Sister ["It is the first mild day"]; Lines written in early Spring; Expostulation and Reply; The Tables turned; To a Young Lady; To Hartley Coleridge; "O Nightingale, thou surely art"; "Strange Fits of Passion have I known"; "Three Years she grew"; "She dwelt among the untrodden Ways"; "A Slumber did my Spirit seal"; "I travelled among unknown Men"; To the Cuckoo ["O blithe New-comer!"]; To a Sky-Lark ["Ethereal Minstrel!"]; "She was a Phantom of Delight"; To a Highland Girl; Stepping Westward; The Solitary

Reaper; At the Grave of Burns; Thoughts suggested the day following; Yarrow Unvisited; Yarrow Visited; Yarrow Revisited; To May.

Poems Akin to the Antique, and Odes

Laodameia; Dion; Character of the Happy Warrior; Lines on the
expected Invasion; The Pillar of Trajan; September 1819; Ode to
Lycoris ["An age hath been"]; Ode to Duty; Ode on Intimations of
Immortality.

Sonnets

I. Composed by the Sea-side, near Calais, August 1802; II. Calais,
August 1802; III. On the Extinction of the Venetian Republic; IV.
To Toussaint l'Ouverture; V. September 1802; VI. Thought of a
Briton on the Subjugation of Switzerland; VII. Written in London,
September 1802; VIII. "The World is too much with us"; IX. Lon-
don, 1802; X. "It is not to be thought of"; XI. "When I have borne
in Memory"; XII. October 1803 ["These times"]; XIII. To the Men
of Kent. October 1803; XIV. In the Pass of Killicranky, an Invasion
being expected, October 1803; XV. "England! the time is come";
XVI. November 1806; XVII. To Thomas Clarkson; XVIII. 1811
["Here pause"]; XIX. "Scorn not the Sonnet"; XX. "Nuns fret
not"; XXI. "Pelion and Ossa flourish"; XXII. "Adieu, Rydalian
Laurels!"; XXIII. Personal Talk ["I am not"]; XXIV. Continued
["Wings have we"]; XXV. Concluded ["Nor can I"]; XXVI. To
Sleep ["A flock of sheep"]; XXVII. "It is a beauteous Evening";
XXVIII. "Where lies the Land?"; XXIX. Composed upon West-
minster Bridge, Sept. 3, 1803; XXX. "I watch, and long have
watched"; XXXI. Scenery between Namur and Liege; XXXII. Com-
posed at Neidpath Castle ["Degenerate Douglas!"]; XXXIII. "Sole
listener, Duddon!"; XXXIV. Seathwaite Chapel; XXXV. "Return,
Content!"; XXXVI. After-Thought; XXXVII. Seclusion ["Lance,
shield, and sword"]; XXXVIII. Rush-Bearing [also called "Rural
Ceremony"]; XXXIX. Inside of King's College Chapel, Cambridge
["Tax not"]; XL. To the Author's Portrait; XLI. Mary, Queen of
Scots, Landing at the Mouth of the Derwent, Workington; XLII.
"Most sweet it is"; XLIII. On the Departure of Sir Walter Scott
from Abbotsford, for Naples; XLIV. To B. R. Haydon, Esq.
["High is our calling"]; XLV. "They called Thee MERRY ENGLAND";
XLVI. "The Pibroch's Note, discountenanced or mute"; XLVII.
"*A Poet!*"; XLVIII. The Pine of Monte Mario at Rome; XLIX.

To the Memory of Raisley Calvert; L. To Rotha Quillinan; LI.
The Trossachs; LII. Composed on a May morning, 1838; LIII.
Highland Hut; LIV. "*There!* said a Stripling"; LV. To a Painter
["All praise"]; LVI. On the same Subject ["Though I beheld"];
LVII. In Sight of the Town of Cockermouth; LVIII. Tranquillity
["Tranquillity! the sovereign aim"]; LIX. Admonition; LX.
"Wansfell! this Household has a favoured Lot."

Reflective and Elegiac Poems

"If Thou indeed"; Influence of Natural Objects; "There was a Boy";
Yew-Trees; Lines composed a few miles above Tintern Abbey;
Address to my Infant Daughter Dora; Lines left upon a Seat in a
Yew-Tree; French Revolution ["Oh! pleasant exercise"]; The
Simplon Pass; Fragment from *The Recluse* ["On Man, on Nature,"];
The Old Cumberland Beggar; Animal Tranquillity and Decay;
Nutting; To Joanna; The Fir-Grove Path ["When, to the attrac-
tions"]; A Farewell; Stanzas written in Thomson's Castle of Indol-
ence; Tribute to the Memory of a Dog; The Small Celandine
["There is a Flower"]; Beggars; Sequel to the Foregoing; Matthew;
The two April Mornings; The Fountain; Lines written on the ex-
pected death of Mr. Fox; Elegiac Stanzas, suggested by a Picture of
Peele Castle; Glen-Almain, or, the Narrow Glen; Written on a
Blank Leaf of Macpherson's Ossian; The Wishing-Gate; To the
Lady Fleming ["Blest is this Isle"]; To the Rev. Dr. Wordsworth;
Evening Voluntaries—I. "Not in the lucid intervals of life"; II. "The
Sun, that seemed so mildly to retire"; To Mary Wordsworth ["O
dearer far"]; To a Child ["Small service"]; Extempore Effusion
upon the Death of James Hogg; Devotional Incitements; Inscription
for a Stone in the Grounds of Rydal Mount ["In these fair vales"].

Subsequent editions added another poem "To the Daisy" ["In
youth from rock to rock"]; "The Green Linnet"; "The Cuckoo
Again" ["Yes, it was"]; "The Primrose of the Rock." Sonnets XXI,
XXII, XXXII, XXXIV, XLV, and LI were dropped and replaced
by: XXI. Catherine Wordsworth ["Surprised by joy"]; XL. [King's
College Chapel] Continued ["They dreamt not"]; XLV. Mutability;
LI. To Lady Fitzgerald, in her seventieth Year ["Such age how
beautiful!"]; LIX. Death ["Methought I saw"]; LX. The Everlasting
Temple ["In my mind's eye"]. In the final section, "A Poet's Epitaph"
is added.

II.   Arnold's Selection from Byron's Poems

Personal, Lyric, and Elegiac

Loch Na Garr [also called "Lachin y Gair"]; "Well! thou art happy"; Epistle to a Friend; To Thomas Moore ["My boat is on the shore"] Childe Harold's Departure [I, iv–xi]; Stanzas composed during a Thunderstorm; "Maid of Athens"; To Inez ["Nay, smile not"]; "One struggle more"; Euthanasia; "And Thou art Dead"; "When We Two Parted"; Stanzas for Music ["There's not a joy"]; Stanzas to Augusta ["Though the day"]; Solitude [*Childe Harold*, II, xxv–xxvi]; Nature the Consoler [*CH*, III, xiii–xv]; The Same [*CH*, III, lxxi–lxxv]; The Poet and the World [*CH*, III, cxiii–cxiv]; Bereavement [*CH*, II, xcviii]; Last Leaving England [*CH*, III, i–ii]; England [*CH*, IV, viii–x]; Ruins to Ruins [*CH*, IV, cxxx–cxxxi]; The Dream ["I saw two beings" to end]; The Poet's Curse [*CH*, IV, cxxxiv–cxxxvii]; Nature to the Last [*CH*, IV, clxxv–clxxxiv]; "She Walks in Beauty"; "Oh! Snatch'd Away"; Song of Saul; Vision of Belshazzar; Destruction of Sennacherib; Ode to Napoleon Buonaparte; Ode on Waterloo ["We do not curse thee,"]; Napoleon's Farewell; Lament of Tasso [lines 1–42]; Dante in Exile [*Prophecy of Dante*, I, 130–78]; The Isles of Greece; Lines to a Lady Weeping; Death of the Princess Charlotte [*CH*, IV, clxvii–clxxii]; Immortality [*CH*, II, vii–viii]; "On this Day I complete my Thirty-sixth Year"; Life [*Don Juan*, XV, xcix].

Descriptive and Narrative

Greece [The Corsair, III, 1–54]; The Same [*The Giaour*, 7–141]; The Same [*CH*, II, lxxiii–lxxvii]; The Same [*CH*, II, lxxxiv–lxxxviii]; Hellespont [*Bride of Abydos*, II, 1–27]; Troy [*DJ*, IV, lxxvi–lxxviii]; The Drachenfels [*CH*, III, 496–535]; Waterloo [*CH*, III, xxi–xxx]; Lake of Geneva.—Calm [*CH*, III, lxxxv–lxxxvii]; Lake of Geneva.—Storm [*CH*, III, xcii–xcvi]; Clarens [*CH*, III, xcix–civ]; Italy [*CH*, IV, xlii–xlvii]; Venice [*CH*, IV, i–iv]; The Same [*CH*, IV, xi–xiii]; The Same [*CH*, IV, xviii]; An August Evening in Italy [*CH*, IV, xxvii–xxix]; The Ave Maria [*DJ*, III, cii–ciii, cv–cix]; Arqua [*CH*, IV, xxx–xxxii]; Clitumnus [*CH*, IV, lxvi–lvii]; Terni [*CH*, IV, lxix–lxxii]; Rome [*CH*, IV, lxxviii–lxxix]; The Coliseum [*CH*, IV, cxxxix–cxlv]; Tomb of Cecilia Metella [*CH*, IV, xcix–ciii]; Grotto of Egeria [*CH*, IV, cxv–cxxiv]; Sonnet on Chillon; Bonnivard and his Brothers [*The Pris-*

oner of Chillon, 107–218]; Bonnivard alone [*The Prisoner of Chillon*, 231–392]; The East [*Bride of Abydos*, I, 1–19]; Journey and Death of Hassan [*The Giaour*, 519–619, 655–674]; Hassan's Mother [*The Giaour*, 689–722]; The Giaour's Love [*The Giaour*, 1099–1130]; Death of Selim [*Bride of Abydos*, II, 491–620]; Corsair Life [*The Corsair*, I, 1–42]; Parting of Conrad and Medora [*The Corsair*, I, 466–504]; Conrad's Return [*The Corsair*, III, 567–625]; Alp and Francesca [*Siege of Corinth*, 424–677]; The Assault [*Siege of Corinth*, 680–722, 769–70, 775–93, 847–878]; Parisina [*Parisina*, 1–28]; The Last of Ezzelin [*Lara*, II, 550–93]; Mazeppa's Ride [*Mazeppa*, 358–568, 574–75, 579–641, 643–715, 718–21, 783–847]; The Streamlet from the Cliff [*The Island*, III, 63–72]; The Shipwreck [*DJ*, II, xlix–liii]; Haidée [*DJ*, II, cxi–cxviii]; Haidée again [*DJ*, III, lxx–lxxv]; Aurora Raby [*DJ*, XV, xliii–xlvii].

Dramatic

Manfred and the Seven Spirits [*Manfred* I, i, 1–231]; Manfred on the Cliffs [I, ii, 1–125]; The Witch of the Alps [*Manfred*, II, ii, 1–204]; Astarte [*Manfred*, II, iv, 28–167]; Manfred's Farewell to the Sun [III, ii, 3–30]; Manfred's End [III, iv, 1–151]; Dying Speech of the Doge of Venice [*Marino Faliero*, V, iii, 26–79, 84–101]; Death of Salemenes [*Sardanapalus*, V, i, 88–133]; Death of Jacopo Foscari [*The Two Foscari*, IV, i, 177–217]; Cain and Lucifer in the Abyss of Space [*Cain*, II, i, 26–135]; Cain and Adah [III, i, 1–161].

Satiric

Fame ["Oh, talk not to me"]; Written after Swimming from Sestos to Abydos; On my thirty-third Birthday ["Through life's dull road"]; To Mr. Murray ["For Orford and for Waldegrave"]; Epistle from Mr. Murray to Dr. Polidori ["Dear Doctor, I have read," lines 1–66, 83–90]; To Mr. Murray ["Strahan, Tonson,"]; Holland House [*English Bards*, 540–59]; Epilogue to *English Bards and Scotch Reviewers* [1037–66]; The Landed Interest [*The Age of Bronze*, 568–631]; Italy [*Beppo*, xli–xlv]; England [*Beppo*, xlvii–xlix]; Wanted—a Hero [*DJ*, I, i–v]; London [*DJ*, X, lxxxi–lxxxii]; Things Sweet [*DJ*, I, cxxiii–cxxvii]; Lambro's Return [*DJ*, III, xxvii, xxix–xli]; A Stormed City [*DJ*, VIII, cxxiii–cxxvii]; Exhortation to Mr. Wilberforce [*DJ*, XIV, lxxxii—lxxxiv]; Exhortation to Mrs. Fry [*DJ*, X, lxxxv–lxxxvii]; Satan claims, at Heaven's Gate, George the Third [*The Vision of Judgment*, xlii–xlix]; The

Sex [*CH*, II, xxxiv]; Our Children [*DJ*, III, lix—lx]; Soul [*DJ*, XIV, lxx—lxxii]; Mobility [*DJ*, XVI, xcvi—xcviii]; Great Names [*DJ*, III, xc—xcv, xcviii—c]; Poetical Commandments [*DJ*, I, cciv—ccvi]; Byron and his Contemporaries [*DJ*, XI, liii—lx]; Poetical Production [*DJ*, XIV, x—xi]; The Lighter Side [*DJ*, IV, iii—iv].

III. Arnold's Selection from Gray in Ward's *English Poets.*

Ode on the Spring; Ode on a distant prospect of Eton College; Hymn to Adversity; The Progress of Poesy; The Bard; Elegy written in a Country Churchyard; Sonnet on the death of Mr. Richard West; Sketch of his own Character; Impromptu, on Lord Holland's Seat at Kingsgate.

IV. Arnold's Selection from Keats in Ward's *English Poets.*

Beauty [*Endymion*, I, 1—24]; Endymion ["I stood tip-toe," lines 193-204]; Hymn to Pan [*Endymion*, I, 279—92]; Bacchus [*Endymion*, IV, 193—203]; Cynthia's Bridal Evening ["I stood tip-toe," lines 215—38]; Saturn [*Hyperion*, I, 1—51]; Coelus to Hyperion [I, 309—57]; Oceanus [*Hyperion*, II, 167—243]; Hyperion's Arrival [II, 346—78]; The Flight ["Eve of St. Agnes," xxv—xlii]; Ode to a Nightingale; Ode on a Grecian Urn; Ode ["Bards of Passion and of Mirth"]; To Autumn; Lines on the Mermaid Tavern; Sonnets: I, On First Looking into Chapman's Homer; II, Written in January, 1817 ["After dark vapours"]; III, Written in January, 1818 ["When I have fears"]; IV, Addressed to Haydon ["Great spirits"]; V, On the Grasshopper and Cricket; VI, The Human Seasons ["Four Seasons fill"]; VII, On a Picture of Leander ["Come hither, all sweet maidens"]; VIII, Keats's Last Sonnet ["Bright star!"]; The Bard Speaks ["Epistle to my Brother George," lines 71—109].

V. Arnold's Selection from Burke.

Tracts on the Popery Laws; A Letter to Sir Charles Bingham, Bart., on the Irish Absentee Tax; A Letter to the Honourable Charles James Fox; Two Letters to Gentlemen in Bristol; Mr. Burke's Speech at the Guildhall, in Bristol, 1780; A Letter to a Peer of Ireland on the Penal Laws against Irish Catholics; A Letter to Sir Hercules Langrishe, M.P., 1792; A Letter to the Right Honourable Edmund Pery; A Letter to Thomas Burgh, Esq.; A Letter to John Merlott, Esq.; A Letter to William Smith, Esq.; A Second Letter to Sir Hercules Langrishe; A Letter to Richard Burke, Esq.; A Letter on the Affairs of Ireland, 1797.

Private Letters: To the Duke of Portland, September 14, 1794; To the Rev. Dr. Hussey, February 4, 1795; To Hussey, May 18, 1795; To Thomas Keogh, Esq., November 17, 1796; To Hussey, December, 1796; To the Right Honourable Wm. Windham, March 30, 1796; To Dr. Laurence, June 5, 1797.

Critical and Explanatory Notes

References to Arnold's diary-notebooks are drawn from H. F. Lowry, K. Young, and W. H. Dunn, eds., *The Note-Books of Matthew Arnold* (London: Oxford University Press, 1952), supplemented by W. B. Guthrie, ed., *Matthew Arnold's Diaries: the Unpublished Items* (Ann Arbor: University Microfilms, 1959). Arnold's correspondence with his publishers is quoted from W. E. Buckler, ed., *Matthew Arnold's Books* (Geneva: Droz, 1958). Most quotations from his other letters are taken from the collected edition by G. W. E. Russell, where they can be found under their dates; the collection has been published in so many editions that page references are not helpful. A very few quotations are from unpublished letters; most of these can be traced through Arthur Kyle Davis's *Matthew Arnold's Letters: a Descriptive Checklist* (Charlottesville: The University Press of Virginia, 1968). Notes to canceled passages are placed in the same sequence as notes to the final text; when the parenthetical word "(variant)" appears, the note is in explanation of a passage that will be found only in the Textual Notes.

[IRISH ESSAYS]

Arnold's interest in the political affairs of Ireland, forecast as early as the Introduction to *On the Study of Celtic Literature* (1867), intensified markedly in the latter part of the following decade. On October 9, 1881, he wrote to George Smith, of Smith, Elder, & Co.: "I find I have accumulated—on Ireland, theatres, education, the future of Liberalism, and other matters,—enough for another volume of Essays, which might come out, with the title of 'Irish Essays &

Others' (?) in February. Would you like to add this to the too numerous series of my prose volumes?"—Buckler, *Matthew Arnold's Books*, p. 160. *Irish Essays* were published about February 21, 1882, at 7 *s*. 6 *d*. They were printed with *Mixed Essays* in the edition of Arnold's works prepared for the American market in 1883 and in a "Popular Edition" by the original publishers in 1891, three years after Arnold's death. The contents were: "The Incompatibles," "An Unregarded Irish Grievance," "*Ecce, Convertimur ad Gentes*," "The Future of Liberalism," "A Speech at Eton," "The French Play in London," "Copyright," and "Prefaces to Poems [1853, 1854]." (These Prefaces were published in the first volume of the present edition.) Except for the three *Discourses in America* this was the last collection of Arnold's prose published in his lifetime.

[ESSAYS IN CRITICISM. SECOND SERIES]

On January 18, 1888, George Craik, administrative partner to the firm of Macmillan, asked Arnold: "Is it not time for you to make a volume of collected papers? You must have a great many Magazine articles that ought to be reprinted & we should much like to publish them." Arnold promptly (January 20) proposed a collection of his essays in literary criticism, for publication by Whitsuntide of 1889: "I have lately thought that a purely literary volume to go with 'Essays in Criticism' and to be called 'Essays in Criticism Second Series'—might do. I should like to include the Wordsworth and Byron Prefaces and the three Essays from Ward's book, then the Amiel, Tolstoi, two Shelley articles and one or two more literary articles which I hope to produce this year." Arnold's sudden death on April 15 curtailed the volume, but its publication proceeded apace with the help of Arnold's son and widow. It was printed entirely from the already existing printed texts and appeared on November 6, 1888, priced at 7 *s*. 6 *d*.—Buckler, *Matthew Arnold's Books*, pp. 75–80. Unlike the *Essays in Criticism* of 1865 (from 1888 designated the "First Series"), the new book consists, not of a series of essays composed over a comparatively short period with essentially a single purpose, but of two clusters of essays, one group (dating from 1879–81) written to introduce English poetry or poets to a literate but not sophisticated audience, the other group (of 1887–88) of very miscellaneous purpose indeed. The four essays of the second group will appear in the final volume of the present edition.

["ECCE, CONVERTIMUR AD GENTES"]

Arnold long cherished the idea of lecturing before a group of working men, but the proper circumstances did not present themselves until his friend Foster Barham Zincke, vicar of Wherstead, invited him to address the Ipswich Working Men's College, of which Zincke had been principal since about 1876. It was, Arnold told his sister, Susanna Cropper, "the largest College of the kind in England. The inducement to me was that I might try and interest them in founding a system of public education for the middle classes, on the ground that the working class suffered by not having a more civilised middle class to rise into, if they *do* rise; this is in my opinion a very true plea, but you may imagine the difficulty and delicacy of urging it in a public meeting in a provincial town, where half the audience will be middle class. However, the speech is meant for the working men, the hands in the great factories for agricultural implements there. They are said to be an intelligent set, and I do not despair of making them follow me."—January 6, 1879. He delivered his lecture on Wednesday, January 8. A week or so later he forwarded to another sister, Mrs. W. E. Forster, "a note from dear old Barham Zincke, by which you will see that the lecture was a success. There were about 600 people present, and they listened very well. I hear that some in the body of the room showed great signs of irritation at times, but they did not break out. The local reporters reported the address, and a man came to me afterwards for my manuscript, to send a condensed report to the London papers. But this was just what [John] Morley had deprecated, so I refused, saying the address was promised to the *Fortnightly*, and the editor did not wish it published in part beforehand. I have so much more the feelings of a literary than of a political man, that I confess, unless one could be reported as only political personages of the very first class are reported, I would sooner keep out of the newspapers altogether, I so hate to see myself put all amiss. . . . I think I am gradually making an impression about public secondary schools. This reform interests me as the first practicable of those great democratic reforms to which we must, I believe, one day come. And they call me a bad Liberal, or no Liberal at all!"—January 16, 1879. Her reply must have coincided with his view: "You so entirely enter into my feelings about this reform," he wrote again, "which seems to me the pressing reform for our own present time to accomplish. At bottom I greatly sympathise also with what you say about the religion of the

middle classes, nor in the Ipswich address have I said anything on
this point which you will dislike, I think. I never read St. Paul on the
Jews but I feel how exactly his sentiment about the Jews answers to
mine about our middle class—'My heart's desire and prayers', etc.
etc. ['to God for Israel is, that they might be saved.'—Romans 10:1]
There is a moderate and pleasing article on 'Porro' ['Porro Unum
Est Necessarium,' on the same subject] in the *British Quarterly*. It
shows the stirring, even in those quarters [the Congregationalists],
of a sense that something *must* be done." And to a third sister, Frances,
he wrote: "I am very glad you liked my Ipswich discourse,
and the praise you give to it as being well adapted to its audience
pleases me particularly. I was careful to try and so adapt it, and
therefore refrained from all irony and playfulness, because these
are so often misunderstood by people who have not had a literary
training. Mr. Barham Zincke tells me that they had a number of
copies struck off from the report in the Suffolk paper, at a penny
apiece, for sale among the working men, and that they were all
bought directly. The *Western Morning News* is really valuable in
its support, especially in these early days when the newspaper press
is as yet apathetic upon the subject. . . . Maine and Lecky both said
to me, only yesterday, that the work I was doing by forcing the
question of middle-class education and civilisation upon people's
thoughts was invaluable, and that they were heartily with me. But
I want other people to talk about the matter rather than to talk
about it myself, for fear of its getting to pass for a hobby of mine."—
c. February 12, 1879; *Letters*, ed. Russell. It is true, as Arnold said in
the lecture, that it concerns a matter he had been devoted to for
twenty years; one has, indeed, heard a good deal of it from him
before, and most recently in "Equality" and " 'Porro Unum.' " "One
main reason why I am so little available for letters is that these educational
questions have laid their hold upon me—in great measure
from accident, in the first instance—and I cannot shake it off, nor
perhaps ought I to wish to. What is a poem or an essay more or less,
compared with the civilisation of the English middle class?" He received
£25 for it from the *Fortnightly Review*, where it appeared in
February, 1879.

Title: Paul and Barnabas to the Jews: "It was necessary that the
word of God should first have been spoken to you: but seeing ye
put it from you, and judge yourselves unworthy of everlasting life,
lo, we turn to the Gentiles."—Acts 13:46.

1:5–8. Arnold was a foreign assistant commissioner to the Newcastle
Commission in 1859 and to the Schools Enquiry (Taunton)

Commission in 1865; his reports were published separately as *The Popular Education of France* (1861) and *Schools and Universities on the Continent* (1868).

1:9–10. The Committee of Council on Education was the supervisory body that carried out the provisions of the education statutes; it was represented in the upper house of Parliament by the lord president of the Privy Council and in the Commons by the vice-president of the Council, both members of the ministry in power. The Committee of Council worked through the Education Department, which had as its permanent administrative head the Committee's secretary.

2:3–4. Late in 1878 three British armies invaded Afghanistan to forestall Russian influence in this area on India's northwest frontier. The initial operations—those that had occurred when Arnold wrote—were successful, but the war was unpopular in England and contributed to the fall of Beaconsfield's government in March, 1880.

2:11–12. When Arnold wrote, only two members of the cabinet were not members of the hereditary aristocracy.

2:33–36. The letter was to Arnold himself; see "Schools in the Reign of Queen Victoria," *Prose Works*, ed. Super, vol. XI.

2:36–37. Archdeacon Denison's letter is quoted by G. W. E. Russell much later. "My dear Bellairs,—I love you very much; but, if you ever come here again to inspect, I lock the door of the school, and tell the boys to put you in the pond."—*Collections and Recollections* (New York, 1898), p. 336; reprinted from *The Manchester Guardian*, 1897. George Anthony Denison (1805–96) was a strenuous high churchman doctrinally who in the early days of parliamentary grants joined with the still Anglican H. E. Manning in resisting the regulation of parochial schools by the state.

3:28. "Know thyself," one of the inscriptions over the door of the temple of Apollo at Delphi, became a principal doctrine of Socrates and of the Stoics. Arnold himself added "and the world" in defining the aim of the critical power: "A poet . . . ought to know life and the world before dealing with them in poetry."—"The Function of Criticism at the Present Time" (1864), *Prose Works*, ed. Super, III, 261.

3:28–29. See p. 19:10–12 and p. 4:37 (variant).

4:1–3. The Institut de France, officially established in the national constitution, included the Académie francaise, the Académie des inscriptions et belles-lettres, the Académie des sciences, the Académie des beaux-arts, and the Académie des sciences morales et politiques. The Académie française has forty members only, elected for life. Renan, elected on June 13, 1878, to the place vacated by the death of the physiologist Claude Bernard, was received into the Academy on April 3, 1879. His address in praise of French culture, an encomium of the unifying effects of an Academy in which the long view of all questions must be taken and an optimistic glorification of the innate goodness of man, was reported in *The Times* on April 4, p. 5, cols. 1–2, and was published separately in Paris.

4:12–13. The first public meet of the season for Her Majesty's Buckhounds was held on November 5, 1878, and was so well attended as to require a special train from London to Slough. Two nights later the annual banquet was given at Willis's Rooms, St. James's, to the farmers who permitted the Royal Buckhounds to hunt on their fields. Four royal princes, including the Prince of Wales, were present, and the report of the speechifying required more than a column of *The Times*.—November 6, p. 9, col. 6 and November 8, p. 3, cols. 5–6.

4:17–31. The London Mechanics' Institution was opened in 1823 under the direction of George Birkbeck and with warm support from Brougham. An article by the latter in the *Edinburgh Review* for October, 1824, republished in January, 1825, as a pamphlet entitled *Practical Observations upon the Education of the People*, gave great impetus to the founding of mechanics' institutes in all the larger towns of England; Brougham and others prepared lecture courses and also founded the "Society for the Diffusion of Useful Knowledge" to promote the composition, publication, and diffusion of elementary textbooks. Brougham's work was anonymously attacked by John Bird Sumner, later archbishop of Canterbury, in the *Quarterly* as early as October, 1825; Brougham himself was disappointed to see that the members of the institutes were not laboring men but from rather higher social levels. Within a decade the movement lost its impetus and altered its direction.

4:37 (variant). Herbert, "The Church-Porch," lines 333–34; quoted in "A Speech at Westminster" (1874), *Prose Works*, ed. Super, VII, 87. For Dante, see p. 19:10–12.

5:9–11. "Greek intelligence has obviously for its essence the instinct for what Plato calls the true, firm, intelligible law of things," said Arnold in *Culture and Anarchy*, with reference to Plato *Republic* VII, 532.—*Prose Works*, ed. Super, V, 178. And he jotted five times in his pocket diaries from 1867 to 1882 the phrase from Epictetus *Encheiridion* xlix: "What do I want? To learn to understand the nature of things and to follow it."—*Note-Books*, ed. Lowry, pp. 54, 68, 100, 217, 375.

5:15–19. "Alle Engländer sind als solche ohne eigentliche Reflex-ion; die Zerstreuung und der Parteigeist lassen sie zu keiner ruhigen Ausbildung kommen. Aber sie sind gross als praktische Mensch-en."—J. P. Eckermann, *Gespräche mit Goethe*, ed. E. Castle (Berlin, 1916), I, 116 (in a conversation upon Byron, February 24, 1825). Arnold quoted the same sentence in the same way ("Intel-ligenz" for "Reflexion") and glossed it in much the same way at the opening of "The Bishop and the Philosopher" (1863), an essay he never reprinted.—*Prose Works*, ed. Super, III, 40.

7:13–16. For the first of these points, see, for instance, "Equality" (1878); for the third, *A French Eton* (1864).—*Prose Works*, ed. Super, VIII, 277–305; II, 262–325. A "municipal system" is a system of local government or administration that includes rural areas as well as towns and is able to bring national policy effectively and equitably to the people; see pp. 12–13. Arnold warmly advocated a modern municipal organization for England in *Schools and Uni-versities on the Continent* (1868), *Prose Works*, ed. Super, IV, 306–7.

7:26–30. "The County Franchise," *Nineteenth Century* II, 547 (November, 1877), quoted by Arnold in "Equality," *Prose Works*, ed. Super, VIII, 279.

7:32. Arnold's opposition to the Real Estates Intestacy Bill, which he criticized in *Culture and Anarchy* (1868) and "Equality," was that by leaving the right of bequest unlimited it did nothing to re-duce the cumulative wealth of the very rich or to alleviate the in-herent poverty of the poor. The bill regularly failed to pass in Parliament. See *Prose Works*, ed, Super, V, 200–205; VIII, 280.

8:11–12. Arnold used these phrases in "Equality" and "Irish Ca-tholicism and British Liberalism" (1878), *Prose Works*, ed, Super, VIII, 299, 302, 345.

8:30–9:14. Arnold treated this idea of the three classes and their "aliens" in *Culture and Anarchy*, *Prose Works*, ed. Super, V, 145–46.

10:1–3. A.-N. de Condorcet, "Vie de M. Turgot," *Oeuvres* (Paris, 1847), V, 196, jotted in Arnold's pocket diary for March 23, 1878.—*Note-Books*, ed. Lowry, p. 297. Anne-Robert-Jacques Turgot, comptroller-general of France from August, 1774, to May, 1776, seemed to Arnold especially interesting as the type of intelligent and conscientious government administrator who could perceive the needs of the modern world.

10:13–20. *De la Démocratie en Amérique* (Paris, 1836), I, 40–41 (two-thirds through chapt. i), quoted by Arnold in "Democracy" (1861) and in the Preface to *Mixed Essays*.—*Prose Works*, ed. Super, II, 9; VIII, 371.

10:24–34. "The Peasants of the Limagne," *Fortnightly Review* XXX, 646–60, 821–35 (November, December, 1878); Arnold quotes from p. 835. The Limagne is a plain in the Auvergne, in central France, some eighty miles southeast of George Sand's home at Nohant. Zincke was an indefatigable traveller and observer.

10:35–11:2. Arnold alluded to Bismarck's view in " 'Porro Unum Est Necessarium' " (November, 1878), *Prose Works*, ed. Super, VIII, 361. It was mentioned in *The Times*, October 12, 1878, p. 5, col. 3.

11:2–11. "Le socialisme contemporaine en Allemagne," *Revue des Deux Mondes*, 3rd ser., XVIII, 882 (December 15, 1876), jotted in Arnold's *Note-Books* at the end of 1877 and cited in the essays on "George Sand" (1877), "Equality" (1878) and " 'Porro Unum Est Necessarium' " (1878).—*Note-Books*, ed. Lowry, pp. 289–90; *Prose Works*, ed. Super, VIII, 232, 290, 361.

11:12–15. P. G. Hamerton, *Round My House* (3rd ed.; London, 1876), p. 230, cited in Arnold's essays on "Equality" and " 'Porro Unum Est Necessarium.' "—*Prose Works*, ed. Super, VIII, 290, 361.

11:27–28. The Introduction to *The Popular Education of France* (1861), reprinted as "Democracy" in *Mixed Essays.*—*Prose Works*, ed. Super, II, 3–29.

11:29–31. In a letter to Arnold, mentioned in "Equality."—*Prose Works*, ed. Super, VIII, 283.

12:1–2. "The *Code Napoléon*, the actual law of France, forbids entails altogether, and leaves a man free to dispose of but one-fourth of his property, of whatever kind, if he have three children or more, of one-third if he have two children, of one-half if he have but one child."—"Equality," *Prose Works*, ed. Super, VIII, 280. Barham Zincke's Limagne peasant, who had been reading Scott's novels in French translation, "was glad to meet an Englishman, that he might learn why the estate, which always appeared enormously large, always went the whole of it to the eldest son. Was this the practice of Englishmen, and permitted by the law? Or was it the invention of the writer for the purposes of his tale?"—"The Peasants of the Limagne," p. 654.

12:3–4. J. S. Mill, *Principles of Political Economy*, Book II, chapter ii, section 4; *Collected Works* (Toronto: University of Toronto Press, 1965), II, 224–25; cited in "Equality," *Prose Works*, ed, Super, VIII, 305.

12:19–22. Cited in " 'Porro Unum Est Necessarium,' " *Prose Works*, ed. Super, VIII, 367–68. Arnold presumably drew his pictures from John Morley, "Turgot in Limousin," *Fortnightly Review* XXVII, 728 (May, 1877); reprinted in his *Critical Miscellanies*, Second Series (London, 1877), p. 205.

13:28–30. Léon Gambetta, speaking at Grenoble on October 10, 1878, said: "We wish that, under the shield of the Republic, the capacities of all citizens may freely develope; and it is certainly not at Grenoble, where I testified to the accession of a new social stratum, that I could say our task is completed. It never will be. After a first stratum will come a second; then others; for the effort of peoples now consists in drawing those who are below and constantly making them to ascend towards light, well-being, and morality."—*Times*, October 17, 1878, p. 5, col. 4; alluded to also by Arnold in " 'Porro Unum Est Necessarium,' " *Prose Works*, ed. Super, VIII, 367.

13:37–14:2. Zincke, "The Peasants of the Limagne," p. 827. The cost of the *lycée* was about 1000 francs, or £40, a year (p. 654). Clermont was some thirty miles from the village where Zincke stayed.

14:14. Local school boards, elected by the ratepayers, were set up gradually under the supervision of the Education Department to carry out the provisions of the Elementary Education Act of 1870.

14:32–35, 15:3–7. Henry Fawcett, "The Recent Development of Socialism in Germany and the United States," *Fortnightly Review* XXX, 610–11, 614–15 (November, 1878). Fawcett, professor of political economy at Cambridge, was a Benthamite member of Parliament. In this essay—the introductory lecture of a course on modern socialism he was giving at Cambridge—Fawcett cautions against free schooling provided by the State: "Even the slightest assault upon the principle of individual responsibility may exert a most disastrous influence. Self-reliance, which is the chief antidote to Socialism, may thus be weakened." For the overtones of Arnold's calling Fawcett "an excellent man," see the first version of *St. Paul and Protestantism* (1870), *Prose Works*, ed. Super, VI, 126, 530.

15:21–27. Delivered September 18, 1878; J. Reinach, ed., *Discours et plaidoyers publiques de M. Gambetta* (Paris, 1883), VIII, 236–37. The speech was reported in *The Times*, September 20, p. 3, col. 1, but without the passage Arnold quoted.

15:36–38. Arnold uses this definition as Burke's again and again in his essays, though according to one student of the subject, the precise phrase is not Burke's.—R. C. Tobias, *Matthew Arnold and Edmund Burke* (Ann Arbor: University Microfilms, 1958), p. 173n. See the quotation from Burke at p. 141:34n.

16:4–8. Fawcett, "Socialism," p. 613.

16:33–37. Bright's millennial hopes are subject to frequent comment in *Culture and Anarchy*, V, 108, 142, 209–10 *et passim*.

17:25–26. See p. 3:28 and note.

17:36–37. The Elementary Education Act of 1870 was sponsored by Arnold's brother-in-law W. E. Forster.

18:30. See note to p. 1, Title.

19:10–12. Dante, *Inferno*, XXVI, 118–20 (the words of Ulysses); see p. 4:37 (variant).

[A SPEECH AT ETON]

Arthur Christopher Benson, son of a future archbishop of Canterbury, relates how as eighteen-year-old president of the Eton Literary Society he used the services of a fellow member of the school, Francis Sorell Arnold, to procure his uncle Matthew as one of that season's lecturers.—*Memories and Friends* (New York, 1924), p. 21. Arnold delivered his talk on April 5, 1879. "I was allured to the 'Speech at Eton' by being told that you had addressed the boys there shortly before, and never in my life did I find a more agreeable audience," Arnold told Gladstone as he sent him a copy of *Irish Essays* on April 3, 1882. He forwarded the manuscript to the *Cornhill Magazine* immediately after delivering the lecture, corrected its proofs before April 14, and received £21 for its appearance in the May number of that journal. There are a good many echoes of his reviews of Curtius's *History of Greece* and of parts of *God and the Bible*.

20:5–19. *Discourses* II, xxi, 11–14. Nicopolis was founded by Augustus at the site of Actium, in northwestern Greece, to commemorate his victory there.

21:16–19. Arnold employs the same irony in *Culture and Anarchy* when he speaks of being educated at Oxford "in the bad old times, when we were stuffed with Greek and Aristotle."—*Prose Works*, ed. Super, V, 126. And see p. 22:16–19.

21:33–37. For the first axiom, see " 'Ecce, Convertimur ad Gentes,' " p. 3:28; for the second, "The Function of Criticism at the Present Time" (1864), *Prose Works*, ed. Super, III, 282–84.

22:31–37. Summary of Goethe's review of Weber's *Die elegischen Dichter der Hellenen* in *Über Kunst und Alterthum* V, iii, 183–87 (1826); *Werke* (Weimar, 1903), XLI (2), 211–13.

23:3–6. Georg von Bunsen (1824–96) was the son of Dr. Arnold's friend Christian Karl von Bunsen. His schooling was at Schulpforta, the most famous of the German secondary schools, which he completed in the spring of 1843; that summer he spent with his parents in England, before entering the University of Berlin in October.

He was a member of the Prussian House of Deputies and then of the German Reichstag for nearly a quarter of a century from 1862.

23:36–24:4. Thucydides II, xli, 1.

24:12–18. Ernst Curtius, *History of Greece,* tr. A. W. Ward (New York, 1871), II, 567 (Book III, chapt. iii, three-fifths through: "The Attic dialect"), with omissions.

24:34–25:16. Friedrich von Hellwald, *The Russians in Central Asia,* tr. Theodore Wirgman (London, 1874), pp. 308, 306–7, the translation improved stylistically by Arnold. He jotted the first passage in his pocket diary for February 8, 1879.—*Note-Books,* ed. Lowry, p. 315. Hellwald (1842–92) was author of books on a wide variety of subjects and editor of the geographical review *Ausland.*

25:18. Turkestan is a region of Central Asia, largely Russian territory; the Oxus and Jaxartes rivers flow westward through it to the Aral Sea. In 1879 this region, and especially the adjoining Afghanistan, were areas of conflict between Russia and England. Arnold set "The Sick King in Bokhara" and "Sohrab and Rustum" in Turkestan.

25:24–28. *Nicomachean Ethics* II, vii, 13 (1108a).

25:30–32. *Republic* VIII, 563 A–B.

26:5–7. Ephesians 5:4.

26:18–22. *Pythian Odes* IV, 102–6.

26:36–27:2. Arnold listed these "instincts" or "powers" in "Equality" and in the Preface to *Mixed Essays.*—*Prose Works,* ed. Super, VIII, 287, 372.

27:24–29. *Panegyricus* 50. Arnold quoted this sentence in "Equality" (1878) and jotted Sainte-Beuve's French translation of it in his pocket diary for August 8–9, 1877.—*Prose Works,* ed. Super, VIII, 287; *Note-Books,* ed. Lowry, p. 281.

27:31–29:26. Arnold repeats here nearly *verbatim* the account of Greek religion he gave in *God and the Bible* (1875), *Prose Works,* ed. Super, VII, 208:6–209:23.

28:20–22. The inscriptions on the temple at Delphi included "Know thyself" (which Socrates regarded as identical with "Be temperate") and, later, "Nothing in excess."—Plato *Charmides* 164–65. But Arnold, referring to the pseudo-Platonic *Lovers* (138 A) spoke in *God and the Bible* of "*soberness* and *righteousness,* to which the words written up on the temple at Delphi called all comers."—*Prose Works,* ed. Super, VII, 208–9.

28:36–37. E.g., in *Campagne in Frankreich, 1792:* "Das Studium der Kunst wie das der alten Schriftsteller gibt uns einen gewissen Halt, eine Befriedigung in uns selbst"; and in *Wilhelm Meisters*

Lehrjahre, VIII, iii: "Eben so nöthig scheint es mir gewisse Gesetze auszusprechen und den Kindern einzuschärfen, die dem Leben einen gewissen Halt geben."—*Werke* (Weimar, 1898, 1901), XXXIII, 188; XXIII, 178. Carlyle translated the latter "a kind of hold in life." Arnold used the expression, as Goethe's, in "Maurice de Guérin" (1863) and in his review of Curtius's *History of Greece* (1872).—*Prose Works*, ed. Super, III, 16; V, 274.

29:37–30:2. Ecclesiastes 11:6.

30:13–21. John Hales, *Works* (Glasgow, 1765), III, 150, 152 (Sermon "Of Enquiry and Private Judgment in Religion," on Galatians 6:7, not quite halfway through), or *Sermons Preach'd at Eton* (2nd ed.; London, 1673), pp. 39, 40–41. Hales wrote, "I see you will willingly take up" and "of the true grounds or reasons." Arnold quoted this passage in "Falkland" (1877), *Prose Works*, ed. Super, VIII, 206.

30:22–25. Thucydides II, xl, 2.

30:33–37. Isocrates *Areopagitikos* 49.

31:4–12. Ecclesiastes 11:7–9, the version slightly modified.

32:7–31. Arnold here continues the account he gave of Greek religion and morality in *God and the Bible, Prose Works*, ed. Super, VII, 209–10.

33:7–13. Curtius, *History of Greece*, tr. Ward, IV, 126 (Book V, chapt. ii, nearly three-fifths through), with omission.

33:21–26. *Ibid.*, III, 302 (Book IV, chapt. iv, one-seventh through), the translation somewhat altered.

33:29–30. In his review of Curtius's *History of Greece* (1872), Arnold also referred to Aeschylus' expression, "an unblest escape from all restraint," perhaps alluding to *Eumenides* 526.—*Prose Works*, ed. Super, V, 282.

34:2–3. "Graecia capta ferum victorem cepit."—Horace *Epistles* II, i, 156.

34:12–14. Proverbs 5:6.

35:14. "That dishonest victory | At *Chaeronea*, fatal to liberty."— Milton, Sonnet X ("To the Lady Margaret Ley"), lines 6–7.

[WORDSWORTH]

"I cannot help thinking that a practice, common in England during the last century, and still followed in France, of printing . . . a notice by a competent critic, to serve as an introduction to an eminent author's works, might be revived among us with advantage," wrote

Arnold in 1865 apropos of Shairp's essay on Wordsworth.—*Prose Works*, ed. Super, III, 258. In January, 1877, Macmillan proposed that Arnold edit a selection of Wordsworth's poems. Not surprisingly, the idea caught Arnold's fancy: "I suppose you would want a notice of Wordsworth to begin the volume, but it ought not to be a long one—not such an introduction as those which Jowett & Green bury their authors in." Macmillan agreed—annotation "only to the extent of common intelligence—if one only knew what that is. . . . '*Bottles*' *touched with emotion* is the sort of audience you seek to reach—and create."—Buckler, *Matthew Arnold's Books*, pp. 132–33. In November, 1878, Macmillan jogged Arnold's memory, but was put off; then on February 6, 1879, he tried again at a more propitious moment, and the work began. Arnold was fussy (but not scientific) about the text. As a matter of convenience type was set from a current one-volume edition, then proofs were corrected from the four-volume edition of 1832. But even here there were exceptions to be made: "I shall not invariably keep to the text of the edition of 1832; and then, too, there are some explanatory headings of Wordsworth's own to be introduced from the edition of 1858." On April 21, Arnold wrote to Mima Quillinan, step-daughter of Wordsworth's daughter Dora, who lived near Rydal Mount and Fox How. "I want to restore some of his lines to what they were before he, as dear Mrs. Wordsworth used to say, 'tinkered' them," and so he begged her to send him a passage of "Laodameia" he recalled from the two-volume edition of 1815.—*Letters*, ed. Russell. He insisted that Wordsworth's punctuation be followed throughout. Macmillan suggested that Arnold not bother himself with reading proofs of the poems, but he thought he had better. He was never an expert at that trade; after the book was published he discovered that the lines "We men, who in our morn of youth defied | The elements" were printed "We men, who in the morn of youth defiled | The elements." "This is the sort of thing which hurries the sensitive into suicide," he told Frederick Locker on September 24. And there were other slips.

The list of poems went off to the printer on April 16. A long passage from *The White Doe of Rylstone* had to be omitted for want of space, but at Macmillan's request the "Margaret" story from *The Excursion* was retained. Arnold wished to insert the ode "Composed upon an Evening of Extraordinary Splendour and Beauty" in response to an earnest request of Frederic Myers, but the poem never appeared in the collection. "Yes, it was the mountain Echo" was dropped in favor of "To a Skylark," but was restored to the list in a second edition. The sonnets "Degenerate Douglas" and "Admonition" were afterthoughts; the former disappeared from the second edition.—Buckler, *Matthew Arnold's Books*, pp. 135–37. "The Primrose of the Rock," dropped from the original list, appeared in the later editions as a favorite of his sister Jane: "Mama liked it, and I like it myself," Arnold told her.—*Letters*, ed. Russell. But he was unable to include all the favorites suggested by his friends, even by Wordsworth's grandson.

Having made his choices, "the thing to be done next is most important," said Arnold: "*to fix the order for printing the poems and the categories in which to class them.*" Though his arrangement was not Wordsworthian, it pleased him greatly. "I have always wished to arrange these poems in some natural and logical order, and I could hardly have believed how much their impressiveness and greatness would be brought out by their being so arranged."— Buckler, *Matthew Arnold's Books*, pp. 135–36. "He will come out better, and more effective in my arrangement, I think, than he has ever come out before. I have gone on the plan of throwing pieces of one poetical *kind* together, not of classifying them, in Wordsworth's own intricate way, according to the spiritual faculty from which they are supposed to have proceeded."—*Letters*, ed. Russell; April 14, 1879.

The Preface grew as he worked on it. It "ought not to exceed 5 to 10 pages, or it will be a be a blemish to the book," he wrote in late March; "I shall try to keep my preface within 15 pages," on April 16. "We shall be thankfull for the 15 pages of preface, but shall not be in the least sorry if you find you cannot say all you want under 20 or 30," replied Macmillan.—Buckler, pp. 135–36. It came in the end to 22 pages. The publishers were eager to have the book out by early June, but neither the typesetting nor Arnold's composition of the Preface was rapid enough. From the first Arnold intended that his essay should be published in *Macmillan's Magazine* to prepare the way for the book and to provide him with an additional £20 in payment; it appeared in the July number. The last proofs of the book were corrected before August 8 and it was published early in September at 4 *s.* 6 *d.*

"What I had to think of, both in the preface and in the selection, was the great public; it is this great public which I want to make buy Wordsworth's poems as they buy Milton's." So Arnold wrote to Jemima Quillinan in reply to some comments on the selection by Wordsworth's grandson Willie. And he could report some success: nearly 4000 copies sold in less than five months. A large paper edition with a few corrections was published late in October at 9 *s.*, a second edition of the smaller volume, with some additions, in November. Further corrections were made in 1884 for the reprinting that did not come until 1886. In the sixty-eight years following the second edition, there were thirty-seven reprintings; the book is still in print at its original publisher's, one of the very few volumes of the Golden Treasury series of which this is true. A separate edition was printed off from the plates for Macmillans of New York in crown octavo to match Arnold's other books in America.

Few of his undertakings gave Arnold so much pleasure. "It is delightful to have to occupy oneself with Wordsworth," he told his sister on April 14. ". . . I don't think any of his *best* work will be left out, though a great deal must be left out which is *good* work, especially of his later time. [My introduction will be] a short one, but I hope to do him justice. He can show a body of work superior to what any other English poet, except Shakespeare and Milton, can show; and his body of work is more interesting than Milton's, though not so great. This seems to me to be the simple truth. I hope this collection of mine may win for him some appreciation on the Continent also. I shall send the book to Scherer, and beg him to review it. Wordsworth's body of work, to keep to that phrase, is superior to the body of work of any Continental poet of the last hundred years except Goethe; superior to that of Schiller, Heine, Musset, Victor Hugo. This, again, seems to me to be the simple truth. But I must not run on."—*Letters,* ed. Russell. Nightingales pleased him the more that spring: "The effect of reading so much of Wordsworth lately has been to make me feel more keenly than usual the beauty of the common incidents of the natural year, and I am sure that is a good thing." "He is one of the best and deepest spiritual influences of our century," Arnold told Ernest Fontanès as he sent him a copy of the book. He was pleased to be told by his host at a party "that he meant, through the occasion given by my little book, to make acquaintance with Wordsworth as he had never done before in his life. And certainly a great many people will be led to do this." Scherer reviewed the book in *Le Temps* for June 17 and 24 and July 1, 1881, and paid Arnold a long and handsome compliment before turning to Wordsworth.

The essay is one of Arnold's best-known pieces of literary criticism, one which did indeed materially advance Wordsworth's reputation. But not all Wordsworth's admirers have been pleased with it. Some at least have failed to heed the caution Arnold gave to Professor W. A. Knight: "It is not an elaborate Criticism of Words-

worth's poetry, but the sort of essay which seemed to me best
calculated to introduce and help such a volume. You must read it
with this view of its character and design." Swinburne thought
Arnold valued Wordsworth too highly and often for precisely the
wrong reasons.—"Wordsworth and Byron," *Nineteenth Century*
XV, 583–609, 764–90 (April, May, 1884). Lane Cooper, fresh from
making his Wordsworth Concordance, in 1929 first published an
ill-natured essay that quarrelled with Arnold's textual practice,
seemed displeased that Arnold received "good pay" for the book,
and found that from beginning to end Arnold's assertions were
generally wrong: Wordsworth did indeed talk of glory, for example
—one hundred and thirty-three times.—"Matthew Arnold's Essay
on Wordsworth," *Evolution and Repentance* (Ithaca, N.Y.: Cornell
University Press, 1935), pp. 1–17. G. G. Sedgewick's rebuke of
Cooper's sophomoric pedantry is valuable because it so strongly
emphasizes Arnold's purpose in terms of the audience for whom
he wrote.—"Wordsworth, Arnold, and Professor Lane Cooper,"
Dalhousie Review X, 57–66 (April, 1930). Of the two books on
Arnold and the Romantics, which of course embrace this essay and
much more besides, that by W. A. Jamison (Copenhagen: Rosen-
kilde and Bagger, 1958) is little more than a compilation of opinions
Arnold expressed about the Romantics in verse and prose, often
set beside those of his contemporaries; that by Leon Gottfried (London: Routledge and Kegan Paul, 1963) is more comprehensive in
its approach and more critically imaginative in its assessment of the
impact of the Romantics on Arnold's own poetry. David J. De-
Laura's essay, "The 'Wordsworth' of Pater and Arnold: 'The Supreme, Artistic View of Life,' " *Studies in English Literature 1500–
1900* VI, 651–67 (Autumn, 1966), is a subtle analysis of the way in
which Pater's essay on Wordsworth (1874) uses the critical language
of Arnold's Oxford lectures on poetry (1864–67) but modifies their
intent, and Arnold's essay on Wordsworth in its turn responds to
Pater's.

36:1. Macaulay (not yet a lord) was a friend of the Whig statesman Lord Lansdowne, whose private secretary Arnold was until
about a year after Wordsworth's death on April 23, 1850. Arnold's
brother-in-law John Cropper was connected with Macaulay by
marriage.

36:12–15. Arnold repeats what he told the Copyright Commission
when he testified before it on January 25, 1877: "I think I have
heard [Wordsworth] say that for the first 30 years or so he had
not made enough by his poems to buy shoe strings."—Copyright

Commission, *Report of the Commissioners* (London: H. M. Stationery Office, 1878), p. 197.

37:7. Wordsworth's prose *Guide to the Lakes*, which he first published under his own name as an appendix to the volume of sonnets on *The River Duddon* in 1820, then separately in 1822 and subsequently, was originally the anonymous introduction to Joseph Wilkinson's *Select Views in Cumberland, Westmoreland, and Lancashire*, published for Wilkinson by R. Ackermann in 1810.

37:31–33. F .T. Palgrave's *Golden Treasury of the Best Songs and Lyrical Poems in the English Language*, first published in 1861, contained forty-one poems by Wordsworth. Shakespeare was second with thirty-two. Living poets were excluded.

38:2–4. "Discours de reception à l'Académie française (3 Avril 1879)," *Discours et conférences* (Paris, 1887), p. 3 (end of ¶2).

38:4 (variant). *Ibid.*, p. 6 (¶5). "[Renan's] taking Victor Hugo's poetry so prodigiously *au sérieux* does, I confess, amaze me in so fine and delicate a mind; but Renan is not *sound*, I think, in proportion to his brilliancy," Arnold wrote to Ernest Fontanès on Easter Sunday, 1879.—*Letters*, ed. Russell.

38:8–13. Arnold said this earlier in "The Function of Criticism at the Present Time" (1864), *Prose Works*, ed. Super, III, 284.

38:13. "Ich sehe immer mehr," said Goethe to Eckermann on January 31, 1827, "dass die Poesie ein Gemeingut der Menschheit ist. . . . Wenn wir Deutschen nicht aus dem engen Kreise unserer eigenen Umgebung hinausblicken, so kommen wir gar zu leicht in [einen] pedantischen Dünkel. . . . Nationalliteratur will jetzt nicht viel sagen, die Epoche der Weltliteratur ist an der Zeit, und jeder muss jetzt dazu wirken, diese Epoche zu beschleunigen."—J. P. Eckermann, *Gespräche mit Goethe*, ed. E. Castle (Berlin, 1916), I, 179–80.

38:32. Nebuchadnezzar was the great king of Babylon who early in the sixth century B.C. destroyed Jerusalem and took the Israelites captive to Babylonia. The Bible account has him go mad and live for seven years with the beasts of the field in punishment for his boast: "Is not this great Babylon, that I have built for the house of the kingdom by the might of my power, and for the honour of my majesty?"—Daniel 4:30.

38:32–33. "I pray that our unrivalled happiness may last," said J. A. Roebuck to his constituents in Sheffield on August 18, 1864, in a speech that drew Arnold's best irony from the chair of poetry at Oxford.—"The Function of Criticism at the Present Time" (1864), *Prose Works*, ed. Super, III, 272.

38:33–35. Arnold himself, first in "Equality" (1878), *Prose Works*, ed. Super, VIII, 299–302.

39:17–21. "L'Angleterre, si orgueilleuse de tout ce qu'elle produit, se vanta de son Milton comme de son Shakspeare. Cet enthousiasme, justifié par de véritables beautés, ne fit que s'accroître."—Villemain's article on Milton, *Biographie universelle (Michaud) ancienne et moderne* (nouv. éd.; Paris, 1843–65), XXVIII, 327. And "[Shakspeare] donne à l'imagination anglaise des plaisirs qui ne vieillissent pas: il agite, il attache, il satisfait ce goût de singularité dont se flatte l'Angleterre; il n'entretient les Anglais que d'eux-mêmes, c'est-à-dire de la seule chose à peu près qu'ils estiment ou qu'ils aiment. . . . Élevé dans une civilisation moins heureuse et moins poétique, Shakspeare n'offre pas dans la même proportion que les Grecs de ces beautés universelles qui passent dans toutes les langues, et il n'y a qu'un Anglais qui puisse le mettre à côté d'Homère ou de Sophocle."—Villemain on Shakspeare, *ibid.*, XXXIX, 238.

39:21–24, 27–28. Arnold cites Joseph de Maistre's disparaging remarks on Milton and instances of the French ranking Shakespeare with Corneille and Victor Hugo in "A French Critic on Goethe" (1878), *Prose Works*, ed. Super, VIII, 252–53.

39:30–40:1. Henry Cochin, "Un Poète américain: Walt Whitman," *Le Correspondant* CIX, 651–52 (November 25, 1877); jotted in Arnold's pocket diary at the end of 1878.—*Note-Books*, ed. Lowry, p. 311.

40:5–9. Eckermann, *Gespräche mit Goethe*, I, 310–11 (January 31, 1830).

40:14 (variant). *Histoire de la littérature anglaise* (3rd ed.; Paris, 1873), IV, 330, 378 (Book IV, chapt. i, sect. 5 and chapt. ii, sect. 4). Arnold probably found the quotations in Scherer's review of Taine's *Histoire* in *Le Temps* on June 7, 1864, reprinted in his *Études sur la littérature contemporaine* (nouv. éd.; Paris, 1894), VI, 130, 128. T. Gautier, "Hernani," *Histoire du romantisme* (1872), chapt. xii, ¶5. *Goethes Unterhaltungen mit dem Kanzler Friedrich von Müller*, ed. C. A. H. Burkhardt (Stuttgart, 1904), p. 173 (March 28, 1830).

40:16. Amphictyonies were federations of tribes in primitive Greece; the best known and longest-lived one was that which had its center at the shrine of Apollo in Delphi. "In case of dispute between the Amphictyones, a judicial authority was wanted to preserve the common peace, or punish its violation in the name of the God."—E. Curtius, *History of Greece*, tr. A. W. Ward (New York, 1871), I, 129 (Book I, chapt. iv, one-fourth through).

40:38. Scott's name was not added to this list until the fourth printing of the essay; see Textual Notes.

42:6. To the collected edition of 1836–37 in six volumes which remained (with minor corrections) the basic edition of Wordsworth's life-time was added a seventh volume in 1842.

42:18. "I challenge anyone," said Lane Cooper, "to find a solecism in Wordsworth's prose or verse to match the plural verb 'fill' " in this passage.—p. 11.

42:37–43:3. Among the headings of Wordsworth's classification, first introduced when he collected his poetical works in 1815, were "Poems Written in Youth," "Poems Referring to the Period of Childhood," "Poems Founded on the Affections," "Poems on the Naming of Places," "Poems of the Fancy," "Poems of the Imagination," "Miscellaneous Sonnets," "Poems Dedicated to National Independence and Liberty," "Poems of Sentiment and Reflection," "Sonnets Dedicated to Liberty and Order," "Miscellaneous Poems," and "Poems Referring to the Period of Old Age." For Arnold's classification of Wordsworth's poems, see Appendix.

43:10–13. When Arnold collected his own poems in 1869, his classification was: "Narrative Poems," "Elegiac Poems," "Lyric Poems," and "Dramatic Poems." In his next collected edition, 1877, he added the classifications "Early Poems" and "Sonnets."

44:27–35. *On Translating Homer: Last Words* (1862), *Prose Works*, ed. Super, I, 210–11. Arnold in 1862 misquoted Wordsworth by writing "On God, on Nature, and on human life." The line is the opening one of the fragment of "The Recluse" that Wordsworth in 1814 prefixed to *The Excursion*.

45:3–6. *Siècle de Louis XIV*, chapt. xxxiv, ¶6: "Des beaux-arts en Europe du temps de Louis XIV."

45:21–22. *Paradise Lost*, XI, 553–54.

45:28. "Ode on a Grecian Urn," line 20.

45:30–32. *Tempest*, IV, i, 156–58.

46:12–13. "The end and aim of all literature, if one considers it attentively, is, in truth, nothing but [*a criticism of life*]."—"Joubert" (1864), *Prose Works*, ed. Super, III, 209.

46:21–22. A summary of quatrain 368 in *Les Quatrains de Khèyam*, traduits du persan par J. B. Nicolas (Paris, 1867), p. 182. This French prose translation of 464 quatrains is far more extensive than FitzGerald's *Rubáiyát*. It was on Arnold's reading list for 1876 and his diary shows that he was reading in it from March 18 to April 25.—*Note-Books*, ed. Lowry, p. 591.

46:31–47:16. *Discourses* II, xxiii, 36–47.

47:24–28. Fragment of "The Recluse" prefixed to *The Excursion* in 1814, lines 14–18.

48:8. Vergil *Aeneid* VI, 662.

48:16–21. "Hours in a Library. No. XIII: Wordsworth's Ethics," *Cornhill Magazine* XXXIV, 209–10 (August, 1876); jotted in Arnold's pocket diary for May 24, 1879.—*Note-Books,* ed. Lowry, p. 318. In "A Guide to English Literature" (1877) Arnold remarked: "No one will be much helped by Wordsworth's philosophy of Nature, as a scheme in itself and disjoined from his poems. Nor shall we be led to enjoy the poems the more by having a philosophy of Nature abstracted from them and presented to us in its nakedness." —*Prose Works,* ed. Super, VIII, 250.

49:1–4. IV, 73–76.

49:14–21. IV, 10–17.

50:9–11. I, i, 2.

50:15–24. *The Excursion* IX, 293–302. See p. 230:17.

50:25. "Now, you old lake poet, you rascally poet, why do you call Voltaire dull?" asked Lamb of Wordsworth at a dinner party at Haydon's on December 28, 1817. "We all defended Wordsworth, and affirmed there was a state of mind when Voltaire would be dull," Haydon added in his diary.—*The Autobiography and Journals of Benjamin Robert Haydon,* ed. Malcolm Elwin (London: Macdonald, 1950), p. 317. See *The Excursion* II, 484.

50:27–28. The National Association for the Promotion of Social Science was founded under the leadership of Lord Brougham in 1856. It held annual "Congresses" in one or other of the major cities of Great Britain from 1857 to 1884, with papers in the areas of its principal concern—jurisprudence and law reform, education, punishment and reformation, public health, and social economy— published in its annual *Transactions.* Peacock ridiculed it as the "Pantopragmatic Society" in *Gryll Grange* (1861). The society ran out of funds and was dissolved in 1886. See Brian Rodgers, "The Social Science Association, 1857–1886," *The Manchester School of Economic and Social Studies* XX, 283–310 (September, 1952).

50:36–37. "To the Lady Fleming," line 81.

51:15. See p. 47:28.

51:29. Arnold developed the religious concept of "that power, *not ourselves,* in which we live and move and have our being," the "tendency, which is *not ourselves,* but which appears in our consciousness, by which things fulfil the real law of their being," in *St. Paul and Protestantism* (1869–70) and *Literature and Dogma* (1871–73); see *Prose Works,* ed. Super, VI, 58, 191, and Index (*s.v.* "not ourselves").

51:33. "A Poet's Epitaph," line 58.

51:34–35. Comparable comments of Wordsworth upon Goethe are recorded in Christopher Wordsworth, *Memoirs of William Wordsworth* (London, 1851), II, 438, 478–79.

52:11–13. "This will never do" was the opening sentence of Jeffrey's anonymous review of *The Excursion* in the *Edinburgh Review* XXIV, 1 (November, 1814); as Arnold indicates, Jeffrey's attack was on "that profuse and irrepressible wordiness which deluges . . . the blank verse . . . and lubricates and weakens the whole structure of [the] style." Jeffrey began his review of *The White Doe of Rylstone* less concisely: "This, we think, has the merit of being the very worst poem we ever saw imprinted in a quarto volume."—*Ibid.*, XXV, 355 (October, 1815).

52:20. *Macbeth*, III, ii. 23.

52:22–23. *Paradise Lost*, VII, 25–26.

52:33–35. Fragment of "The Recluse" prefixed to *The Excursion* in 1814, lines 78–80.

53:9. "Michael," line 466.

53:16–21. Burns, "A Bard's Epitaph," lines 19–24.

54:7. I.e., "Ode: Intimations of Immortality from Recollections of Early Childhood."

54:12. Arnold habitually referred to "The Solitary Reaper" as "The Highland Reaper," though the title is correct where the poem is printed in his selection from Wordsworth. Palgrave in *The Golden Treasury* gave it the title simply of "The Reaper."

54:32–33. *The Excursion*, I, 1–37, 443–970.

55:6–7. "To the Spade of a Friend (an Agriculturist) Composed While We Were Labouring Together in His Pleasure-Ground," beginning: "Spade! with which Wilkinson hath tilled his lands."

55:22–25. Letter to Lady Beaumont, May 21, 1807; C. Wordsworth, *Memoirs of W. Wordsworth*, I, 339. Arnold jotted this passage in his pocket diary for September 29, 1867, and a nearby passage from the same letter on December 5, 1879.—*Note-Books*, ed. Lowry, pp. 63, 329.

[THE IRISH UNIVERSITY QUESTION]

Arnold's letter in *The Times* for July 31, 1879, resumes what he said at much greater length a year earlier in "Irish Catholicism and British Liberalism" (*Prose Works*, ed. Super, VIII, 321–47). The Irish University Education Bill passed the Lords on July 15 and had its second reading in the Commons on July 24. Eleven days

after Arnold's letter it passed its third reading in the lower house
and received the royal assent four days later. In the earlier stages
of the discussion, Arnold wrote to his sister with some pride: "I
think about the Irish University Question I have effected some
real good."—May 25; *Letters,* ed. Russell. The letter was reprinted
in Fraser Neiman's *Essays, Letters, and Reviews by Matthew Arnold* (Cambridge, Mass.: Harvard University Press, 1960), pp. 212–
15.

56:1–3. On April 8, 1820.—Henry Grattan, *Memoirs of the Life
and Times of the Rt. Hon. Henry Grattan, by His Son* (London,
1846), V, 543; jotted in Arnold's pocket diary for January 14–15,
1879.—*Note-Books,* ed. Lowry, p. 315.

58:19–20. Trinity College, Dublin, was chartered in 1592 to be
erected on land occupied by the ruins of the Augustinian monastery
of All Hallows, which had been given to the Corporation of Dublin
at the dissolution in the reign of Henry VIII.

58:30–31. In describing the disabilities imposed on Catholics in
the penal code established by the Irish Parliament in the eighteenth
century, W. E. H. Lecky says: "[A Catholic] could not possess a
horse of the value of more than five pounds, and any Protestant, on
giving him five pounds, could take his horse."—"Henry Grattan,"
The Leaders of Public Opinion in Ireland (New York, 1872), p.
122.

59:4–7. Lord Chancellor Cairns, in introducing the Irish University Education Bill in the House of Lords on June 30, 1879, said:
"The [religious] tests for the higher endowments of Trinity College . . . have been entirely removed, and there is absolutely at this
moment no disqualification to any person whomsoever with regard to any endowment or preferment in Trinity College."—*Times,*
July 1, p. 7, col. 2.

59:13–14. Tests and subscriptions were abolished at Oxford and
Cambridge in 1871, at Trinity College, Dublin, by the Fawcett Act
of 1873.

59:35–38. "In point of fact, it is among the mass of those who
are capable of taking creditable degrees, but who are not able to
win the great prizes of a University, that some of the students would
be found who most need such pecuniary assistance as an endowed
college would offer, and who would make the best use of the substitute for such a college now proposed. . . . The contention of the
Government appears at present to be that assistance is undenominational when given to clever young men or boys, but becomes de-
nominational when given to young men who are not clever."—
Times, July 25, 1879, p. 9, columns 3–4.

60:17–18. Sir Edward Knatchbull (1781–1849), ninth baronet, was a leader of the Protestant party that opposed Catholic emancipation in Parliament prior to 1829.

[ON POETRY]

The nineteenth-century love of listing the "greatest" in every category of human endeavor—a fashion from which we have by no means shaken ourselves free—produced the eight-volume quarto collection, *The Hundred Greatest Men: Portraits of the One Hundred Greatest Men of History* (London, 1879–80); represented were poetry, art, religion, philosophy, history, science, politics, and industry. "I have promised to write two pages of introduction to the poets, in a series of photographs of the 100 most remarkable men who have ever lived, which a strange American, Dr. Wallace Wood, is going to bring out. But then it is only two pages, and I was so struck with the man's energy, when I found he had got Renan, Taine, Mommsen, Helmholtz and Max Müller for some of his other introductions, that after refusing at first, I gave way and consented. He gives £50 for two pages, too, which is not bad; some New York publisher is behind him, with many dollars," Arnold wrote on October 22, 1878. In the event, the list of contributors from four nations did not include Mommsen but was rounded out with Noah Porter, A. P. Stanley, Froude, and John Fiske, and the general introduction was written by Emerson. Wood's London address is jotted at the beginning of Arnold's pocket diary for 1878. The poets, dramatists, and novelists introduced by Arnold's essay were Homer, Pindar, Aeschylus, Sophocles, Euripides, Aristophanes, Menander, Lucretius, Vergil, Dante, Rabelais, Cervantes, Shakespeare, Milton, Molière, Goethe, and Scott, not all of whom could be very accurately portrayed by even the most skilful engraver and at least one of whose merits were in 1879 supported by the merest scraps and fragments. The first two volumes were published early in August, 1879; the publisher was a London firm, not a New York one. Arnold's brief essay pleased him enough so that he used it as the starting-point for "The Study of Poetry" the following year. It was reprinted by Fraser Neiman, *Essays, Letters, and Reviews by Matthew Arnold* (Cambridge: Harvard University Press, 1960), pp. 237–39.

61:14–16. *Poetics* 1451 b 6–8.

61:17–21. *The Advancement of Learning*, Book II, iv, 2.

62:2. Arnold quotes Maurice de Guérin as saying: "I owe to

[poetry] whatever I now have pure, lofty, and solid in my soul."—
Prose Works, ed. Super, III, 30.

62:10–14. "Maximen und Reflexionen," *Werke* (Weimar, 1907),
XLII (2), 200; jotted in Arnold's pocket diary at the end of 1877.—
Note-Books, ed. Lowry, p. 290. Between "science" and "Poetry is"
Goethe remarked: "Künste und Wissenschaften erreicht man durch
Denken, Poesie nicht, denn diese ist Eingebung; sie war in der Seele
empfangen als sie sich zuerst regte."

62:15–16. Littré's *Dictionnaire de la langue française* (1873) de-
fines "homme" as "animal raisonnable."

62:19–20. This sentence deliberately suggests Arnold's definition
of religion (p. 63:20–21) as "morality touched with emotion," first
stated in *Literature and Dogma* (1871), *Prose Works,* ed. Super, VI,
176.

63:9–10. Goethe was born in 1749. In the century and a half
thereafter Germany produced such philosophers as Kant (1724–
1804), Fichte (1762–1814), Hegel (1770–1831), Schelling (1775–
1854), and Schopenhauer (1788–1860).

63:29. "To profess to see Christianity through the spectacles of a
number of second or third-rate men who lived in Queen Elizabeth's
time (and this is what office-holders under the Thirty-Nine Articles
do)—men whose works one never dreams of reading for the purpose
of enlightening and edifying oneself—is an intolerable absurdity,
and . . . it is time to put the formularies of the Church of England
on a solider basis," Arnold wrote to his mother on December 17,
1862.—*Letters,* ed. Russell.

[THE FRENCH PLAY IN LONDON]

The six-week visit of the entire company of the Comédie francaise,
from June 2 to July 12, 1879, provided the Londoners with the theatrical sensation of the decade. Performing six nights a week at the
Gaiety Theatre, and giving six Saturday matinée performances (and
one extra matinée to make up for an occasion when the star had been
indisposed), the company displayed a large repertoire of plays from
the classics of the seventeenth century to the works of the contemporary dramatists. The company itself, if one may judge from the
reviews, was uniformly excellent, but the English audience was
especially caught up by Sarah Bernhardt from the moment of her
performance of the second act of *Phèdre* on the opening night,
"writhing and convulsed with shame and passion," as *The Athe-*

naeum admiringly put it. Her performances included *L'Étrangère* of the younger Dumas (June 3 and 25), Octave Feuillet's *Le Sphinx* (June 14, 28; July 10), Victor Hugo's *Hernani* (June 9, 21, 28; July 9 and Act V on the closing night) and *Ruy Blas* (June 30, July 2, 12), Racine's *Phèdre* (June 13, July 5) and *Andromaque* (June 26), and Voltaire's *Zaïre* (June 17). Among the other plays were Balzac's *Mercadet le faiseur* (July 1), Beaumarchais' *Le Barbier de Séville* (June 25), Corneille's *Le Menteur* (June 6), the elder Dumas' *Mdlle. de Belle-Isle* (June 11), the younger Dumas' *Le Fils naturel* (June 4) and *Le Demi-monde* (June 10, 19), Erckmann-Chatrian's *L'Ami Fritz* (June 16, July 8), Marivaux' *Le Jeu de l'amour et du hazard* (June 18), Racine's *Les Plaideurs* (June 14, 26) and George Sand's *Le Marquis de Villemer* (June 7, July 7) and *Le Mariage de Victorine* (July 3). Four plays of Alfred de Musset's were produced, and the Molière performances were: *Le Médicin malgré lui* (June 6), *Tartuffe* (June 7, 21), *Le Misanthrope* (June 2, 14), *Les Précieuses ridicules* (June 2, 17), *L'Avare* (June 27), *Le Dépit amoureux* (June 28), *Les Fourberies de Scapin* (July 3), *Les Femmes savantes* (July 4), and *L'Étourdi* (July 11). After a gala closing night for the visitors, the Gaiety Theatre re-opened with a burlesque, and not long afterwards Mdlle. Bernhardt severed her connection with the Comédie française.

Arnold's venture into dramatic criticism was followed a few years later by his casual articles in *The Pall Mall Gazette* signed "An Old Playgoer." But the present essay comes closer in its tone to the kind of literary evaluation he practised also in "The Study of Poetry." He received £40 from the *Nineteenth Century*, where the article appeared in August, 1879.

64:10–24. Sonnet, "Calais, August, 1802" ("Is it a reed that's shaken by the wind?"). The First Consul was Napoleon.

65:11–12. Bernhardt made herself available, for a fee of £80–£100, to perform, without theatrical costume or properties, at private drawing room entertainments—an offer eagerly taken up by some London hostesses.

65:27–30. Élisa Félix (1820–58), always known simply as Rachel, was one of the greatest French *tragédiennes;* the reviewers of 1879 were full of comparisons between her and Sarah Bernhardt. She made a sensational debut with the Comédie française on June 12, 1838, and first played Hermione in Racine's *Andromaque* a month later. (Bernhardt in London performed the less dramatic role of Andromache in the play.) On her first tour of England Rachel made a triumphant debut as Hermione; Larousse's *Dictionnaire universelle* used precisely the word Arnold chose to describe her reception—"*l'engouement du public.*" Arnold's diaries record that he saw Rachel at the St. James's Theatre in London on July 20 and 22, 1846 (*Andromaque* and *Phèdre*), then in Paris a few months later: December 29 (*Polyeucte*), December 31 (*Andromaque*), January 2 (*Horace*), 6 (*Cinna*), 16 (*Horace*), 19 (*Le Cid*), 23 *(Andromaque*), 25 (Corneille's *Don Sanche d'Aragon*), and 29 (*Phèdre*), and February 1 (*Marie Stuart,* presumably Lebrun's version of Schiller). (This list of performances does not correspond exactly with the list of Rachel's performances in December–February printed in Georges d'Heylli (E. A. Poinsot), *Rachel* [Paris, 1882], p. 278.) Arnold was in Edinburgh on August 23, 1847, when Rachel performed there in *Horace,* a performance he may have seen. His *New Poems* (1867) contains a sequence of three sonnets on Rachel.

65:38. Reviews appeared in *The Times* almost daily during the run. *The Pall Mall Gazette* had a series of three articles on "The Lessons of the Comédie Française" on July 8, 10, and 12, 1879; it was severely critical of the acting of Sarah Bernhardt. *The Daily News* had more than a dozen news items about the company, and especially about Sarah Bernhardt's schemes for augmenting her income.

66:3. Both were legal prosecutions for ritualistic practices, and both were occupying the public press during 1879. Alexander Mackonochie (1825–87) became curate in charge of a new church, St. Alban's, Holborn, in 1862, and was first tried in 1867 on the complaint of a parishioner for deviating from the allowable forms. His case was before the courts in various ways until he resigned his living at the end of 1882. The Clewer case involved Thomas Thellusson Carter, rector of Clewer, Berkshire, charged with administering the sacrament in a ritualistic manner forbidden by the courts. The report on a single aspect of the proceedings occupied a full page of *The Times* for March 10, 1879, and was subject of a leading article on that date.

66:5. See p. 83:11n.

66:13–14. James 1:24.

66:20–24. Quoted in F. W. Riemer, *Mittheilungen über Goethe* (Berlin, 1841), II, 95; jotted in Arnold's pocket diary for March 25, 1871, April 2–3, 1872, at the beginning of 1873, January 7–8, 1875, and in one of his "General Note-Books."—*Note-Books,* ed. Lowry, pp. 152, 176, 191, 226, 522.

66:36–37. Rachel retired at the age of thirty-five; Sarah Bernhardt was thirty-four when she appeared in London in 1879 and continued to act until the year before her death in 1923.

67:25–31. The principal member of this young and stirring generation in Arnold's view was undoubtedly Swinburne, who replied in *A Study of Shakespeare* (1880) by calling Hugo "the common lord and master of all poets born in his age—be they liege subjects as loyal as myself or as contumacious as I grieve to find one at least of my elders and betters, whenever I perceive—as too often I cannot choose but perceive—that the voice is the voice of Arnold, but the hand is the hand of Sainte-Beuve."—p. 158. When he received the *Study of Shakespeare* from its author on December 20, Arnold wrote that he had instantly begun to read it, "and . . . I shall not part with [it] until I have read it through. I always follow you with interest and often with keen pleasure, and it gives me pleasure to have an opportunity of telling you so. Think mercifully of me when I now and then blaspheme Victor Hugo." Swinburne told Arnold, as he sent him a copy of *Songs of the Springtides* on May 13, 1880 (with its 520-line "Birthday Ode for the Anniversary Festival of Victor Hugo") that he was again taking up Arnold's gauntlet in an article on "Victor Hugo: *Religions et Religion*," *Fortnightly Review* XXXIII, 761–68 (June, 1880), and Arnold replied: "I need not say that I have already read the Birthday Ode. You do indeed invest with splendour Victor Hugo and his Opera Omnia; it is impossible to read you without catching some of your glow. And indeed the power of your 'Father and Master and Lord' is undeniable; he has power, pathos, life, all sorts of things; only just the very charm and accent of a poet are what I miss in him. But I shall not fail to read with attention what you put forth on the subject; I wish I could be as sure that it would make me enjoy Victor Hugo's poetry as I am sure that it will make me enjoy your force and eloquence." Swinburne's article, warm in its praise of Hugo, expressed, as he said it would, "my conviction that Goethe's verdict on *Hernani* [see p. 40:14, variant] is worth just exactly as much, and for exactly the same reasons, as Voltaire's on *Hamlet*, when holding exactly the same place as Goethe after him in the curule chair of European letters."—C. Y. Lang, ed., *The Swinburne Letters* (New Haven: Yale University Press, 1960), IV, 117, 142, 145. See the excellent article by S. M. B. Coulling, "Swinburne and Arnold," *Philological Quarterly* XLIX, 211–33 (April, 1970).

68:15–21. See pp. 39:35–40:1.

68:26–30. *Henry V*, IV, i, 315–19.

69:25. See p. 46:13n.

69:28–29. *The Athenaeum* remarked that Arnold "must needs be a bold man" not to have done so, but its review of the *Wordsworth*

Selections appeared after the present essay was published.—September 27, 1879, p. 393.

69:34–35. V, iii, 60–61.

69:37–38. V, i, 58–59.

70:5–6. *Richard II*, II, i, 46, 50.

70:8–10. Sonnet, "It is not to be thought of," lines 11–13.

70:12–13. Copied at the end of Arnold's pocket diary for 1877.— *Note-Books*, ed. Lowry, p. 291.

70:28–31, 71:2–4. *Ruy Blas*, I, iii, 139–42; II, iv, 50–52.

71:21–28. *1 Henry VI*, IV, iii, 39–46.

72:30. *George Dandin* (1668), a comedy in prose, was not in the repertoire of the Comédie française in London, and would not now be singled out as a masterpiece of Molière's to compare with *Othello* as a masterpiece of Shakespeare's.

73:18–19. "Sein grosses Talent ist das eines Epitomators, und da der Dichter überhaupt als Epitomator der Natur erscheint, so müssen wir auch hier Shakespeare's grosses Verdienst anerkennen, nur läugnen wir dabei und zwar zu seinen Ehren, dass die Bühne ein würdiger Raum für sein Genie gewesen."—"Shakespeare und kein Ende!" *Über Kunst und Alterthum* V (1826); *Werke* (Weimar, 1902), XLI (1), 67.

74:12–15. Arnold saw Sainte-Beuve several times in Paris in August, 1859, April–May, 1865, and May, 1866.

74:17–20. *Siècle de Louis XIV*, chapt. xxxii, three-fifths through. —*Oeuvres complètes* (Paris, 1878), XIV 548.

74:25–35. *Lettres et opuscules inédits* (3rd ed.; Paris, 1853), I, 57.

75:9. François Joseph Talma (1763–1826), one of the greatest of French tragic actors, was on the stage before and throughout the Revolution and the Napoleonic eras and well into the Restoration. He was much admired by Napoleon.

75:24–25. The roles of Phèdre and Doña Sol were Bernhardt's most famous while she was in the company of the Comédie française. "For the sombre *femme fatale* of Hugo she substituted an adorable creature all tenderness and charm," says *The Oxford Companion to the Theatre*.

75:28–29. The distant sounding of the horn is the summons to Hernani to commit suicide, according to his agreement. It is the night of his wedding to Doña Sol, converted by that sound into the catastrophe of the play.

75:30–31. F. L. Z. Werner's one-act tragedy, *Die vierundzwanzigste Februar* (1810) started the vogue of the "fate drama" in Germany. Sir Walter Scott's gothic tragedy in prose, *The House of Aspen* (written in 1799) was described by the author as a *rifacimento* of "Veit Weber's" (i.e., Leonhard Wächter's) *Die heilige Vehme;* it was first published late in 1829 and was produced with some success in the Edinburgh theater that winter.

75:33–38. Letter to *Le Temps* from London, June 16, 1879, reprinted in Georges d'Heylli (E. A. Poinsot), ed., *La Comédie française à Londres, 1871–1879* (Paris, 1880), p. 111; jotted in Arnold's pocket diary for August 8, 1879.—*Note-Books*, ed. Lowry, p. 322.

76:26–77:1. V, vi, 52–54, 60, 63; V, v, 31; V, vi, 72–73, 16. The Surrey Theatre in Blackfriars Road was throughout most of the century the most popular of the minor theaters in London, especially for its production of melodrama.

77:6–7. *Bombastes Furioso* (1810) was a burlesque opera by William Barnes Rhodes, a parody of Ariosto's heroic poem *Orlando Furioso.*

77:31–32. For the company's performances of plays by Octave Feuillet (1821–90) and the younger Alexandre Dumas (1824–95), see p. 349. It performed *Le Post Scriptum* (June 12), *Les Fourchambault* (June 20, July 5), and *Philiberte* (July 11) by Émile Augier (1820–89), and *Le Gendre de M. Poirier* (June 12) by Augier and Jules Sandeau.

77:36–78:1. Arnold quotes his own characterization of Paris in *Literature and Dogma* (1873). His phrase *"homme sensuel moyen"* occurs again in "George Sand" (1877).—*Prose Works,* ed. Super, VI, 390–91; VIII, 223:38 and n.

78:31. The French company performed Théodore de Banville's *Gringoire* (1866) in London on June 23.

78:35. See p. 64:22.

79:3. *Les Dominos roses,* by Alfred Delacour and Alfred Hennequin, opened in Paris on April 17, 1876, and its adaptation by James Albery, *The Pink Dominos,* was produced at the Criterion Theatre, London, on March 31, 1877. "It is a three-act farce, the not too reputable incidents in which spring from the freak of two wives, who, to test their husbands, send them invitations to a masked ball." "If not exactly childlike in innocence, the intrigue . . . has, at least, no absolute wickedness. . . . The English version is a capital instance of successful adaptation. In some respects, indeed, it is better than the original."—*Athenaeum,* April 29, 1876, p. 610; April 7, 1877, p. 459. But *The Daily Telegraph* was scandalized that such indecency should appear on the London stage. It had 555 consecutive performances there until December 20, 1878, crossed the Atlantic and the Pacific, and was revived at the Criterion as late as the autumn of 1892.

79:21–23. First in "Heinrich Heine" (1863), then in *Literature and Dogma* (1873), "Falkland" (1877), and "Equality" (1878).— *Prose Works*, ed. Super, III, 121; VI, 390; VIII, 201, 294.

79:36–38. Arnold was in Shrewsbury on August 19, 1853, but the Shrewsbury newspapers of that date throw no light on the performance he describes.

80:14–16. For convenient lists of the theaters in London and Edinburgh in the latter half of the nineteenth century, see Allardyce Nicoll, *A History of Late Nineteenth Century Drama, 1850–1900* (Cambridge: at the University Press, 1946), I, 215–22, 224.

80:31–34. A doctrine Arnold expressed in "Equality" (1878) and elsewhere.—*Prose Works*, ed. Super, VIII, 287, 371–72.

81:18–22. Arnold alludes especially to *The World* and *Truth;* see p. 91:25n.

82:18–83:18. Arnold repeats much of what *The Times* said of the advantages and organization of the Comédie francaise on June 3, 1879, p. 5, col. 5.

83:9. Edmund Got (1822–1901) and Louis-Arsène Delaunay (1826–1903) were members of the company that visited London in 1879. By that time François Régnier de La Brière (1807–85) had retired from the stage, but he continued as professor at the Conservatoire. Louis Barizain, known as Monrose (1811–83), the principal *comédien* in the company until his retirement in 1869, was professor at the Conservatoire until 1880. The Conservatoire national de musique et de déclamation was founded in 1795 and when Arnold wrote offered free instruction to about 600 pupils, under the supervision of the Ministry of Fine Arts. "To supply the Pensionnaires, the engaged actors not yet belonging to the Société, from whom the Sociétaires are recruited, there are not only all the theatres of France, but the classes of Declamation at the Conservatoire, with the best old actors for professors, and yearly competitions under careful judgment, certain successes in which give a right to a *début* at the Théâtre Français."—*Times*, June 3, 1879, p. 5, col. 5.

83:11–12. The Comédie francaise, known also as the Maison de Molière or the Théâtre francais, was officially founded in 1680, seven years after Molière's death. It received a substantial subvention from the government.

83:29–31. The Theatres Royal, Drury Lane and Covent Garden, by patents dating from 1660, claimed exclusive rights to the performance of plays in London. These rights were more and more strenuously contested in the nineteenth century, in the courts, in the parliamentary debates, and in practice by the production in other theaters of "burlettas" which often were not significantly different from plays. The patents were repealed by the Act of 1843 for regulating the theaters.

83:35–36. See p. 66:23–24.

84:8–12. Arnold echoes some of his key phrases from *Culture and Anarchy;* see *Prose Works,* ed. Super, V, 128, 123, 147.

84:21–22. See p. 15:36–38.

84:27. The Science and Art Department, like the Education Department, was administered under the Committee of Council on Education. It provided instruction in science and art in schools throughout the kingdom and had under its superintendence various museums and libraries, chief of which was the South Kensington Museum (now the Victoria and Albert Museum).

84:28. Edward Frederick Smyth Pigott became examiner of stage plays on August 25, 1874.

84:33. *The Modern British Drama* (London: printed for William Miller, Albermarle Street, by James Ballantyne and Co., Edinburgh, 1811), consisted of five large octavo volumes, two of tragedy, two of comedy, and one of operas and farces, from the seventeenth and eighteenth centuries, excluding Shakespeare.

85:5. *Romeo and Juliet,* III, i, 100.

85:25. The Gaiety Theatre in the Strand (1868–1902) stood not far from the site of its modern successor and namesake in Aldwych; but this too has now vanished.

85:29. In much the same way, Arnold returned from his tour of France in 1859 with the message: "Organize your secondary instruction," and from the principal Continental countries in 1865 saying: "Organize your secondary and your superior instruction." In the latter report, as here, he concludes rhetorically with those words.—*Prose Works,* ed, Super, II, 90; IV, 328.

[JOSEPH DE MAISTRE ON RUSSIA]

In 1863, when Arnold was reading in Eugénie de Guérin and drawing subjects for his Oxford lectures from Sainte-Beuve, he wrote at the head of a list of books he planned to read "Joseph de Maistre's Correspondence," which had been the subject of a *Causerie* on June 2, 1851, collected with others into the fourth volume of the

Causeries du lundi. But the correspondence may have been unread that year, for the name of de Maistre continues to crop up on Arnold's reading lists in his pocket diaries at intervals, until finally from June 1 to December 1, 1877, he actually did read in the work. He promised an article on it to Dr. William Smith, editor of the *Quarterly Review*, in June, 1879, and jotted brief excerpts from it in his pocket diary later that summer. There were the inevitable delays, but his manuscript went from Fox How to the printer about September 18. The essay appeared in the *Quarterly* for October, anonymous by the *Quarterly*'s rule like his two previous contributions (the essays on Scherer, "A French Critic on Milton" and "A French Critic on Goethe"). But unlike his other two, this essay was never reprinted and was not known as Arnold's until its separate but simultaneous discovery by Professor Fraser Neiman and the present editor in 1959. The *Wellesley Index to Victorian Periodicals* then revealed that Arnold's name was set beside the article in the publisher's list of contributors. He received £26. 5s. in payment. The title does not appear at the beginning of the article, but is taken from the running heads at the tops of the pages.

As usual Arnold owes little to Sainte-Beuve beyond the suggestion of a subject, unless Sainte-Beuve's opening remark that one could not fail to recognize in de Maistre a political philosopher of the first order led Arnold to his comparison with Burke. Sainte-Beuve was most concerned to give a sympathetic picture of de Maistre's character: "Longtemps on ne crut avoir dans le comte Joseph de Maistre qu'un homme d'un esprit supérieur et qu'un cerveau de génie; aujourd'hui on est heureux de trouver tout simplement en lui un homme et un coeur," and (a sentence Arnold copied in his pocket diary in 1879) "Son innocence de vie le soutient, sa gaieté naturelle ne l'abandonne pas." John Morley published a comparable but much longer study of de Maistre in the *Fortnightly Review* in 1868.

The essay has been reprinted in Neiman's *Essays, Letters, and Reviews by Matthew Arnold* (Cambridge: Harvard University Press, 1960), pp. 216–35; the steps of its conception are traced from Arnold's diaries and his letters to Smith by Roger L. Brooks, "Matthew Arnold's 'Joseph de Maistre on Russia,' " *Huntington Library Quarterly* XXX, 185–88 (February, 1967).

86:1–5. "Maximen und Reflexionen," *Werke* (Weimar, 1907), XLII (2), 151. The first sentence was jotted in Arnold's pocket diary for September 2, 1879, and several times thereafter.—*Note-Books*, ed. Lowry, pp. 323, 335, 372, 427, 546.

87:35–36. Burke died in 1797, de Maistre in 1821.

88:4–5. *Lettres et opuscules inédits* (3rd ed.; Paris, 1853), II, 494.

88:9–11. In 1790 de Maistre composed, out of a vast number of revolutionary clichés he had collected, an imaginary "Discourse of Citizen Cherchemot on the Festival of the Popular Sovereignty." This phrase appears in *Lettres et opuscules*, II, 222.

88:19–21. *Lettres et opuscules*, I, 382.

88:21–22. See his *Apologia, passim*, and especially its Note A: "Liberalism."

88:34. Newman defends his conception of an infallible Church early in chapt. v of the *Apologia*, "Position of My Mind since 1845."

88:36. *Macbeth* II, i, 47.

89:9–10. Henry Brougham, Baron Brougham and Vaux (1778–1868), one of the founders of the *Edinburgh Review*, was a member of Parliament from 1810 and became Lord Chancellor in the reforming Whig ministry of Lord Grey in 1830, a post he held for four years. He was generally sympathetic to the Utilitarians and has left his mark in the improvement of the English legal system.

89:14–31. *Lettres et opuscules*, I, 508, 381, 508, 452 (363–64). George Hammond Whalley (1813–78), member of Parliament from 1859 until his death, "was an ardent protestant, and made himself notorious by the frequency and bitterness of his denunciations of the Jesuits, whom he suspected of all manner of intrigues."— *D.N.B.* He spoke from the same platform from which Murphy delivered himself of the riot-inciting anti-Catholic diatribes in Birmingham that Arnold commemorated in *Culture and Anarchy*. The quotation is from Horace *Carmen Saeculare* 74.

90:2–91:8. Arnold draws upon the "Notice biographique" which de Maistre's son prefixed to the *Lettres et opuscules*. For his education by the Jesuits, see I, 387; and his familiarity with languages depends also on the authority of his own statement, I, 223. The latter was repeated by Sainte-Beuve, *Causeries du lundi* (3rd ed.; Paris, 1859), IV, 195. Chambéry, capital of Savoy, was ruled by the House of Savoy, as were Piedmont, with its capital at Turin, and Sardinia, with its capital at Cagliari. Restored to the king of that house in 1815, Chambéry was again ceded to France in 1860 as part of the price for French support of the House of Savoy in unifying Italy.

91:9–11. The book was first published in 1851. The sixth edition appeared in 1873, the seventh in 1880.

91:19. "Ma plume ressemble un peu (et en cela seul) à celle de madame de Sévigné: elle a la bride sur le cou," wrote de Maistre to his daughter.—*Lettres et opuscules*, I, 172 (and see I, 114). Marie de Rabutin-Chantal, Marquise de Sévigné (1626–96), a friend of La Rochefoucauld and Madame de La Fayette, was a prolific letter-writer whose correspondence was published in numerous editions after her death.

91:25. See p. 286:1–4.

91:25–28. A rash of weekly "journals of society" followed the founding of *Vanity Fair* on November 7, 1868. Two of the most successful were *The World*, a Wednesday paper founded by Edmund Yates on July 8, 1874, and *Truth*, a Thursday paper founded on January 4, 1877, by Henry Labouchere, who had been on the staff of *The World* from its beginning. See "Equality" (1878), *Prose Works*, ed. Super, VIII, 303.

91:33–92:7. *Lettres et opuscules*, I, 450–51, quoted also by Sainte-Beuve, *Causeries*, IV, 213–14. Arnold jotted the final sentence in his pocket diary for August 3, 1879.—*Note-Books*, ed. Lowry, p. 321. "Pertransivit benefaciendo" is "he went about doing good" (said of Christ by Peter in Acts 10:38). The italics are de Maistre's.

92:8–10. Arnold quoted this maxim in letters of December 24, 1862, May 14, 1863, and February 28, 1866.—*Letters*, ed. Russell, and one unpublished.

92:17–18. Because of the conflict of Russian and British interests in Afghanistan.

93:3–19. *Lettres et opuscules*, I, 86–87. "Chassez ... galop" is from Philippe Néricault ("Destouches"), *Le Glorieux* (1732), Act III, scene 5.

93:23–25. *Ibid.*, I, 269. Arnold jotted this sentence in his pocket diary for September 14, 1879.—*Note-Books*, ed. Lowry p. 324.

93:34–94:21. *Ibid.*, I, 50, 114. De Maistre wrote: "A foreigner who has three children here cannot educate one."

94:30–95:11. *Ibid.*, I, 115–16, with omission; quoted also in part by Sainte-Beuve, *Causeries*, IV, 210.

95:17–34. *Ibid.*, I, 220–21, dated "December, 1809."

95:37–96:15. *Ibid.*, I, 260, 265–66. "Je me défie donc de toute loi constitutionelle *écrite*."

96:15–97:6. *Ibid.*, I, 264–65, 352; II, 286. The schism which separated the Eastern from the Roman church is commonly dated from 1054, when papal legates excommunicated the patriarch of Constantinople. The Tartars, a Mongol horde, conquered Russia in 1238 and dominated it until 1380.

97:9–15. *Ibid.*, I, 405–6. "Pope" here means simply "priest."

97:18–98:2. *Ibid.*, I, 362, 405.

98:6–15. *Ibid.*, I, 306–7, 311.

98:20–99:13. *Ibid.*, I, 352, 266–67, 325, 267. "Raisonneuses" means "argumentative." The Latin is Vergil *Aeneid* VI, 86–87, substituting "Neva" (the river at St. Petersburg) for "Tiber."

99:19–100:19. *Ibid.*, I, 367–68. After "not less serious" Arnold has omitted the sentence, "Je ne sais quel esprit de mauvaise foi et de tromperie circule dans toutes les veines de l'État." Numa Pompilius, the second king of Rome (traditionally 715–673 B.C.) was a reformer of religion and morals. The Decemvirs were two successive Roman committees of ten, the first appointed in 451 B.C., to codify the laws; they prepared the Twelve Tables.

100:24–32, 101:6–10. *Ibid.*, I, 366; II, 312. De Maistre himself, in his fourth "Letter on Public Education in Russia," quotes the passage from Bacon's *De Augmentis Scientiarum*, Book I, nearly one-third through. Agesilaus, king of Sparta, at a meeting in 395 B.C. with the Persian satrap Pharnabazus, whose territory he had invaded, spoke admiringly to his enemy: "Would that a man like yourself were on our side."—Xenophon *Hellenica* IV, i, 38.

101:18–102:14. *Ibid.*, I, 366; II, 281–83.

102:24–103:24. *Ibid.*, II, 283–85, with omissions.

103:25–104:3. *Ibid.*, II, 282 (342), 286–87. The Dvina River flows north into the Gulf of Riga and thus comes between the Polish cities and St. Petersburg and Moscow.

104:5–24. *Ibid.*, II, 287–88. It is Arnold who specifies "ce qu'ils ont de plus cher" as "their children."

104:25–36. *Ibid.*, I, 311–12, 455, 405.

105:2. Dr. Adolf Neubauer (1832–1907), Hungarian-born scholar of Hebrew manuscripts, was sub-librarian of the Bodleian Library, Oxford.

105:10–11. *Lettres et opuscules*, I, 359.

105:20–106:19. *Ibid.*, I, 352–53, with omissions; II, 379, 395; I, 406, 322, 353.

106:23–33. *Ibid.*, II, 369–71. For "le venin germanique," see II, 392.

107:12–16. *Ibid.*, I, 448, with omissions; quoted in part also by Sainte-Beuve, *Causeries*, IV, 199–200. The family of Brignola was one of the most distinguished of Genoa, politically and intellectually. Antonio Brignole-Sale (1786–1863) represented Genoa at the Congress of Vienna. When, over his protest, Genoa was joined to Piedmont and Sardinia under the House of Savoy, he became head of the royal university in 1816, and thereafter was ambassador to Rome and Paris and a minister of state.

107:16–18. Essay "Of Truth," ¶1.

107:21–108:2. *Lettres et opuscules*, I, 391–95; II, 394.

107:23. The Illuminati, a Russian sect founded about 1790, were dominated by the ideas of Jakob Boehme and Emanuel Swedenborg.

107:33–36. The Convention of Paris was the so-called Holy Alliance, signed on September 26, 1815, by the Orthodox Alexander I of Russia, the Catholic Francis I of Austria, and the Protestant Frederick William III of Prussia, at the proposal of the first. It declared that the three nations would regard themselves as members of a single Christian nation whose only sovereign was "God, our Divine Saviour, Jesus Christ, the Almighty's Word, the Word of life."

108:4–12. *Ibid.*, I, 438, 421 (445: II, 390–91).

108:16–33. *Ibid.*, I, 392–93. St. Teresa of Avila (1515–82), St. Francis of Sales (1567–1622), François de La Mothe-Fénelon (1651–1715) and his friend Jeanne Marie Bouvier de La Mothe Guyon (1648–1717) were all Roman Catholic mystical writers.

108:37–109:16. *Ibid.*, I, 322, 386.

109:18–110:10. *Ibid.*, I, 18–19, 418–19, 386–88, 440–41, 444 (where de Maistre quotes "Rome's doctrine,"—"Hors de l'Église point de salut"), I, 300. "Extra ecclesiam nulla salus" ("Outside the Church no salvation") was a dogmatic axiom first formulated by Origen and Cyprian (mid third century); it is still the doctrine of Catholic theologians.

110:15–111:15. *Ibid.*, II, 340–42, with omissions. Simon Strogonoff was the youngest of three brothers who conquered Siberia for the Russians in the late sixteenth century. Alexander Vasilievich Suvarov (1729–1800), Russian field marshal, suppressed the rebellion of Pougatscheff in 1775 (see p. 99:14–15), subdued the Poles, and in the last year of his life led the Russian troops against the French Revolutionary armies in Italy.

[COST OF ELEMENTARY SCHOOLS]

In his General Report to the Department of Education for 1878, Arnold compared the average cost per child for elementary education in France (18s. 1d.) with the cost per child in the board schools of London, which he calculated at 55s. 11d. That his figures were slipshod is patent from the ease with which he is willing to assume that the French average is the cost of a child's education in Paris: "It cannot be right, it is extravagant and absurd, that the London boy's education should be so managed as to cost three times as much as that of the Paris one." Because he still looked forward to the day when secondary education would also become a state function and its cost be added to that of elementary education, he protested against the Utopian extravagance of the school boards: "It is only during the last year that the operations of the London School Board have come much under my immediate notice in Westminster. I am quite sure that the board needs the advice, *simplify*. I am quite sure that they ought to conceive in a simpler way the problem before them, and the means of working it out. I am quite sure that their conception of what is requisite in the way of accommodation, studies, salaries, administration, is pitched too high."—Arnold, *Reports on Elementary Schools, 1852–1882*, ed. Francis Sandford (London, 1889), pp. 220–21; ed. F. S. Marvin (London, 1908), pp. 196–97. "They have given people such a handle [with their extravagance] that the public institution of secondary schools is made harder than ever," Arnold told his sister on October 13, 1879. "That is my great cause of quarrel with them."—*Letters*, ed. Russell.

When Sir Charles Reed, chairman of the London School Board, on October 1, 1879, opened its last session before a new election with an elaborate statement of its accomplishments, he alluded in passing to Arnold's suggestion that the program be marked by greater simplicity.—*Times*, October 2, p. 4, cols. 3–5. There followed some correspondence in *The Times*, and a leading article that dwelt at some length on Arnold's statement that "we spend, on the whole, for each child more than France spends for two children, and the London School Board spends for each child more than France spends for three children"; the article acknowledged that in France "no doubt this cost varies in different districts as it does in England."—October 13, p. 9, col. 4. Next day (p. 8, col. 2), "Teacher" published a letter quoting some very marked corrections of Arnold's figures from *The Teacher* newspaper of October 4, which added that "The ignorantins have had their day, and by a decree of a Republican majority a system of education will soon be in working order which will cost more than half as much again as the system which Mr. Arnold regards with such approving complacency." Arnold's letter appeared in *The Times* on October 20.

113:7–12. Arnold explained in *The Popular Education of France* (1861) that the teaching brethren, established by Lasalle in 1679, were variously known as the Frères de Saint Yon, the Frères Ignorantins, and the Frères des Ecoles Chrétiennes.—*Prose Works*, ed. Super, II, 40. He mentions his meeting with Frère Philippe (Matthieu Bransiet), *ibid.*, II, 71, 77. "You must not pay much attention to attacks on the Christian Brothers' Schools such as you sent me," Arnold wrote to his sister early in February, 1879. "To call them *frères ignorantins* is a mere renewal of the abuse and ridicule of the teaching clergy at the time of the Reformation; it is a mere common-place. The Brothers have to get the Government certificate just like other teachers, and their schools are not, or were not, on the whole, inferior to the lay schools, though neither are particularly good. Of the French it is particularly true that a great deal of their civilisation is got outside the school. The Brothers teach more of what they call 'religion and morals' than the lay schools do, and, of course, a great deal of what they teach under this head is rather childish, but then, on the other side, you have the lay teacher saying, according to Guizot's report, when asked how he provided for teaching religion and morals, 'Je n'enseigne pas ces bêtises-là,' and between the two one does not know which to think least eligible, but I am inclined to prefer the Christian Brothers."—*Letters*, ed. Russell.

[COPYRIGHT]

The question of Copyright was actively discussed on both sides of the Atlantic; English authors were inclined to feel put upon by the American failure to grant them the protection (and hence royalties) their own country provided, but the hearings of the Copyright Commission, which sat from 1876 to 1878, gave evidence of a good deal of confusion in English law as well. At the end of his pocket diary for 1879 Arnold jotted a list of half-a-dozen titles "to read for Article on Copyright"; all these are alluded to in the article he published in the *Fortnightly Review* for March, 1880. He received £30 in payment. "I rather rely on [William] as to this question," he wrote to his sister, William E. Forster's wife, soon after the article appeared. "[G. W.] Smalley tells me I have put the thing better than any one else for the purpose of really getting the Americans to do something." But this was wishful thinking, as was his request of Gladstone two years later: "If you ever have half an hour to spare in the Easter holidays, you will perhaps kindly glance at the essay on 'Copyright' in the accompanying volume [*Irish Essays*], and consider whether an English author ought not to have property in his work for a longer term after death than he has now. For many good books the sale commences late, their author has to create, as Wordsworth said, the taste by which he is to be enjoyed; such an author is surely the very man one would wish to protect, but at present the law is far more unfavourable to him in England than in France, Germany, or Italy."

114:1–12. George Sand, "Michel Lévy," *Dernières pages* (Paris, 1877), pp. 269–76.

114:18. Gervais Charpentier, also a Paris publisher, was another pioneer in bringing out inexpensive books.

114:27–115:17. *Dernières pages*, pp. 271–72. "Man shall not live by bread alone" were Jesus' words to the devil in the wilderness, Matthew 4:4 (Luke 4:4).

115:18–116:2. *Dernières pages*, pp. 272–73.

116:32–33. Arnold mentioned these "instincts" frequently in his writings; see pp. 26–27 and *Literature and Dogma* (1871), *Prose Works*, ed. Super, VI, 174.

116:37. The franc was worth about 9½ *d*; Arnold's rough conversion equated "two-and-sixpence or three shillings" with "three francs or three francs and a half."

117:5–10. The first part of *The Memoirs of Prince Metternich*, tr. Robina Napier, was published in two volumes by Richard Bentley and Sons on December 29, 1879. The French version was published in Paris by E. Plon in December, 1879.

117:27–32. The Copyright Commission, under the chairmanship of Lord John Manners, was appointed on April 17, 1876, supplanting one designated the preceding October 6 under the chairmanship of Earl Stanhope, who died on December 24, 1875. The commissioners included Sir James Fitzjames Stephen, James Anthony Froude, Anthony Trollope, and eleven others besides the chairman. Their report was submitted on May 24, 1878. Arnold quotes, not the "opening sentence," but ¶ 16, the first substantive paragraph of the report.—Copyright Commission, *Report of the Commissioners* (London: H. M. Stationery Office, 1878), p. ix. The "proprietary right" gives the author or owner of the copyright an absolute right, for the term of the copyright, to control reproduction of the work; the "right to a royalty defined by statute" (Arnold omits three words) would give any person the right to reproduce provided only he paid the owner whatever royalty was fixed by law.

118:3–5. *Pensées*, sect. v, no. 295; ed. L. Brunschvicg (Paris, 1908–21), XIII, 222. Quoted also in "The Church of England" (1876), *Prose Works*, ed. Super, VIII, 72.

118:7–10. T. H. Huxley testified before the commission on April 13, Herbert Spencer on March 6 and 20, 1877, and T. H. Farrer on eight separate occasions. Farrer also wrote a statement on "The Principle of Copyright," *Fortnightly Review* XXX, 836–51 (December, 1878), which Arnold read in preparation for this article. Sir Louis Mallet, a member of the commission, so little agreed with the report that he declined to sign it and submitted a separate report of his own, printed along with the commission's report. Thomas Henry Farrer (1819–99), later Baron Farrer, was permanent secretary of the Board of Trade from 1865 to 1886, duing which period "almost all the reforms of and additions to our system of commercial law were only brought about with [his] concurrence."—William Carr in *D.N.B.* Mallet (1823–90) was a grandson of Mallet du Pan, whom Arnold mentioned in "A Genevese Judge" (p. 290). He had formerly served with the Board of Trade and was currently permanent undersecretary of state for India. The principal discussion of the absolute natural right of an author to control his production is in Copyright Commission, *Minutes of Evidence* (London, 1878), pp. 304–6, and *Report*, pp. xlvii–xlix.

118:15–18. Arnold repeatedly stated this conviction: in *Culture and Anarchy* (1868), "Endowments" (1870), *Literature and Dogma* (1871), *God and the Bible* (1874), and "Equality" (1878).—*Prose Works*, ed. Super, V, 201; VI, 134, 188; VII, 145; VIII, 285. Burke said: "Government is not made in virtue of natural rights, which may and do exist in total independence of it; and exist in much greater clearness, and in a much greater degree of abstract perfection: but their abstract perfection is their practical defect. . . . Government is a contrivance of human wisdom to provide for human wants."—*Reflections on the Revolution in France*, nearly one-fourth through.

119:13–25. The principal concern of Arnold in his testimony before the Copyright Commission was to urge "above all the lengthening of the time, after the author's death, during which the property in his works remains to his family," and the provision that all his copyrights should lapse simultaneously, not one by one.—*Minutes of Evidence*, pp. 196–97. He informed himself more accurately about the terms of foreign copyright before publishing his article, but in general depends on the report of the Copyright Commission, p. xi.

119:31–120:4. *Minutes of Evidence*, pp. 267, 272–73, 275, and *Report*, p. xlviii (¶ 7). Mallet's remark is quoted in the article by Froude (see p. 122:17, 33n.), p. 175. Farrer lived at Abinger Hall, near Dorking, Surrey; Professor John Tyndall concluded his testimony before the Copyright Commission with the remark: "I hold my right to my own intellectual work to be at least as sacred as is the right of my excellent friend, whose propositions have been discussed here, to Abinger Hall."—*Minutes of Evidence*, p. 316.

122:17–25. *Report*, p. lvi (¶ 79); *Minutes of Evidence*, Appendix H, p. 374, both quoted in "The Copyright Commission," *Edinburgh*

Review, American ed., CXLVIII, 175, 161 (October, 1878). Farrer's word was "undesirable," not "intolerable," but the *Edinburgh* was responsible for Arnold's misquotation.

122:33–35. The article was anonymous, but its authorship was no secret. Froude was himself a member of the Copyright Commission.

123:19–24. *Minutes of Evidence*, Appendix I, p. 375, in support of Farrer's answers to questions 3931–33, pp. 208–9. The editions bought in Paris were published by Tauchnitz of Leipzig. But Arnold's figures are not a strictly accurate statement of the matter: the American edition of Trevelyan's *Life of Macaulay* cost nearly 18 *s.* (*Minutes*, p. 203), the Tauchnitz only 8 fr., or 6*s.* 8*d.* *Middlemarch* was available in England at 7*s.* 6*d.* and *Daniel Deronda* at a guinea.

124:1–19. Sir Louis Mallet's dissenting report is the most vigorous argument for the royalty system, which he seems to fix at a payment to the copyright owner of 20 percent.—*Report*, pp. l–li. That Arnold was not being entirely preposterous in his picture of the hapless author pursuing his royalty around the world is illustrated by the fate of a Canadian law permitting cheap American reprints of English copyright works to be imported upon payment of a duty of 12½ percent, to be collected by the Canadian Customs and forwarded to the British Government for the benefit of the authors. "The Act has proved a complete failure. . . . [In ten years] no returns, or returns of an absurdly small amount, have been made to the authors and owners."—*Report*, p. xxxi. And Froude also declares that collecting the royalty would be impossible.—*Edinburgh Review*, American ed., CXLVIII, 165.

124:20–30. *Report*, pp. viii–xii. The Copyright Act of 1842 was the principal statute governing copyright in the United Kingdom at this date.

124:31–37. *Edinburgh Review*, American ed., CXLVIII, 176.

125:13–25. The "three-decker" novel so typical of the century, published in three volumes at a guinea and a half, aimed primarily at sale to the rental lending libraries, of which Mudie's was chief; and so did a great many other books published at a comparatively high price.

125:29–37. *Edinburgh Review*, American ed., CXLVIII, 178. Froude was editor of *Fraser's Magazine* from 1860 to 1874.

126:2–7. "The proposal [of fixed royalty] really amounts to this, that whereas, at present, the poorer class of readers are inconvenienced by having to wait for a cheap edition a certain number of years, they shall, by this arrangement, be advantaged by having a cheap edition forthwith; which is to say that people with smaller amounts of money shall have no disadvantages from their smaller amounts of money. It is communistic practically: it is simply equalizing the advantages of wealth and poverty."—Spencer before the commission, March 20, 1877; *Minutes of Evidence*, p. 284. Arnold embellishes Spencer's statement with illustrations.

126:20–23. *The Memoirs of Madame de Rémusat, 1802–1808*, tr. Mrs. Cashel Hoey and John Lillie, was published by Sampson Low, Marston & Co., in two volumes. The Paris edition published by Calmann Lévy was in three volumes.

127:20–23. In November, 1878, Harper and Brothers addressed a note to the Secretary of State in Washington suggesting that the copyright question be referred to an international conference, and published the proposal as *Memorandum in Regard to International Copyright Treaty between Great Britain and the United States* (New York, 1879). Conant referred to this proposal in his article, pp. 156, 161 (see note to p. 127:23–29).

127:23–29. S. S. Conant, "International Copyright: I. An American View," *Macmillan's Magazine* XL, 151–61 (June, 1879); "C," "II. An Englishman's View of the Foregoing," *ibid.*, pp. 161–66. Samuel Stillman Conant (1831–?1885) had been managing editor of the *New York Times* and was after 1869 managing editor of *Harper's Weekly*. Leonard Henry Courtney (1832–1918), later Baron Courtney, was a member of Parliament and one of the chief writers of leading articles for *The Times* (London).

127:31–128:3. George Haven Putnam, *International Copyright Considered in Some of Its Relations to Ethics and Political Economy* (New York: G. P. Putnam's Sons, 1879), p. 15.

128:4–12. *Ibid.*, pp. 24, 21, 23. A draft proposal of "An Act to Grant Copyright to Foreign Authors" adopted at a meeting of the New York Booksellers and Publishers on February 6, 1872, would grant copyright to a foreign author upon condition of his work's being manufactured in all its parts in the United States and distributed by a publisher who was a citizen of the United States.—*The Publishers' . . . Weekly Trade Circular*, n.s. I, 91 (February 8, 1872).

128:18–30. Conant, pp. 153–54, 153.

128:31–129:16. *Ibid.*, pp. 152, 159–60, the last portion somewhat paraphrased.

129:25. An aside of Don Bazile's (not Figaro's) in Beaumarchais' *Le Barbier de Séville*, III, xi; quoted by Arnold in *Culture and Anarchy* (1868).—*Prose Works*, ed. Super, V, 152.

129:33–36. In 1864; ridiculed by Arnold in "My Countrymen" (1866).—*Prose Works*, ed. Super, V, 10, 15.

130:11–15. Conant, pp. 154–55.

130:21–24. English copyright law was far from clear on this matter, but the digest made by Sir James Stephen for the Copyright Commission indicates that copyright might be obtained for any book published in the United Kingdom before or at the same time as its publication elsewhere, by an author who was a British subject or who "owes local and temporary allegiance to Her Majesty by residing at that time in some part of Her Majesty's dominions." A judicial decision seemed to have removed even this token residence requirement, but had not clearly decided the point.—*Report*, pp. lxviii–lxix.

130:37–131:6. Both T. H. Huxley and John Tyndall testified before the Copyright Commission in mid-April, 1877, that they received regular remittances from their American publishers.—*Minutes of Evidence*, pp. 308, 314–16.

131:11–14. Arnold testified before the Copyright Commission on January 25, 1877: "I am told [my works] are a good deal sold [in America]." For this he received, he said, no remuneration, "but Ticknor and Field[s] once sent me, I think, 50 *l*. as a kind of honorarium, to acknowledge the profit which they had got from me." He believed that if there were copyright privileges available to him in America, he "(like all other authors, I suppose) should gain immensely."—*Minutes of Evidence*, p. 198. In one respect his negative was not entirely accurate: both his London publishers, Smith, Elder and Macmillan, were in the habit of sending a stock of his works, with specially printed American title pages, to Macmillan of New York, and for these copies he was paid by his London publishers.

The payment of £50 he mentioned was made in September, 1866, at the prodding of Macmillan, who had supplied early sheets of *Essays in Criticism* (1865) and of "Thyrsis," the latter of which appeared in Ticknor and Fields' *Every Saturday* in Boston on March 10, 1866, some three weeks in advance of the first appearance in England; £30 was reckoned for the *Essays*, £20 for "Thyrsis." Ticknor and Fields' single-volume edition of *Essays in Criticism, On Translating Homer*, and *A French Eton* (1865) sold at $1.75, then $2.00; 3060 copies were printed by early 1874, and still more thereafter when the plates were sold to Henry Holt & Co. of New York (1876) and ultimately to Macmillan & Co. of New York (1880). Arnold no doubt forgot that in the autumn of 1867 he received a further £20 from Ticknor and Fields for their edition of his *New Poems*. Still in the future when he testified were £10 from Harpers late in 1878 for their publication of his *Selected Poems* in their ten-cent "Franklin Square Library" and the sum of £78. 16s. 1d. described in his diary merely as "From Publishers. America" in December, 1880—chiefly from the Macmillan (New York) one-volume edition of his *Poems* (1878). Harpers seem to have made no payment to him for reprinting his selections from Wordsworth and Byron in their Franklin Square Library (1879, 1881). In the late summer of 1878 Roberts Brothers of Boston wished to buy a set of plates for Arnold's edition of Johnson's *Six Lives of the Poets*, but demurred at paying Arnold a royalty of 10 percent, or even 5 percent, and the proposal was dropped.—Buckler, *Matthew Arnold's Books*, p. 129. Thereupon an edition was printed for and published by Holt in New York and from it Arnold received nothing.

Other works of his produced and published in America without payment to him were his *Poems*—his 1853 and 1855 volumes combined into one—by Ticknor and Fields in October, 1856 (2000 copies), *Literature and Dogma* by James R. Osgood of Boston in April, 1873 (2650 copies), and *God and the Bible* by Osgood at the end of 1875 (1500 copies). Both the latter passed·shortly to Holt and then to Macmillan in New York; there are no figures available for the number of copies they distributed. See Roger L. Brooks, "Matthew Arnold and Ticknor and Fields," *American Literature* XXXV, 514–19 (January, 1964); his "A Neglected Edition of Matthew Arnold's Poetry and a Bibliographical Correction," *Papers of the Bibliographical Society of America* LV, 140–41 (April, 1961), and his "An Unrecorded American Edition of the *Selected Poems of Matthew Arnold*," *The Library*, 5th ser., XVI, 213–14 (September, 1961); William E. Buckler, "An American Edition of Matthew Arnold's *Poems*," *PMLA* LXIX, 678–80 (June, 1954), and R. H. Super, "The First Publication of 'Thyrsis,' " *Notes and Queries* CCVI, 229 (June, 1961) and his "American Piracies of Matthew Arnold," *American Literature* XXXVIII, 123–25 (March, 1966). Since Arnold drew considerable income from the sale of his work to periodicals, it might be added that up to this time he had received nothing from American journals that reprinted his writings, except for "Thyrsis."

Spokesmen for the American publishers made it appear that there was entire harmony among them in their publication of British books, but the case of Arnold's books shows matters somewhat otherwise, and here no doubt American consciences were clear, since they were competing with copies printed in England and imported by a branch of an English firm. Macmillans of New York published *Literature and Dogma* at $2.00 (the copies sent from England) while Osgood sold his edition at $1.50. In 1877 Macmillans were selling *God and the Bible* in New York at $2.00 (copies from England) and across the street Holt was offering the unauthorized reprint at $1.50. The acquisition by Holt of the Osgood *Literature and Dogma* forced Macmillans to reduce their price to $1.50, and a few years later they reduced *God and the Bible* to the same price. Almost simultaneously in October, 1878, Macmillans and Holt advertised competing editions of Arnold's collection of Johnson's *Six Lives of the Poets* at $2.00. Macmillans' copies came from England, Holt's were made in New York, and since Holt added Carlyle's and Macaulay's essays on Boswell to his edition, Macmillans were forced to cut their price to $1.50.

132:17–20. As Arnold testified before the Copyright Commission: "I do not understand the insurmountable obstacle to effecting anything with America, after the experience of the success of France in getting rid of what the French call the *contra-façon Belge*. I can imagine no interest that the Americans have in continuing to pirate our books that the Belgians had not in continuing to pirate French books. Balzac and men like him complained that their bread was taken out of their mouth by the Belgians, and yet France has now made a satisfactory arrangement with Belgium. I no longer see the Belgian editions of French works which I used to see and buy. The Belgians undersold the French by a franc or two a volume, I believe, even with books that only cost four or five francs in France. They had the market of their own country and of Europe for these books."—*Minutes of Evidence*, p. 198.

132:20–22. There simply was no clear and enforceable copyright legislation that applied uniformly to the whole empire, and both Canada and India were cited again and again before the Copyright Commission as importers of cheap editions of British works for which the copyright owners received nothing.

133:1. Manchester, the great industrial city, is cited as the center of *laissez-faire* economic theory and practice.

133:12–32. Conant, p. 159; Putnam, p. 53. The "absurdly cheap editions" were produced chiefly in Chicago, St. Louis, and to some extent Toronto. Harper's "Franklin Square Library," in which Arnold's *Selected Poems* were reprinted for a dime, was New York's answer, designed to drive the cheap competition out of business.

133:34–134:4. Conant, pp. 156–57.

134:30–37. Courtney (p. 162) takes the view that the present American interest in "international copyright" was only a move on the part of the New York publishers to protect their interest against the competition of those in the West. Froude, looking (as Arnold says) to a gradual change in American opinion, believes that "the question should still, for the present, be allowed to rest."—p. 174.

135:4–17. Arnold was quite right. The American Copyright Act of 1891 still contained the manufacturing provision of the New York publishers' proposal of 1872 (see p. 128:4–12n).

[THE FUTURE OF LIBERALISM]

"Perhaps there is nothing in which one may more safely employ oneself, or which brings one, and properly brings, so much happiness as beneficence. But do not you feel sometimes anxious to attack the condition of things which seems to bring about the evils on which your beneficence has to be exercised? When once you have got it into your head that this condition *does* in great measure bring the evils about, and that it is in great measure remediable, I think one can hardly rest satisfied with merely alleviating the evils that arise under it. But I am sure women do not in general feel this—and perhaps it is as well not to feel it. Here is a long prose!" So Arnold wrote to his sister Susy in January, 1879.—*Letters*, ed. Russell. About that time he promised John Morley for the *Fortnightly* a pair of articles on "The Future of Liberalism," "which will, I hope, be the last of my publications about politics and social matters," but which he found himself "disinclined to set about" and therefore postponed in favor of his Wordsworth selections.—Buckler, *Matthew Arnold's Books*, p. 133. The Liberal victory in the general election of 1880 revived the idea, though now it was only a single article promised to James Knowles for the *Nineteenth Century* in July. The Liberals "at best . . . are in a very crude state," Arnold told his sister Jane, who was married to one of their leaders, "and with little light or help in them at present. But through their failing, and succeeding, and gradual improvement lies our way, our only way; I have no doubt of that. But that they will yet fail more than once, and give other chances to the Tories and to future Lord B[eaconsfield]s, I think too probable."—*Letters*, ed. Russell. He received £50 for the article.

136:1–8. William Cobbett, *Rural Rides* (London: Macdonald & Co., 1958), pp. 167–68 (Tenterden, Kent, August 31, 1823). The *Rural Rides* was on the list of books "To read—1880" at the beginning of Arnold's pocket diary for that year, and frequent entries early in the year show him carrying out his plan.—*Note-Books*, ed. Lowry, p. 598. Cobbett's attack was upon the current Lord Camden, who because of his father's distinction received one of the most profitable sinecures in England. "The merit of Pratt was, that he was constantly opposed to the principles of Yorke. Yorke was called a *Tory* and Pratt a *Whig;* but, the devil of it was, *both* got to be *Lords;* and, in one shape or another, the families of *both* have, from that day to this, been receiving *great parcels of public money!* Beautiful system! . . . The people of the present day would laugh at disputes (carried on with so much *gravity!*) about the *principles* of Pratt and the principles of Yorke." Sir Charles Pratt (1714–94), a popular Whig lawyer and judge, as Lord Camden was lord chancellor from 1766 to 1770 in the administration of the elder Pitt. Philip Yorke (1690–1764), as Lord Hardwicke, was lord chancellor from 1737 to 1756. Both were Whigs, but of different factions. The opposition between the younger Pitt, a Tory, and Charles James Fox, a Whig, took place at the turn of the century, a generation later than Pratt and Yorke.

136:16–17. Sir Roundell Palmer (1812–95) as Lord Selborne was lord chancellor under Gladstone in 1872–74 and 1880–85. Hugh McCalmont Cairns (1819–85) as Lord Cairns was lord chancellor under Disraeli in 1868 and 1874–80.

137:21–22. "Mildness and sweet reasonableness" was Arnold's translation of the attributes of Jesus as St. Paul describes them in II Corinthians 10:1.—*St. Paul and Protestantism, Prose Works,* ed. Super, VI, 115.

137:23–24. *Republic* IX, 591 B, adjoining a passage jotted in Arnold's pocket diary for July 4, 1880, and several times thereafter.—*Note-Books,* ed. Lowry, pp. 339, 386, 402, 408, 540.

137:35–38. In the Preface to *Higher Schools and Universities in Germany* (1874), *Prose Works,* ed. Super, VII, 122.

138:1–8. Gladstone's government was defeated over the Irish University Education Bill in March, 1873. Because Disraeli declined to form a government without an election, Gladstone continued as prime minister, but when he appealed to the nation in a general election in February, 1874, the Conservatives were returned with a clear majority. Arnold presumably alludes to his critique of the Liberals in *Culture and Anarchy* (1867–68).

138:25–27. Plato *Republic* VII, 540 A.

138:35–37. In "The Function of Criticism at the Present Time" (1864), Arnold defined the function of the critical power as "in all branches of knowledge, theology, philosophy, history, art, science, to see the object as in itself it really is."—*Prose Works,* ed. Super, III, 258. The expression "a mind which sees things as they really are" occurs in Joseph Butler's Sermon XV, ¶4; *Works*, ed. Gladstone (1896), II, 262. In his review (1864) of Taine's *Histoire de la littérature anglaise*, Edmond Scherer quotes "le mot de Chamfort: 'Le grand art, c'est de n'être dupe de rien!' "—*Études sur la littérature contemporaine* (nouv. éd.; Paris, 1894), VI, 134. See the beginning of " 'Porro Unum Est Necessarium' " (1878), *Prose Works*, ed. Super, VIII, 348.

139:10–11. On March 8, 1880, Beaconsfield dissolved Parliament, primarily on the issue of Home Rule for Ireland; the general election a month later gave the Liberals a very substantial majority, along with 65 seats to the Irish nationalists.

139:11–14. The idea caught Arnold's fancy. When he wrote on April 2, 1880, to congratulate his sister Mrs. W. E. Forster on her husband's victory in the polls at Bradford, he remarked: "Lord B. was demoralising for our people, and the Tories show their bad side more and more the longer they stay in; and then the Tory *Bottles*, the shoddy Conservative, Stock Exchange or commercial, is terrible. Still, the Radical Bottles, and middle-class Liberalism in general— you know my opinion of them—at best they are in a very crude state, and with little light or help in them at present."—*Letters*, ed. Russell. Perhaps, indeed, the suggestion that he portray the Tory Bottles had been hers.

139:14–20. The Conservatives claimed that the educated class voted in support of them, the uneducated in support of the Liberals: "The result in the City, Westminster, and the metropolitan counties, so different from that elsewhere, proves this statement conclusively," as the Conservative apologists are quoted by John Morley in his analysis of the elections of 1880; he denied their explanation.— "Home and Foreign Affairs," *Fortnightly Review* XXXIII, 729 (May, 1880). The City is the commercial part of London, from Temple Bar to the Tower, that includes the Bank, the Royal Exchange, and St. Paul's.

140:4–13, 141:1–3. The franchise was extended to the agricultural laborer by Gladstone's Reform Act of 1884. It had been gained by the entire urban male population by what its enemies called a "leap in the dark," Disraeli's Reform Act of 1867. For Arnold on "natural rights" see p. 118:15n.

141:6–8. There was a remarkable alternation between the parties in power in the latter third of the century: Liberals governed from 1868 to 1874, Conservatives from 1874 to 1880, Liberals from 1880 to 1885, Conservatives from 1885 to 1892 (with a Liberal interlude from

February to August, 1886), Liberals from 1892 to 1895, then Conservatives to 1905.

141:27–32. In "Civilisation in the United States" (1888) Arnold attributes to Plato (perhaps *Gorgias* 512 E or *Republic* I, 352 D) the notion that "Man's study is to discover the right answer to the question *how to live*"; in the essay on Wordsworth (p. 46) he founds the proposition on Epictetus *Discourses* II, xxiii. The statement about the science of politics is a commonplace among the Greeks; see Aristotle *Nicomachean Ethics* 1094 a–b.

141:34–36. Men "think themselves bound, not only as individuals . . . but also in their corporate character to perform their national homage to the institutor, and author, and protector of civil society; without which civil society man could not . . ." etc.— *Reflections on the Revolution in France*, two-fifths through.

142:10–15. See pp. 26:36–27:2.

143:27–29. Edward Henry Stanley (1826–93), fifteenth Earl of Derby, was eldest son of the Conservative prime minister who retired in favor of Disraeli in February, 1868, and died in October, 1869. As Lord Stanley, he sat in the House of Commons from late in 1848 until he succeeded to the earldom. He was a member of the cabinet in his father's governments and in Disraeli's government of 1874, but resigned in March, 1878, openly opposed the government's foreign policy, and finally on March 12, 1880, announced his severance from the Conservative party. Thereafter he held office in Gladstone's second administration, but broke from Gladstone on the Irish home rule issue.

144:1–5. The language of Bright speaking at a Reform demonstration at Leeds, reported in *The Morning Star*, October 9, 1866, p. 2, jotted in Arnold's pocket diary for October 12, and quoted in *Culture and Anarchy* (1867).—*Note-Books*, ed. Lowry, pp. 36–37 and *Prose Works*, ed. Super, V, 108.

144:5–6. See p. 154:26.

144:10–18. In a speech before the Huddersfield Chamber of Commerce, January 8, 1880, reported in *The Times*, January 9, p. 8, col. 3, and jotted in Arnold's pocket diary for January 3–4.—*Note-Books*, ed. Lowry, pp. 333–34.

144:30–32. The road from Liverpool to Manchester traverses the heavily industrial south Lancashire region; it goes through St. Helen's, a glass, iron, and brick manufacturing city in the heart of a coal mining district, and passes near Wigan, in the center of a rich coal field and with important iron, steel, and engineering industries.

Bolton, practically contiguous with Manchester, is one of the oldest seats of the English textile industry. The large estate of the Earls of Derby, Knowsley Park, of some 2000 acres, is only about three miles from St. Helen's. Arnold spent the nights of September 30 and October 1, 1882, as guest of Lord and Lady Derby at Knowsley.

145:8 (variant). Blackburn, 25 miles north of Manchester and 14 miles north of Bolton, was the center of the cotton-weaving industry. It was the birthplace of John Morley, editor of the *Fortnightly Review*, biographer of Cobden, etc. (see p. 146:30).

145:16–21. Sir Frederic Leighton's first presidential address to the students of the Royal Academy on the occasion of the awarding of prizes, December 10, 1879.—Leighton, *Addresses Delivered to the Students of the Royal Academy* (2nd ed.; New York, 1897), p. 9. Arnold jotted eight passages from this address, but not what he here quotes, in his pocket diary for July 30–August 9, 1880.—*Note-Books*, ed. Lowry, pp. 340–41.

146:10–11. "The manufactures, which bring new citizens into existence just as much as if they had actually begotten them, bring more of them into existence than they can maintain, or are too precarious to go on maintaining those whom for a while they maintained."—"Our Liberal Practitioners," *Culture and Anarchy* (1868), *Prose Works*, ed. Super, V, 219.

146:31–33. Jotted in Arnold's pocket diary for February 8, 1880, as the view of a New York Trades' Union.—*Note-Books*, ed. Lowry, p. 335.

147:3–5. The tram line formerly ran from Holborn along Gray's Inn Road to King's Cross railway station, then along Pancras Road, Great College Street, Kentish Town Road, Prince of Wales Road, and Malden Road to the Hampstead Heath station of the North London Railway. Camden Town is a notably shabby district created by the Lord Camden referred to at the beginning of this essay. It was Dickens's first London home.

147:15–20. *Addresses*, p. 9.

147:24–25. See p. 144:13–14.

148:3–14. J. H. M. Busch, *Graf Bismarck und seine Leute* (Leipzig, 1878), I, 313 (November 3, 1870). Arnold used the authorized English translation, *Bismarck in the Franco-German War* (London, 1879).

148:24–26. Arnold used this description of the middle class in "Equality" (1878), "Irish Catholicism and British Liberalism" (1878), and " 'Porro Unum Est Necessarium' " (1878), and jotted it in his pocket diary for March 22, 1879, and June 13, 1880, as well as in one of his "General Note-Books."—*Prose Works*, ed. Super, VIII, 302, 322, 362, 369; *Note-Books*, ed. Lowry, pp. 317, 339, 542.

149:1–3. M. E. Grant Duff, who frequently made himself spokesman for the Liberals in foreign policy, early in February, 1880, published *Foreign Policy*, a pamphlet in the "Practical Politics" series issued by the National Liberal Federation.

149:4–5, 16–18. Earl Granville (1815–91) was foreign secretary under Gladstone in 1870–74 and 1880–85. Arnold ridiculed the ineffectiveness of Liberal foreign policy in the Prusso-Danish conflict of 1864 and over the Russian introduction of warships into the Black Sea in 1870 in the essay on "My Countrymen" (1866) and in *Friendship's Garland*, Letter X.—*Prose Works*, ed. Super, V, 10, 334–39.

149:20–23. "That is the sort of phraseology a man employs when he means to do nothing," said Bismarck of Granville's representations about the Russian Black Sea action in 1870. "There is as little to fear from these English now, as there was to hope from them four months ago."—*Times*, November 19, 1878, p. 3, col. 2 (Busch's *Graf Bismarck und seine Leute*, II, 9 [November 17, 1870]).

150:11–13. By the Elementary Education Act of 1870.

150:36–151:2. Plato *Republic* VIII, 556 B–C.

152:24–29. On April 20, 1653, Cromwell entered the House of Commons with a handful of musketeers and forcibly dissolved the Long Parliament. Pointing to the Mace, he said: "What shall we do with this bauble? There, take it away." Henry Dunckley, a Manchester journalist better known by his pen-name of "Verax," published an article on "The Progress of Personal Rule" in the *Nineteenth Century* IV, 785–808 (November, 1878), in which he traced a zeal for the re-establishment of an early Stuart view of the prerogatives of the throne to the teachings of the Queen's former adviser, Baron Stockmar, and to the efforts of her current prime minister, Lord Beaconsfield (Disraeli). Citing a passage from Disraeli's novel *Coningsby*, Dunckley remarked: "[Nothing] could be more candid. You must begin by gradually discrediting and disregarding the House of Commons, and then, when the hour is ripe, you may remove the mace, clear the benches, lock the doors, and send a royal proclamation to the newspapers." "The gaunt outlines of Personal Rule can already be discerned through the thin veil of constitutional forms, and the reality of power is slipping from our hands."—pp. 794, 808. M. W. L. Corry, nephew of the Lord Shaftesbury of Arnold's trinity, was Lord Beaconsfield's private secretary and in-

separable companion in public appearances from 1866 until Beaconsfield's death nine months after the publication of this essay. He was
created Baron Rowton in May, 1880, on the fall of the Tory administration. Beaconsfield never became an octogenarian.

154:12–14. See "Our Liberal Practitioners," *Culture and Anarchy*
(1868), and Preface to *Higher Schools and Universities in Germany*
(1874), *Prose Works*, ed. Super, V, 193–99; VII, 128–30.

154:18–21. As he did in his speech of January 8, 1880; see p.
144:10–18n.

154:26–29. John Bright, despite ill health, on February 10, 1880,
took the chair for the first of a course of four lectures delivered by
R. W. Dale on "The Rise of Evangelical Nonconformity" in the
Union Chapel, Islington, in the presence of the leading Nonconformist ministers of the London region. Bright's remarks were reported in *The Times* next day, p. 11, col. 2, and were subject of a
leading article, p. 9, col. 5–6.

155:7–8. Arnold concluded his essay on "The French Play in
London" with warm advocacy of government support of the theater; see pp. 82–85.

155:14–18. All three of these recurrent proposals were brought
forward by private members, not the Liberal ministry, though
among the matters Gladstone once listed as subjects his party must
deal with were liquor laws and burial laws.—"England's Mission,"
Nineteenth Century IV, 582 (September, 1878); jotted in Arnold's
pocket diary for November 9, 1878. Arnold frequently ridiculed the
Liberal proposals respecting marriage with a deceased wife's sister
and the burials law. "Local option" referred to the laws governing
the sale of alcoholic beverages. On June 18, 1880, the temperance
advocate Sir Wilfrid Lawson successfully moved a resolution in the
Commons calling for revision of the licensing act to give "the inhabitants themselves . . . protection from the injurious consequences
of the present system by some efficient measure of local option," a
proposal he had brought forward in various forms for nearly two
decades. John Bright spoke in favor of one of Lawson's proposals,
just as he had supported permitting marriage to a deceased wife's
sister.

155:24–37. Bright's remark was made in the House of Commons
on April 21, 1869, and reported in *The Times* next day, p. 6, col. 5;
see *Friendship's Garland*, Letter VIII (1869).—*Prose Works*, ed.
Super, V, 315 and n. Herod the Tetrarch imprisoned and ultimately
beheaded John the Baptist because when he wished to marry Hero-

dias, his brother Philip's wife, "John said unto him, It is not lawful for thee to have her."—Matthew 14:4. Arnold used the word "delicacy" somewhat ironically in this context in the *Friendship's Garland* letter, p. 316.

156:24–27. Médoc is a district on the left bank of the Gironde north of Bordeaux, where the very finest of the Bordeaux wines are produced. Benjamin Ward Richardson (1828–96), a distinguished physician, "was an ardent and determined champion of total abstinence, for he held that alcohol was so powerful a drug that it should only be used by skilled hands in the greatest emergencies."— *D.N.B.*

156:31–35. In "Irish Catholicism and British Liberalism" (1878), *Prose Works*, ed. Super, VIII, 344.

157:2–6. *The Life of Edward, Earl of Clarendon*, written by himself (Oxford, 1857), I, 61 (Part I, ¶69), jotted in Arnold's pocket diary for August 31, 1873, and quoted in "A Last Word on the Burials Bill" (1876).—*Note-Books*, ed. Lowry, p. 199, and *Prose Works*, ed. Super, VIII, 102. Convocation is the assembly of bishops and representative clergy of each of the two provinces of the Church of England, Canterbury and York; the bishops sit in the upper house, the rest of the clergy in the lower house.

158:6. Germany's principal difficulty of the preceding decade was the *Kulturkampf*, Bismarck's struggle against the Roman Catholics.

158:14–17. In "Equality" (1878), "Irish Catholicism and British Liberalism" (1878), and " 'Ecce, Convertimur ad Gentes' " (1879),— *Prose Works*, ed. Super, VIII, 299, 302, 345; IX, 8.

158:27–29. Edward Stanley, 12th Earl of Derby (1752–1834) was a well-known sportsman best remembered for establishing the Oaks and the Derby sweepstakes at Epsom in 1779 and 1780. Preston, a manufacturing town some thirty miles to the north of Derby's estate at Knowsley, customarily sent nominees of the Derby family to Parliament; the son of the 12h earl sat for Preston from 1796.

159:5. The seventy-two-year-old third Earl of Leitrim was shot dead along with a clerk and the driver of their cart in the country near Milford, Donegal, on April 2, 1878. A rigorous landlord, he had already evicted many tenants and some eighty more evictions were said to be in process when the murder occurred; it was only the most striking of the agrarian assassinations up to that time. At the end of his pocket diary for 1878 Arnold jotted "P.M.G. on Ld. Leitrim," referring to an article on Leitrim's murder, "Agrarianism in Ireland," *Pall Mall Gazette*, April 4, 1878, pp. 1–2.—*Note-Books*, ed. Lowry, p. 308. Gladstone's first Irish Land Act was passed in 1870.

159:27. The mythological Medusa turned to stone all who looked in her eyes, and therefore Perseus, in order to kill her, had to turn his head away and guide his sword by the reflection in the mirror of his polished shield.

160:7–8. Peter preached of "the times of restitution of all things," and Daniel foresaw that "the saints of the most High shall take the kingdom, and possess the kingdom for ever, even for ever and ever."—Acts 3:21, Daniel 7:18 (22, 27).

[THE STUDY OF POETRY]

When T. Humphry Ward, the husband of Arnold's niece Mary, approached Arnold with proposals for his anthology of the English Poets in late October, 1878, Arnold expressed warm approval but declined to participate: "Plans in which I could join if I were a man of letters purely and simply, I cannot join in now that I am a school-inspector with a very limited time at my disposal for letters. I am obliged to keep, for work which has suggested itself to my own mind, the little time which I have free." And therefore he had de-clined John Morley's proposal to do a monograph on Shakespeare for the English Men of Letters series; his single recent commitment for work on commission, he said, was a two-page Introduction to the poets in Wood's *The Hundred Greatest Men*. Four days later, however, on October 26, Arnold held out the hope that he might write a general introduction for Ward after all. Ward, disappointed by the initial refusal, meanwhile proposed alternative authors; Ar-nold replied on the 30th: "Stopford Brooke would be more *accept-able* than Palgrave. I should not like you to have to drop your plan, and sooner than you should do this, would see whether I could pos-sibly manage the introduction; the selecting part I could not under-take. Try the publishers first with Stopford Brooke or Palgrave, and if you cannot succeed, then write to me again. My notion is that the publishers would take your scheme gladly with such a list, in general, as you proposed, whether I were in it or not." Five months later, Arnold wrote again (March 10, 1879): "I will not go back from my promise to help you if my aid was seriously wanted, and I will write your Introduction. But do not count on me for any-thing more; for to accomplish even so much as that, I must give up something which I had planned to execute this year. You shall have the Introduction by the beginning of October; when you come to us, you must tell me the sort of thing you wish it to be." A letter of August 8 carried a familiar request: "Don't forget to let me know what is the latest date you can give me for the Preface, the paging being in roman numerals. I have corrected the last revise of my Wordsworth, but have still got a thing to do for the Quarterly, and am feeling a little tired and good for nothing." A month later (September 11) he wrote: "Unless something unforeseen happens, I will be ready for you by the end of October. At the present moment I have no notion what I shall say, but Providence will, I hope, make my way plain before my face." In November he was still making preparation for the essay: "I have been reading Chaucer a great deal, the early French poets a great deal, and Burns a great deal. Burns is a beast, with splendid gleams, and the medium in which he lived, Scotch peasants, Scotch Presbyterianism, and Scotch drink, is repulsive. Chaucer, on the other hand, pleases me more and more, and his medium is infinitely superior. But I shall finish with Shakespeare's *King Lear* before I finally write my Introduction, in order to have a proper taste in my mind while I am at work."—*Letters*, ed. Russell, to his sister Frances (misdated 1880). Corrected proofs went back early in February, 1880. "I have put translations; perhaps it is best," he wrote to Ward. "I am very glad you are pleased with what I have done; I assure you I was very anxious to produce something that would serve your book, not disserve it; and on looking it carefully through, I think this Preface will be found interesting, although, as the Americans acutely observe, 'there is a set of critics in England who seem to be perpetually hostile to Mr. Arnold.' The type is very good—much better than I expected." By this time, he had already committed himself to doing the introductory notes to the poems of Gray and Keats for Ward. The first two volumes of *The English Poets* were published by Macmillan about the middle of May. On February 7, 1881, the publisher sent Arnold a copy of his contributions for revisions for a second edition, but no significant changes were made.—Buckler, *Matthew Arnold's Books*, p. 75.

From the very first Arnold's Introduction was regarded as the most important part of the anthology; it remains one of his best-known critical essays, one subsequent students have most liked to sharpen their claws on. It is admirably conceived for its purpose— to give some guidance to a middle-class public not sophisticated in the reading of poetry; to treat it as if it were addressed to an audience of scholars and professional critics is a mistake. An essay of this sort must not be "eccentric and startling. You do not want to startle," said Arnold. Nevertheless the discrimination of two common

grounds of misjudgment of poetry—personal and private associations on the one hand, the historical significance of the work on the
other—is both perceptive and useful; many of Arnold's severest
scholarly critics fall quite simply into the latter error. The touchstone method—which perhaps is faulty because it probably requires
some sense of the context of the touchstone passages—was one Arnold evolved as early as his Oxford lectures *On Translating Homer*
(1860–61). An interesting study of these passages for what they reveal of Arnold's taste is J. S. Eells, *The Touchstone of Matthew
Arnold* (New York: Bookman Associates, 1955).

Arnold's conception of eighteenth-century poetry met with vocal
opponents from the first. W. J. Courthope, one of the editors of
Pope, wrote to demonstrate, in contradistinction to Arnold, that
Dryden and Pope are classics of our *poetry.*—"The Liberal Movement in English Literature," *National Review* III, 633–44 (July,
1884), and letter to *The Pall Mall Gazette,* July 4, 1884, p. 6. More
recently, E. K. Brown assembled Arnold's comments on the prose-
writers and poets of the century to demonstrate that "he spoke of
the eighteenth century from the outside, with no faculty for identi-
fying himself with its modes of thinking, feeling, living. . . . He was
himself a Romantic; . . . he never lost his sense of intimacy with"
figures like Wordsworth, Goethe, Emerson, and Newman.—"Arnold and the Eighteenth Century," *University of Toronto Quarterly*
IX, 202–13 (January, 1940). In a more precisely argued essay, Geof-
frey Tillotson prefaces his remarks with the observation that while
Arnold was well informed and intelligent when he dealt with his
own age, "he tells us little that we cannot dispense with about earlier
ages." Certainly Arnold was a rapid, not a meticulous, reader of
poetry: he "does not seem to have given Pope's poetry the attention
necessary for experiencing it as it is."—"Matthew Arnold and
Eighteenth Century Poetry," *Criticism and the Nineteenth Century*
(London: Athlone Press, 1951), pp. 61–91.

Lovers of Chaucer have always been outraged by what they consider Arnold's undervaluing of him; the fault is not in what Arnold
thought about Chaucer, but in any attempt at rank ordering of poets.
Perhaps the most surprising omission in Arnold's essay, from the
point of view of the twentieth century, is the name of Donne; but
Ward's selections suggest the prevailing taste (with which Swinburne and his friends would have disagreed): his anthology prints
only five of Donne's poems, preceded by a mere two pages of introduction.

161:1–11. The final paragraph of Arnold's Introduction on Poetry in *The Hundred Greatest Men* (1879), revised; see p. 63:25–37. The thesis of *Literature and Dogma*, as indeed its title indicates, may be summed up in these words: "The language of the Bible . . . is literary, not scientific language; language *thrown out* at an object of consciousness not fully grasped, which inspired emotion. Evidently, if the object be one not fully to be grasped, and one to inspire emotion, the language of figure and feeling will satisfy us better about it, will cover more of what we seek to express, than the language of literal fact and science. The language of science about it will be *below* what we feel to be the truth."—*Prose Works*, ed, Super, VI, 189.

162:3–7. Preface to the second edition of *Lyrical Ballads* (1800), nearly three-fifths through; jotted in Arnold's pocket diary for January 14, 1878, and December 14, 1879.—*Note-Books*, ed. Lowry, pp. 294, 329.

162:20–27. *Les Cahiers de Sainte-Beuve* (Paris, 1876), p. 51, jotted in Arnold's pocket diary at the beginning of 1879.—*Note-Books*, ed. Lowry, p. 313.

163:2–4. See Arnold's essays on "Wordsworth" (where he drew upon his own lectures *On Translating Homer*) and on "Joubert" (1863), where he says of the men of genius in literature and the men of ability in literature: "The work of the two orders of men is at bottom the same,—*a criticism of life.*"—*Prose Works*, ed. Super, IX, 44–46; III, 209.

163:37, 164:7. "To see the object as in itself it really is" is for Arnold the true function of criticism.—*On Translating Homer* (1860) and "The Function of Criticism at the Present Time" (1864); *Prose Works*, ed. Super, I, 140; III, 258.

164:29–165:10. For somewhat the same idea in quite different language, see Charles d'Héricault, ed., *Oeuvres de Clément Marot* (Paris, 1867), p. iii.

165:15–16. "Le mot *classique* . . . commence à paraître chez les Romains. Chez eux on appelait proprement *classici*, non tous les citoyens des diverses classes, mais ceux de la première seulement. . . . Tous [les autres] étaient désignés par la dénomination *infra classem*, au-dessous de la classe par excellence. Au figuré, le mot *classicus* se trouve employé dans Aulu-Gelle, et appliqué aux écrivains: un écrivain de valeur et de marque, *classicus assiduusque scriptor*, un écrivain qui compte, qui a du bien au soleil, et qui n'est pas confondu dans la foule des prolétaires."—Sainte-Beuve, "Qu'est-ce qu'un classique?" *Causeries du lundi* (4th ed.; Paris, 1869), III, 38–39 (October 21, 1850).

166:30–31. *De imitatione Christi* III, xliii, 11–12, jotted in Arnold's pocket diary for December 7, 1879, and five times during the following decade.—*Note-Books*, ed. Lowry, pp. 329, 402, 412, 421, 426, 435.

167:2–3. Since in "A Guide to English Literature" (1877) Arnold praised Stopford Brooke's handling of Caedmon's Old English versification of Genesis (c. 670 A.D.), he may only indirectly be glancing at such a statement as the following in Brooke's *English Literature:* "The most famous passage of the poem not only illustrates the dark sadness, the fierce love of freedom, and the power of painting distinct characters which has always marked our poetry, but it is also famous for its likeness to a parallel passage in Milton. It is when Caedmon describes the proud and angry cry of Satan against God from his bed of chains in hell."—(New York, 1879), p. 12.

167:7–16. The last line of the Oxford manuscript of the *Chanson de Roland* reads: "Ci falt la geste que Turoldus declinet," which may mean that Théroulde was author or merely scribe. The *jongleur* or *joculator* commonly recited the work of others, whereas the *trouvère* or troubadour was an original poet. The account of Taillefer's singing of Roland at the battle of Hastings comes from Wace, *Roman de Rou*, Part III, 8035–40. Arnold perhaps drew information from the Introduction to George Ellis, ed., *Specimens of Early English Metrical Romances* (new ed.; London, 1848), p. 9, and George Saintsbury, *A Short History of French Literature* (Oxford, 1882), p. 13. The former was on Arnold's reading list for 1880, and an earlier version of the latter book was quoted in his pocket diary for that year.—*Note-Books*, ed. Lowry, pp. 597, 344–45. But his immediate source was Vitet's essay (see note to p. 167:17–23).

167:17–23. Louis Vitet, "La Chanson de Roland," *Revue des Deux Mondes, nouv. pér.* XIV, 851, 860 (June 1, 1852); reprinted in his *Essais historiques et littéraires* (Paris, 1862), pp. 73–74.

167:31–34. Lines 2377–80.

168:4–5. Arnold cited these lines in his first lecture *On Translating Homer* (1860), in order to illustrate the romantic falsity of Ruskin's comment on them. Thereafter they became in the lectures one of the touchstones for testing a good translation; Arnold quoted as excellent the translation of them by E. C. Hawtrey, provost of Eton College, in the volume called *English Hexameter Translations* (London, 1847).—*Prose Works*, ed. Super, I, 101–2, 149, 164, 196, 203.

168:26–28, 169:2. Arnold used both passages as touchstones in his lectures *On Translating Homer* (1860–62); he gave his own hexameter translation of the former, and of the latter he remarked: "In the original this line, for mingled pathos and dignity, is perhaps without a rival even in Homer." His prose translation there differs slightly from the present version: "in times past wert" for "in former days wast."—*Prose Works*, ed. Super I, 100, 115, 129, 161, 177, 213–14; 212.

169:13. "In la sua" is the reading of several manuscripts and no doubt of the edition Arnold used. Other authoritative readings are "E la sua" and "E'n la sua."

169:16–18. *2 Henry IV*, III, i, 18–20.

169:20–170:2. *Hamlet*, V, ii, 357–60.

170:4–14. *Paradise Lost*, I, 599–602, 108–9; IV, 271–72.

171:17–18. *Poetics* IX, 3 (1451 b 6).

171:19–37. In his final lecture *On Translating Homer* ("Last Words"), a rather similar discussion of the "grand style" laid down this definition: "The grand style arises in poetry, *when a noble nature, poetically gifted, treats with simplicity or with severity a serious subject*."—*Prose Works*, ed. Super, I, 188.

172:17–18. The terms *langue d'oc* and *langue d'oïl* discriminate between the words used to express "yes" in the tongues current south and north of the Loire, and hence denote the two dialects. The language of "oïl" ("oui") prevailed and is the modern French.

173:1–4. *Li Livres dou trésor*, ed. P. Chabaille (Paris, 1863), p. 3 (Book I, part I, chapt. i, end). Brunetto (c. 1220–94), a Florentine, is greeted warmly by Dante as his master in the *Inferno*, canto XV.

173:8–17. *Cligés*, lines 30–39. Chrétien de Troyes lived in the latter half of the twelfth century, about a hundred years before Brunetto.

173:31–34. The seven-line stanza, "rime royal" (ababbcc), which Chaucer used in *Troilus and Criseyde* and "The Prioress's Tale."

173:36. Wolfram von Eschenbach was author of the German romance *Parzeval* at the beginning of the thirteenth century.

174:19–21. "Preface to the *Fables*," ¶12, 10; *Essays*, ed. W. P. Ker (Oxford, 1900), II, 262, 257. Dryden's *Fables* included some versions of Chaucer.

174:29. John Lydgate, *The Life of Our Lady* (c. 1410), II, 1633. The passage was often printed as a separate poem in the early editions of Chaucer; see *Chaucerian and Other Pieces*, ed. W. W. Skeat (Oxford, 1897), p. 450.

174:29–33. In "The History of the English Language" prefixed to his *Dictionary* (1st ed.; London, 1755), I, 9.

174:37. Spenser, *Faerie Queene*, IV, ii, 287.

175:11, 20–26. "The Prioress's Tale" (from *The Canterbury Tales*), lines 92, 162–68. Since no manuscript of the tale reads "in virginitee," Arnold's text has been corrected to "to virginitee." Despite Arnold's Preface, Ward did not include this tale in his selection from Chaucer for *The English Poets*.

175:27. Wordsworth modernized the tale in 1801 and published the version in 1820.

176:24–25. Dante died in 1321, Chaucer in 1400.

177:9–11. "Les regrets de la belle Heaulmière" is the title commonly given to the poem which makes up stanzas xlvii–lvi (lines 453–532) of Villon's *Le Testament* (1461); Swinburne published a verse translation of it in the second series of *Poems and Ballads* (1878). François de Montcorbier (1431–63 or later) took the name of Villon from his guardian.

178:13–16. *Essay of Dramatic Poesy*, ¶10; *Essays*, ed. Ker, I, 35.

178:16–21. "Preface to the Fables," ¶14, 11; *Essays*, ed. Ker, II, 264–65, 258–59. It is Dryden who reports that Cowley "declared he had no taste of" Chaucer.

178:30–31. Wordsworth said that, with two slight exceptions, "the poetry of the period intervening between the publication of the 'Paradise Lost' and the 'Seasons' does not contain a single new image of external nature; and scarcely presents a familiar one from which it can be inferred that the eye of the Poet had been steadily fixed upon his object, much less that his feelings had urged him to work upon it in the spirit of genuine imagination."—"Essay, Supplementary to the Preface" (1815), half-way through. Coleridge's estimate of Pope in the middle of chapt. i of *Biographia Literaria* is much like Arnold's.

179:8–14. *The Iliads of Homer, Prince of Poets* . . . Done According to the Greek by George Chapman, ed. Richard Hooper (2nd ed.; London, 1865), I, 23 (Commentarius on Book I). Arnold quoted the passage in his first lecture *On Translating Homer* (1860), and there, as here, he made a difficult passage incomprehensible by omitting "her" after "confirm."—See Textual Notes and *Prose Works*, ed. Super, I, 114.

179:15–18. *An Apology against a Pamphlet Call'd A Modest Confutation of the Animadversions upon the Remonstrant against Smectymnuus* (London, 1642), ¶6; *Works*, ed. H. M. Ayres *et al.* (New York: Columbia University Press, 1931), III (1), 303.

179:20–24. The opening words of the "Postscript to the Reader" of Dryden's translation of the *Aeneid* (1697); *Essays*, ed. Ker, II, 240. Though Dryden's life overlapped Milton's by 43 years and he was therefore indeed "Milton's contemporary," these two passages were separated by more than half a century.

180:18–19. *The Hind and the Panther* (1687), first two lines.

180:23–24. Imitation of *The Second Satire of the Second Book of Horace* (1734), lines 143–44.

181:32–182:2. "On the Death of the Late Lord President Dundas," lines 25–30.

182:4–5. "Clarinda" was Agnes Craig M'Lehose, to whom Burns addressed such conventionally sentimental songs as "Clarinda, mistress of my soul." Their correspondence, signed "Clarinda" and "Sylvander," survives.

182:5–10. Letter to George Thomson, October 19, 1794; *Letters of Robert Burns*, ed. J. DeLancey Ferguson (Oxford: at the Clarendon Press, 1931), II, 268. Burns wrote "that command of" and "deplorably stupid."

182:36–183:7. "The Holy Fair," lines 163–71.

183:19–26. Lines 25–32.

183:30–184:2. "Epistle to a Young Friend," lines 41–48.

184:4–11. "Address to the Unco Guid, or the Rigidly Righteous," lines 57–64.

184:14–17. Epistle to Dr. Thomas Blacklock ("Wow, but your letter made me vauntie!"), lines 51–54.

184:21–22. Arnold seems to allude to Xenophon *Memorabilia* I, ii, 48, jotted in his pocket diaries for August 22, 1875, at the end of 1876, at the beginning of 1877, and in one of his "General Note-Books."—*Note-Books*, ed. Lowry, pp. 233, 263, 270, 541, 544.

185:17–20. "Song" ("Ae fond kiss, and then we sever"), lines 13–16. The poem is sometimes called "Farewell to Nancy."

185:28–31. "Winter, A Dirge," lines 17–20.

186:17. In Part I.

186:24–25. "To a Mouse, On turning her up in her Nest, with the Plough, November, 1785."

186:36–187:2. "Auld lang syne," lines 17–20.

187:9, 12–15. *Prometheus Unbound*, III, iv, 204; II, v, 1–4.

187:18–21. "Tam Glen," lines 13–16.

188:22–23. "Menander has perished, and Aristophanes has survived. And to what is this to be attributed? To the instinct of self-preservation in humanity. The human race has the strongest, the most invincible tendency to *live*, to *develop* itself. It retains, it

clings to what fosters its life, what favours its development, to the
literature which exhibits it in its vigour; it rejects, it abandons what
does not foster its development, the literature which exhibits it
arrested and decayed."—"On the Modern Element in Literature"
(1857/1869), *Prose Works*, ed. Super, I, 29–30.

[THOMAS GRAY]

The first book Arnold edited, apart from Isaiah, was the *Six Chief
Lives from Johnson's Lives of the Poets,* no doubt a surprising choice
for one who is generally held to have little sympathy with the
eighteenth century. His interest in the period, difficult as was the
critical task of explaining it in terms compatible with the romantic
critical theories of the Victorians, was genuine. And therefore when
Ward asked him to introduce selections from several authors for
his anthology of *The English Poets*, Arnold opted for Gray as well
as Keats. "That century is very interesting, though I should not like
to have lived in it; but the people were just like ourselves, whilst the
Elizabethans are not," he wrote to his wife on December 22, 1880.—
Letters, ed. Russell. He had already stated briefly what he thought
of Gray in "A Guide to English Literature" (1877).—*Prose Works*,
ed. Super, VIII, 249–50. The new undertaking, however, was not
easy: he worked at it from the latter part of March until May 8,
1880, when his diary records: "Work at Gray & send it." On May 1
he wrote to Ward: "I am well into my notice of Gray, but, 'more
meo,' I have on this provocation been reading up my English 18th
century again, and have spent much time over what is, after all, a
depressing business. Gray is a very depressing man, himself, and it
will be months before I recover from him." And on May 20 he
wrote: "I have shortened Gray as much as I can, but I give you free
leave to shorten it more, if you like, and are able." His selection from
Gray's poems and from those of Keats went to the publisher about
the same time. The essay is perhaps too dependent on Gray's letters,
too biographical, too little substantial as a piece of criticism. But
Arnold must have viewed his task in terms of his function—to give
appropriate introductory matter to help the uninformed reader understand what sort of man wrote the poems; like Johnson's own
Lives, this was a preface biographical and critical, not a critical
essay. Even its length was obviously limited by its purpose. Two
years later, after reading Edmund Gosse's little book on Gray in the
English Men of Letters series, Arnold wrote to him: "I must [tell]

you what satisfaction your performance has given me. 'Simonidean' is the right word to express the note struck by Gray—you could not have taken a better. Collins, at his best, strikes the same note, and perhaps we must own that the diction of Collins in his Ode to Evening is more Simonidean, more pure, than Gray's diction—but then the Ode to Evening has not the evolution of Gray and of Simonides—like the rivers of central Asia, it loses itself in the sand. As to the Ode to Liberty, to speak of it as Swinburne does is really to talk nonsense. You are right in remarking that the secret of Gray's superiority lies in his having read, thought and felt so very much more than Collins. The bad side of Gray's reading,—that he used it as 'a narcotic,'—you have well seized at page 67. But perhaps he did all he could, and for him to do without an anodyne was impossible, and reading was the best anodyne at his command. He is one of the most interesting figures in our literary history. His scantiness of production was a misery to him, but has it hurt his fame? I sometimes think that if Tennyson had delivered himself of nothing Arthurian except the first fragment he gave us, the Morte d'Arthur, he himself would have lost much occupation, indeed, and the reading world a good deal of pleasure, but we should have had a grander sense of his possibilities in Arthurian story. You are not quite just to Bonstetten: have you read Ste. Beuve's delightful *causeries* about him?" (The allusion to Swinburne refers to his introduction to Collins for Ward's *English Poets:* "No cleverness can make up for such an outrage on all truth and proportion as Swinburne's over-praise of Collins. . . . Except a poetic diction comparatively pure (for that age), Collins has not, I think, much merit. The Ode to Evening leads nowhere, has no internal development; you finish it with a sense of flatness. The Ode to Liberty has positively no merit at all." When Swinburne reprinted his introduction to Collins in his *Miscellanies* [1886], he added a few sentences to regret Arnold's preference of Gray over Collins.)

The volume containing the Gray poems was published about December 11, 1880. Arnold received £50 for writing his prefaces to and making his selections from Keats and Gray.—Buckler, *Matthew Arnold's Books*, p. 74.

189:5–12. *Correspondence of Thomas Gray*, ed. Paget Toynbee and Leonard Whibley (Oxford: at the Clarendon Press, 1935), III, 1275 (August 17, 1771); *Works of Thomas Gray*, ed. J. Mitford (London, 1835–43), IV, 207. Gray died late on the night of July 30, at the age of fifty-four. Both James Brown and Thomas Wharton had been friends of his from his undergraduate days. Brown wrote "melancholly at Mr. Gray's Room," and "those about him apprehended it."

189:21–24. Johnson spoke coolly of Gray's poetry in his "Life of Gray" and even more vigorously in conversation. "Sir, he was dull in company, dull in his closet, dull every where. He was dull in a new way, and that made many people think him GREAT. He was a mechanical poet," Johnson told Boswell on March 28, 1775; and see Boswell's *Life of Johnson, passim.* Norton Nicholls, a young friend of Gray's later years, wrote: "[Gray] disliked Doctor Johnson, & declined his acquaintance; he disapproved his style, & thought it turgid, & vicious; but he respected his understanding, & still more his goodness of heart."—*Correspondence of Gray,* ed. Toynbee, III, 1290.

190:1–4. Printed from the manuscript of William Cole in the British Museum in *The Works of Gray,* ed. Mitford, I, civ. This is the edition of Gray Arnold used; to it is prefixed a biographical memoir of Gray by Mitford.

190:8. "Among the Lives the best are perhaps those of Cowley, Dryden, and Pope. The very worst is, beyond all doubt, that of Gray."—Macaulay's *Encyclopaedia Britannica* article on Johnson, near the end; reprinted in Arnold's edition of *The Six Chief Lives from Johnson's "Lives of the Poets."* Arnold's six lives included Dryden, Pope, and Gray, but not Cowley.

190:10–14. William Mason, Gray's executor and biographer, in 1778 composed these lines for a monument to Gray in Westminster Abbey. They are quoted in Mitford's biographical memoir, three-fifths through (I, lvii).

190:22–25. Mitford's biographical memoir, two-fifths through, in a paragraph on the publication of Collins' *Odes* (I, xxxix).

190:27. Robert Potter, *An Inquiry into Some Passages in Dr. Johnson's Lives of the Poets, particularly . . . Gray* (London, 1783), p. 16; quoted by Mitford, three-fourths through (I, lxviii).

190:28–30. William Forbes, *An Account of the Life and Writings of James Beattie* (2nd ed.; Edinburgh, 1807), I, 205 (May 4, 1770, a year before Gray's death); quoted by Mitford, one-third through (I, xxviii).

190:31–34. *The Correspondence of William Cowper,* ed. Thomas Wright (London, 1904), I, 141 (to Joseph Hill, April 20, 1777); partially quoted at the end of Mitford's biographical sketch (I, xcii).

190:34–191:2. Adam Smith, *Theory of Moral Sentiments,* Part III, chapt. ii; ed. Dugald Stewart (London, 1875), p. 180; quoted by Mitford, nearly two-thirds through (I, lviii).

191:3–6. R. J. Mackintosh, *Memoirs of the Life of Sir James*

Mackintosh (London, 1835), II, 172, quoted near the end of Mitford's sketch (I, lxxxix).

191:14–18. Forbes, *Beattie*, I, 106 (John Gregory to Beattie, January 1, 1766); quoted by Mitford, one-third through (I, xxviii).

191:23–24. Beattie, in the letter quoted at p. 190:28, remarked that the "Elegy" was "by no means the best of [Gray's] works."

192:4–11. William Johnson Temple in the *London Magazine* for March, 1772; quoted by Mitford, nearly four-fifths through (I, lxx–lxxi).

192:11–25. Mitford, immediately following the preceding (I, lxxiii–lxxiv). He quotes Mackintosh's *Life*, II, 427.

192:32–193:5. Letter to Thomas Wharton, September 11, 1746; ed. Toynbee, I, 241; ed. Mitford, III, 12. Gray wrote "suffer'd vastly by the Transcribblers."

193:7–16. Letter to Norton Nicholls, April 14, 1770; ed. Toynbee, III, 1121–22; ed. Mitford, V, 107, and IV, 195. Gray wrote "if I should blame you for."

193:19–27. Letter to Nicholls, January 26, 1771; ed. Toynbee, III, 1157–58; ed. Mitford, V, 120–21, and IV, 194–95.

193:32–194:16. Richard West to Gray, April 4, 1742; Gray to West, April 8; ed. Toynbee, I, 190, 192–93; ed. Mitford, II, 148, 152–54. *Cato* was Addison's tragedy (1713). Gray quotes from the opening scene of *Richard III*. Arnold omits parts of Gray's remarks, and Gray wrote "where the thought or image does not support it." "And what follows" means "and the rest of the passage," "*et seqq.*"

194:24. Gray to Wharton, February 21, 1764; ed. Toynbee, II, 832; ed. Mitford, IV, 29. " 'Tis true Cambridge is very ugly, she is very dirty, & very dull; but I'm like a cabbage, where I'm stuck, I love to grow."—Gray to Horace Walpole, March 20, 1738; ed. Toynbee, I, 82.

194:31–195:7. August 15, 1771; ed. Mitford, V, 148.

195:14–17. September 26, 1753; ed. Toynbee, I, 384; ed. Mitford, III, 117–18, where it is dated December 26, 1753. Gray wrote "have seen, what you describe."

195:19–27. To Nicholls on the death of his uncle, September 23, 1766; ed. Toynbee, III, 935–36; ed. Mitford, V, 63, where it is dated September 2, 1766.

195:31–196:3. March 28, 1767; ed. Toynbee, III, 953; ed. Mitford, IV, 85–86. Gray wrote "preserve and support you."

196:6–16. Norton Nicholls' manuscript reminiscences of Gray, printed in Mitford's ed., V, 32; *Correspondence*, ed. Toynbee, III, 1289.

196:16–22. Recounted in Mitford's memoir of Gray, half-way

through (I, xlviii); see *Correspondence*, ed. Toynbee, II, 896 and n. (Gray to Beattie, October 2, 1765).

196:23–26. December 19, 1757; ed. Toynbee, II, 544; ed. Mitford, III, 187.

196:29–32. Letter to Beattie, July 2, 1770; ed. Toynbee, III, 1141; ed. Mitford, IV, 190.

197:1–8. Gray to Wharton, enclosing his journal for October 3, 1769; *Correspondence*, ed. Toynbee, III, 1089; ed. Mitford, IV, 151–52. The words in italics are from Milton's *Samson Agonistes*, lines 86–89. *Les Rêveries du promeneur solitaire* (1782) are by Rousseau.

197:11–13. Quoted in Mitford's sketch, nearly four-fifths through (I, lxx).

197:20–24. August 22, 1737; ed. Toynbee, I, 66; ed. Mitford, II, 19.

197:25–198:3. May 27, 1742; ed. Toynbee, I, 209; ed. Mitford, II, 165. Gray wrote "has somewhat in it." Tertullian's words, usually quoted in this form, were actually "Certum est, quia impossibile est."—"De Carne Christi," cap. v, *Opera*, ed. F. Oehler (Leipzig, 1854), II, 434.

198:6–18. April 25, 1749; ed. Toynbee, I, 317–18; ed. Mitford, III, 62. The mock obituary concludes: "His death is supposed to have been occasion'd by a Fit of an Apoplexy, being found fall'n out of Bed with his Head in the Chamber-Pot." Mitford prints "spirit of the place" and "reconcile my languid companion; we shall."

198:21–23. Wednesday, January 1, 1775; printed in "Gray's Diary for 1755," *Gentleman's Magazine* CLXXIX, 229 (September, 1845); reprinted in Roger Martin, *Chronologie de la Vie et de l'Oeuvre de Thomas Gray* (Paris, 1931), p. 152. Gray wrote "doloris sensus circa renes," but Arnold follows the text in Mitford's sketch, one-third through (I, xxxiii).

198:24–30. Stoke, August 25, 1757; ed. Toynbee, II, 520; ed. Mitford, III, 167–68. Gray wrote "not extraordinary, ever since I came hither."

199:1–3. May 24, 1771; ed. Toynbee, III, 1189; ed. Mitford, IV, 200–201.

199:12–14. July 23, 1756; ed. Toynbee, II, 466; ed. Mitford, III, 152 (dated July 25, 1756).

199:14–19. February 25, 1768; ed. Toynbee, III, 1018; ed. Mitford, IV, 111. Gray wrote "so civilly" and "till fourscore-and-ten," and Arnold omits a passage that says: "What has one to do, when *turned of fifty*, but really to think of finishing?"

199:28–29. To Nicholls, January 6, 1770; ed. Toynbee, III, 1112; ed. Mitford, V, 102. Charles Victor de Bonstetten (1745–1832),

Swiss man of letters, was the subject of a series of Sainte-Beuve's *Causeries* that Arnold quoted frequently in his pocket diaries.

199:30–200:3. Bonstetten, *Souvenirs, écrites* [*sic*] *en 1831* (Paris, 1832), pp. 117–19, quoted by Mitford, V, 180–81. Arnold jotted a sentence from this sketch in his pocket diary for January 29, 1854.— *Note-Books*, ed. Lowry, p. 1.

200:3–8. *Causeries du lundi* (3rd ed.; Paris, 1869), XIV, 431.

200:13–16. J. P. Eckermann, *Gespräche mit Goethe*, ed. E. Castle (Berlin, 1916), I, 300, 323 (December 20, 1829; March 21, 1830). The latter passage contains one of Arnold's favorite quotations: "Die Hauptsache ist, dass man lerne, sich selbst zu beherrschen."

200:18. "Epistle to Dr. Arbuthnot," line 132 ("this long disease").

200:22–24. See pp. 179–81.

201:9–12. *Causeries du lundi*, XIV, 418–19.

201:32–38. "Life of Dryden," nine-tenths through and four-fifths through.

202:17–18. See p. 178:30n.

202:36. See p. 317:5–6n.

202:37–203:1. Goldsmith reviewed Gray's *Odes* anonymously in the *Monthly Review* XVII, 239–43 (September, 1757); *Collected Works of Oliver Goldsmith*, ed. Arthur Friedman (Oxford: at the Clarendon Press, 1966), I, 112–17. The review was not really disparaging, though Gray regarded it so, as is plain from his remark to Wharton on October 7, 1757; *Correspondence*, ed. Toynbee, II, 532–33. Norton Nicholls records that Gray "thought Goldsmith a genuine poet" and was delighted with *The Deserted Village.—Ibid.*, III, 1291; ed. Mitford, V, 36. Gray's "Alliance of Education and Government," a fragment of 107 lines, was published posthumously in 1775, well after *The Traveller* (1764), but Mitford cites a parallel between the two that is the basis for Arnold's remark.—I, 148.

203:4. *The Deserted Village*, line 126.

203:8. *2 Henry IV*, III, i, 20, one of Arnold's "touchstone" passages; see p. 169:16–18.

203:10–12. "Life of Dryden," two-thirds through.

203:16–22. "To the Pious Memory of the Accomplish'd Young Lady, Mrs. Anne Killigrew, Excellent in the Two Sister-Arts of Poesy and Painting. An Ode," lines 92–98.

203:26–33. *Pythian Odes* III, 153–55 (Arnold's translation continues to line 161).

204:7–9. From a letter to Mason, January 13, 1758, quoted by Mitford in an "Essay on the Poetry of Gray," II, ii; ed. Toynbee, II, 551.

[JOHN KEATS]

Arnold sent off his essay on Gray on Saturday, May 8, 1880; on Monday, May 10, he began his work on Keats. By the twenty-first he had forwarded his selections from the poems; on July 5 he completed the essay. Like the introduction to Gray, this depends heavily on the poet's letters, and aims at showing the reader of the selections what sort of man the poet was and what he thought about his art. It fulfills its proper function well; but when separated from the work for which it was written and published in a collection of critical essays, it leads its readers to expect something it does not provide. Its very brief critical discussion echoes what Arnold had already said of Keats, with somewhat greater *éclat*, in "Maurice de Guérin" (1862).—*Prose Works*, ed. Super, III, 13, 31–34. The volume of Ward's *English Poets* that contained Keats was published together with the one that contained Gray, about December 11, 1880.

A well-known letter from Arnold to Clough in 1848 or 1849, soon after the first publication of the book which was his principal source for this essay, makes an interesting contrast between a young man's response (when he was not much older than Keats was) and the mature man of the essay: "What a brute you were to tell me to read Keats' Letters. However it is over now: and reflexion resumes her power over agitation. What harm he has done in English Poetry. As Browning is a man with a moderate gift passionately desiring movement and fulness, and obtaining but a confused multitudinousness, so Keats with a very high gift, is yet also consumed by this desire: and cannot produce the truly living and moving, as his conscience keeps telling him. They will not be patient neither understand that they must begin with an Idea of the world in order not to be prevailed over by the world's multitudinousness: or if they cannot get that, at least with isolated ideas: and all other things shall (perhaps) be added unto them. . . . I have had that desire of fulness without respect of the means, which may become almost maniacal: but nature had placed a bar thereto not only in the conscience (as with all men) but in a great numbness in that direction. But what perplexity Keats Tennyson ed id genus omne must occasion to young writers of the ὁπλίτης sort: yes and those d----d Elizabethan poets generally. Those who cannot read G[ree]k sh[ou]ld read nothing but Milton and parts of Wordsworth: the state should see to it."—*The Letters of Matthew Arnold to Arthur Hugh Clough*, ed. H. F. Lowry (London: Oxford University Press,

1932), pp. 96–97. Arnold as a young poet faced the same problems Keats articulated so sensitively and at such length, but his solution was one Arnold rejected; hence the slightly disparaging reference also in the Preface to Arnold's *Poems* of 1853. By 1880 Arnold no longer was vitally touched by these problems, but the old affection for Keats remained, and a little something of the old distress. His acknowledgment of Sidney Colvin's *Keats* in a letter of June 26, 1887, contains some very interesting comments on individual poems. —E. V. Lucas, *The Colvins and Their Friends* (New York, 1928), pp. 192–94. A valuable study of Keats's impact on Arnold may be found in G. H. Ford, *Keats and the Victorians* (New Haven: Yale University Press, 1944), pp. 49–89.

205:1–2. *Of Education*, two-thirds through; *Works*, ed. Allan Abbott *et al* (New York: Columbia University Press, 1931), IV, 286. Milton wrote "simple, sensuous and passionate."

205:8–9. To Benjamin Bailey, November 22, 1817; printed in R. M. Milnes, *Life, Letters, and Literary Remains of John Keats* (London, 1848), I, 65. Arnold used a later edition: *The Life and Letters of John Keats*, by Lord Houghton. A new edition in one volume (London: Edward Moxon & Co., Dover Street, 1867).

205:9–12. To George and Thomas Keats, December 22 [21], 1817; Milnes, *Life*, I, 94. This is the famous "negative capability" passage.

205:12–19. *Life of Benjamin Robert Haydon, from His Autobiography and Journals*, ed. Tom Taylor (London, 1853), II, 9.

205:20. Vergil *Aeneid* XII, 435.

205:24. Fanny Brawne, five years younger than Keats, died in 1865, her husband Louis Lindon in 1872. Six years later Harry Buxton Forman published from the original manuscripts *Letters of John Keats to Fanny Brawne, Written in the Years MDCCCXIX and MDCCCXX* (London: Reeves and Turner, 1878). On November 9, 1878, Arnold agreed to sign a memorial to Lord Beaconsfield drawn up by Forman on behalf of Keats's impoverished sister Fanny, and when the Government granted only a single gift of £150 he responded to Forman's further appeal in April, 1879, with the promise of a guinea toward a subscription on her behalf.

206:8–23. October 13, 1819. The quotation is from John Ford, *'Tis Pity She's a Whore*, I, iii.

206:29. "Give me that man | That is not passion's slave."—*Hamlet* III, ii, 76–77.

206:30–33. *Blackwood's* twitted Keats with being an apothecary's student; Milnes turned the phrase to Keats's credit: "Here is a surgeon's apprentice, with the ordinary culture of the middle classes, rivalling in aesthetic perceptions of antique life and thought the most careful scholars of his time and country."—*Life*, II, 104.

207:13–14. The opening lines of a sonnet of 1817.

207:31–208:4. Milnes, *Life*, II, 42, 44. George Keats wrote "courage and manliness." *Blackwood's* addressed him derisively as "good Johnny Keats." Before Keats's death, Byron expressed himself in most irreverent terms about his poetry, and these expressions were made public in Moore's *Letters and Journals of Lord Byron* (1830): "Instead of [Scott's *Monastery*], here are Johnny Keats's *piss-a-bed* poetry, and three novels by God knows whom," and "Why don't they [the *Edinburgh* reviewers] review and praise *Solomon's Guide to Health?* It is better sense, and as much poetry as Johnny Keats" (October 12, November 18, 1820). The latter is quoted by Milnes, *Life*, I, 205.

208:7–14. January 13, 1818; Milnes, *Life*, I, 105, 104, misdated April 21, 1818.

208:24–39. January 23, 1818; Milnes, *Life*, I, 77.

209:1–4. Joseph Butler, *The Analogy of Religion, Natural and Revealed*, I, v, 7; *Works*, ed. W. E. Gladstone (Oxford, 1896), I, 110.

209:8–21. September 23, 1819; Milnes, *Life*, II, 29.

209:28. In a letter to Bailey, August 14, 1819, Keats speaks of "the drawling of the blue-stocking literary world."—Milnes, *Life*, II, 11.

209:31–210:4. To his publisher J. A. Hessey, October 9, 1818; Milnes, *Life*, I, 214. Keats wrote "my own domestic criticism." "J. S." was author of a letter in *The Morning Chronicle* of October 3, 1818, defending Keats against the *Quarterly*.

210:7–12. To Haydon, October 3, 1819; Milnes, *Life*, II, 10.

210:17–18. To C. W. Dilke, September 22, 1819; Milnes, *Life*, II, 17–18.

210:20–21. " 'Tis strange the mind, that very fiery particle, | Should let itself be snuff'd out by an article."—Byron, *Don Juan*, XI, 479–80, quoted by Milnes, *Life*, I, 206.

210:22–23. To John Taylor, August 23, 1819; Milnes, *Life*, II, 12.

210:26–211:3. To Reynolds, April 9, 1818; Milnes, *Life*, I, 120–21. Keats wrote "least Shadow of public thought," not "least shadow of thought about their opinion."

211:7–11. To Taylor, August 23, 1819; Milnes, *Life*, II, 13.

211:12–15. July 8, 1819.

211:18. Keats's letters to Reynolds, April 9 and 10, 1818, show him discarding his first Preface to *Endymion* on the advice of his friends and writing the new one that was actually published. The earlier one disappeared, but was later discovered and printed in Milnes' edition of 1867.—Milnes, *Life* (1848), I, 120–26; (1867), pp. 101–3.

211:25–27. To George and Georgiana Keats, October 14, 1818; Milnes, *Life*, I, 229–30. The words "a fine thing" apply to a young lady Keats had met; the other words characterized both the lady and Byron.

211:33–36. To John Taylor, April 24, 1818; Milnes, *Life*, I, 129–30. The quotation is from Proverbs 4:5 ("Get wisdom" in the Bible, "get learning" in Milnes).

212:2–3. To Bailey, August 14, 1819; Milnes, *Life*, II, 11.

212:4–12. MS notes written in a copy of *Paradise Lost*, printed in Milnes, *Life*, I, 274–75.

212:16–18. "To J. H. Reynolds, Esq.," lines 72–74, first printed in Milnes, *Life*, I, 115. Though the earlier editions read "and so philosophise," the edition of Milnes Arnold used prints, as he does, "and to philosophise."

212:21–23. To Reynolds, August 24, 1819; Milnes, *Life*, II, 15.

212:27–29. To George and Georgiana Keats, October 14–31, 1818; Milnes, *Life*, I, 235–36. Only a few weeks before Arnold first read Keats's letters, he himself wrote to Clough from Switzerland on September 29, 1848: "Of [Béranger] I am getting tired. . . . In the reste, I am glad to be tired of an author: one link in the immense series of cognoscenda et indagenda despatched. More particularly is this my feeling with regard to (I hate the word) women. We know beforehand all they can teach us: yet we are obliged to learn it directly from them."—*Letters of Arnold to Clough*, ed. Lowry, pp. 92–93.

212:30–34. To Charles Brown, August, 1820; Milnes, *Life*, II, 67.

213:1–7. August 16, 1819.

213:8–15. To George and Georgiana Keats, October 14–31, 1818; Milnes, *Life*, I, 236, 235. Keats wrote "of my intellect."

213:15–19. To Fanny Brawne, February, 1820 (?); H. B. Forman's Letter XVII.

213:24–25. To Bailey, November 22, 1817; Milnes, *Life*, I, 64.

213:27–28. "Ode on a Grecian Urn," lines 49–50.

214:7–10. To Bailey, November 22, 1817; Milnes, *Life*, I, 67.

214:11–18. August 24, 1819; Milnes, *Life*, II, 15. Keats wrote "and strive to be nothing," but Arnold prints it as Milnes gives it.

214:20–22. To Brown from Naples, November 1, 1820; Milnes, *Life*, II, 78.

214:37. Arnold first used Keats as an example of "natural magic" in "Maurice de Guérin" (1862), *Prose Works*, ed. Super, III, 13–14.

214:38–215:6. "On Edmund Kean as a Shakespearian Actor," an anonymous paper written at Reynolds' request for *The Champion* of December 21, 1817; printed in the Appendix to Milnes's ed. of 1867, p. 336.

215:10–11. To George and Georgiana Keats, October 14–31, 1818; Milnes, *Life*, I, 227.

215:12–15. See "Maurice de Guérin," *Prose Works*, ed. Super, III, 30, 33.

215:15–17. "What distinguishes the artist from the mere amateur, says Goethe, is *Architectonicè* in the highest sense," remarked Arnold in his Preface to *Poems* (1853: republished 1882), in a passage where he used Keats's "Isabella" as an example of incoherent beauty of language.—*Prose Works*, ed. Super, I, 9–10.

215:35–216:7. "Ode to May. Fragment," lines 5–14.

[BYRON]

In the "Memorial Verses" (1850) with which Arnold commemorated Wordsworth's achievement and death, he linked him with Goethe and Byron as the contemporaries who most set the tone for their age. And so it is not surprising that, having completed the Wordsworth volume for the Golden Treasury series, he should propose to the publishers that he undertake a similar selection from Byron. (The publisher's suggestion that he do Burns came to nothing.) It has been said that the Byron volume was first suggested to him by Disraeli. In any case the agreement with the publisher was reached late in May, 1880. Arnold forwarded the poems, "arranged and *titled*," to the printers on December 2, "and hope they will not be long in beginning," he told Macmillan. The volume was more difficult to prepare than the Wordsworth "because *bits* of poems must constitute the main part of the volume," but "it will be a beautiful and powerful volume of poetry; much more beautiful and powerful than I had expected."—Buckler, *Matthew Arnold's Books*, p. 148. The text used was the 17-volume edition published by Murray in 1832. His Preface, like the Preface to Wordsworth, was first published as an essay in *Macmillan's Magazine* for March, 1881, and brought Arnold £20. The book itself was slow to appear; in its Golden Treasury form it was published at 4 s. 6 d. and on large paper at 9 s., early in June. The book's success was very unlike the Wordsworth volume: "The sale is very small & the returns consequently a long time in coming," his publishers told him on January 18, 1888.—Buckler, p. 146. One of his selections was the death speech of Marino Faliero, for which Arnold at fourteen won a competition in elocution at Winchester by the "simplicity and distinctness of his delivery."—Thomas Arnold, *Passages in a Wandering Life* (London, 1900), p. 15.

Arnold's work was more controversial than he may have supposed. It was greeted almost instantly by a published note from the hand of William Hale White that demonstrated at great length how Arnold underrated Goethe's esteem for Byron and ended with a firm declaration that "energy, power, is the one thing after which we pine, especially in a sickly age. We do not want carefully-constructed poems of mosaic, self-possessed and self-conscious. Force is what we need and what will heal us. In so far as it is force, it is the true morality, the true beauty, and the only revelation."—"Byron, Goethe, and Mr. Matthew Arnold," *Contemporary Review* XL, 179–85 (August, 1881). Then came Swinburne's long, amusing, but in the long run quite meaningless blast against Byron and Arnold's overpraise of him; Swinburne exalted Shelley in compensation. "If the author of *Thyrsis* be the real Mr. Arnold, I cannot avoid the inference that the critic who places Byron above Shelley and Wordsworth above Coleridge is something not himself—something, shall we say, definable as a stream of tendency making for unrighteousness in criticism and inconsistent with righteousness in poetry?"—"Wordsworth and Byron," *Nineteenth Century* XV, 583–609, 764–90 (April, May, 1884), and *Miscellanies* (London, 1886), p. viii. (How little Arnold was able to predict Swinburne is evident from his remark to Ward when he saw Swinburne's dithyramb on Collins: "It would have been so much better to give to Swinburne Byron, where over-praise would be, at any rate, not eccentric and startling.") H. J. C. Grierson's Warton Lecture for 1920, "Lord Byron: Arnold and Swinburne" (reprinted in his *The Background of English Literature* [London: Chatto and Windus, 1950], pp. 68–114) is less concerned with the debate between Victorian critics than with the attempt to estimate Byron justly, and highly. "The issue between Arnold and Swinburne was the ever-recurring one of the relative values in poetry of technique and inspiration, art and life." (p. 108)

217:1–2. See pp. 54, 338.

217:16–19. Brooke's selection of *Poems of Shelley* was published in the Golden Treasury series by Macmillan in 1880. In December, 1877, Arnold published an article on Brooke's *Primer of English Literature;* see *Prose Works,* ed. Super, VIII, 237–51 and IX, 167:2n.

217:26–218:2. For Shelley's many expressions of admiration of Byron's poetry, see Appendix VIII, *s.v.* Byron, of *The Letters of Percy Bysshe Shelley,* ed. F. L. Jones (Oxford: at the Clarendon Press, 1964), II, 470–71. "Shelley, . . . certainly the most modest of great poets, contemplates Byron in the fixed attitude of a literary worshipper," writes John Nichol, and among other passages of Shelley's praise of Byron, Nichol somewhat misquotes a letter to John Gisborne, January 26, 1821: "In my opinion [Lord Byron's last volume] contains finer poetry than has appeared in England since the publication of *Paradise Lost.* Cain is apocalyptic; it is a revelation not before communicated to man."—*Byron* (New York, 1880), pp. 125, 147.

218:9–12. "His love of that which is indefinite and changeful made him enjoy and describe better than any other English poet that scenery of the clouds and sky which is indefinite owing to infinite change of appearance. . . . He describes not only the momentary aspect, but also the change and progress of the sunset or the storm," wrote Brooke in the Preface to his *Poems of Shelley.* But like Arnold he admitted that "a great deal of his poetry of Nature has no ground in thought, and consequently wants power."—pp. xxxv, xxxi.

218:18. In 1840 Mary Shelley published in two volumes Shelley's *Essays, Letters from Abroad, Translations and Fragments* (London: Edward Moxon). Included was the translation of Plato's *Symposium* Arnold was fond of quoting.

218:29–32. In 1866 Swinburne edited for Moxon *A Selection from the Works of Lord Byron.* When he reprinted his Preface in *Essays and Studies* (London, 1875), he added three introductory sentences by way of apology for his earlier venture; Arnold quotes from these (p. 238). *Essays and Studies* also reprinted Swinburne's article on "Matthew Arnold's New Poems."

219:12–13. Letter to John Murray, November 29, 1813; *The Works of Lord Byron: Letters and Journals,* ed. R. E. Prothero (London: John Murray, 1898–1901), II, 291.

219:16–18. To Thomas Moore, June 8, 1822; ed. Prothero, VI, 81.

219:18–24. To John Murray, June 6, 1822, and to Thomas Moore, March 3, 1814; ed. Prothero, VI, 77; III, 56. The two letters are combined and given as Arnold quotes them in Nichol, *Byron,* p. 75.

221:3–4. *Hamlet,* I, v, 79. "To know or to honour him aright he must be considered with all his imperfections and with all his glories on his head," said Swinburne of Byron.—*Essays and Studies* (1875), p. 238.

221:28–222:4. Review of Taine's *Histoire de la littérature anglaise*, first published in *Le Temps*, May 24 and June 7, 1864; *Études sur la littérature contemporaine* (nouv. éd.; Paris, 1894), VI, 130–33. The quotation is from Taine's *Histoire* (3rd ed.; Paris, 1873), IV, 330 (Book IV, chapt. i, sect. 5). See p. 40:14, variant—a passage doubtless removed because Arnold wanted to use it here. Nichol quotes Taine's judgment in the final chapter of his *Byron*. More than thirty years before Scherer, Macaulay wrote that Byron "was himself the beginning, the middle, and the end, of all his own poetry, the hero of every tale, the chief object in every landscape."— "Byron," ¶8 from end.

221:33–34. When Clovis presented himself to Saint Remigius for baptism on Christmas Day, 496, the Saint commanded him: "Humbly bow thy head, Sicambrian; adore what thou hast burned, burn what thou has adored."—Gregory of Tours, *Historia Francorum*, II, 31. The expression became proverbial; Arnold used it in his *Last Words on Translating Homer* (1862), *Prose Works*, ed. Super, I, 200.

222:8–12, 17–19. "Death of Lord Byron," *Edinburgh Weekly Journal*, 1824; *Miscellaneous Prose Works of Sir Walter Scott* (Edinburgh, 1834), IV, 348, 375.

222:15–17. Letter to John Murray, December 17, 1821, acknowledging Byron's dedication to Scott of *Cain;* printed in Lockhart's *Life of Scott*.

222:22–27. *Cain,* I, i, 138–40; II, ii, 403–4. Byron wrote "Souls who dare."

222:30–33. "On a souvent remarqué cette alliance, au premier abord singulière, du génie poétique et du génie philologique."— "Leopardi" (1844), *Portraits contemporains* (nouv. éd.; Paris, 1882), IV, 366.

223:11–12. *Werner,* V, i, 383–84.

223:14–15. *Heaven and Earth,* lines 359–60.

223:17–18. *The Prisoner of Chillon,* lines 42–43. Byron wrote "so rise."

223:20. *Childe Harold,* IV, 1620.

223:22. *The Giaour,* line 68. Nichol says this passage "strike[s] deeper than any verse of either" Scott or Moore.—*Byron,* p. 74.

223:26. *Tempest,* I, ii, 50.

224:1–2. Milton, "Il Penseroso," lines 99–100.

224:7, 9. "The Longest Day," line 3 (1820 version), and "Inscriptions Supposed to Be Found in and near a Hermit's Cell," IV, 9.

224:8. Ruskin used the quatrain beginning "Parching summer" as epigraph to the third installment of "Fiction—Fair and Foul," which at this point is a severe critique of Wordsworth. And in making the contrast of Wordsworth with Byron, Scott, and Burns, he remarked: "Does not a sense come upon you of some element in their passion, no less than in their sound, different, specifically, from that of 'Parching summer hath no warrant'? Is it more profane, think you—or more tender—nay, perhaps, in the core of it, more true?"—*Nineteenth Century*, VIII, 394, 399 (September, 1880). In the preceding installment, Ruskin remarked: "I have lately seen, and with extreme pleasure, Mr. Matthew Arnold's arrangement of Wordsworth's poems; and read with sincere interest his high estimate of them. But a great poet's work never needs arrangement by other hands; and though it is very proper that Silver How should clearly understand and brightly praise its fraternal Rydal Mount, we must not forget that, over yonder, are the Andes, all the while."—P. 204 (August, 1880). Silver How is a hill west of Grasmere, not far from Wordsworth's home at Rydal Mount and Arnold's family home at Fox How, Ambleside.

224:25–27. Arnold contrasts "euphuia," the finely tempered nature with its harmonious perfection in which the characters of beauty and intelligence are both present, with the "aphuia" of the British Philistine, in "Culture and Its Enemies," his final lecture from the chair of poetry at Oxford (1867).—*Prose Works*, ed. Super, V, 99.

224:30. "I do not know that I resemble Jean-Jacques Rousseau. I have no ambition to be like so illustrious a madman," Byron wrote to his mother on October 7, 1808, and Moore, when he printed this letter, printed also an elaborate comparison Byron drew up of himself with Rousseau in one of his journals.—*Letters*, ed. Prothero, I, 192–93. Arnold alludes especially to the sentence quoted by Nichol: "He was of the people—I of the aristocracy."—*Byron*, p. 37.

224:31–225:1. Moore tells the story that Byron, seeing his younger friend Lord Delawarr on the monitor's list for punishment, asked the monitor not to "lick him" because he was a brother peer.—*Letters and Journals of Lord Byron, with Notices of His Life* (3rd ed.; London, 1833), I, 60–61; Nichol, *Byron*, p. 29.

225:2–3. Byron's letters were full of such expressions when he wrote to close friends like Moore and Murray from mid 1813 to early 1815, when he was an exuberant young man with the world at his feet.

225:4–5. "He is a Greek temple, with a Gothic Cathedral on one hand, and a Turkish Mosque and all sorts of fantastic pagodas and conventicles about him."—Letter to Moore, May 3, 1821; *Letters*, ed. Prothero, V, 274.

225:29–36. Both Eckermann and Müller record recurring banter between Goethe and his daughter-in-law Ottilie over her admiration of Byron; e.g., Eckermann, *Gespräche mit Goethe*, ed. E. Castle (Berlin, 1916), I, 138–39 (March 26, 1826) and *Goethes Unterhaltungen mit dem Kanzler Friedrich von Müller*, ed. C. A. H. Burkhardt (Stuttgart, 1904), p. 38 (January 2, 1820). Arnold cites Tieck's preference for Byron over Goethe in "A French Critic on Goethe" (1878), *Prose Works*, ed. Super, VIII, 253–54.

226:17–19, 30–31. John Nichol (1833–94), professor of English literature at Glasgow, early published a review of Arnold's *Merope* in *Undergraduate Papers* (Oxford), I, 166–79 (1858). His *Byron* was published in the "English Men of Letters" series in 1880; Arnold quotes from his final chapter, p. 205. In the same chapter of evaluation of Byron, Nichol draws on Arnold's "Stanzas in Memory of the Author of 'Obermann'" and "Memorial Verses."

226:25–26. J. P. Eckermann, *Gespräche mit Goethe*, ed. E. Castle (Berlin, 1916), I, 201 (July 5, 1827).

226:27–30. *Ibid.*, I, 139 (March 26, 1826).

227:9–10. *Ibid.*, I, 41 (October 19, 1823).

227:11–15. *Ibid.*, I, 243 (December 16, 1828); quoted also by Nichol, *Byron*, p. 205.

227:17–21. *Ibid.*, I, 115–16, 117 (February 24, 1825).

227:23. *Ibid.*, I, 142–43 (November 8, 1826).

227:31–32. *Ibid.*, I, 109 (January 18, 1825). But then, as Arnold pointed out elsewhere, Goethe also said: "Alle Engländer sind als solche ohne eigentliche Reflexion."—I, 116.

228:8–9. *Ibid.*, I, 115 (February 24, 1825).

228:24–25. "Joubert" (1863); *Prose Works*, ed. Super, III, 209.

228:31–36. See pp. 163, 171.

229:13–18. Count Leopardi was born at Recanati, Ancona, on June 29, 1798, and died at Naples on June 14, 1837. As a lad he developed a twisted spine, and Ste.-Beuve draws the parallel with Byron.—*Portraits contemporains*, IV, 388.

229:23–25. An echo of I Samuel 18:7: "Saul hath slain his thousands, and David his ten thousands."

229:35–36. The Scottish physician James Kennedy published

Conversations on Religion, with Lord Byron and Others (London, 1830). Nichol gives a summary of the debates in his *Byron*, pp. 184–86.

230:5–.9 "La Ginestra, o il fiore del deserto," one of the *Canti*. The passage Arnold alludes to is lines 158–201. Although modern editions read "in queste rive," that of 1877 (Leipzig: Brockhaus) gives Leopardi's earlier version, "in queste piagge."

230:17. *The Excursion*, IX, 293. See p. 50:15–24. The passage, 43 lines long, is an argument for the State's responsibility for elementary education, and Arnold's citing it—doctrinally sound as he must have regarded it, pompously dull as it certainly is—is mildly humorous.

230:26. "The Recluse," line 771. The passage in which this line occurs was published with *The Excursion* in 1814. See pp. 47:28, 51:15.

231:11. "The fates have bestowed an enduring soul upon men." —*Iliad* XXIV, 49.

231:13. Dante, *Paradiso*, III, 85; see p. 169:13.

231:15–17. *King Lear*, V, ii, 9–11.

232:2–6. "Byron," *Essays and Studies* (1875), p. 239. The italics are Arnold's.

232:17. Almack's Assembly Rooms, in King Street, St. James's, were the scene of fashionable social functions in the late eighteenth and early nineteenth centuries. Sarah, Countess of Jersey (1785–1867), a leader of London society during the Regency, was a friend of Byron's. At one of her large assemblies, Byron was cut by most of the guests after his separation from his wife, but conspicuously not by his hostess.

232:29–31. Letter to Murray on *Don Juan*, August 1, 1819; ed. Prothero, IV, 327.

232:28–233:2. "It is always thus in the long run:—Time, the Avenger."—Letter to Murray, August 12, 1819; ed. Prothero, IV, 344–45.

233:5–7. Journal, January 16, 1814; ed. Prothero, II, 381.

233:7–10. Journal, November 23, 1813, and January 13, 1821; ed. Prothero, II, 339; V, 173. The passages are quoted by Nichol, *Byron*, p. 178, and jotted in Arnold's pocket diary for January 16–17, 1881. —*Note-Books*, ed. Lowry, p. 351.

233:15–16. The Address is the reply of the Houses of Parliament to the sovereign's speech that opens each session of Parliament. The sovereign's speech is in fact a statement of the legislative program of the ministry; the Address in each House is moved by one of the loyal followers of the party in power, and debate on it is a means of formally discussing the entire government policy.

233:20. Subjects of poems by Shelley.

233:29–31. Marguerite, Countess of Blessington, *Conversations of Lord Byron*, ed. E. J. Lovell, Jr. (Princeton: Princeton University Press, 1969), p. 7 (bis).

234:4–6. Quoted by Scherer, *Études sur la littérature contemporaine*, VI, 129.

234:7–8. *Byron*, p. 211.

234:25–26. "Le fait est que le talent de Byron est moins poétique qu'oratoire. Il a moins d'imagination que de rhétorique."—*Études sur la littérature contemporaine*, VI, 132.

234:32–35. Eckermann, *Gespräche*, ed. Castle, I, 200 (July 5, 1827).

234:38. *Childe Harold*, II, 230.

235:5. "The Solitary Reaper," line 17; (variant) "Michael," line 466.

235:7–8. *Childe Harold*, IV, 1261–62.

235:20. *Ibid.*, IV, 1173.

235:32. Disraeli's (Lord Beaconsfield's) last novel, *Endymion* (1880), dealt with the social and political life of mid nineteenth-century England, with recognizable persons from that life thinly disguised.

236:12–13. "A few years [after the age of Shakespeare] the great English middle class, the kernel of the nation, the class whose intelligent sympathy had upheld a Shakespeare, entered the prison of Puritanism, and had the key turned on its spirit there for two hundred years."—"Heinrich Heine" (1863), *Prose Works*, ed. Super, III, 121. Arnold was fond of quoting this sentence; see p. 79:21–23.

236:15–17. See pp. 8:11–12, 158:16–17.

236:18–21. This passage is reminiscent of what Arnold said of Heine, and is based on what Heine said of himself: "He is significant because he was, if not pre-eminently a brave, yet a brilliant, a most effective soldier in the Liberation War of humanity."—*Prose Works*, ed. Super, III, 107. At the close of that essay, Arnold drew at length the parallel between Heine and Byron that foreshadows the present essay.

237:3–4. In his essay on "Joubert" (1863), Arnold translated a passage from that author: "Plato loses himself in the void, but one sees the play of his wings, one hears their rustle." And of Marcus Aurelius he said (1863): "In his character, beautiful as it is, there is something melancholy, circumscribed, and ineffectual."—*Prose*

Works, ed. Super, III, 203, 146. "I therefore so run, not as uncertainly; so fight I, not as one that beateth the air."—I Corinthians 9:26. As part of an earlier (1869) debate with Arnold about the merits of Shelley and Byron, Swinburne wrote: "Shelley was born a son and soldier of light, an archangel winged and weaponed for angel's work."—"Notes on the Text of Shelley," *Essays and Studies* (London, 1875), p. 216.

[THE INCOMPATIBLES]

The Liberal victory of April, 1880, brought with it the appointment of Arnold's brother-in-law W. E. Forster to the chief secretaryship for Ireland, an arduous post in one of the most troublesome of times. An invitation to visit at the chief secretary's lodge Arnold turned down for the time being: "I want . . . to unite our visit to Ireland with our visit to Fox How next autumn," Arnold wrote to his son in Australia in December, 1880; "then I should get a sight of the west of Ireland, which I have never seen, and probably get some sea-trout fishing, which is excellent there, and at its best in September. But really Ireland is in such a state that what will happen there, or what will become of the Ministry which has to deal with its affairs, or how far travelling in Connemara will be profitable next autumn, no one can now say." And so when the Liberals announced that they were bringing in a new Land Bill that would remedy the defects of that of 1870, Arnold wrote his longest and most fundamental discussion of Anglo-Irish relations without yet having looked for himself at the state of affairs. His comment to his wife on the Liberal policy is apparently far less sensitive than the essays themselves, something of an echo of his earlier "force till right is ready": "I don't think the stopping an isolated meeting makes the slightest impression over here [in England], though you seem to think a great deal of it over there [in Ireland, where she was visiting]. What people are wanting here is a totally different system of government—an *état de siège,* in short—only carried out with perfect humanity and quietness. But the Radical masses of the large towns in the north approve, I believe, of the Government doing nothing; they don't wish anarchy to be strictly dealt with anywhere, because they wish for no precedents or dispositions of interference if they choose to be anarchical themselves; and this is perhaps the most formidable thing in the present situation—this feeling in the proletariate of the large towns, and the complicity of the Government with this feeling." What the article shows so clearly is the strong sense, so out of keeping with the imperialist temper, that an alien government cannot legislate for a people according to its own standards, even when these may be demonstrably more forward-looking than the probable policy of the indigenous masses; and it was in addition far from Arnold's opinion that the Liberal policies were as unselfish and forward-looking as they claimed to be. At the end of the year 1881, after his visit to "this fascinating but troublesome country" as he called it in a letter to Gladstone ("The Forsters, . . . poor people, experience much more of its troublesomeness than of its fascination"), he wrote encouragingly to his sister: "I do indeed feel for you in the present condition of things in Ireland—the more so as a beginning of the better state of things is all that we shall probably be permitted to see in our time; but it will be something solid to look back upon if William has been instrumental in forwarding even this beginning. For my part, the immense revolution which is actually in progress in Ireland, and which is before us in England too, though it has not actually commenced, carries me back continually to the great Hebrew prophets, with their conviction, so distasteful to the rulers and politicians of their times, of the inevitability of a profound revolution; their conviction, too, of the final emergence of a better state of things. 'O that thou hadst hearkened to My commandments! then had thy peace been as a river, and thy righteousness as the waves of the sea.' [Isaiah 48:18] The world is always thinking that the 'peace as a river' is to be had without having 'hearkened to the commandment,' but the prophet knows better." Forster was not the leader to better things for Ireland; he and his party had felt obliged to introduce even before their Land Bill a Coercion Bill to enforce law and order, and its unpopularity was such as to compel Forster's resignation only a few months after Arnold wrote this letter. But these events were still in the future when "The Incompatibles" appeared in April and June, 1881, in the *Nineteenth Century*. Each part brought Arnold £50. The title is only another way of phrasing a title Arnold had already used: "Irish Catholicism and British Liberalism." The frequent citation of Burke goes hand in hand with the volume of selections from Burke's writings on Ireland that Arnold was working on at the same time.

238:16–21. Robert Lowe, speaking at Sheffield on September 4, 1873, reported in *The Times* next day, p. 3, col. 3. Arnold jotted the expression in his pocket diary for August 10, 1873, and quoted it in his Preface to *Higher Schools and Universities in Germany* (1874). —*Note-Books*, ed. Lowry, p. 199; *Prose Works*, ed. Super, VII, 129.

238:21–26. "The cleverest, most liberal, most upright man, can do nothing for his country as things stand. Unless prepared to fly at the throat of England, he is no fit tool for the people."—Charlotte G. O'Brien, "Eighty Years," *Nineteenth Century* IX, 411 (March, 1881). The expression "ravin as a wolf" occurs in Genesis 49:27.

239:26–27. Burke, "A Letter to a Noble Lord," three-fifths through. Arnold jotted this expression in his pocket diary for July 17, 1869, and seven times thereafter in the next decade, as well as in one of his "General Note-Books."—*Note-Books*, ed. Lowry, p. 105, etc. He quoted it frequently in his writings from 1871 onward.

240:1–4. J. P. Eckermann, *Gespräche mit Goethe*, ed. E. Castle (Berlin, 1916), I, 149 (December 20, 1826), jotted in Arnold's pocket diary at the beginning of 1881 and in one of his "General Note-Books."—*Note-Books*, ed. Lowry, pp. 350, 529.

240:5–9. See p. 248:36.

240:10–15. "Letter to Thomas Burgh, Esq." (1780), half-way through.

240:21–24. "Speech at the Guildhall, in Bristol, Previous to the Late Election" (1780), more than one-fourth through; jotted at the end of Arnold's pocket diary for 1886.—*Note-Books*, ed. Lowry, p. 424. Burke wrote "fond desires."

241:15–17 (variant). In the same month with Arnold's article appeared one by Lord Sherbrooke (formerly Robert Lowe), the Liberal politician; earlier in the year there were articles by Sir Bartle Frere, formerly governor of the Cape of Good Hope, and by Lt.-Gen. Sir Garnet Wolseley.

242:9–17. Arnold visited the schools of Alsace in the latter part of June, 1859, as an assistant commissioner for the Newcastle Commission; his report was published as *The Popular Education of France* (1861); *Prose Works*, ed. Super, vol. II. Arnold's comment on Germany's annexation of Alsace-Lorraine after the war of 1870–71, with the contrast he draws between the attitudes of the Alsatians toward the French and of the Irish toward the English, echoes a remark he made in his review of Renan's *La Réforme* (1872), in "Equality" (1878) and in "Irish Catholicism and British Liberalism" (1878).—*Prose Works*, ed. Super, VII, 47; VIII, 291, 322.

242:36. Strasbourg, a free imperial city, was seized by Louis XIV in 1681, in a time of peace; French rule was recognized by the treaty of Ryswick sixteen years later.

243:27–35. *A View of the Present State of Ireland* (1596), *Prose Works*, ed. Rudolf Gottfried (Baltimore: The Johns Hopkins Press, 1949), p. 158.

243:36–244:2. *A Short View of the State of Ireland* (1727), *Prose Works*, vol. XII: *Irish Tracts, 1728–33*, ed. Herbert Davis (Oxford: Basil Blackwell, 1955), p. 10.

244:3–7. *A Modest Proposal* (1729), *ibid.*, p. 114, slightly altered by Arnold.

244:18–20. C. G. Gordon, letter printed in *The Times*, December 3, 1880, p. 6, col. 5, jotted in Arnold's pocket diary for August 16, 1880.—*Note-Books*, ed. Lowry, p. 342. Gordon, returning from a brief mission in China, in October visited Ireland to ascertain on his own account the state of affairs there.

245:12–14. Plutarch *Life of Caesar* xxxv, quoted in *On the Study of Celtic Literature* (1866), *Prose Works*, ed. Super, III, 298.

245:17–19. Henri Martin, *Histoire de France depuis le temps les plus reculés jusqu'en 1789* (4th ed.; Paris, 1865), I, 36; quoted *ibid.*, III, 344.

245:28. "Cath-loda: A Poem," Duan II, *The Poems of Ossian*, translated by James Macpherson, ed. William Sharp (Edinburgh, 1896), p. 14; jotted in Arnold's pocket diary at the end of 1865 and used as epigraph for *On the Study of Celtic Literature.—Note-Books*, ed. Lowry, p. 34; *Prose Works*, ed. Super, III, 291.

246:13–16. Charles James Fox (1749–1806) and the younger William Pitt (1759–1806) were the leaders of the Whig and Tory parties in the last decades of the eighteenth century. Both were second sons of influential politicians; Fox entered the House of Commons at nineteen, Pitt at twenty-one, and Pitt became prime minister at twenty-four, a post he held (with the intermission of a three-year period) until his death. Fox, who had been foreign secretary in the Whig ministry before Pitt took office, resumed that post on Pitt's death, but himself died eight months thereafter.

246:27–29. "Letter on the Affairs of Ireland" (1797), final paragraph.

246:29–33. John Morley's *Burke* was published in Macmillan's "English Men of Letters" series (of which Morley himself was general editor) in August 1879. Arnold here is also giving advance notice of his own edition of Burke's *Letters, Speeches and Tracts on Irish Affairs* which appeared at the beginning of June, 1881.

246:36–247:2. "Tracts Relative to the Laws against Popery in Ireland," chapt. iii, pt. 2, ¶5.

247:8–22. First "Letter to Sir Hercules Langrishe, Bart." (1792), half-way through.

247:23–27. "Letter to a Peer of Ireland on the Penal Laws against Irish Catholics" (1782), ¶21 and final paragraph.

247:28–36. "Letter to Richard Burke, Esq.," ¶¶25, 23, 21.

248:1–7. First Letter to Langrishe, ¶7. Burke wrote "one of these bodies was . . ." The final phrase is an adaptation to the Irish of the biblical "hewers of wood and drawers of water" (i.e., slaves).— Joshua 9:21, 23.

248:11–15. First Letter to Langrishe, five-sixths through.

248:15–20. "Two Letters to Gentlemen in the City of Bristol" (1778), I, ¶6.

248:20–25. "Second Letter to Sir Hercules Langrishe" (1795), ¶4; "Letter to William Smith, Esq." (1795), ¶8.

248:30–31. "The King said to everybody who came near him that the book was a good book, a very good book, and every gentleman ought to read it."—Morley, *Burke*, p. 152.

248:32–35. "Letter on the Affairs of Ireland" (1797), ¶5.

248:36–249:2. Eckermann, *Gespräche*, I, 204 (July 9, 1827), jotted in Arnold's pocket diary at the beginning of 1881.—*Note-Books*, ed. Lowry, p. 350.

249:3. In 1800, largely through the efforts of Pitt in London, the Irish Parliament voted to end its independent existence and to unite the Kingdom of Ireland with the already United Kingdom of England and Scotland. Thereafter Ireland would send representatives to the Parliament in Westminster.

249:13–15. "Letter on the Affairs of Ireland," ¶13.

249:17–18. "In fact the Union of 1800 was not only a great crime, but was also, like most crimes, a great blunder. . . . [But] I cannot agree with those who believe that the arrangement of 1782 could have been permanent. . . . A Union of some kind was inevitable. It was simply a question of time, and it must some day have been demanded by Irish opinion. At the same time it would not, I think, have been such a Union as that of 1800."—W. E. H. Lecky, "Henry Grattan," *The Leaders of Public Opinion in Ireland* (New York, 1872), pp. 194–96.

249:30. In 1793 Roman Catholics gained the franchise in Ireland but were still denied the right to sit in the Irish Parliament. One of the promises made to induce them to support the Union in 1800 was that this restriction would be removed. George III, however, declined to permit his ministers to keep their promise and Roman Catholics were barred from the Imperial Parliament until an act of 1829 finally granted them "emancipation."

249:32–33. Lecky, *Leaders of Public Opinion*, p. 132. The "penal laws" against the Roman Catholics were imposed during the reigns of William III and his successors; they were for the most part relieved in 1774–92. See p. 58:30n.

250:8–10. Tithes—compulsory taxes to support the (Episcopalian) Church of Ireland—were collected directly from the peasantry until 1838, when they became a charge upon the landlords and were thereafter concealed in the rents. In 1869 the Church of Ireland was disestablished. The Land Act of 1870 provided that when a tenant not in debt gave up his land he must be compensated for improvements he had made. It did not prevent the landlord from fixing the level of rents at his will and evicting tenants who were in arrears. It gave the force of law everywhere (as Arnold points out on p. 254) to the custom which had grown up in the northern province of Ulster by which the tenant was recognized as having something salable in the intangible values and condition of the farm, distinct from the landlord's rights in the land itself.

250:26. "Doing As One Likes" is Arnold's title for the second chapter of *Culture and Anarchy*.

251:25–27. "Letter to Richard Burke," last paragraph.

251:34–36. "Tracts on the Popery Laws," chapt. iii, pt. 2, ¶4.

252:31–36. "Reflections on the Revolution in France," two-fifths through.

253:18–22. "Letter to Richard Burke," ¶25. Burke does not name Cromwell; he says merely "a regicide usurper."

254:16–22. "Tracts on the Popery Laws," chapt. iv, ¶6.

256:14–15. Morley speaks of Burke's *Address to the King* (1777), "where each sentence falls on the ear with the accent of some golden-tongued oracle of the wise gods."—*Burke*, p. 212.

256:17–22. "Letter on the Affairs of Ireland," ¶5.

256:32–34. See p. 240:10–15.

257:20–21. Arnold's close friend John Duke Coleridge became Lord Chief Justice of England on November 29, 1880. On October 12, 1881, after a visit to Ireland, Arnold wrote to Coleridge: "The Irish press was a new thing to me: it is like the Jacobin press in the heat of the French Revolution. I don't see how Ireland is to settle down while such stimulants to the people's hatred and disaffection are applied every day. But our English pedants will continue to believe in the divine and saving effect, under all circumstances, of right of meeting, right of speaking, right of printing. As long as it is a game of words between Gladstone and Parnell, the English constituencies may be delighted, but the temper of Ireland will be neither cowed nor improved."—E. H. Coleridge, *Life & Correspondence of John Duke Lord Coleridge* (London, 1904), II, 307.

Samuel Morley (1809–86), one of England's largest textile manufacturers and a staunch Congregationalist, was a member of Parliament for Nottingham in 1865–66 and for Bristol from 1868 to 1885.

Originally opposed to state intervention in education, he changed his ground, supported the Elementary Education Act of 1870, and sat on the London School Board from 1870 to 1876. Intelligent and generous, he stood nevertheless for many of the Liberal programs Arnold tended to ridicule. He was an admirer of Dr. Thomas Arnold and named one of his sons Arnold.

258:29–31. See p. 269:8–10.

258:36–259:1. "Eighty Years," *Nineteenth Century* IX, 412 (March, 1881).

259:10–14. John Bright (1811–89), a Quaker and a Lancashire industrialist, was the most vigorous spokesman for the Nonconformists among the Liberal leaders in Parliament. John Carvell Williams (1821–1907) was for more than fifty years a leader of the Liberation Society, which aimed at Church disestablishment, and was an influential writer for *The Nonconformist* newspaper. Jesse Collings (1831–1920) was one of the founders of the National Education League that advocated free and non-sectarian elementary education, was associated with Joseph Chamberlain in the municipal reform movement in Birmingham, and entered Parliament in 1880.

259:16–17. See p. 266:34–35.

259:23–25. See p. 238:16–21.

259:35–36. A phrase attributed to *The Daily Telegraph* in Arnold's Preface to *Higher Schools and Universities in Germany* (1874), *Prose Works*, ed. Super, VII, 129.

260:4–5. See p. 240:21–22.

260:13. Charles Haddon Spurgeon (1834–92) was a popular Baptist preacher whose Metropolitan Tabernacle in Southwark (Surrey) held more than 7000 persons. In *Culture and Anarchy* Arnold alluded to a meeting in the Tabernacle, presided over by John Bright, in support of the resolutions looking forward to disestablishment of the Church of Ireland.—*Prose Works*, ed. Super, V, 194–98.

206:25–26. See p. 239:26–27.

260:27. "And the Word was made flesh, and dwelt among us, . . . full of grace and truth."—John 1:14.

260:38–261:1. An expression of Bishop Butler's that Arnold was fond of quoting: "Things and actions are what they are, and the consequences of them will be what they will be; why then should we desire to be deceived?"—Sermon VII, "Upon the Character of Balaam," ¶16; *Works*, ed. W. E. Gladstone (Oxford, 1896), II, 134.

261:24. John Morley, one of the most energetic and intelligent of the Liberals, was a friend of Arnold's and editor of the *Fortnightly Review*.

261:29–30. For the Penal Code, see p. 249:32n. Louis XIV in 1685 revoked the 87-year-old Edict of Nantes, which had granted religious toleration to the French Protestants.

262:2–3. See p. 248:19–20.

262:8–9. Gladstone introduced his new Irish Land Bill in the House of Commons on April 7, 1881.

262:30–33. First Letter to Langrishe, ¶9 from end.

263:4–5. See p. 247:28–29.

263:11–16. "Letter to a Peer of Ireland," final paragraph. The first sentence is paraphrase, not quotation.

263:16–17. "Letter to Richard Burke, Esq.," ¶25.

264:2–4. See p. 251:34–36.

264:34–35. Arnold described Stein's Prussian land reforms of 1811 in two letters to *The Pall Mall Gazette* in November, 1866.—*Prose Works*, ed. Super, V, 57–64.

265:3–4. Gladstone's bill set up a three-man court with the power, if appealed to, to fix a fair rental for a piece of land which should be unchanged for fifteen years, and which would have the effect of a fifteen-year lease on behalf of the tenant. The same court would have the power to fix the value of the tenant-right in case of dispute over it with the landlord. Acting as a Land Commission, the three-man tribunal might also advance up to three-fourths of the purchase price to any tenant who wished to buy from a willing landlord, and might itself buy from a willing landlord for resale. It could likewise advance money for purposes of emigration.

265:16–19. The right of the tenant to transfer, for a consideration, the good will and other intangible values inherent in the land he held was, said Gladstone in presenting his new bill, "rooted in the history of Ireland and in the ideas of the Irish people," and was "recommended by a multitude of practical advantages."—*Times*, April 8, 1881, p. 7, col. 4.

266:10–14. Letter of November 25, 1793; *Correspondence of Edmund Burke*, ed. Charles William, Earl Fitzwilliam, and Richard Bourke (London, 1844), IV, 201–2, with omissions; partially jotted in Arnold's pocket diary at the beginning of 1886.—*Note-Books*, ed. Lowry, p. 423.

266:28–29. In a letter to *The Daily News* on January 22, 1881, Robert Lowe, Lord Sherbrooke, contended for the "observation of the commandment 'Thou shalt not steal' " in the handling of the Irish land question and denounced the lawless tyranny of Land League or Parliament which tends to destroy "security of the fruit of labour and enterprise, on which the whole structure of society reposes." *The Pall Mall Gazette* thereupon with some amusement

referred to Sherbrooke as "a champion of the eighth commandment."—January 22, 1881, p. 4.

266:30–31. The sovereign at his coronation took an oath to
"maintain the laws of God, the true profession of the gospel, and the
Protestant reformed religion as it is established by law." Burke discussed the impact of this oath on the treatment of Irish Catholics in
the middle of his first Letter to Sir Hercules Langrishe.

266:31–33. *The Times*, February 6, 1873, p. 9, col. 3 (leading
article), quoted by Arnold in his Preface to *Higher Schools and
Universities in Germany* (1874), *Prose Works,* ed. Super, VII, 121,
128–29.

266:33–35. Quoted *ibid.,* VII, 121.

267:17–19. See p. 240:12–15.

267:20–27, 268:1–3. Letter of September 26, 1775; *Correspondence,* II, 72.

268:6–9. Plato *Gorgias* 521 D, jotted in Arnold's pocket diary
for September 26, 1872, and February 23, 1873, and quoted in his
Preface to *Higher Schools and Universities in Germany* (1874).—
Note-Books, ed. Lowry, pp. 183, 196; *Prose Works,* ed. Super, VII,
130.

268:30. See p. 138:36.

269:8–10. "Playing Mr. Parnell's Game" (on his speech at Waterford, December 5), *Pall Mall Gazette,* December 7, 1880, p. 1; jotted
in Arnold's pocket diary for August 19.—*Note-Books,* ed. Lowry,
p. 342.

269:10–13. Speaking at Waterford, December 5, 1880; reported in
The Times next day, p. 10, col. 3, and jotted in Arnold's pocket
diary for September 7.—*Note-Books,* ed. Lowry, p. 344.

270:9. "Consummation" and "millennium" are both terms from
the apocalyptic books of the Bible: Daniel 9:27; Revelation 20:2,
3, 4, 7.

270:14–15. See p. 248:19–20.

271:8–10. "One obvious criticism on Cobden's work, and it has
often been made, is that he was expecting the arrival of a great social
reform from the mere increase and more equal distribution of material wealth. . . . He wrote to a friend: 'Nations have not yet learnt
to bear prosperity, liberty, and peace. They will learn it in a higher
state of civilization.' . . . He conceived a certain measure of material
prosperity, generally diffused, to be an indispensable instrument of
social well-being."—John Morley, *The Life of Richard Cobden*
(London, 1879), concluding paragraphs.

271:15–20. Arnold repeatedly listed these "powers"; see pp. 26–27.

271:24. Matthew 4:4 (Luke 4:4).

271:27–28. Eugène Goblet, comte d'Alviella, "La Mission de l'Angleterre dans l'Inde," *Revue des Deux Mondes,* 3d. pér., XVI, 620 (August 1, 1876); quoted at the beginning of Arnold's essay on "Falkland" (1877), *Prose Works,* ed. Super, VIII, 188.

271:31–32. Psalm 37:11 (Vulgate 36:11); see Matthew 5:5.

271:34–37. "La Révolution pour l'idéal," *Impressions et souvenirs* (Paris, 1896), p. 254; jotted in Arnold's pocket diary at the beginning of 1882 and quoted in his essay on "George Sand" (1877).— *Note-Books,* ed. Lowry, p. 367; *Prose Works,* ed. Super, VIII, 232.

272:4–5. "Réflexions sur divers sujets," no. 37; *Oeuvres,* ed. D.-L. Gilbert (Paris, 1857), I, 96; jotted in Arnold's pocket diary for April 2, 1882, and at the beginning of 1887 and 1888.—*Note-Books,* ed. Lowry, pp. 372, 427, 435.

272:23–26. "Daniel O'Connell," *Leaders of Public Opinion in Ireland,* pp. 252–54.

273:5–6. See pp. 8, 38, 158.

273:22. In order to recuperate from a serious illness, Gladstone on August 26, 1880, sailed from Gravesend on the steamer *Grantully Castle* for a cruise around the British Isles. On the first day out, he sat on the bridge "all the morning, laughing over 'David Copperfield.' "—*Times,* August 28, p. 8, col. 3. On October 14, Arnold wrote to his colleague Joshua Fitch: "I have this year been reading David Copperfield for the first time. [He was reading it aloud to his younger daughter Nelly in the evenings.] Mr. Creakle's school at Blackheath is the type of our ordinary middle-class schools, and our middle class is satisfied that so it should be."—*Letters,* ed. Russell. Arnold's pocket diary, however, indicates that he may have read *David Copperfield* in 1852.—*Note-Books,* ed. Lowry, p. 551. See J. Lucas, "Dickens and Arnold," *Renaissance & Modern Studies,* XVI (1972).

274:4. "This is now bone of my bones, and flesh of my flesh (Adam of Eve).—Genesis 2:23.

274:10–13. The description comes from *David Copperfield,* beginning of chapter vi and of chapter ix.

274:15–25. *David Copperfield,* end of chapter vii.

274:26–275:7. Sabine Baring-Gould devotes half his chapter on German education to the experiences reported by a German university graduate as foreign language teacher in English private academies. "I have compared his experiences with those of another German, and I find the report of both is the same."—*Germany, Present and Past* (London, 1879), I, 261–82. (Variant) Baring-Gould in fact lived until 1924.

276:2–3. See p. 148:24–26.

276:30–277:8. Edward Murdstone, a wine merchant, was David Copperfield's stepfather; Jane Murdstone was Edward's sister. Arnold quotes from the latter part of chapt. x and the early part of chapt. iv.

277:23. See p. 159:5.

277:24. William Bence Jones, a landowner in the western part of County Cork, who claimed to have spent £25,000 in the improvement of his estate, dated from the Athenaeum Club a long letter to *The Times* couched in unmitigated language of the free-trade political economists; the essence of it was that most Irish landlords were very fair, that most Irish tenants had no grievance, and that the new proposals of the Land Bill, by removing the competitive incentive to hard work, by rewarding even the tenant "who has wholly run out his land, as is quite without exception the case with those who are turned out for non-payment of rent, or if he has drunk himself to ruin," were simply catastrophic. Jones also believed firmly in emigration to thin out the population, relieve the charge upon the boards of guardians, and get rid of the criminal class. "Every one who gets into any trouble, social, criminal, or any other, goes at once, women as well as men."—April 21, 1881, p. 10, cols. 5–6. The *D.N.B.* remarks that Jones "was never popular" in his district of Ireland.

278:26–33. *Prose Works*, ed. R. Gottfried, p. 96. Spenser wrote "can find."

278:33–38. "We have in this kingdom but about 600 incumbents, and I fear 3000 popish priests, and the bulk of our clergy have neither parsonage-houses nor glebes: and yet till we can get more Churches or Chapels and more resident clergymen, instead of getting ground of the papists, we must lose to them, as in fact we do in many places, the descendants of many of *Cromwell's* officers and soldiers here being gone off to popery."—Boulter to the Duke of Newcastle, March 7, 1727; *Letters Written by His Excellency Hugh Boulter, D.D., Lord Primate of All Ireland, &c., to Several Ministers of State in England* (Dublin, 1770), I, 179.

279:12. Quinion is first described in *David Copperfield*, chapt. ii.

279:25–26. See p. 145:5–6.

279:26–27. "The dissidence of dissent and the Protestantism of the Protestant religion," an expression drawn from Burke's speech, "On Conciliation with the Colonies," one-fourth through, was the motto of *The Nonconformist*, weekly newspaper of the Dissenters. Arnold ridiculed the motto in the first chapter of *Culture and Anarchy* (1867) and frequently thereafter.—*Prose Works*, ed. Super, V, 101.

279:29–30. A letter signed "E. B." in *The Nonconformist*, January 29, 1873, p. 113; quoted by Arnold in his Preface to *Higher Schools and Universities in Germany* (1874) and in "Irish Catholicism and British Liberalism" (1878); *Prose Works*, ed. Super, VII, 106; VIII, 326, 339.

279:32–33. The City Companies are descendants of the guilds, societies of men engaged in the same occupation within the City of London (that part of the metropolis north of the Thames that had been enclosed within the old city walls and extends from the Tower of London on the east to Temple Bar on the west); their annual banquets are matters of great ceremony. On the site of the demolished Temple Bar at the western end of Fleet Street there was erected in 1880 a stone shaft surmounted by a bronze Griffin (symbol of the City of London) that caused a great deal of merriment; it still stands.

279:36. Dublin Castle, seat of the lords lieutenant of Ireland and place of confinement of many an Irish rebel patriot, was the administrative center of the British government in Ireland. It is architecturally undistinguished enough to make clear the irony of Arnold's remark.

280:20–23. In the House of Commons, April 8, 1881; reported in *The Times* next day, p. 9, col. 6, and jotted in Arnold's pocket diary for January 30.—*Note-Books*, ed. Lowry, p. 352.

280:24–26. Speaking at Birmingham, October 26, 1880; reported in *The Times* next day, p. 10, col. 4, and jotted in Arnold's pocket diary at the beginning of that year.—*Note-Books*, ed. Lowry, p. 333.

281:3–6. Fourteen members of the Irish Land League, including five members of Parliament headed by Parnell, were tried at the Court of Queen's Bench in Dublin on nineteen counts of conspiracy by entering into an illegal combination to induce by threats the Irish tenants to withhold their rents and to bring pressure that would dissuade persons from bidding for goods taken in execution for rent and from hiring any farm from which a tenant had been evicted. The language Arnold cites is printed in *The Times* of November 4, 1880, p. 6, col. 1. After a trial that consumed twenty-one days and cost vast sums of money, the jury on January 25, 1881, could not agree and the defendants were released. As Arnold indicates, the defendants were commonly referred to as "the traversers."

281:8–9. Tennyson, "You ask me, why, tho' ill at ease," lines 11–12.

281:17–18. Leading article on the Boer insurrection in the Transvaal, January 10, 1881, p. 9, col. 4; jotted in Arnold's pocket diary at the beginning of that year.—*Note-Books*, ed. Lowry, p. 351.

281:29–32. "The first thing a white person of any class at all does here, is to set up Kafirs under him, whom he knocks about as much as he dares, complaining all the time of their ignorance and stupidity. Everybody turns at once into a master and an independent gentleman with black servants under him, and the result is that it is impossible to get the simplest thing properly done, for the white people are too fine, and the black ones too ignorant or too lazy."— Mary Ann, Lady Barker, *A Year's Housekeeping in South Africa* (London, 1877), pp. 207–8.

282:7. John Gordon Sprigg (1830–1913), son of a Baptist minister at Ipswich, emigrated to the Cape Colony, where he received a free farm in 1861. He became prime minister of the colony during the Kafir War of 1877–78, and held that post for thirteen of the next twenty-six years. The *D.N.B.* describes him as "completely lacking in humour."

282:8. Graham Berry (1822–1904), educated in Chelsea and a shopkeeper in the King's Road, emigrated to Victoria (Australia) in 1852 and became a general storekeeper and wine and spirit merchant there. He bought a newspaper, entered politics, and was prime minister from August to October, 1875; from May, 1877, to March, 1880; and from August, 1880, to July, 1881. When an administrative deadlock with the upper house of the legislature left the colony without money, Berry preferred dismissal of the public servants to borrowing.

282:11–12. The Society of Arts, chartered in 1847 under the presidency of the Prince Consort, was the moving force behind the Great Exhibition of 1851 and the International Exhibition of 1862. "[Creakle] is not a schoolmaster now," David Copperfield tells Traddles near the end of his history. "He is retired. He is a Middlesex Magistrate."—chapt. lxi.

283:10–15. Arnold dwelt at greater length on Carlyle's general doctrines, especially as they are presented in *Sartor Resartus*, in his essay on "Emerson" (1883), *Prose Works*, ed. Super, vol. X. In an article on Thomas Carlyle in *Le Temps* of February 11, 1881, Edmond Scherer spoke of the devastating influence of Carlyle's mannered style upon his successors, and praised those few who remained content to be simple and sincere. "M. Matthew Arnold a, j'imagine, autant d'idées dans la tête que Carlyle et autant de poésie dans l'âme que M. Ruskin, et il ne se croit pas obligé pour cela de parler comme un mystagogue."—*Études sur la littérature contemporaine* (Paris, 1886), VII, 67. Arnold thought this a "charming compliment."

283:31. Arnold dated his satirical *Friendship's Garland* letters from Grub Street, the proverbial residence of the London hack writer. See *Prose Works*, ed. Super, V, 32.

284:3–6. Plato *Republic* VI, 493 A-B.

284:19–26. On March 3, 1882, Arnold sent Lady Frederick Cavendish a copy of *Irish Essays* with a note: "I promised that I would some day send you my attack on Lord Frederick, and now I send you not only one attack upon him, but two! [See p. 305:10.] I wish he would be Christian enough to return good for evil, by saying a word some day for middle class education." About two months later, Lord Frederick was assassinated in Dublin, where he had gone to succeed Arnold's brother-in-law, W. E. Forster, as Chief Secretary.

285:5–16. George Berkeley's *The Querist* was published anonymously in three parts in 1735, 1736, and 1737; it consisted solely of 895 rhetorical questions on the condition of Ireland, without discussion. In a version published with the author's name in 1750, a good many queries were omitted, a few added, and the final number became 595. Arnold quotes nos. 90, 436, 444, and from the cancelled queries, pt. ii, no. 253.

285:22–23. See p. 267:26–27.

[PREFACE TO BURKE]

Lord Coleridge once recalled seeing Matthew Arnold as a seven-year-old lad at Laleham placed upon a table to recite Burke, which he did with great gusto. Burke was always a favorite political philosopher of Arnold's: his wisdom and insight transcended the practical failure to perceive the direction of events in the future of Europe. On January 21, 1880, Arnold wrote to Ernest Fontanès: "You should order a small volume on Burke by John Morley, published by Macmillan, London. It is a cheap book, costing but half-a-crown, and you will find it very suggestive. Burke, like Wordsworth, is a great force in that epoch of concentration, as I call it, which arose in England in opposition to the epoch of expansion declaring itself in the French Revolution. The old order of things had not the virtue which Burke supposed. The Revolution had not the banefulness which he supposed. But neither was the

Revolution the commencement, as its friends supposed, of a reign of justice and virtue. It was much rather, as Scherer has called it, 'un déchaînement d'instincts confus, un aveugle et immense besoin de renouvellement.' An epoch of concentration and of resistance to the crude and violent people who were for imposing their 'renouvellement' on the rest of the world by force was natural and necessary. Burke is to be conceived as the great voice of this epoch. He carried his country with him, and was in some sort a providential person. But he did harm as well as good, for he made concentration too dominant an idea with us, and an idea of which the reign was unduly prolonged. The time for expansion must come, and Burke is of little help to us in presence of such a time. But in his sense of the crudity and tyranny of the French revolutionists, I do not think he was mistaken."—*Letters*, ed. Russell.

As matters in Ireland became more and more critical, Arnold was more and more drawn to Burke's views of the state of that unhappy country in its relation with England; here Arnold found him a less blind prophet than he was about the fate of the French Revolution. The idea of bringing out a selection of Burke's principal writings on Ireland was presumably Arnold's, not his publisher's. Proofs of the text began to reach him about April 20, 1881; the Preface was not sent off until about May 10. The volume was published about June 4 at 6 *s.*; as a publishing venture it was not a success. A careful study of the impact of Burke on Arnold is the doctoral dissertation by R. C. Tobias, *Matthew Arnold and Edmund Burke* (Ann Arbor: University Microfilms, 1958).

286:1. Burke, attacking the "atheistic and infidel" philosophic writers of France, says of those of England at the beginning of the eighteenth century: "At present they repose in lasting oblivion. Who, born within the last forty years, has read one word of Collins, and Toland, . . . and that whole race who called themselves Freethinkers? Who now reads Bolingbroke? Who ever read him through?"—*Reflections on the Revolution in France*, one-third through; quoted by Arnold in "Falkland" (1877), *Prose Works*, ed. Super, VIII, 200.

288:17. Henry Grattan (1746–1820) as a member of the Irish Parliament opposed the Union in 1800, then as a member of the Imperial Parliament urged Catholic emancipation. He was buried in Westminster Abbey.

288:23–28. William Wentworth Fitzwilliam, fourth Earl Fitzwilliam (1748–1833), nephew of the Whig prime minister Rockingham (to whom Burke was at one time private secretary), like Burke left the Whig opposition and supported Pitt in the war against revolutionary France. He was lord lieutenant of Ireland for three months in 1795, but was recalled for expressing sympathy with demands for Catholic emancipation.

289:2–4. *Correspondence of the Right Honourable Edmund Burke; between the Year 1744 and the Period of His Decease, in 1797*, edited by Charles William, Earl Fitzwilliam, and Sir Richard Bourke (London: Francis and John Rivington, 1844). 4 vols.

289:7–12. "The [Irish Land] Bill of the Government, as you may be sure, is in all circumstances the best Bill that could be offered to Parliament. You do not suppose that 14 members of the Government spend days and weeks in the consideration of a measure of this kind without ascertaining in connexion with it everything everybody else can know."—Speech at the banquet of the Fishmongers' Company, April 27, 1881, reported in *The Times* next day, p. 10, col. 4.

289:15–21. November 7, 1796; *Correspondence*, IV, 351.

[A GENEVESE JUDGE]

Arnold always had a high regard for the intellectual life of Geneva. From 1864 onward the name of Alexandre Vinet frequently appeared on his reading lists and among the subjects on which he planned to write, though he never did so. Edmond Scherer he met in 1859 and corresponded with thereafter; Scherer is the subject of two of Arnold's *Mixed Essays*. One might add the name of Joseph de Maistre, a Savoyard and a Catholic, but a correspondent of the Genevese group, who caught Arnold's attention at least as early as 1863 and is also the subject of an essay in the present volume. The essay on Amiel, of course, was still in the future (1887). In 1873 Arnold referred to the *Bibliothèque universelle et revue suisse* as "one of the most seriously conducted and trustworthy reviews in Europe."—"A Speech at Westminster," *Prose Works*, ed. Super, VII, 80. And so it is not surprising that he should have undertaken to call the attention of his countrymen to the obscurely published memorial volume on Eugène Colladon, with its reprinting of all or parts of eight of Colladon's essays of 1831–51 from the *Bibliothèque universelle*. How Arnold came upon the volume we do not know— probably through Scherer, perhaps through his acquaintance Sir Louis Mallet, a British civil servant, grandson of Mallet du Pan and hence a cousin of Colladon's. His pocket diary shows him reading the little volume on June 7, 13–15, 17, and 20, and working on the article on June 18, 22, and 24; he finished it on July 6 and it appeared anonymously in *The Pall Mall Gazette* for Wednesday, July 13, 1881. He was paid 4 gns. for it—about a guinea more than he might have expected in terms of its length and the *Gazette's* rate of pay. It has been republished by Fraser Neiman, *Essays, Letters, and Reviews of Matthew Arnold* (Cambridge: Harvard University Press, 1960).

290:1. The article is a review of *Un Petit-fils de Mallet du Pan:* Eugène Colladon, *Études et fragments litteraires,* précédés d'une notice par Édouard Humbert (Genève: J. Sandoz, 1881). Arnold draws this statement and his other biographical information from Humbert's prefatory notice; see pp. viii–ix.

290:2–6. De Maistre was a correspondent of Mallet du Pan's. Sainte-Beuve's essays on the two men (1851) were collected in the fourth volume of his *Causeries.* For Arnold's parallel between de Maistre and Burke, see "Joseph de Maistre on Russia," pp. 87–88.

290:7–8. Mallet du Pan published his royalist *Considerations sur la revolution française* in 1793.

290:11–12. Colladon was born on February 1, 1805, in Lyon, and died on January 25, 1880, in Geneva. The independent republic of Geneva, in which Mallet du Pan was brought up, came to an end with annexation to revolutionary France in 1798. After the Napoleonic wars, Geneva became one of the Swiss cantons.

290:20–22. Humbert's "Notice," p. xlviii.

290:24–291:1. *Ibid.,* p. xxxiv.

291:32–292:2. *Ibid.,* pp. lx–lxi. Châtelard is about a mile and a half west of Montreux.

292:12–25. *Ibid.,* pp. lxiii–lxiv.

292:26. Selborne and Cairns, as lords chancellor in the alternating Liberal and Conservative administrations of this period, were the highest judges in England. See p. 136:16–17.

293:10–30. From Colladon's review of Jules Janin's edition of *Lettres de Mademoiselle de Lespinasse* (1848).—Colladon, pp. 105–6.

293:31–33. This echoes the apology with which Colladon begins his essay on Mlle. de Lespinasse, p. 83. "Se ruer sur cette facile pâture" is the phrase Arnold translates as "fling themselves on that easy food for talk."

294:3–12. Colladon's review of Balzac's *La Peau de Chagrin* (1831), pp. 51–52.

[AN UNREGARDED IRISH GRIEVANCE]

Arnold's concern for secondary education in England necessarily extended itself to Ireland, where the entire educational picture was in far worse state. J. P. Mahaffy's report on grammar schools for the Endowed Schools, Ireland, Commission, which Arnold read from May 31 to June 2, 1881, gave him material for an article on "Irish Grammar Schools," written from July 16–21, read in proof on July 24, and published in the August number of the *Fortnightly Review;* he was paid £25 for it. When he reprinted the piece in *Irish Essays* he altered its title to "An Unregarded Irish Grievance."

295:1–26. To the Reverend Dr. Thomas Hussey, December, 1796; *Correspondence of Edmund Burke,* ed. Charles William Earl Fitzwilliam and Richard Bourke (London, 1844), IV, 400–401, or *Letters, Speeches and Tracts on Irish Affairs by Edmund Burke,* ed. Matthew Arnold (London, 1881), pp. 435–36.

296:26–28. See pp. 148:24–26, 276:1–3.

297:13. John Pentland Mahaffy (1839–1919), professor of ancient history and later provost of Trinity College, Dublin, was an occasional correspondent of Arnold's, who among other things seconded Mahaffy's nomination for membership in the Athenaeum Club. His report as inspector of grammar schools is Appendix A (pp. 233–62, dated October 7, 1880) of the *Report* of the Endowed Schools, Ireland, Commission (Dublin, 1881). It was reviewed at some length in *The Athenaeum,* June 4, 1881, pp. 748–49.

297:28–33. The division Arnold indicates is that of the main body of the Commisioners' report, as well as of Mahaffy's portion. The Commissioners of Education in Ireland, established by statutes of 1813 and 1822, show up in the *Report* as utterly ineffective and indifferent. There were only seven Royal Free Schools in all Ireland; six of these were grammar schools, educating in all 347 pupils in 1879 (and only 28 of these were educated free); five of the schools were within the range of 16 to 46 pupils. The Erasmus Smith's schools were endowed from lands given by Smith in 1657. In 1879 there were four grammar schools (i.e., secondary schools), two Dublin intermediate schools, and 105 elementary schools. (The rules of the governing board provided that in these last there should be only three holidays in the year—a week at Christmas, a week at Easter, and a fortnight in the autumn—and that "Parents or Friends of Children shall not interfere in the Course of Education in any manner whatever," except that they might, if not members of the Church of England, withdraw their children from the catechetical instruction.) The Incorporated Society in Dublin for Promoting English Protestant Schools in Ireland, incorporated in 1733, had 16 schools in operation in 1879, ranging from 16 to 78 pupils.

298:5–7. See p. 266:31–35.

298:21–36. *Report*, p. 234.

298:37–299:20. *Report*, pp. 236, 246, 247, 251.

299:21–30. *Report*, p. 255.

299:31–300:38. *Report*, pp. 247, 255–56, the language slightly modified. Arnold uses "failing of the stock" where Mahaffy wrote "failing of the race."

301:1–19. *Report*, pp. 235, 251 and 253, 237, 240.

301:19–302:6. *Report*, pp. 240, 237, 239, 238.

302:12–21, 30–303:10. *Report*, pp. 254, 258.

303:12–15, 28–34. *Report*, p. 260.

304:5–9. Léon Gambetta (1838–82) was the son of a grocer in Cahors, in southwestern France. He was leader of the radical republicans in France and one of the most influential forces in the Chamber of Deputies after the fall of Napoleon III. He was premier of France for two months in the winter of 1881–82. Arnold's *A French Eton* (1864) is a sustained development of the thesis that the French *lycée* offers to the French middle class an education the equal of that available only to the wealthiest in England.—*Prose Works*, ed. Super, II, 262–325.

304:32–33. See p. 15:36–38n.

304:33–34. "Popular" (i.e., elementary) education was first made "a public service" in England by the Elementary Education Act of 1870.

305:10. See p. 284:19–26.

305:11–13. See p. 296:26–28 and note.

307:25–26. See p. 303:5–6.

307:36–308:7. *Report*, p. 256.

308:13–15. *Report*, p. 252. The new Royal University of Ireland, established by the Conservative government in 1879, was an examining body that incorporated the former Queen's colleges, the Catholic University of Dublin, and Trinity College, Dublin.

309:3–8. "We do not find much in the volume [Arnold's selections from Burke] applicable to the present condition of Ireland, or to recent land legislation. Most of the abuses which Burke so eloquently and powerfully denounced have passed away."—"Edmund Burke on Ireland," *The Nonconformist and Independent,*

September 15, 1881, p. 868. From its date, this cannot be the article to which Arnold refers, but the sentiment is the same.

309:20. For Murdstone and Quinion, see pp. 276–77, 279.

310:6. For Dublin Castle, see p. 279:36.

[PREFACE TO *Irish Essays*]

312:3–5. The Preface to *Poems* (1853) was in fact reprinted in the second and third editions (1854, 1857) of that work, with a few alterations, and the Preface to the Second Edition was reprinted in the third edition. Both appear in Volume I of the present edition of Arnold's *Prose Works*.

314:17–19. *Coriolanus*, I, i, 181–83.

314:36. "A politician, to do great things, looks for a *power*, what our workmen call a *purchase;* and if he finds that power, in politics as in mechanics, he cannot be at a loss to apply it."—Burke, *Reflections on the Revolution in France*, three-fifths through; cited by Arnold, with acknowledgment to Burke, in "Falkland" (1877); *Prose Works*, ed. Super, VIII, 204.

315:14–35. *Theaetetus* 174–75. Thales, the sixth century (B.C.) Ionian philosopher who was regarded as one of the Seven Sages of the ancient world, "fell into a well as he was looking up at the stars," whereupon a "clever witty Thracian handmaid . . . said, that he was so eager to know what was going on in heaven, that he could not see what was before his feet."

316:1–3. See pp. 266:33–35, 143:3.

316:8–10. This was the sense of Wellington's comment in Parliament on the Reform Bill of 1832; Arnold quoted it in *Culture and Anarchy* (1868), *Prose Works*, ed. Super, V, 135–36.

316:21–23. Ernest Renan, "Lettre à un ami d'Allemagne," *Journal des Débats*, April 16, 1879; *Discours et conférences* (Paris, 1887), p. 61; jotted in Arnold's pocket diary for May 4, 1879, March 26, 1882, January 20, 1883, and February 7, 1885.—*Note-Books*, ed. Lowry, pp. 318, 372, 390, 415.

316:24–25. Psalm 37:11 (Vulgate 36:11); see Matthew 5:5.

316:27–28. John 12:31.

316:36–317:1. Luke 17:22–23 and "Ye blind guides," Matthew 23:16, 24.

317:5–6. Perhaps "Love that will be annihilated sooner than treacherous has already made death impossible, and affirms itself no mortal but a native of the deeps of absolute and inextinguishable being."—"Heroism" (conclusion); *Essays, First Series.* Quoted also in "Thomas Gray" (1880), p. 202:36.

317:12–14. Luke 9:60, Vulgate version, jotted in Arnold's pocket diary at the beginning of 1882 and of 1887.—*Note-Books,* ed. Lowry, pp. 366, 427. See also Matthew 8:22.

Textual Notes

[TEXTS]

79w*   Poems | of | Wordsworth | Chosen and Edited by | Matthew Arnold | London | Macmillan and Co. | 1879
         Also issued with the imprint: New York | Macmillan and Co., | 1879
         Preface, pp. v–xxvi. Reprinted with alterations on large paper, September 20, 1879 (79wlp); with further alterations, November, 1879 (79wnov); 1880, 1882, with further alterations 1886, 1888, etc.

79whar Poems of Wordsworth, chosen and edited by Matthew Arnold. New York: Harper & Brothers, 1879. [Franklin Square Library, no. 82; paperbound quarto.]
         Not collated. From the first English edition; successive reprintings did not embody Arnold's subsequent alterations.

81by   Poetry | of | Byron | Chosen and Arranged by | Matthew Arnold | London | Macmillan and Co. | 1881
         Also issued with the imprint: New York | Macmillan and Co., | 1881
         Preface, pp. vii–xxxi. Reprinted on large paper, June 4, 1881.

81byhar Poetry of Byron, chosen and arranged by Matthew Arnold. New York: Harper & Brothers, 1881. [Franklin Square Library, no. 208; paperbound quarto.]
         Not collated.

81bu   Letters | Speeches and Tracts | on Irish Affairs | by | Edmund Burke | Collected and Arranged by | Matthew Arnold | with a Preface | London | Macmillan and Co. | 1881
         Preface, pp. v–x.

* For 79 read 1879, etc.

82   Irish Essays | and Others | by | Matthew Arnold | London | Smith, Elder, & Co., 15 Waterloo Place | 1882 | *All rights reserved*

83m   Mixed Essays | Irish Essays | and Others | by | Matthew Arnold | New York | Macmillan and Co. | 1883

91   Irish Essays | and Others | by | Matthew Arnold | Popular Edition | London | Smith, Elder, & Co., 15 Waterloo Place | 1891 | *All rights reserved*
         This edition has no textual authority and is not collated.

88   Essays in Criticism | Second Series | by | Matthew Arnold | London | Macmillan and Co. | and New York | 1888 | *All rights reserved*
         Posthumously collected and published.

["ECCE, CONVERTIMUR AD GENTES"]

Fortn.   "'Ecce, Convertimur ad Gentes,'" *Fortnightly Review* XXXI (n.s. XXV), 238–52 (February, 1879)
       Reprinted 82, 83m, 91 (not collated)

1:11. to its inspectors   *Fortn.*

2:11. *no ¶ Fortn.*

2:18. of individuals and of localities   *Fortn.*, 82; of individuals and localities   83m

2:19. in that; the State   *Fortn.*

2:31. *no ¶ Fortn.*

3:1. it is abundantly   *Fortn.*

3:8. *no ¶ Fortn.*

3:24. are a testimony, as it seems to me,   *Fortn.*

3:27. of intelligence and knowledge,   *Fortn.*

3:28–29. *to follow . . . knowledge   not in Fortn.*

3:30. *no ¶ Fortn.*

3:35. the performance . . . the promise,   *Fortn.*

4:29. Institute; they   *Fortn.*

4:32. *no ¶ Fortn.*

4:37. have been right. Something is always gained by setting our mark high. George Herbert says—

"Who aimeth at the sky
Shoots higher much than he that means a tree."

And I was pausing the other day, for other and personal reasons, over a passage in an earlier and much greater poet than George Herbert—the Italian Dante, when it occurred to me that the passage had a good application to such institutions as this College of yours, which I had then been just invited to address. The passage 5 is one describing the end of a favourite hero of old Greek poetry, the much-enduring and ingenious Ulysses, whose end is also the subject of one of Mr. Tennyson's finest poems. Ulysses and his men had been all through that long ten years' war in Troy; they had been battered about for ten years more on their way home, 10 and at last they had got home to their Greek island. But Ulysses was possessed with the longing still to see and know more of men and of men's doings, more of nature; he proposed to go *after the sun*, as he expressed it, outside the Mediterranean, the inland sea on whose shore the Greeks lived, out over the great and wide 15 ocean towards the west and south, and to acquaint himself with the unexplored and unknown world. "I and my companions were old and slow," he says, when this desire came upon him. He imparted it to them in an earnest speech, exhorting them to bestow, with him, the little of life which remained to them upon this high 20 enterprise; and he concluded with these words: "Consider whereunto ye are born; made ye were not to live like brutes, but to follow virtue and knowledge." And this speech so moved his hearers, that after it, says Ulysses, "even if I had wanted to turn them back from the enterprise, I could not have done so." 25

This is the story, and now for the application. The application lies in the appeal to the natural desire for virtue and knowledge in men, and in its force even amidst many and great discouragements. "I and my companions are old and slow," a man of imperfect training and scanty leisure who joins one of these Working 30 Men's Colleges may say; "we have not the helps and aptitudes which come of constant instruction, constant mental practice; our time has been spent on other things; our leisure is short, there are plenty of other calls on it which are attractive; and yet here I am, with all this to dissuade me, going after the sun, setting off into the 35 vast and untried ocean of knowledge, where so many have foundered, at a high, half-understood call to know myself and the world. What can be driving me?" What is driving him is the correspondence of the call, however often neglected and however imperfectly obeyed, with the genuine aspiration of human nature. 40 To arrive at a *Fortn.*

5:3. of man. "Consider whereunto ye are born; ye were not made

to live like brutes, but to follow virtue and knowledge."
All this some of you may think vague and highflown, but I shall
be prosaic enough presently. And all the   *Fortn.*
5:12. is sound, it is   *Fortn.*
5:15. *no* ¶ *Fortn.*
5:20. stupid; all   *Fortn.*
5:21. was singularly   *Fortn.*
6:10. as they are,   *Fortn.*
6:23. politician; I   *Fortn.*
6:25. have very little interest —   *Fortn.*
6:30. *no* ¶ *Fortn.*
7:3. should lay them before you with   *Fortn.*
7:11. since that period I   *Fortn.*
7:24. are not dreamed of   *Fortn.*
8:20. *no* ¶ *Fortn.*
8:21. reason—it worked well.   *Fortn.*
8:38. *no* ¶ *Fortn.*
9:8. further   *Fortn.*, 82
9:15. *no* ¶ And the word vulgarised as   *Fortn.*
9:18. them. Whether   *Fortn.*
9:21. not, however, whether   *Fortn.*
9:30–31. inequality. They may   *Fortn.*
9:36. statesman that France   *Fortn.*
10:15. in any others,   *Fortn.*, 82
10:21. *no* ¶ *Fortn.*
11:6. anywhere, except in   *Fortn.*
11:37–38. and . . . *Equality   not in Fortn.*
12:5. or . . . manner   *not in Fortn.*
12:12. measure of reform.   *Fortn.*, 82; measure to reform.   83m
13:14. must soon come   *Fortn.*
13:27, 37. *no* ¶ *Fortn.*
14:14. *no* ¶ *Fortn.*
14:17–18. limited; those   *Fortn.*
14:27–28. Discourage them in their   *Fortn.*
15:2–3. turn out untrue; and at any   *Fortn.*
15:8. *no* ¶ *Fortn.*
15:29. and of self-assertion.   *Fortn.*
15:34. *no* ¶ *Fortn.*; yourselves to be   *Fortn.*
15:35. against the State, bureaucracy, centralisation,   *Fortn.*
17:4. it so mars and   *Fortn.*
17:7–8. ruling class which . . . much; they have them, but on the
    whole   *Fortn.*

17:12. *no* ¶ *Fortn.*
17:16. But, as it is at present, our middle class *cannot* *Fortn.*
17:18. may be said *Fortn.*
17:28. have really no *Fortn.*
17:32. *no* ¶ *Fortn.*
17:36. every year among *Fortn.*
18:6. most inferior that *Fortn.*
18:7–8. And this must tell *Fortn.*
18:27. looked round, and saw *Fortn.*
19:1. carrying it on. *Fortn.*
19:8. having striven to know *Fortn.*
19:10. to . . . designs, *not in Fortn.*
19:10–11. "Consider, consider whereunto *Fortn.*

[A SPEECH AT ETON]

Cornh. "A Speech at Eton," *Cornhill Magazine* XXXIX, 538–49 (May, 1879).
Ecl. "A Speech at Eton," *Eclectic Magazine*, n.s. XXX, 13–21 (July, 1879). Not collated.
   Reprinted 82, 83m, 91 (not collated)

20:9–10. have entered here *Cornh.*
20:26–27. here, no more could they at *Cornh.*
21:8. schoolboy: this *Cornh.*
21:13. *no* ¶ *Cornh.*
21:25. nervously what is *Cornh.*
21:33. to me that what *Cornh.*
21:34–35. world; that for *Cornh.*
22:3. *no* ¶ *Cornh.*
22:30. everything he read *Cornh.*
22:38. Theognis in that *Cornh.*
23:33. just for one lecture, *Cornh.*
24:6. from prejudice, freedom *Cornh.*
24:37–38. the Asiatic more tractable." *Cornh.*, 82, 83m; *corrected from Hellwald*
26:4–5. to be once named *Cornh.*
26:19. me. These twenty *Cornh.*
27:18. is three-fourths *Cornh.*
27:30. *no* ¶ *Cornh.*, 82
27:31. for us, as I have more than once had occasion to say, with the *Cornh.*

27:37. genius. And so   *Cornh.*
28:21. temple there called   *Cornh.*
28:28. *no* ¶   *Cornh.*
29:5. a Hellenic state,   *Cornh.*
29:33. forth; the   *Cornh.*
30:21. to me probable that   *Cornh.*
30:22. the words of   *Cornh.*
30:30. *no* ¶   *Cornh.*
31:8. is to come is vanity.   *Cornh.*; All that cometh is vanity.   *A.V.*
31:12–13. Let . . . people.   *not in Cornh.*
31:14. *no* ¶   The old rigid order breaks   *Cornh.*
31:15. scene; it   *Cornh.*
32:9–10. had, in the shadow of   *Cornh.*
32:14. order, outweighing all other   *Cornh.*
32:17. and after   *Cornh.*
32:19–20. Attic nation, the Hellenic people, could not   *Cornh.*
32:22. mind set on other   *Cornh.*
32:24–25. which had not been enough followed, of which it strongly
  felt   *Cornh* .
32:26. It gave its   *Cornh.*
32:29. It allowed itself to   *Cornh.*
33:27. people, too, oscillated and   *Cornh.*
33:38. rolled on, and the Hellenic   *Cornh.*
34:15. reforming spirit, which was   *Cornh.*
34:20. there you have the   *Cornh.*
34:31. from the moral that   *Cornh.*
35:7–8. though not many,   *Cornh.*
35:8–9. think that that is   *Cornh.*
35:9–10. Probably you will have   *Cornh.*
35:14–15. the century . . . power,   *not in Cornh.*
35:27. proceed to have more   *Cornh.*
35:28–29. certainly to hear a great many scientific lectures,   *Cornh.*

[WORDSWORTH]

Macm.   "Wordsworth," *Macmillan's Magazine* XL, 193–204 (July,
          1879).
Appl.   "Wordsworth," *Appleton's Journal,* n.s. VII, 138–46 (Au-
          gust, 1879). Not collated.
Lit.   "Wordsworth," *Littell's Living Age* CXLII, 323–32 (Au-
          gust 9, 1879). Not collated.

Ecl.   "Wordsworth," *Eclectic Magazine*, n.s. XXX, 333–45 (September, 1879). Not collated.
Reprinted 79w, 79wlp, 79wnov (&c.), 88.

36:13. him say, that,   *Macm.*
37:22. in 1852,   *mispr. Macm.*, 79w; *corr.* 79wlp
37:26. waned; Wordsworth's   *Macm.*
37:31. undetermined. The abundance   *Macm.*
37:33–34. offence to some.   *Macm.*
38:4. vanity." And when M. Renan presents himself to the French
Academy,—the only authentic dispensers, he says, of glory, of   10
"this grand light,"—he presents himself supported by M. Victor
Hugo, his "dear and illustrious master," a poet irradiated with it; a
poet "whose genius has throughout our century struck the hour
for us, has given body to every one of our dreams, wings to every
one of our thoughts." Yet probably not twenty people in that   15
magnificent assemblage, all coruscating with the beams of the
"grand light," had ever even heard of Wordsworth's name.
¶Wordsworth was   *Macm.*
38:4–5. and would certainly   *Macm.*
38:7. vanity. And it is quite impossible for us to esteem recognition   20
by the French Academy, or by the French nation, or by any single institution or nation, as so decisive a title to glory as M. Renan
supposes it. Yet we may well allow him, after these reserves, that
few   *Macm.*
38:16–17. even as seriously and eminently worthy, in   *Macm.*
39:28. and Victor   *Macm.*
39:36. thought. Along   *Macm.*
40:3–4. in one short sentence, more felicitously.   *Macm.*
40:9. all respect,"   *Macm.*
40:14. ¶Or, again, judgment may go the other way. Byron has   30
had an immense reputation, not in England only, but on the Continent. M. Taine, in his history of English literature, takes Byron
as seriously as he takes Shakspeare. Byron is the supreme and incomparable expression of the English genius after eight centuries
of preparation; he is the one single contemporary author who has   35
atteint à la cime, "reached the summit;" *Manfred* is the twin
brother of *Faust*. But then M. Scherer strikes in with his words of
truth and soberness. Remarking that "Byron is one of our French
superstitions," he points out how Byron's talent is oratorical rather
than poetical; he points out how to high and serious art, art im-   40
personal and disinterested, Byron never could rise; and how the

man in Byron, finally, is even less sincere than the poet. And by
this we may perceive that we have not in Byron what we have in
Milton and Shakspeare—a poetical reputation which time and the
authentic judgment of mankind will certainly accept and con-
secrate.

So excellent a writer and critic as M. Renan sees in M. Victor
Hugo a "beloved and illustrious master, whose voice has throughout our century struck the hour for us." Of these "strikings of the
hour" by the voice of M. Victor Hugo, none certainly was more
resonant, none was hailed with more passionate applause by his
friends, than *Hernani*. It is called for again, made to strike over
again; we have the privilege of hearing it strike in London. And
still there is no lack of applause to this work of a talent "combining," says Théophile Gautier, "the qualities of Corneille and of
Shakspeare." But I open by chance a little volume, the conversations of Goethe with the Chancellor von Müller. There I come
upon this short sentence: "Goethe said, 'Hernani' was an absurd
composition." *Hernani sei eine absurde Composition.* So speaks
this great foreign witness; a German, certainly, but a German favourable to French literature, and to France, "to which," said he,
"I owe so much of my culture!" So speaks Goethe, the critic who,
above all others, may count as European, and whose judgment on
the value of a work of modern poetry is the judgment which will,
we may be almost sure, at last prevail generally.

I come back to *Macm.*

40:38. Scott, *first added in* 79wnov
41:15. Racine, Boileau *not in Macm.*
42:22. is constantly dulled *Macm.*
42:25. is not much of an exaggeration *Macm.*, 79w; *revised* 79wlp
42:30. chilling the high-wrought *Macm.*
43:23. ¶Naturally grouped, and disengaged, moreover, from
Macm., 79w; *revised* 79wlp
43:30. remains of him, after *Macm.*
43:36. or Coleridge, *not in Macm.*, 79w, &c.; *added in* 1886
43:38. good work, his *Macm.*
44:21. that superior *Macm.*
44:26. what they will not. *Macm.*
46:9. to the word ideas *Macm.*
48:18–19. capable of exposition *all edd.; corrected from* 49:12 *and*
Stephen.
48:25–28. his philosophy the illusion. *Macm.*
48:29. more general, *Macm.*
48:31. dismiss his philosophy. *Macm.*

49:8. further *Macm.*
49:11. of the philosophy, *Macm.*
49:12. systematical *all edd.; corrected from Stephen.*
49:23. the Wordsworthian *Macm.*
51:4–5. It is great *Macm.*
51:7. simple elementary affections and *Macm.*, 79w; *revised* 79wlp
53:7–8. like this: — *Macm.*
54:10–11. pick out the kind of poems which most perfectly show *Macm.*
54:14. these he produced *Macm.*
54:18. eminent because of the *Macm.*
54:19. eminent, also, because of the *Macm.*
54:24–25. Dante, Shakspeare, Milton, even Goethe, are *Macm.;* Dante, Shakspeare, Molière, Milton, even Goethe, are 79w; *revised* 79wlp
54:28–39. *not in Macm.*
54:31–37. interesting. But it contains, I think, 79w, 79wlp (Except ... the volume *added* 79wnov)
55:5. with pleasure *Peter Bell*, *Macm.*
55:10. worthy of it; *Macm.*

[THE IRISH UNIVERSITY QUESTION]

Times "The Irish University Question," *The Times*, July 31, 1879, p. 10, cols. 4–5. Not reprinted by Arnold.
56:2. not one country *mispr. Times*

[ON POETRY]

Hundr. The | Hundred Greatest Men | Portraits | of the | One Hundred Greatest Men of History | *Reproduced from fine and rare steel engravings* | Volume I | Poetry | Poets, Dramatists, Novelists | London | Sampson Low, Marston, Searle, and Rivington | Crown Buildings, 188 Fleet Street | 1879 | (*All rights reserved*)
"Introduction to Volume I," pp. i–iii(bis)
Title: *supplied by editor*

[THE FRENCH PLAY IN LONDON]

Ninet. "The French Play in London," *Nineteenth Century* VI, 228–43 (August, 1879).

Ecl. "The French Play in London," *Eclectic Magazine*, n.s. XXX, 400–411 (October, 1879). Not collated.
Reprinted 82, 83m, 91 (not collated)

64:5, 6; 66:7. enjouement   *mispr.* 82, 83m
65:1. has just   *Ninet.*
65:16, 18. were exhibiting . . . were conducting   *Ninet.*
65:22. ¶The sense of   *Ninet.*
65:23. children; but   *Ninet.*
65:23–24. in it, we have all of   *Ninet.*
65:30–31. I will not   *Ninet.*
66:22. for the future; that   *Ninet.*
66:32. peril; perilous   *Ninet.*
67:6. all; one   *Ninet.*
67:11–12. mannerism: that something   *Ninet.*
67:21. of French   *Ninet.*
68:22. no¶   *Ninet.*
68:23. reverence   *mispr.* 82, 83m
68:24. matter; we   *Ninet.*
69:16. may assert the   *Ninet.*
69:20. if our estimate   *Ninet.*
69:21. to have been much   *Ninet.*
69:22–24. ways. We may compare the production of Corneille and Racine which we are said to underrate, we may compare it in power, in   *Ninet.*
70:9. Which Shakspeare   *Ninet.*, 82, 83m; *corrected by ed.*
70:17–18. have been attending to the contents of the   *Ninet.*
70:21. We want an   *Ninet.*
70:25. in a silver   *mispr.* 82, 83m
70:27. *Hernani:*—   *Ninet.*, 82, 83m; *corrected by ed.*
71:18. of Shakspeare, adopted or   *Ninet.*
71:29. of it remain   *Ninet.*
72:6. just use of   *Ninet.*
72:7. Chaucer; as   *Ninet.*
72:14. He is   *Ninet.*
72:25. life; comedy   *Ninet.*
72:34. him; and if   *Ninet.*
72:38. he had not   *Ninet.*
73:6–7. but . . . comedy   *not in Ninet.*
73:26-27. by virtue of   *Ninet.*
73:27–28. makes itself felt,   *Ninet.*
73:37. poet; and . . . where he   *Ninet.*

74:13. I ventured   *Ninet.*
74:23. is not inclined   *Ninet.*
75:7. Pope, but   *Ninet.*
75:21. worthy of better.   ¶*Phèdre*   *Ninet.*
75:26. *no*¶   *Ninet.*
75:34–35. that we are   *Ninet.*
76:9. of Dante or Milton.   *Ninet.*
77:8. sense for   *Ninet.*
77:10. may retain our   *Ninet.*
77:12. the classic tragedy . . . We may keep,   *Ninet.*
77:15. delightful, edifying and   *Ninet.*
77:16. even he, in   *Ninet.*
77:19. life that remain to   *Ninet.*
77:20–21. the turbulent young generation around us, that   *Ninet.*
77:23. ¶What are   *Ninet.*
77:35. all; it   *Ninet.*
78:1. ideal life is   *Ninet.; ideal is   82, 83m
78:1–4. an ideal . . . work for.   *not in Ninet.*
78:13–14. expression; it . . . drama, I say, of the   *Ninet.*
78:17–19. passions and *dévouement*, lighting   *Ninet.*
78:26–27. not homogeneous enough, not sufficiently   *Ninet.*
78:38–79:1. notwithstanding . . . generation,   *not in Ninet.*
79:5–6. is unreal,   *Ninet.*
79:9. from exercising a great   *Ninet.*
79:19. in the movement,   *Ninet.*
79:23–24. It forsook the theatre. The theatre reflected the   *Ninet.*
79:26. existence no more.   *Ninet.*
79:27. *no*¶   It came afterwards to reflect   *Ninet.*
79:29. it also recalled and   *Ninet.*
79:31. as 'the town' ceased   *Ninet.*
79:32–33. repeated the old with   *Ninet.*
79:33–34. talent, but the mass of the British middle class kept quite aloof   *Ninet.*
79:36. *no*¶   I remember that,   *Ninet.*
80:2. were some half-dozen   *Ninet.*
80:23, 25. was beginning . . . was seeking   *Ninet.*
80:30–31. live right if . . . by one point . . . by several points   *Ninet.*
81:1–3. We . . . irresistible.   *not in Ninet.*
81:4. *no*¶   *Ninet.*
81:17–18. Paris; the emancipated   *Ninet.*
81:34–35. right conclusion that we   *Ninet.*
81:36–37. the ideal of the life of the . . . of its drama.   *Ninet.*

82:8. the like defect: both   *Ninet.*
82:11. ¶What *are* we to learn then from   *Ninet.*
82:13. Theatre; what *is*   *Ninet.*
82:23–24. be played more, it . . . a lower drama still   *Ninet.*
82:34. of sound and pleasing   *Ninet.*
82:37. ¶Secondly, the   *Ninet.*
83:7. self-governing. In connexion with it is   *Ninet.*
83:12–13. from the great century, and has traditions,   *Ninet.*
83:15. results which have   *Ninet.*
83:23–24. later drama which   *Ninet.*
83:29–31. organisation which we had, in the patent . . . Shakspeare,
  we find   *Ninet.*
83:35. way, and devoid   *Ninet.*
83:37. attack; they   *Ninet.*
84:2. greatness it has   *Ninet.*
84:6. abandoned; and then,   *Ninet.*
84:12. and to press him to   *Ninet.*
84:17–18. impulse to do so, and with   *Ninet.*
84:26. them Drury Lane Theatre. Let   *Ninet.*
84:37. company; it   *Ninet.*
85:12. theatre, and then   *Ninet.*

[JOSEPH DE MAISTRE ON RUSSIA]

Quart.   "Joseph de Maistre on Russia," *Quarterly Review* CXLVIII,
    432–52 (October, 1879). Anonymous. Not reprinted by
    Arnold.

103:28. Slave   *mispr. Quart.*
108:38. invisible attraction   *Quart.; corrected from de Maistre*

[COST OF ELEMENTARY SCHOOLS]

Times   "Cost of Elementary Schools," *The Times*, October 20,
    1879, p. 6, col. 5. Not reprinted by Arnold.

[COPYRIGHT]

Fortn.   "Copyright," *Fortnightly Review* XXXIII (n.s. XXVII),
    319–34 (March, 1880).

Ecl. "Copyright," *Eclectic Magazine*, n.s. XXXI, 513–24 (May, 1880). Not collated.
  Reprinted 82, 83m, 91 (not collated)

114:16. this name, *Fortn.*, 82; his name, *mispr.* 83m
114:21–22. books of an outward . . . fashion to satisfy *Fortn.*
115:33. appetite for knowing and judging *Fortn.*
115:35–36. require for catching the first gleam; the day will dawn for *Fortn.*
116:4. 1920, *Fortn.*
116:10. *no¶ Fortn.*
116:28. a great deal *Fortn.*, 82; a good deal 83m
117:6–7. volumes of *Prince Metternich's Memoirs and Correspondence* in French, which have *Fortn.*
117:13. give the public new *Fortn.*
117:31. substitute a right *Fortn. and Commission Report*
118:11. that he can have *Fortn.*
118:13. the real point at issue between these distinguished and *Fortn.*
118:27, 36. *no¶ Fortn.*
119:1. reward; but *Fortn.*
119:6. appropriate; but then, *Fortn.*
119:8. nemesis *Fortn.*
119:11. taken him under *Fortn.*
119:12. sanctioned his *Fortn.*
119:25. ¶And this, *Fortn.*
119:30–31. *no¶ Fortn.;* But . . . it? *not in Fortn.*
119:32. is haunted by *Fortn.*
119:33–34. between things as belonging *Fortn.*
119:35. in itself and as belonging *Fortn.*
119:36. itself. His *dog,* his *Fortn.*
120:5. *no¶ Fortn.*
120:15. only; and *Fortn.*
120:20–21. say, in ideas, in spoken *Fortn.*
120:23–24. property in ideas and in spoken *Fortn.*
120:32. ownership, and a disposition *Fortn.*
121:9. meanwhile, he retains *Fortn.*
121:18–19. denies him the . . . of the pheasants *Fortn.*
121:21. appropriate; and other *Fortn.*
121:23. ownership, because of *Fortn.*
121:24–25. ownership which the law does allow him it has to *Fortn.*
121:28. to let him *Fortn.*

121:36-38. natural difficulties; but the special measures are far less *Fortn.*

122:2–3. and profit from that   *Fortn.*

122:8–9. ownership. His production is a production particularly difficult to . . . , particularly easy for   *Fortn.*

122:17. contention, and Mr. Farrer's.   *Fortn.*

122:30. easy to appropriate.   *Fortn.*

122:32–33. reasoning of Professor Huxley and of Mr. Herbert Spencer, and even the   *Fortn.*

122:38. in itself;" only,   *Fortn.*

124:12. dominions; what   *Fortn.;* Dominions; what   82

124:25. arrangement: instead   *Fortn.*

124:32. withdrawal, in effect, from the author of the   *Fortn.*

125:4. The strength of the dissatisfaction of   *Fortn.*

125:29. *no*¶   *Fortn.*

125:32. those that one has   *Fortn.*

126:30–31. their contents. The contents offered us for   *Fortn.*

127:3–5. it still, even when we have reformed our book-trade. For reforming it, the   *Fortn.*

127:16. have been saying   *Fortn.*

127:23. Copyright; Mr. Conant,   *Fortn.*

128:4. is well known,   *Fortn.*

128:8. good of our   *Fortn.,* 82, 83m; *corrected from Putnam*

128:15. in principle, but he   *Fortn.*

128:26. He alleges that   *Fortn.*

128:31. says Mr. Conant,   *Fortn.*

129:17. us; not only   *Fortn.*

129:28. place; why   *Fortn.*

129:33. as when we   *Fortn.*

130:5. as they are; our   *Fortn.*

130:8. *no*¶   *Fortn.*

130:11–12. Conant's own statement, appears   *Fortn.*

130:17. for it; if   *Fortn.*

130:21. far from true,   *Fortn.*

130:26. histories; Mr. Henry James   *Fortn.*

131:9–10. hear it said that in truth   *Fortn.*

131:17. And according to   *Fortn.*

131:18. may be true; only, if one had not   *Fortn.*

131:22. never have dragged on,   *Fortn.*

131:33. of honesty; they call   *Fortn.*

131:34. stealing; if   *Fortn.*

131:37. false; there is   *Fortn.*

132:2. respect the sense of delicacy in itself not less *Fortn.*
132:7. is highly esteemed, *Fortn.*
132:15–16. must not expect *Fortn.*
132:17. take; we *Fortn.*
132:19. stopped the Brussels *Fortn.*
132:25–26. consideration and delicacy; and, so far as it depends *Fortn.*
132:36. acts they showed, *Fortn.*
132:37. delicacy; certainly they *Fortn.*
133:6. delicacy; nor is *Fortn.*
133:11. delicacy, and English *Fortn.*
134:20. and authors cry out *Fortn.*
134:27–28. ask whether the English author can reasonably expect *Fortn.*
134:29. to copyright in America without *Fortn.*
134:32. pressing; that opinion in *Fortn.*
134:34. which it is now *Fortn.*
135:11. to the dearness *Fortn.*
135:18. *no*¶ Here, where lies *Fortn.*
135:20. books; I am *Fortn.*
135:22–23. hope they will give us copyright; but I hope, also, they will *Fortn.*

[THE FUTURE OF LIBERALISM]

Ninet. "The Future of Liberalism," *Nineteenth Century* VIII, 1–18 (July, 1880).
Reprinted 82, 83m, 91 (not collated)

136:4. parties which *Ninet.*
136:26, 28. the bad condition . . . that bad condition *Ninet.*
137:10. his; I see *Ninet.*
137:32–34. succeeded in . . . had quite . . . which they themselves supposed. *Ninet.*
137:35. *no* ¶ *Ninet.*
137:35–36. remarking, at the very most *Ninet.*
138:1. their disaster came, I kept assuring the Liberals *Ninet.*
138:9–10. successfully; but they have been *Ninet.*
138:11–12. in the days when I exhorted *Ninet.*
138:15. rather than of the *Ninet.*
138:35. who happen *Ninet.*
139:4. future; and, although *Ninet.*

139:9. ¶Let us begin by making ourselves as pleasant as we can *Ninet.*

139:10. and conceding *Ninet.*

139:24. demoralising. I will not *Ninet.*

139:32. were both very attractive and *Ninet.*

139:34–35. profoundly Liberal; and by a *Ninet*

139:37. so thinking; it turns to them from *Ninet.*

140:26–27. capable of speaking for *Ninet.*

140:29. one is quite *Ninet.*

141:9. not so. Unremittingly, however *Ninet.*

142:21. them, or impediment and *Ninet.*

142:26–27. ease; at times they get *Ninet.*

142:34. in England. The Liberals *Ninet.*

142:38. much; but *Ninet.*

143:17. Liberals, not the *Ninet.*

143:27. ¶And Liberal statesmen like *Ninet.*

143:30. are in fact continually *Ninet.*

144:2. told, of 'the cities *Ninet.*

144:37. beauty, to his *Ninet.*

145:9. such as Blackburn, Bolton, *Ninet.*

145:11. beauty, and his instinct *Ninet.*

145:13. these instincts, *Ninet.*

145:33. produce what is not *Ninet.*

146:2. say, the leaders *Ninet.*

146:5. so that it lasts long *Ninet.*

146:6. by it, or thinking, *Ninet.*

146:7–8. doing, or concerning themselves *Ninet.*

146:9–10. like St. Helens and Blackburn to *Ninet.*

146:23. begotten; but these *Ninet.*

146:26. trade, complaints of *Ninet.*

146:34. visit what Cobbett called *Ninet.*

146:36. far as Blackburn; we Londoners *Ninet.*

147:8. And at this season of *Ninet.*

147:28. we see; and his instinct for *Ninet.*

147:29. starved, for the schools *Ninet.*

147:31–32. anywhere; and its provision for *Ninet.*

148:15–16. account of *public opinion,* as it forms *Ninet.*

148:18–19. nay amongst the English *Ninet.*

148:22. *no*¶ And this great *Ninet.*

148:27. all these, to this Philistine middle class it is that a Liberal *Ninet.*

149:5–6. will deny the *Ninet.*

149:12–13. Duff's study by *Ninet.*
149:14. and the hot *Ninet.*
149:17–18. dealings . . . dealings *Ninet.*
149:34–35. dissatisfaction there may be, too, and at *Ninet.*
150:11. it; for giving the mere rudiments of knowledge to *Ninet.*
150:12. lowest class they have, indeed, sought to *Ninet.*
150:15–16. again, the great . . . community has scarcely *Ninet.*
150:28. obscurely in it all *Ninet.*
150:31–33. neglected. [*no¶*] To the need in man for *Ninet.*
151:12. for the country *Ninet.*
151:18. and starved instinct by the *Ninet.*
151:22. give satisfaction too. *Ninet.*
151:23–25. *no¶* To the instinct for intellect and knowledge they give none. To large *Ninet.*
151:26–27. abroad, they are by nature, as a class, inaccessible; *Ninet.*
151:29. yet, as they *Ninet.*
151:32–33. for the communication and *Ninet.*
152:7. turn has come to them now. *Ninet.*
152:10. so often and so much already — *Ninet.*
152:32. secret of its life, the secret of the future. *Ninet.*
152:35–36. what that secret of the community's life really is, and of the life of *Ninet.*
152:38. Hitherto they themselves have conceived it *Ninet.*
153:4–5. adversaries. With one *Ninet.*
153:6. they are in *Ninet.*
153:13–14. Let . . . light. *not in Ninet.*
153:20. his simple tools *Ninet.*
153:36. general; but *Ninet.*
154:4–5. such a line . . . such as *Ninet.*
154:15. will turn *Ninet.*
154:16–17. face, and see their imperfections and try *Ninet.*
154:18. *no¶ Ninet.*
155:5. statesmen neglect for *Ninet.*
155:12. they may have *Ninet.*
155:14–17. objects, of legalising . . . sister, of permitting . . . and of granting *Ninet.*
155:23. *no¶* Some Liberals misconceive these objects *Ninet.*
155:33–34. been in the wrong. *Ninet.*
155:35. but it takes more *Ninet.*
156:28. *no¶ Ninet.*
157:9. better to have *Ninet.*

157:21. the past, which consist *Ninet.*
157:28–29. expansion they have not *Ninet.*
157:29. adequately. For the need *Ninet.*
158:1. befalling it that cause [*sic*]; and the *Ninet.*
158:5–6. suffers signal *Ninet.*
158:9. We have *Ninet.*
158:11–12. satisfied, we have admirable political liberty and free *Ninet.*
158:14–15. ¶For our present . . . may be summed up in this: that *Ninet.*
158:28. great-grandfather, whose *Ninet.*
159:13. real remedy like the reform of the law of bequest, but invent *Ninet.*
159:19. though not so glaringly as in *Ninet.*
159:26–27. they shut their eyes to, as if *Ninet.*
159:28. like ours, inevitably *Ninet.*
159:31. ¶Not until the need in man for *Ninet.*
159:32–33. statesmen—that it includes equality as *Ninet.*
159:34. them, but cared *Ninet.*
160:1–2. to go on unto civilisation, *Ninet.*
160:9. will not satisfy *Ninet.*
160:10. Tories will from time to *Ninet.*

[THE STUDY OF POETRY]

Ward   The | English Poets | Selections | with Critical Introductions | by Various Writers | and a General Introduction by | Matthew Arnold | edited by | Thomas Humphry Ward, M.A. | Late Fellow of Brasenose College, Oxford | Vol. I | Chaucer to Donne | London | Macmillan and Co. | 1880 [1883, 1887, 1891, &c.] | [*All rights reserved*]
General Introduction, pp. xvii–xlvii. Reprinted 88
Title: Introduction *Ward;* General Introduction *Ward, Contents page; present title perhaps not Arnold's*
161:28–29. *not in* Ward
167:15. chaunt *Ward;* chant 88
169:25. xxxiii. 39, 40. *mispr.* Ward, 88
173:16. ja meis *inserted by ed.*
175:11, 181:4. in virginitee!' *Ward, 88; corrected from Chaucer*
178:1. ¶But for my *Ward*
179:12. confirm, that *Ward, 88; corrected from Chapman*

185:14–15. motto for *The Giaour,*   Ward (*1880*), *erroneously*
186:26.   *Whistle and*   Ward, 88; *O Whistle and*   Burns

[THOMAS GRAY]

Ward   The | English Poets | . . . | Vol. III | Addison to Blake | . . .
              Arnold's Introduction to Gray, pp. 303–16; reprinted 88

189:28–29. *not in* Ward; vol. iv.   *mispr.* 88
192:33. dry consciousness   *mispr. Ward*
194:15. follows?   *mispr.* 88
195:25. partly left   Ward, 88; *corrected from Gray*
195:34. an idea   *mispr.* 88
196:31. has unhappily   Ward, 88; *corrected from Gray*
197:1. down alone   Ward, 88; *corrected from Gray*
197:2. colouring of light   *mispr. Ward,* 88
204:12. in his style   *Ward*

[JOHN KEATS]

Ward   The | English Poets | . . . | Vol. IV | Wordsworth to Do-
           bell | . . .
              Arnold's Introduction to Keats, pp. 428–37; reprinted 88

205:28–29. *not in Ward*

[BYRON]

Macm.   "Byron," *Macmillan's Magazine* XLIII, 367–77 (March,
              1881)
Lit.   "Byron," *Littell's Living Age* CXLIX, 131–39 (April 16,
              1881). Not collated
              Reprinted 81by, 88

217:28–29. *not in Macm.,* 81by
218:2–3. himself. At a thousand points Shelley was immeasurably
    Macm.
218:23–24. is a belief   *Macm.*
219:9–10. stanza and verse by verse from   *Macm.*
221:26–27. The . . . it.   *not in Macm.*
221:33. idol which M. Taine   *Macm.*

222:3. poet. This *beau ténébreux* hides a coxcomb. *Macm.*
223:1. instances that will   *Macm.*
224:3. ridiculous. These poets, with their   *Macm.*
225:22. His admirers   *Macm.*
227:28. quoted anywhere in English words, Goethe   *Macm.*
231:32. he is   *Macm.*
233:11–15. *no* ¶   *Macm.;* Byron . . . for him.   *not in Macm.;* This
   is not the sort of Liberal peer to move   *Macm.*
233:18. suit it. Byron threw   *Macm.*
234:2. Leopardi, may   *Macm.*
234:17–20. The way . . . seeing it.   *not in Macm.*
234:20. True, as a   *Macm.*
235:1–2. Nature takes   *Macm.*
235:5. "And never lifted up a single stone," [*instead of* 'Will . . .
   sings?'] *Macm.*
235:9. ¶Of verse   *Macm.*
235:15. itself, would be to do a   *Macm.*
235:17–24. *no*¶   *Macm.;* Such . . . himself.   *not in Macm.*
236:28–29. place his poetry,   *Macm.*
236:30–32. and although . . . easily.   *not in Macm.*

[THE INCOMPATIBLES]

Ninet. "The Incompatibles," *Nineteenth Century* IX, 709–26,
   1026–43 (April, June, 1881). [In this edition, pp. 238–62,
   262–85.]
   Reprinted 82, 83m, 91 (not collated)

238:2–8. appearance, and it seems we are not to set eyes upon it until April is a week old. An additional paper on Irish affairs, even if
the Land Bill could be discussed in it, is an offering which, perhaps, people may be expected to receive with weariness and terror
rather than with a cheerful welcome. And above all, they may resent being troubled with a paper on these grave and sad affairs by
an insignificant person, and one who has no special connexion with
Ireland. *Ninet.*
238:16. of the Irish. 'The *Ninet.*
238:23. Miss O'Brien, *Ninet.*
238:27. way; obstruct *Ninet.*
239:12. tell me *Ninet.*
239:12–13. governed as a *Ninet.*

239:13–14. I am entirely indisposed *Ninet.*
239:15. tell me that Ireland is irresistibly *Ninet.*
239:19–20. colonies or to be *Ninet.*
239:22. were irresistibly *Ninet.*
239:28. world; — in presence *Ninet.*
240:4–6. are pedants. Elsewhere he attributes *Ninet.*
240:8. of their public *Ninet.*
240:9. amongst them *Ninet.*
240:18. current. We are pedants, as Goethe says; we adopt *Ninet.*
240:24. These . . . by us. *not in Ninet.*
240:38–241:2. movements, unclassed and . . . but who are . . . country, of the humane *Ninet.*
241:4–5. sentiment, and appalled *Ninet.*
241:12. let them pass for *Ninet.*
241:15–17. told. The editor of this Review is a kind and charitable soul, and he is willing to make room, among his statesmen and   15
generals, for an insignificant outsider who proposes only to talk
to other insignificant outsiders like himself in a plain way, and to
perish in the light, at any rate (if perish we must), and not in a
cloud of pedantry. But we must take the benefit of our kind editor's charity when we can, and he insists on extending it to us at   20
this moment, when the Land Bill is not yet made known. However, it is possible that a knowledge of the Land Bill might not
much help us; at all events, it is not essential to our purpose, which
is to look fairly into the incompatibility, alleged *Ninet.*
241:20. have possessed ever *Ninet.*
242:3. insecurity, and reason for *Ninet.*
242:4. this, at least, *Ninet.*
242:18–19. and its *Ninet.*
242:28–29. proceedings. People, however, go about *Ninet.*
242:37–38. history; it . . . act, but it long ago ceased *Ninet.*
242:38–39. On . . . hand, *not in Ninet.*
243:9–11. them, continued to burn, and burns still; the present *Ninet.*
243:17. with the conquered. *mispr. Ninet.*
243:18. as the first and *Ninet.*
243:19. well-being, and justice. Never *Ninet.*
243:23. *no¶ Ninet.*
244:5. upon that matter, *Ninet. and Swift;* upon the matter, 82, 83m
244:15. ¶Next, after *Ninet.*
244:26. *no¶* English opinion attributes *Ninet.*

244:28. religion. However the *Ninet.*
244:29–30. be fusion and forgetfulness of *Ninet.*
244:31. while it lasts. Still, if it is *Ninet.*
245:1–2. which we attribute to them and a good many more besides. Undoubtedly *Ninet.*
245:5. and it makes *Ninet.*
245:17. remedy for them? *Ninet.*
245:29. true; but *Ninet.*
245:33–34. due, in whole or in *Ninet.*
245:35. by us altogether, *Ninet.*
245:38. *footnotes not in Ninet.*
246:4. will be most anxious, as I *Ninet.*
246:5. and wrongs of England's *Ninet.*
246:6–7. hands; and *Ninet.*
246:9. frankly. Burke is *Ninet.*
246:10. trust. He is the greatest *Ninet.*
246:11–12. statesmen — the only one, it seems to me, who *Ninet.*
246:21. spirit; still, *Ninet.*
246:22. which he does not *Ninet.*
246:36. misgovernment than to *Ninet.*
248:9–11. Now . . . kindness. *not in Ninet.*
248:16. answer that Bristol Philistine who *Ninet.*
248:23. ascendency; but *Ninet.*
248:31. while the book *Ninet.*
248:32–33. he writes *Ninet.*
248:34–35. views he would *Ninet.*
249:20–22. interest adverse to Great Britain; they had acted together on behalf *Ninet.*
249:26. Parliament. The Union *Ninet.*
249:27–28. personage, the British Philistine. For thirty *Ninet.*
249:30–32. emancipation. Wesley wrote, *Ninet.*
250:7. steam *Ninet.*; stream 82, 83m
250:10. of 1870 — but *Ninet.*
250:22. is, much disorder. *Ninet.*
250:36–251:2. do otherwise; not to make governments irresolute in repressing disorder, but to make them resolute, also, in redressing injustice. *Ninet.*
251:4–6. Ireland . . . memory. *not in Ninet.*
251:6. We do not *Ninet.*
251:12. seems impossible to *Ninet.*
251:15–17. land in Ireland, is not to confer *Ninet.*
251:19. bad or good, *Ninet.*, 82

251:24. the length and   *Ninet.*
251:30. these violences.   *Ninet.*
251:31. But here things   *Ninet.*
251:34–35. says . . . again,   *not in Ninet.*
252:2. order. In   *Ninet.*
252:9–10. them, declares   *Ninet.*
252:13–14. root, general well-being, that necessary   *Ninet.*
252:26. at this day   *Ninet.*
252:27–29. expropriating   religious . . . expropriating   individual   *Ninet.*
253:5. compensation; of   *Ninet.*
253:13. has been this: *Ninet.*
253:14–15. The confiscations   *Ninet.*
253:33–34. seriously. They must be brought to acquiescence in   *Ninet.*
253:35–36. by good treatment. The acquiescence   *Ninet.*
254:3. expropriating them, which   *Ninet.*
254:8. can, and another   *Ninet.*
254:36. is not before us,   *Ninet.*
254:36–37. as I perfectly well   *Ninet.*
255:1. which are manifest,   *Ninet.*
255:4–12. Landowners . . . laid down.   *not in Ninet.*
255:12. It is evident that ownership   *Ninet.*
255:13. will thus be made   *Ninet.*
255:32–33. ¶Landowners hate . . . [*see lines 4–12*] . . . laid down. ¶However,   *Ninet.*
256:16. directing matters,   *Ninet.*
257:2–3. be tried and succeed.   *Ninet.*
257:17. to them, though   *Ninet.*
257:24. list to London   *Ninet.*
258:6–7. naturally be expected to have done so. The   *Ninet.*
258:14. to interfere to relieve   *Ninet.*
258:20. land; our middle   *Ninet.*
258:25–26. do right with religion.   *Ninet.*
258:29. discontent; even the   *Ninet.*
258:31. talks as if   *Ninet.*
258:34. can be done only by   *Ninet.*
259:27. there was   *Ninet.*
259:31. they could not   *Ninet.*
260:1–2. and they thought that   *Ninet.*
260:13. ask yourself   *Ninet.*, 82; ask yourselves   83m
260:36. which classes and   *Ninet.*

261:30–31. French Protestantism, and maintained   *Ninet.*

261:33–34. and turning up   *Ninet.*

262:2. healing; 'the temper,   *Ninet.*

262:3. bring them   *Ninet.*

262:4–5. enough to make well-being general and to do justice, we and our   *Ninet.*

262:7. must say something hereafter. For the present I have said enough. When a good-natured editor, with all kinds of potentates pressing to speak in his Review, allows an insignificant to talk to 10   insignificants, one should not abuse his kindness.   *Ninet.*

262:8–11. ¶'Sir, it is proper to inform you that *our measures must be healing.*' The Irish Land Bill is now before the world, and it is easy enough, no doubt, to pick holes in its claim to be called *Ninet.*

262:12. For . . . thus.   *not in Ninet.*

262:13. *no*¶   *Ninet.;* country; they   *Ninet.*

262:19. Britain. The grievance   *Ninet.*

263:2. forgotten; and a   *Ninet.*

263:6. so long a favourite,   *Ninet.*

263:8–11. Instead . . . before us.   *not in Ninet.*

263:12. 'of this contempt and   *Ninet.*

263:19. *no*¶   *Ninet.*

263:25. out; and   *Ninet.*

263:31. one would think,   *Ninet.*

263:37. would be   *Ninet.*

264:2–4. "The . . . order."   not in 82, 83m

264:6. order; things   *Ninet.*

264:12–13. imprisonment . . . trial,   *not in Ninet.*

264:31. To commute the   *Ninet.*

264:35. to give   *Ninet.*

265:1–2. likely to be   *Ninet.*

265:9. alike; but   *Ninet.*

265:13. if . . . done,   *not in Ninet.*

265:17–18. by which they themselves   *Ninet.*

265:23. question; tenant-right   *Ninet.*

265:29–31. would please him far better than . . . might now give it *Ninet.*

265:32. *no*¶   *Ninet.*

265:34. inconvenient; it   *Ninet.*

265:39. *no*¶ *Ninet.;* a measure healing.   *Ninet.*

266:8. in the former part   *Ninet.*

266:16. telling us when   *Ninet.;* telling when   *mispr.* 82, 82m

266:29. *commandment; if* Ninet.
266:33. or that Ninet.
267:1. one of the formulas Ninet.
267:6. and choosing Ninet.
267:7. *no* ¶ Ninet.; Bill does not Ninet.
267:9–10. are hard upon good landlords; but Ninet.
267:11. fashion, and in Ninet.
267:11–12. the presentation of Ninet.
267:14. *no*¶ Ninet.
267:31–32. They acquiesce . . . mass of us being, Ninet.
268:12–13. quiet people at . . . day, who have no . . . them, may well
  be inclined at any rate Ninet.
268:20. *no*¶ Ninet.
268:23. Probably if Ninet.
268:25–28. routine. We do not suppose, even, that we can point out   15
  courses which politicians and newspapers, as people and parties
  now are, will be at all likely to entertain. But we may be able to
  suggest, perhaps, courses which quiet people may think over in
  their minds as possible means to help us out of our difficulties, and
  which will remain to be tried, and to save us from despair, if the   20
  means which politicians and newspapers are now recommending,
  and of which the public mind is full, should prove, when they are
  tried, not to be successful. In this way we were led to suggest a
  mode of dealing with the agrarian trouble in Ireland which our
  politicians and newspapers are not at all likely to entertain, but   25
  which to quiet, simple people may perhaps commend itself as reasonable enough, and as offering refuge and hope if other courses,
  when they are tried, fail.
    Meanwhile, however, let us treat the endeavours and Ninet.
268:29. prejudice, remembering Ninet.
268:30. Ireland is to Ninet.
268:35. so; but . . . whether it proposes Ninet.
269:8–9. The *Pall Mall Gazette* says indeed, or did say formerly, for
  we will by no means oblige it to remain in a particular opinion
  which seems unsound — the *Pall Mall Gazette* said formerly: 'A   35
  good Ninet.
269:10. mouth.' Now Mr. Parnell Ninet.
269:13–14. have at present. A good Ninet.
269:17. not; much Ninet.
269:21. too; the present Ninet.
269:29. please; but if, Ninet.
269:34–35. *endowment,* you give Ninet.

269:36. influence, you   *Ninet.*

270:13. than healing measures   *Ninet.;* mis-usage   *Ninet.,* 82

270:14. wrong; 'their   *Ninet.*

270:16. *no¶   Ninet.*

270:19. treated fairly.   *Ninet.*

270:21–23. excite, the mere calculation of . . . is not sufficient   *Ninet.*

270:29–30. attached in spirit still;   *Ninet.*

271:1. attractive; the   *Ninet.*

271:10. always; and for   *Ninet.*

271:12. before they imply   *Ninet.*

271:14. of old. They are   *Ninet.*

271:21. to evolve them; if   *Ninet.*

271:23. evolve all these powers.   *Ninet.*

271:25. one of the factors of   *Ninet.*

271:30. of this element   *Ninet.*

271:33. strong; but   *Ninet.*

272:1. peculiarly sensible. They . . . sentiment, they have   *Ninet.*

272:4. *no¶   Ninet.*

272:5. it.' If   *Ninet.*

272:11–12. to the politeness to be found amongst them, and to the great value of it, will be . . . minds: *Ninet.*

272:18. aristocracy which have,   *Ninet.*

272:22. Its members   *Ninet.*

272:26. rate, it is capable   *Ninet.*

272:31. *no¶   Ninet.*

272:33. that if it were   *Ninet.*

273:5. in the happy possessorship   *Ninet.*

273:17–18. which they form of the   *Ninet.*

273:25–26. has ever happened to me before to comment   *Ninet.*

273:28. merits,   *Ninet.*

273:32. all round   *Ninet.,* 82; all around   83m

274:8. immortal; the . . . perish, but   *Ninet.*

274:9. drawing which Dickens has given of it cannot   *Ninet.*

274:26–27. intelligence, who died not long ago, Mr. Baring Gould, shortly before his death published a book   *Ninet.*

274:28. he gave testimony   *Ninet.*

274:30–31. spoken of, and the   *Ninet.*

274:33–34. in their schools,   *Ninet.*

275:2, 4. disgusted; they . . . bringing up; but   *Ninet.*

275:11. term is taken   *Ninet.*

275:12. true, and therefore,   *Ninet.*

275:20. though *Ninet.*

275:22–23. mass are badly taught, and brought *Ninet.*

275:26. *no¶ Ninet.*

275:27. are conscious *Ninet.*

275:33. Creakle, are some *Ninet.*

276:4. *no¶ Ninet.*

276:5–6. not disposed . . . of them, really see in them. This is what *Ninet.*

276:7–8. them. The Scotch of the Lowlands, of far the *Ninet.*

276:10–11. ourselves, and breed Murdstones as naturally as we do. Wales is *Ninet.*

276:12. ardour the Murdstonian religion, *Ninet.*

276:16. which to them, *Ninet.*

276:18–19. civilisation seems to have. *Ninet.*

276:24–25. of that valuable and instructive *Ninet.*

276:25–26. *Copperfield*, and may . . . finger on the *Ninet.*

276:30–34. hand, Mr. Murdstone, with his *Ninet.*

277:4–5. firmness, with her 'uncompromising *Ninet.*

277:6–7. black nails,' her 'hard steel purse,' and her 'numerous little steel fetters and rivets'; severe and *Ninet.*; black nails;" severe and 82, 83m; brass nails *David Copperfield*

277:8. These people, with *Ninet.*

277:12–13. energy, industry, religion, *Ninet.*

277:16. *no¶* Now Murdstone may be called the natural product of a course of Salem House and of Mr. Creakle acting upon hard, stern, and narrow natures. A disposition *Ninet.*

277:32. see him too much and too often; and he *Ninet.*

278:4. religion false and *Ninet.*

278:8. astonishment that 'even *Ninet.*

278:17–18. community, it has no *Ninet.*

278:20. *no¶ Ninet.*; dulness; if *Ninet.*

278:22. itself; in *Ninet.*

278:32–33. did indeed happen so. *Ninet.*

278:38–279:1. hardness; it grows irksome to itself, *Ninet.*

279:8. side. That *Ninet.*

279:9. side; and this *Ninet.*

279:10–11. in our all-containing treasure-house of the *History Ninet.*

279:16–17. Quinion was not precisely and literally Murdstone's partner, for Grinby, we are told, was his partner; but Quinion was his manager, and is truly *Ninet.*

279:20. manners. To a *Ninet.*

279:22. He produces *Ninet.*
279:25–27. *Hell-holes,* and the dissidence of *Ninet.*
279:32. art, made the City *Ninet.*
280:9. they are conspicuous *Ninet.*
280:17–18. may at least say, *Ninet.*
280:29. it seems we *Ninet.*
280:32–35. It is . . . relish them. *not in Ninet.*
280:35–36. gainers by it, laugh *Ninet.*
281:22–24. religion, and in . . . geniality. Wherever *Ninet.*
281:25. civilisation, and our governing *Ninet.*
281:26–28. watch their ways and wishes, and back up . . . can, but it does not prove attractive. *Ninet.*
281:29. *no¶ Ninet.*
281:30–32. Barker, their wives will be ladies, they will not even *Ninet.*
281:37–38. in general. They have *Ninet.*
282:1. be sure, *Ninet.*
282:2–3. stamp of Murdstone or *Ninet.*
282:13. tell him of *Ninet.*
282:16. civilisation, and gives *Ninet.*
282:22. hear of what is *Ninet.*
282:23. determine to perish, as I say, in *Ninet.*
282:26. Irish. Even if we *Ninet.*
282:27. estranged as they now are, *Ninet.*
282:37. not now much *Ninet.*
282:38–283:1. make them judged *Ninet.*
283:5. governs in a *Ninet.*
283:7–8. *no¶ He has got . . . again!* I think I hear people saying. Really they ought *Ninet.*
283:21. *no¶ Ninet.*
283:23. ills, but they *Ninet.*
283:35. of a matter *Ninet.*
283:37. in; if I *Ninet.*
284:2. notice; but then the middle *Ninet.*
284:6. which might please *Ninet.*
284:12. proceedings, so far as his *Ninet.*
284:18. panderer *Ninet.*
284:23–26. and to . . . Creakle. *not in Ninet.*
284:31. must we give healing *Ninet.*
284:36. civilisation; and *Ninet.*
285:1. remedying the failure. *Ninet.*

285:4. recommending them to their attention: — *Ninet.;* recommending these to their attention:— 82; recommending these to our attention:— 83m

285:12. ¶Perhaps, also, they might do well to *Ninet.*

285:19–20. our countrymen insist upon it. that attractive . . . is, or ought to be, *Ninet.*

[PREFACE TO BURKE]

Text: 81bu. Not reprinted by Arnold.

[A GENEVESE JUDGE]

PMG "A Genevese Judge," *Pall Mall Gazette*, July 13, 1881, pp. 11–12. Anonymous. Not reprinted by Arnold.

[AN UNREGARDED IRISH GRIEVANCE]

Fortn. "Irish Grammar Schools," *Fortnightly Review* XXXVI (n.s. XXX), 137–48 (August, 1881) Reprinted 82, 83m, 91 (not collated)

Title: Irish Grammar Schools *Fortn.*

295:1. the year before *Fortn.*

295:24. be sure and *Fortn.*, 82, 83m; *corrected from Burke*

295:28–29. hour, I will not judge. *Fortn.*

296:1. needs, and pursue *Fortn.*

296:8–9. pleasures by raising its . . . , by extending and deepening its *Fortn.*

296:10. *no*¶ *Fortn.;* True, . . . done. *not in Fortn.*

296:12. class, and this class, *Fortn.*

296:14. of it; its *Fortn.*

296:16. independence." Not Ireland alone *Fortn.*

296:18. class; the part *Fortn.*

296:29. *no*¶ *Fortn.*

296:37. class in England and *Fortn.*

297:4. boy is taken through *Fortn.*

297:10. *no*¶ *Fortn.*

297:13. very competent observer, *Fortn.*

298:8. We . . . of them. *not in Fortn.*

298:9. Schools were not   *Fortn.*

299:12. attention. He complains bitterly of the low standard of the prize and scholarship examinations at the Queen's Colleges of Cork and Galway, boys having obtained *distinctions* there, whom he had resolved to send home to their parents on account of their stolid and invincible ignorance. He objects   *Fortn.*

300:2. are not enslaved   *Fortn.*

300:16–17. Ireland, and England   *Fortn.*, 82, 83m; *corrected from Mahaffy*

301:19. He finds fault   *Fortn.*

301:22–23. reforms, and perpetuates inefficient arrangements and incompetent   *Fortn.*

302:20. versatility; if   *Fortn. and Mahaffy*

302:30–31. (to . . . sons)   *not in Fortn.*

303:12. us them. "The   *Fortn.*

303:17. have good   *Fortn.*

303:28. not the least   *Fortn. and Mahaffy;* not in the least   82, 83m

303:34. enormous advantages."   *Fortn. and Mahaffy;* enormous superiority."   82, 83m

303:35. *no¶   Fortn.*

303:37–38. public schools, and if the whole middle class in Ireland could afford to . . . bemoan their   *Fortn.*

304:2. instruction amongst them. But they cannot.   *Fortn.*

304:4. either; the   *Fortn.*

304:9. a teaching as good.   *Fortn.*

304:13–15. class, as well as for the . . . is wholly inadequate.   *Fortn.*

304:19. expounded; to me   *Fortn.*

304:29. dislike of   *Fortn.*

304:31. alone; no doubt   *Fortn.*

304:34. difficult; it   *Fortn.*

305:1. overcome, and, so far as popular   *Fortn.*

305:4. *no¶   Fortn.*

305:6. service; but,   *Fortn.*

305:18. *no¶   Fortn.*

305:23. faith; he   *Fortn.*

305:24. is a fine thing,   *Fortn.*

305:31. this consummation it is not   *Fortn.*

305:34. *no¶   Fortn.*

306:3. them; and to this   *Fortn.*

306:4. the State, the nation acting   *Fortn.*

306:7–8. favourable; as indeed to   *Fortn.*

306:8. of life—now become a second nature to them and much endeared to their hearts—arising out   *Fortn.; see lines 11–12*

306:10–12. lives, religion; they are apprehensive *Fortn.*

306:16. do so; and although *Fortn.*

306:17. and the pressing *Fortn.*

306:21. may not . . . life-time. *not in Fortn.*

306:23–24. by our own doing *Fortn.*

306:24–25. governing class is not *Fortn.*

306:26–29. do so. It will do what the middle class, the class on whose favour political power depends, it will do what this class demands, but it will do no more. *Fortn.*

306:31. to demand public *Fortn.*

306:36. govern it, whenever *Fortn.*

306:37. education; its *Fortn.*

307:4. no¶ *Fortn.*

307:8–9. it does, respects them. He *Fortn.*

307:10. examinations; but *Fortn.*

307:11. instruction, but *Fortn.*

307:14. Something had to be *Fortn.*

307:15. instruction, but the Protestant *Fortn.*

307:20–21. respect to these Protestant feelings; hence *Fortn.*

307:23. no¶ *Fortn.*

307:32. responsibility; hence *Fortn.*

308:10. when it institutes *Fortn.*

308:13–15. that "the new . . . like the intermediate system," and not *Fortn.*

308:20. means set seriously *Fortn.*

308:20–21. round; it *Fortn.*

308:23. doing so, who see what it loses by doing so, can only *Fortn.*

308:27. rise in *Fortn.*

308:28. however, it sacrifices *Fortn.*

308:30. also; and *Fortn.*

308:33. to its education. *Fortn.*

309:1. endowment; the Protestants of Great Britain are emphatically hostile to the endowment of Catholicism in any shape or form." And this when we have in Britain *Fortn.*

309:14–15. Great Britain, she *Fortn.*

309:18. as . . . said, *not in Fortn.*

309:22–23. which the Murdstones and *Fortn.*

309:24. Quinions, with their *Fortn.*

309:27–28. character; they . . . theatres; they *Fortn.*

309:29. and . . . meeting, *not in Fortn.*

309:32. so; but *Fortn.*

309:35. *no¶   Fortn.*
309:37. power; and such   *Fortn.*
309:38. is more   *Fortn.*
310:1. people, than the   *Fortn.*
310:4–5. operation; but not in this sense of   *Fortn.*
310:6. The Castle   *Fortn.*
310:9. and better   *not in Fortn.*
310:13. wishes listened to; and   *Fortn.*
310:20. their minds   *Fortn.*
310:24–25. as its aged   *Fortn.*
310:31. honest, logical, single-minded aim   *Fortn.*
310:33. *no¶   Fortn.*
311:3. herself by making such a demand; she will   *Fortn.*

[PREFACE TO *Irish Essays*]

Texts: 82, 83m, 91 (not collated)
Title: Preface. 82; Preface to Irish Essays.   83m

Index

A reference to a page of text should be taken to include the notes to that page.

DATE DUE

GAYLORD			PRINTED IN U.S.A.